Sir William Borlase's Grammar School

The First 400 Years

EDITED BY GREGORY B. S. LIM

© Sir William Borlase's Grammar School 2023
Published by
Gresham Books Ltd
The Carriage House
Ningwood Manor
Ningwood
Isle of Wight
PO30 4NJ
www.gresham-books.co.uk

All rights reserved. No part of this publication which is copyright may be reproduced, stored in a retrieval system, or transmitted, in any form or by any means — electronic, mechanical, photocopying, recording or otherwise — without the prior permission of Gresham Books Ltd or the appropriate copyright owner. Full particulars of copyright are given in the acknowledgements.

Text set in 9pt Source Sans Pro (TT)
Printed in the UK
ISBN: 978-0-946095-97-1

CONTENTS

Preface from the Headteacher — V
Introduction from the Editor — VI

Chapter 1
Foundation and the First 250 Years (1624–1874) — 1

Sir William's Ancestors — 2
Sir William Borlase (c.1564–1629) — 4
Sir William's Descendants — 6
The Borlase Coat of Arms — 10
Sir William's Will — 11
The First Century — 13
Thomas Heather I (1735–1759) — 14
William Heather (1759–1782) — 15
Thomas Heather II (1782–1793) — 17
Rev. H. H. Gower (1793–1809) — 17
Rev. Stephen Gage (1809–1814) — 19
William Francis (1814–1835) — 20
George Gale (1835–1844) — 24
Charles T. Wethered (1844–1850) — 25
Edwin Segrave (1850–1880) — 26

Chapter 2
Revival and Renewal (1874–1974) — 29

The New Scheme — 30
Rev. Michael Graves (1881–1895) — 32
E. W. Clark (1896–1901) — 42
E. H. Blakeney (1901–1904) — 44
Rev. Albert J. Skinner (1904–1927) — 47
World War I (1914–1918) — 56
The Post-War Period — 61
William S. Booth (1927–1956) — 68
World War II (1939–1945) — 76
Ernest M. Hazelton (1956–1974) — 79
Boarders at Sentry Hill — 87

Chapter 3
The Modern Era (1974–2024) — 95

Roy R. Smith (1974–1988) — 96
Laurence A. Smy (1989–1996) — 104
Dr Peter A. Holding (1997–2018) — 110
Kay L. Mountfield (2018–2023) — 113
Performing Arts and Specialist School Status — 123
Foreign Languages — 130
School Curriculum and Pedagogy — 132
Aspects of School Life — 134
Sport — 144

Chapter 4
The Old Borlasian Club and Alumni — 161

A Brief History of the Club — 162
Officers of the Club — 167
Stuart Lever Room — 168
Borlase Masonic Lodge — 170
Old Borlasians — 170

Chapter 5
Staff — 197

Long-serving Teaching Staff — 198
Trustees, Governors and Staff — 200

Acknowledgements — 203

Contributors — 204
Picture Credits — 205
Subscribers — 208

PREFACE FROM THE HEADTEACHER

Mr Ed Goodall
Headteacher

If Sir William Borlase could see now the School that bears his name, 400 years since he founded it and secured its continuation through his will, one hopes that he would delight at its vibrant, diverse community and be proud of the opportunities that have been afforded to so many through the School's rich history. That Sir William Borlase's Grammar School continues to thrive is no matter of fortune; it is down to the inspiration, determination and commitment to the benefit of others — values which the School seeks to uphold and inculcate in its students today — of so many people through the ages whom this book recognises and honours.

To consider the four centuries of change and progress during which the School has borne witness to wars, societal transformation, and advancement in technology is a reminder that we walk on ancient ways; where we stand now, others have stood and will stand in the future. However, while an individual's time at the School may be only fleeting, their association with it whether as a former or current student, member of Staff, parent or governor will always endure.

The Borlase motto, *Te Digna Sequere*, remains the clarion call for all in the School community and encapsulates the essence of our educational philosophy. It provides validation for the Staff through whose dedication and service the School seeks to provide the best education possible, and it is also an exhortation to the students, encouraging them to discover their passions and pursue their aspirations to enrich their own lives and the lives of others.

While this book chronicles and rightly celebrates the *first* 400 years of Sir William Borlase's Grammar School, education is a forward-looking pursuit and the next chapters are already being written by the Staff and students in our midst. May the spirit of *Te Digna Sequere* always be sustained so that current and future generations are inspired and empowered to shape the world for the better.

INTRODUCTION FROM THE EDITOR

*Dr Gregory B. S. Lim (OB 1997–2003)
President of the Old Borlasian Club and School Trustee*

"A knight there lived in days of old, when James the First was King." The opening lines of the School Song, written by the Rev. A. J. Skinner (Headmaster 1904–1927), evoke a time 400 years ago when Sir William Borlase founded a School in Marlow in memory of his second son, Henry, who died at a young age in 1624. In Sir William's will, the School was endowed "to teach twenty four poor children to write, read and cast accounts". Only boys would have attended school, so Sir William also made provision for "twenty-four poor women children of the Borough of Great Marlow only to make bone lace, to spin or knit". The curriculum at Borlase has evolved considerably over the past four centuries, and Sir William could scarcely have imaged the size and scope of the twenty-first-century educational establishment that still proudly bears his name. Nevertheless, the School remains faithful in many ways to the objectives laid down by Sir William: to educate local children so that they may be better equipped to succeed in the world. As is inscribed on the front of the School, "If any will not worke neither shall he eate" (2 Thess. 3:10) or, perhaps more encouragingly, "Ye shall know the truth, and the truth shall make you free" (John 8:32).

That a School should still exist in Marlow after 400 years was not an inevitability, and Borlase has been threatened with closure at various points in its history. Dwindling numbers of students, financial insolvency and even a Headmaster convicted (perhaps unjustly) of assault and libel all very nearly resulted in the demise of Borlase School. However, each period of adversity was met with resolute determination from those who loved the School to see it endure, and Borlasians of today owe these individuals a great debt. Some are mentioned in this book, but countless others surely also contributed.

This book is being published to celebrate the 400th anniversary of the School's foundation, a milestone that few institutions achieve. The first three chapters give an historical account of the School up to the present day and describe some unique aspects of Borlase School life. The prominent roles of Rowing, Hockey and the Performing Arts in the Borlase experience are highlighted. The fourth chapter describes the activities of The Old Borlasian Club and profiles various alumni of the School.

While editing this book, I have discovered many facts about the School, and I hope you find it similarly informative. I have repeatedly been struck by how special Borlase has been to so many people, whether they be teachers who have taught at the School for most of their careers, or students who have remained in contact with the School throughout their lives. There is something ineffable about Borlase that keeps people engaged. Perhaps it is the beautiful and historic Cloisters and Chapel; maybe it is the sense of community and what Mr W. S. Booth (Headmaster 1927–1956) called 'The Borlase Spirit'. Whatever it is, generations of Borlasians have gone forth from Borlase and followed things worthy of themselves. *Te Digna Sequere*!

CHAPTER 1
FOUNDATION AND THE FIRST 250 YEARS (1624–1874)

SIR WILLIAM'S ANCESTORS

Sir William Borlase could trace his descent from the Norman Conquest of 1066. Taillefer of Angoulême had joined the contingent of his neighbour, Roger Montgomeri, and had fought at the Battle of Hastings. Taillefer was rewarded for his services by William Rufus (King William II) with the estate of Borlase in the parish of St Wenn, near Bodmin in mid-Cornwall. From the Cornish words *bor* and *glas*, Borlase is thought to mean 'the green hillside'.

Even today, in the hamlet of Rosenannon, there is a signpost that reads 'Borlase 1' and, this distance away, along a leafy, winding and very narrow road, there are a couple of houses, some barns and a fine old farmhouse that clearly bears the name 'Borlase' on its gateway. This farmhouse is what remains of the ancient manor of the Borlase family, from whom Sir William Borlase is descended.

Wool for export and cheese for home consumption would have been the main produce of West Country farmers in those days, and Borlase Farm is still a working farm. The family remained on the estate, retaining the name Taillefer or Tailfer, until the fourteenth century, when the last of the direct line, Alice Frank Tailfer, died. The estate then descended to Andrew Borlas, her first cousin, and from him to a long line of Borlases.

When the direct line became extinct in the sixteenth century, the estate was sold but the family name continued to flourish. A younger brother of the House, Walter Borlase, who died in 1550, continued the Cornish branch of the family. Walter established himself at the nearby Treluddrow Manor in St Newlyn East and gained substantial wealth from selling mining rights. His son, also called Walter, had an impressive home on the cliffs of Pendeen, West Cornwall, later to be the birthplace of the noted eighteenth-century antiquary, geologist and naturalist, Dr William Borlase FRS (1696–1772).

1.1.1. King William II granted an estate in Cornwall to Sir William Borlase's ancestor

1.1.2. A signpost in Cornwall pointing to Borlase Farm

 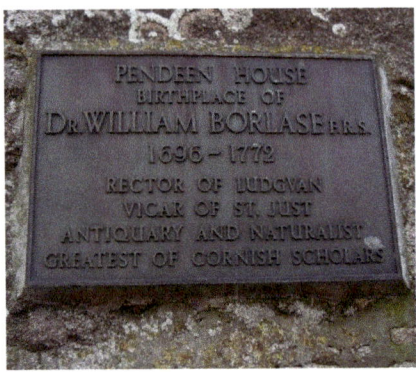 

1.1.3. The Borlase house in Pendeen, birthplace of Dr William Borlase FRS, the Cornish antiquary, geologist and naturalist

It was an illustrious family and, in the centuries ahead, the Borlases made their mark in Cornwall and beyond as lawyers, admirals, members of parliament (MPs), mayors and vicars. There are memorial plaques and windows to various members of the Borlase family in St Michael's Church, Helston, and St Anietus' Church, St Neot.

Walter's younger brother, Edward, ventured 'up country' to London. Having served his apprenticeship to Thomas Maynard, he was admitted to the freedom of the Mercers' Company in 1514. Edward Borlase became a successful textile merchant, specializing in silk and very expensive materials. He was also a wine merchant and apparently supplied the wine to Henry VIII on the Field of the Cloth of Gold. Edward died in 1544. In about 1559, his son, John Borlase, bought Westhorpe Manor House in Little Marlow, which previously belonged to a convent of Benedictine nuns, and the estate at Bockmer in the parish of Medmenham. John was MP for Buckinghamshire in 1586 and Sheriff in 1588, the year of the Spanish Armada. He died in 1593. Both he and his wife, Anne (daughter of Sir Robert Litton of Knebworth), were buried in St John the Baptist Church, Little Marlow.

1.1.4. Memorials to George Simon Borlase FRS (1792–1837), John Borlase (died 1843, aged 80 years) and Henry Borlase (died 1846, aged 82 years) in St Michael's Church, Helston; the Borlase coats of arms above the memorials are enlarged. The stained-glass window depicting the Transfiguration of Christ is dedicated to George Simon Borlase; it was placed in the east window in 1837, but was restored in the 1990s and is now above the main entrance to the church.

Foundation and the First 250 Years (1624-1874)   CHAPTER 1 | 3

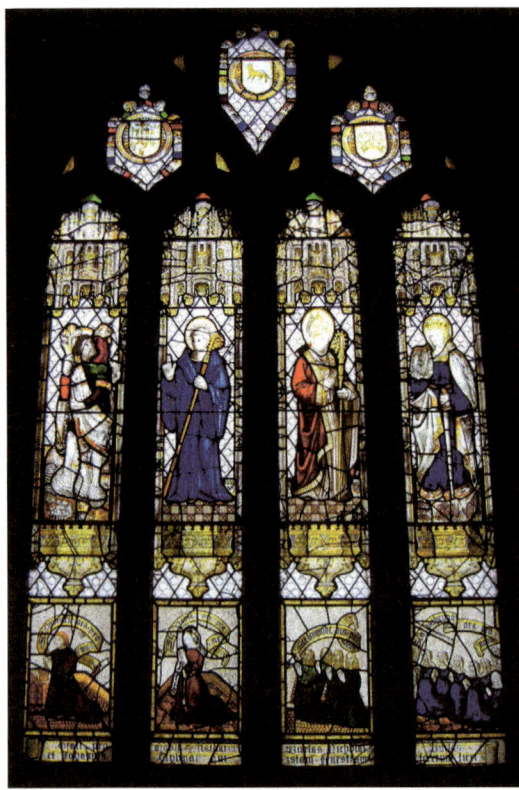 

1.1.5. The Borlase (or Burlas) window in St Anietus' Church, St Neot, depicting (from left to right) St Christopher, St Neot, St Leonard and St Catherine; below are members of the Borlase family who donated the window: Nicholas, his wife Catheine, and their four sons and eight daughters

SIR WILLIAM BORLASE (c.1564–1629)

The School's Founder, Sir William Borlase, was the only son of this John Borlase. He had two sisters, Elizabeth and Dorothie. He matriculated to Magdalen College, Oxford, on 17 November 1581, aged 17 years. In 1594, he was admitted as a member of Gray's Inn. In 1601, he was High Sheriff of Buckinghamshire, and in 1602, MP for Aylesbury. On 28 June 1603, he was knighted by James I at Sir John Fortescue's at Beddington in Surrey. In 1604, he was elected MP for Aylesbury, and in 1614, for Buckinghamshire.

In 1610, Sir William was at loggerheads with King James I over the old question of the boundaries of the royal forests. The needy king wished to make Sir William pay for his lands on the basis that they had previously been royal forest and, therefore, royal property. The king naturally won, and Sir William was graciously allowed to recover his lands on payment of compensation. No wonder he wished to raise the matter in Parliament and to proceed "by bill rather than by petition". In 1623, the Duke of Buckingham was pressing for subsidies to fit out his famous and futile Cádiz expedition. Sir William (as Deputy Lieutenant for the county) was one of the assessors, and his sympathies were with the taxpayers. He wrote a letter to protest against the heavy assessment on his neighbour, Mr John Hampden, who was to pay £13 6s. 8d., and on his mother, who was to pay £10.

1.2.1. King James I of England knighted Sir William Borlase in 1603

1.2.2. Ben Jonson: playwright, poet and friend of Sir William Borlase

Sir William was a friend of the poet and dramatist Ben Jonson (1572–1637). He painted a portrait of Ben and presented him with this "attempt at verse":

*To paint they worth, if rightly I did know it,
And were but painter half like thee, a poet;
Ben, I would shew it.*

Perhaps the portrait did not do justice to the burly Ben, for his answer, entitled "To Burlace" is hardly complimentary:

*Why, though I be of prodigious waist,
I am not so voluminous and vast
But there are lines wherewith I may be embrac'd.*

*'Tis true, as my womb swells, so my back stoops,
And the whole lump grows round, deform'd and droops;
But yet the tun of Heidleb has hoops.*

*You are not tied by any Painter's law
To square my circles, I confess, but draw
My superficies; that was all you saw:*

*Which if in compass of no art it came
To be described, but by a Monogram,
With one great blot you have drawn me as I am.*

*But whilst you curious were to have it be
An Archetype for all the world to see,
You have made it a brave piece, but not like me.*

*Oh, had I now the manner, mastery, might,
Your power of handling shadow, aire and sprite,
How could I draw, behold, and take delight;*

*But you are he can paint, I can but write,
A Poet hath no more than black and white,
Nor has he flattering colours or false light.*

*Yet when of friendship I would draw the face,
A letter'd mind, and a large heart would place
To all posterity, I would write Burlace.*

Sir William's wife, Mary (daughter of Nicholas Backhouse of London), together with 18 others, died from the plague in 1621 and was buried at Little Marlow. Sir William died on 4 September 1629 and was also buried at Little Marlow on 10 September. The site of Sir William's grave is unknown (the level of the nave was raised by the Victorians, and many memorials were removed during this process).

1.2.3. St John the Baptist Church, Little Marlow, where Sir William Borlase and his parents, wife, son and other descendants were buried

SIR WILLIAM'S DESCENDANTS

Sir William Borlase had three sons: William, Henry and John. The first to die was Henry, a barrister, MP for Aylesbury in 1621 and for Marlow in 1624 until his death. As we shall hear, it was in memory of Henry that his father endowed the School.

The youngest son, John, was MP for Marlow in both the Short and the Long Parliaments of 1640.

William, the oldest son and heir, was knighted by James I at Warwick in 1617. Sir William's wife was Amy, daughter of Sir Francis Popham of Littlecote in Wiltshire. Sir William was MP for Wycombe in the Parliament of 1627–1628, when the Petition of Right was carried in the teeth of King Charles I, and when Sir Miles Hobart of Harleyford, MP for Marlow, pocketed the keys of the House of Commons in the face of the King's messenger, and the Speaker, Finch, was held down in his chair while the Commons passed their resolutions. Sir William realized the importance of the occasion and compiled a volume of Parliamentary Notes. On 15 December 1630, one year after his father, he died, without completing the foundation of the School. Although he lived at Bockmer, he wished to be buried at Little Marlow, "at the feet of my Father".

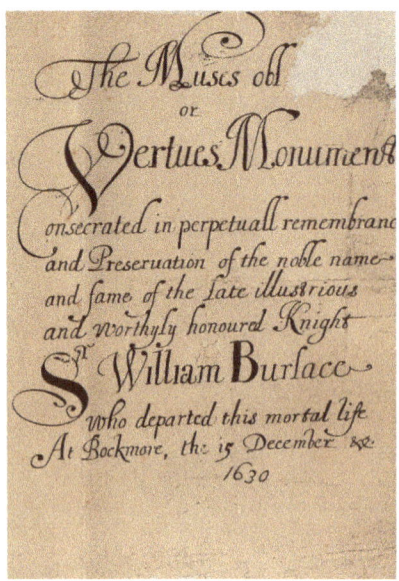

1.3.2. Title page to a poem on the death of Sir William Burlace [Borlase], son of the Founder

After Sir William's death, his wife Amy married secondly the courtier Gabriel Hippesley (died 1659), with whom she had a son, Francis Hippesley. Amy, Lady Borlase was buried at Little Marlow on 1 August 1661.

The second Sir William also had three sons, John, William and Henry, and had two daughters, Anne and Mary. Anne married Richard Grenville and became the ancestress of a line of famous statesmen that included two Prime Ministers. She died on 30 January 1646. Mary died on 27 February 1637 and was buried at Little Marlow. Henry was given an estate in Kent and died in around 1688. William seems to have lived in Marlow, possibly in Widmere, an estate that had previously belonged to the Knights Templar and later to the Knights Hospitaller, and which the Borlases bought from an old family, the Widmers, somewhere around 1630. He was MP for Marlow in the Cavalier Parliament and died in 1665.

John, the heir, who inherited Little Marlow and Bockmer, lived in times of trouble. He was created a baronet by Charles I in 1642, the year the Civil War began. James I had created the rank of baronet to help to fill his treasury, and no doubt John Borlase had to subscribe to Charles's war chest. He attended the Royalist Parliament at Oxford and was consequently deprived of his seat at Westminster. In 1645, although he had not actually fought for the king, he was arrested, sent to Worcester by the victorious Parliamentarians, and was forced to compound for a very large sum before his estates were discharged and he was released. Sir John Borlase died on 8 August 1672 and was buried at Little Marlow on 12 August.

Portraits of Sir John and his wife, Alice Bankes (1621–1683), daughter of Sir John Bankes of Corfe Castle, were painted by Sir Anthony van Dyck (1599–1641) in 1637/1638, shortly after their marriage, and are now in the National Trust Collections and on display at Kingston Lacy.

A copy of the painting of Sir John hangs in the School Reception and is thought to be by Angelica Vanessa Garnett (1918–2012), an artist and writer with links to the Bloomsbury Group. The painting was given to the School in 1951 by Mrs Molloy, who had an ancestral link with the Borlase family. As an aside, Sir John Borlase, 1st Baronet, should not be confused with his cousin and contemporary, Sir John Borlase (1576–1648), who was Lord Justice of Ireland.

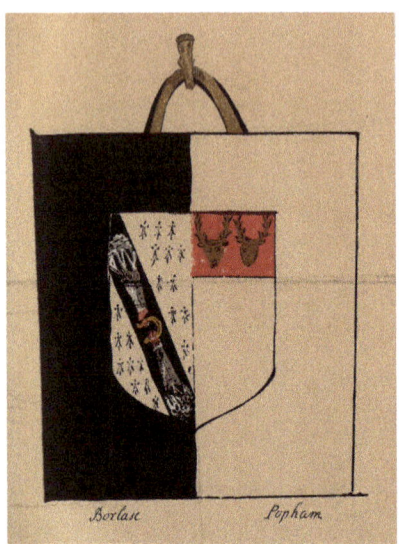

1.3.1. The coat of arms of Borlase impaling those of Popham, the family of Amy, Lady Borlase

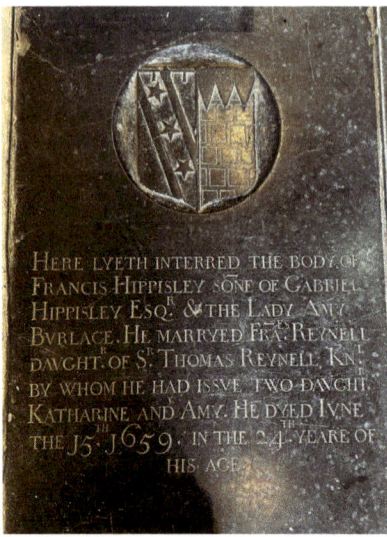

1.3.3. Ledger stone of Francis Hippisley, son of Gabriel Hippisley and the Lady Amy Borlase, in St John the Baptist Church, Little Marlow

1.3.4. Portraits of Sir John Borlase and Alice, Lady Borlase by Sir Anthony van Dyck

1.3.5. Painting of Sir John Borlase, 1st Baronet, undergoing restoration funded by the School Trustees in 2023

1.3.6. Portrait of Sir John Borlase, Lord Justice of Ireland

Foundation and the First 250 Years (1624-1874)   CHAPTER 1

Sir John Borlase, 1st Baronet, had ten children: John, Baldwin, William, Charles, Alexander, Mary, Francis, Alice (also known as Anne), Katherine and Amy. His eldest son, Sir John Borlase, 2nd Baronet, was MP for Great Marlow in the three Short Parliaments of Charles II, in the Parliament of James II, and in the Convention Parliament that settled the crown on William III and Mary II. He died in February 1688 and, his brothers having predeceased him without issue, the Borlase baronetcy became extinct. Sir John was buried in St Mary & St Edburga's Church, Stratton Audley, and he is commemorated with a large, baroque monument. Sir John's brother Baldwin is also commemorated with a cartouche.

The 2nd Baronet's sister Mary married Sir Humphrey Miller, 1st Baronet (1633–1709) and died in 1679. Another sister, Anne, married Arthur Warren of Stapleford Hall, Nottinghamshire, and the Marlow property came to her, the pair living at Bockmer. Their youngest son, Borlase Warren (1677–1747), heir to Stapleford, Little Marlow and Bockmer, was the man who in 1721 was called upon to put the School on a sound foundation, and we shall hear of him later. Borlase Warren was MP for Nottingham and was the father of John Borlase Warren (c.1699–1763) and the grandfather of Admiral Sir John Borlase Warren, 1st Baronet (1753–1822). All three were Governors of the School.

1.3.7. The baroque monument to Sir John Borlase, 2nd Baronet, featuring the Borlase coat of arms, and the cartouche to his brother Baldwin, both in St Mary & St Edburga's Church, Stratton Audley

1.3.8. Portraits of Mary Borlase and Sir Humphrey Miller

8 | CHAPTER 1   Foundation and the First 250 Years (1624-1874)

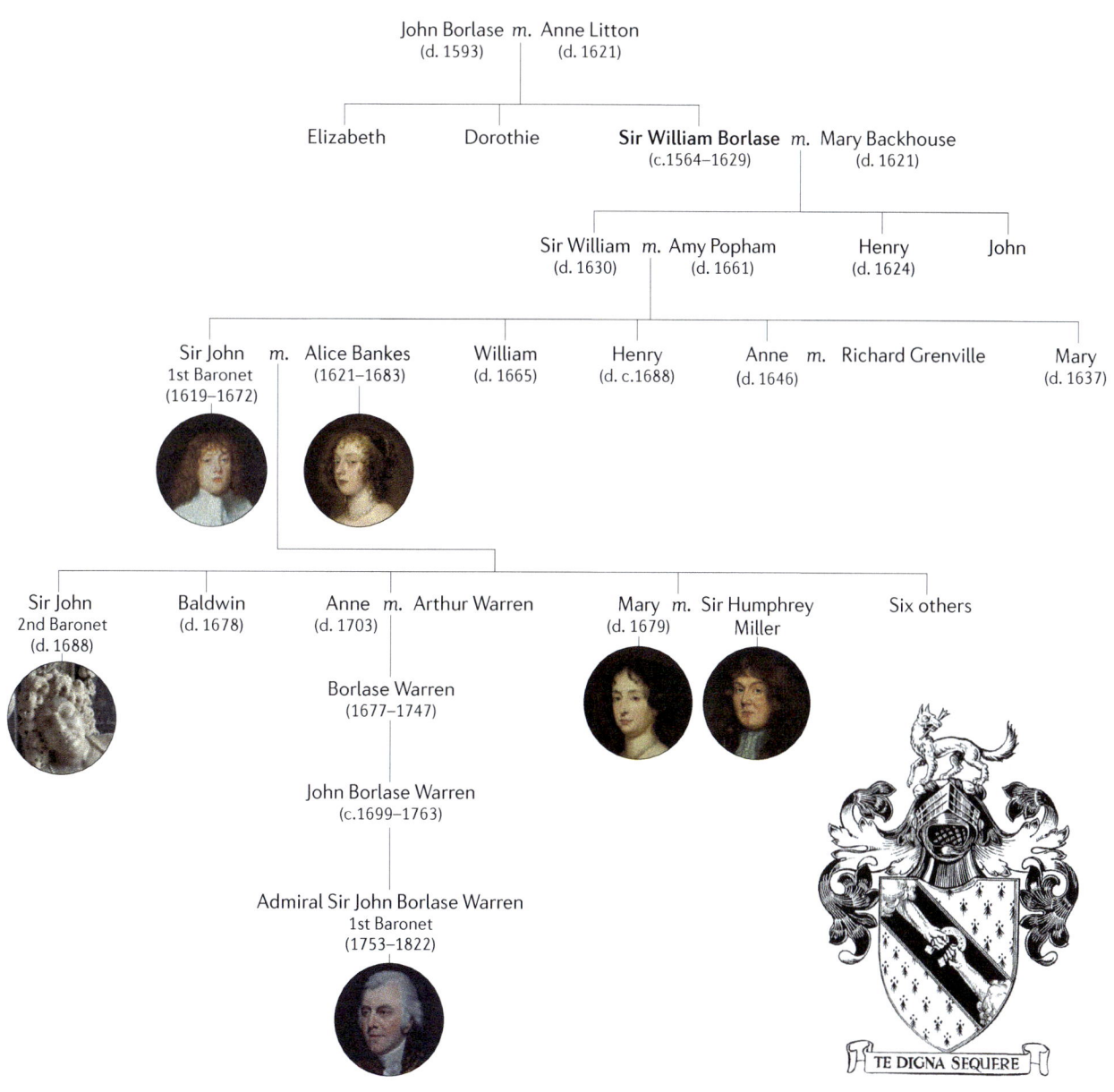

1.3.9. Sir William Borlase and his descendants

Foundation and the First 250 Years (1624-1874)   CHAPTER 1 | 9

THE BORLASE COAT OF ARMS

1.4.1. *The armorial bearings of Sir William Borlase of Marlow in the County of Buckingham, issued by the College of Arms*

1.4.2. *The coat of arms of Taillefer, as recorded in 1318*

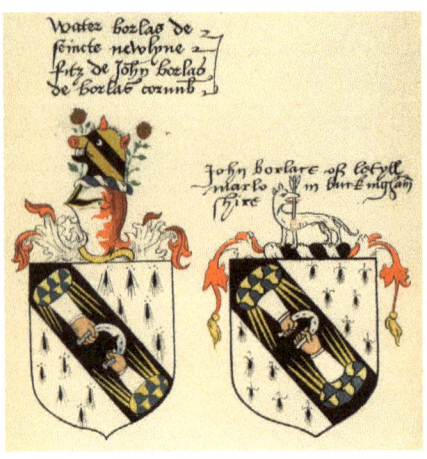

1.4.3. *The coat of arms of Walter Borlase (left), of St Newlyn, son of John Borlase, of Borlase in Cornwall; and of John Borlase (right), of Little Marlow in Buckinghamshire; both from a manuscript in the College of Arms from the reign of Henry VIII*

The origins of the Borlase coat of arms lie with the family's ancestors, the Taillefers of Angoulême in France. The Taillefer coat of arms had a hand coming out of a cloud and holding a badelaire (a kind of cutlass). These were placed over a field (background) of mullets (eight-pointed stars). Legend has it that this sword is the sword of 'Corto' made for William, Count of Angoulême. William assumed the name 'Taillefer' after defeating Storis, a king of the Northmen, in single combat. The legend says that William cut Storis literally in two through breastplate and breastbone, with a single stroke of his sword, Corto. Hence the name 'Taillefer' from *tailler* and *fer* meaning 'cutter of iron'.

This accounts for the arm and cloud in the School's coat of arms, but what became of Corto? A variation of the Taillefer arms is recorded in 1318 as "A hand and arm clothed, holding a sword bendwise [diagonally] cutting asunder a bar of iron between 6 mullets (spur-rowels), 2 in chief, and 3 in point". The bar was perhaps introduced to depict the name Taillefer.

The Borlase coat of arms, as found early in the reign of Henry VIII are "Ermine on a bend [diagonal stripe] Sable [black], two arms clothed Argent [silver] (the hands proper)

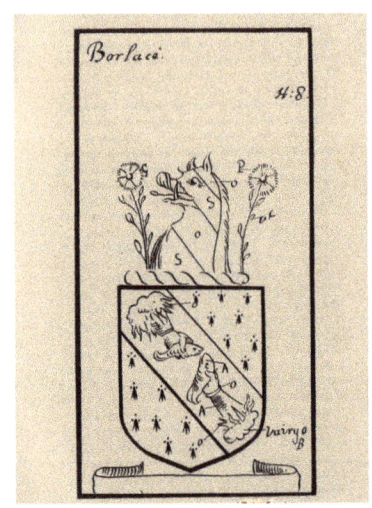

1.4.4. *Versions of the coat of arms of Borlase in the seventeenth century*

1.4.5. *The coat of arms of Borlase with the Taillefer bar erroneously replaced by a scroll (left) and with the horse shoe erroneously replaced by two fish (right)*

issuing from clouds proper ... rendering asunder a horse-shoe (broken in the middle) Or [gold]". If the bar in the 1318 version is enlarged, and another hand holding a sword added, we get the appearance of two arms pulling a horse shoe apart, the two swords making up each half of the shoe.

The sword Corto, therefore, disappeared from the arms to be replaced by a horse shoe (which is now unbroken), and the mullets were replaced by ermine which remains to this day.

When at the close of the fifteenth century the Cornish ancestors of Borlase assumed the coat of arms, English heralds often misunderstood them. In one case, the bar was replaced by a scroll and, in another, the swords were replaced by fish! It is simple to see how easy it was for the cutlasses to be replaced by the familiar horse shoe.

The helm that tops the Borlase shield is that of a knight. Unknighted members of the family would have used the helm of an esquire, which faces to the heraldic dexter (left), and has a closed visor.

The history of the crest (which sits on top of the helm) is not so well detailed. Different members of the family used different crests, such as a boar's head with roses or the familiar wolf carrying an arrow in its mouth.

At the bottom, the motto *Te Digna Sequere* means 'Follow things worthy of thyself'.

1.4.6. The coat of arms of Borlase School depicted in stained glass in the Staffroom and on the cover of The Rover *magazine in July 1953 (top row, second from left)*

SIR WILLIAM'S WILL

The codicil to the will of Sir William Borlase is dated 16 October 1628. Of note, the School was already in existence at the time. It is not correct to say, as some historians of Buckinghamshire have stated, that the School was not founded until 1628. Sir William was a barrister and quite capable of drawing up his own will in the legal language of the day.

"And whereas I have erected a house and bought also some other houses and lands in Great Marlow to be employed for the charitable uses hereafter expressed as a memorial of my late son Henry Borlase, my Will is, the said house and other houses and lands shall wholly be employed for ever for the benefit of the poor of the said Parish of Great Marlow, Little Marlow and Medmenham and none other parish, in manner as hereafter I shall express. And whereas I have already bought as much in houses and lands in Great Marlow as will amount unto fourteen pounds a year, not valuing herein the new house I have built for the School House. And my meaning is, if it please God to give me so long life, to buy twenty pounds a year in lands or rent charge so to lay also to the charitable uses hereafter expressed. And if it should please God to take me out of this miserable world before I can buy the said twenty pounds a year, then I give, bequeathe, and my Will is, four hundred pounds should be bestowed by my Executor for the purchasing of the said twenty pounds a year, more at the least by him.

I have bought at Bix, County Oxon, about twenty pounds a year in lands, and two houses, all which shall be laid for ever to the said House to these uses following, and to be assured with all the said former houses and lands by my Son and Executor to twelve feoffees, whereof eight of them shall be chosen by him in the town and parish of Great Marlow, three in the parish of Little Marlow and one in the parish of Medmenham, and when any of the said Feoffees shall die, that the surviving Feoffees or the greatest part of them shall present the

Foundation and the First 250 Years (1624-1874) | CHAPTER 1 | 11

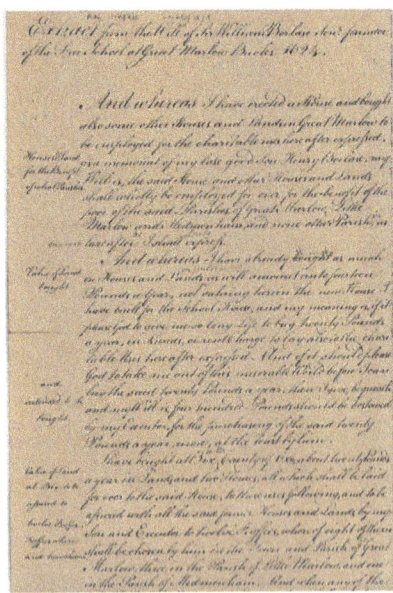

1.5.1. An extract from the will of Sir William Borlase

names of some three other fit persons to succeed in the place of him deceasing to my said Executor, whom I make during his life Governor of the said House and lands, and he shall choose such one of them as he shall think fit to succeed as Feoffees with the rest surviving. And after his decease I appoint the Lord of the Manor of Davers in the parish of Little Marlow for the time being ever hereafter to be Governor of the said House and lands so appointed and hereafter intended to be purchased, the profits whereof I do appoint to be employed as followeth:

Imprimis, twelve pounds a year shall be allowed a Schoolmaster to teach twenty four poor children to write, read and cast accounts, such as their parents and friends are not able to maintain at school, to be taken into the said School between the age of ten and fourteen, and after any of them can read, write and cast accounts, which I conceive in two years they will be ready to do, my will is that the Feoffees, or the greater part of them, shall at every Easter present the number of twelve of the fittest and best learned of them to the Governor for the time being after my Son's decease, and he, the said governor at the time being, shall choose six of them, to whom my Will is shall be given forty shillings apiece towards the binding of them apprentices to some trades; and so likewise I do appoint the said Feoffees or the greater number of them, when any are upon places void, to be put into the School, or any as aforesaid to be preferred at any Easter, to present out to those parishes where the number is void double the number of those that are to be taken in or preferred to the said Governor, and he then shall choose who shall have the benefit of the place void or to be preferred with the forty shillings.

And touching the choice of Schoolmaster for the time being, my Will is, the Governor for the time being, with the consent of the greater part of the Feoffees, shall after my Son's decease, from time to time appoint or remove him. And the said Schoolmaster, besides the twelve pounds a year, shall enjoy and have to himself wholly the new House to dwell in where Smith, now the Schoolmaster, dwelleth, without paying any rent; and also the garden, which he now holdeth, together with sufficient room in the backside to lay wood and fuel in for his own provision, the which house the said Schoolmaster and succeeding schoolmasters shall from time to time repair.

My further Will is, that there shall be yearly bought by Feoffees two reams of paper, to be allowed for the said poor scholars, and primers, psalters and some New Testaments as may serve for the said poor children to learn to write and read.

Further my Will is, that the house where now Hugh Tanner dwelleth, adjoining to the west side of the said School House, shall be for ever employed as a Work House and House of Correction for the said three parishes and none other. And the said Hugh Tanner and his successors shall be chosen into that place, according as the Schoolmaster hereby appointed to be chosen, and he and they shall have for their wages, besides the said house, barn and orchard adjoining to the said barn, the sum of six or eight pounds a year, as the Governor and Feoffees or the greater part of them after my Son's death shall think fit. And he shall teach yearly twenty-four poor women children of the Borough of Great Marlow only to make bone lace, to spin or knit, to be put to him by the Churchwardens and Overseers of the Poor of Great Marlow town and parish with the consent of the greater part of the Feoffees and Governor, as is before appointed. And the said Hugh Tanner and his successors shall whip or cause to be whipped all such offenders as the Petty Constables, Officers, or Tithing Men of the said three parishes shall bring to him by the laws of this Realm are to be whipped for any offence so punishable by the common laws or statutes of this Realm; and shall also punish such delinquents of Great Marlow as the Churchwardens and Overseers thereof, or the greatest part of them shall, with the consent of one Justice of the Peace, deliver over to him, the said Hugh Tanner, or his successors, to be punished according to the statute; and shall keep for four days in his House of Correction

1.5.2. The original School House and the House of Correction

any rogue or vagabond taken within the town and parish of Great Marlow, Little Marlow and Medmenham, or any of them (but not out of other parishes) which by lawful authority are sent to him, and shall use punishment and correction upon the person so sent as may be done by the laws of this Realm.

My Will and meaning is, that if there be any surplusage hereafter of rent to be had out of the houses and lands which are or shall be laid to the aforesaid uses, that the said surplusage shall be bestowed further to such uses for the benefit of the poor aforesaid by the Governor for the time being with the assent of the greater part of the Feoffees shall be thought fit.

And my Will is, they shall let out the said houses and lands at the best and highest rates they can well get, because it is for the good of the said poor.

Provided always and my Will and meaning is, that my Executor, my Son, shall during his life have full and sole power to himself place, remove, prefer, and take in Feoffees, Schoolmaster, Scholars, Masters of the House of Correction, and those aforesaid which he is to teach, without assent of any other at his discretion, and that the manner of election, appointing and removing before herein expressed shall be used in form aforesaid only from and after my said Son's decease."

THE FIRST CENTURY

We see from Sir William's will that the School House was built in 1624, that the first Schoolmaster was called Smith, and that the first Master of the House of Correction was Hugh Tanner. A reference is made to the School in a document of 1640. A lady named Agnes Friar, who had died in Little Marlow in 1615, was to be remembered by an annual gift of twenty shillings to twenty poor widows, to be paid at Christmas, the fund to be raised "out of the revenue of the property of John Borlase lying near the School House".

Little is known of Borlase School during its first century. An undated document of about 1730 explains why. In 1721, a Commission of Charitable Uses issued out of the Court of Chancery had investigated the administration of the Charity. They found that because Sir William Borlase's son had died without making a Deed of Feoffment or appointed feoffees (trustees) according to his father's will, "Several persons had acted as Feoffees in the said Trust without any feoffment or Deed of Appointment", and the Charity had been misapplied. The Commission ordered Borlase Warren, of Little Marlow, Lord of the Manor of Davers (Danvers), to appoint regular feoffees according to the terms of the will. He did so by deed poll, but the Commission was not yet satisfied. Some of the nominees were unsatisfactory. A further order was made that, within two months, Borlase Warren was to surrender all lands mentioned in the will that had been left to maintain the Free School to John Webb, Henry Fletcher, James Harman (Gent.), John Oxlade, William Bradshaw, William Langley, Abel Bird, John Lattimore, Andrew Medwin, Ralph Rose, Thomas Jackson (Clerk), and Gabriel Page, who were to hold the lands "in trust for the several uses mentioned".

Borlase Warren obeyed the order, but by 1730 none of the deeds or other papers could be found. They had been left in the care of James Harman, who refused to deliver them up. After a threat of legal proceedings, he handed over to the other Feoffees the keys of a box kept in the church vestry. But when they went there to open the box, it was empty!

The Feoffees appointed in 1721 administered the Trust and, when any died, others were regularly appointed by Borlase Warren. The Schoolmaster during the period was named Roe. Around 1730, the Feoffees wished to get rid of Roe, and consulted a Windsor solicitor, named R. Crowle, as to the advisability of taking

1.6.1. The original School House, built in 1624, which still forms the heart of the School

Foundation and the First 250 Years (1624-1874)

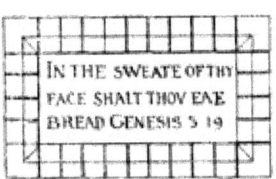

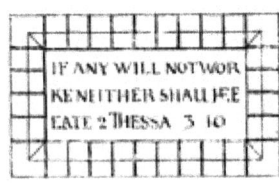

1.6.2. Inscriptions on the front of the original School House

action. Of the Feoffees of 1721, James Harman, William Langley, Andrew Medwin, Ralph Rose and Thomas Jackson were still alive. Thomas Lockwood, Francis Sawyer, John Gibbons, Jonathan Oxlade, Henry Lovegrove, Thomas Keene and William Hawes had since been appointed. It is suggested that James Harman was a friend of Roe, and rather than see him ejected, Harman had destroyed the School documents.

THOMAS HEATHER I (1735–1759)

What happened we do not know, but presumably Roe was ejected before 17 January 1735. On that date, the Feoffees met to set the House in order. The window at the north end of the School was to be taken down and made larger. A new brewhouse was to be erected at the north end of the Schoolroom. The two chamber floors were to be taken up and new ones laid; the old boards, if fitting, were to be used to mend the garrets. Windows and window cases were to be mended and repaired, and the floor of the dwelling-room to be repaved.

On 29 April 1736, the Feoffees, with the approval of Borlase Warren, appointed Thomas Heather, of Hughenden, to be Schoolmaster of the Free School at the salary mentioned in the will, together with £4 per year additional salary. He actually received £20, not £16, during the whole period he was Master.

For the next eleven years, there is little to record. The Feoffees met regularly each Easter to submit to the Governor a list of applicants for places in the School and to inspect the School premises. There was no lack of applicants. In 1742, there were ten boys applying for five places; in 1746, twenty boys for ten places —

six from Medmenham, six from Little Marlow and eight from Marlow. In 1747, one boy was expelled for continued absence. There is evidence that boys stayed on at the School, not for the two years provided for in the will, but for four or five years. Of nine boys admitted in 1742, one remained until 1747, six until 1746 and only two left after two years' schooling. In 1743, the Feoffees met in August, when they resolved to erect "a room and chamber over the drink vault to prevent the running of rain water through the arch in to the vault, at present very troublesome, and also be very convenient and serviceable for the family of the present and succeeding Masters".

In 1747, the Governor, Borlase Warren, died, and was succeeded by his son, John Borlase Warren. Andrew Medwin, the old Treasurer, was followed by William Hawes, who kept the Trust accounts and documents much more carefully than his predecessor.

Perhaps it would be interesting to summarize the bills paid in 1749 as a clue to the value of the Borlase Free School property at the time. Thomas Heather was paid £10 salary each half year, at Easter and Michaelmas, and ten shillings each half year for a ream of paper for use by the boys. At Easter, he bought seven spelling books at 5s. 10d., for the use of the boys admitted that year. James Field, the Master of the House of Correction, received £1 11s. 0d. each half-year. Buckle Hawes receipted a bill for his Uncle William Hawes for 21 yards of blue cloth at 2s. 6d. — £2 12s. 6d.; 5¼ yards of scarlet

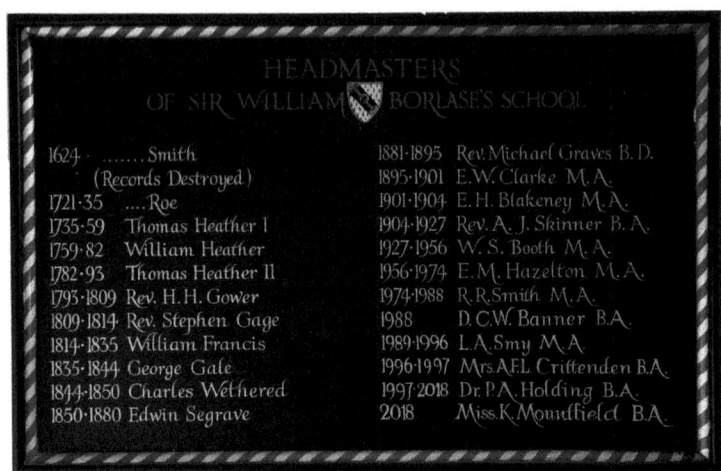

1.7.1. Headteachers of the School; little is known before Thomas Heather I in 1735

quality — 6½d.; 7 half ounces of thread — 7d.; seven blue caps, tassels and strings — 8s. 5½d.; and 8s. 2d. paid to James Field for making the new uniforms for the boys admitted at Easter. Henry Lovegrove signed a receipt for £1 from the Agnes Friar legacy. Elizabeth Cooke made her cross on a receipt for £2 out of Sir William Borlase's legacy to apprentice boys leaving school. Mary Hollis was paid 12s. 3d. for building materials (500 bricks, 300 tiles and 10 bushels of lime delivered at the Free School cost 3s. 3d.). Ann Hobbs was paid £1 2s. 8d. for materials delivered "at Ye Whiping House". Thomas Gray had £2 9s. 8d. for "work done on housen belonging to the Free School". William Lorrance was paid 12s 2½d. for similar work. William Webb was paid £1 16s. 8½d. for work at the School and Chapel End. John Phillips received £13 1s. 3½d. for wood supplied and work done at School, and Thomas Colsil received 9s. 2d. for five days thatching of "Ye Barn" belonging to "Ye Free School". This is an outlay of over £50 — a fair average of the annual payments during the eighteenth century. In this year, we have the earliest extant record of the blue and red School uniform and of the payment of the apprenticeship legacy.

Between 1750 and 1759, we have further evidence of charges upon the Estate. In 1750, £1 12d. 0d. was paid as eight years' quit rent for the houses in Chapel End to Lord Cobham, and in 1755, £1 for five years' quit rent for the same property to Daniel Moore. During the same period, twenty-seven sums of £2 were paid, according to the terms of Sir William Borlase's will, for apprenticing suitable boys after four years at School. The money was usually paid to the parents, but occasionally to the new master who apprenticed the boy. The signatures are some guide to the class of boy at the School. Four parents were unable to sign their names, while many of the signatures are obviously those of people unaccustomed to writing. Some, however, are the signatures of local tradesmen. Before a boy could qualify for the bequest, he had to have a testimonial of his ability and good character signed by Thomas Heather. Usually, Heather baldly stated that the boy had attended school for four years and was generally satisfactory. Occasionally, however, he would open out, as in the case of James Hall, who left in 1753, who was "abundantly qualified as to writing and arithmetic for the business into which he is now apprenticed".

The Governor, John Borlase Warren, one time MP for Nottingham, lived at Stapleford, Nottinghamshire, and never visited Little Marlow. At first, he selected the boys from the lists presented to him by the simple method of taking the first names on the list. After 1755, however, the correspondence with the Feoffees was done entirely by his secretary, John Wilkinson. In 1756, Warren was too afflicted with gout to attend to business and, from that date, he left the choice of boys entirely to the Feoffees. In 1758, after much pressure on the Senior Feoffee, James Harman, who had been Feoffee since 1721, to resign, a new Deed of Feoffment was drawn up in favour of the Feoffees now in office. When Harman's successor was appointed, one of the candidates was Charles Wethered — the first member of the Wethered family to be mentioned in the documents. In 1759, Thomas Heather died. He was succeeded as Schoolmaster by his son, William.

WILLIAM HEATHER (1759–1782)

William's salary was only £12 a year, paid annually at Easter. He ran the School much as his father had done, but charged a penny per book for making the writing paper into exercise books, and 18s. for pens and ink, at the rate of 1s. per boy. There were, therefore, 18 free-place boys in the School in 1760. He occasionally bought Testaments at 1s. 2d. each. He bought two in 1764, five in 1765 and seven in 1766.

In 1763, the Governor died and was succeeded by his ten-year-old son, another John Borlase Warren. During the minority, the business of the Trust was done by his uncle and trustee, James Warren, Vicar of Stretton Abbey.

A bill of 1759 for eleven years' quit rent, due to William Clayton, shows how the School property was assessed at that time. For the Free School, 5s.; for "the Parsonage half-acre and a garden plat next to Birches", 1s.; for three tenements in Chapel End, 8d. per year were paid. In 1762, extensive alterations were made to the House of Correction, and in 1765, two new cottages were built; bills amounting to £134 were paid in this year for building materials and labour.

In 1771, the Feoffees seized the goods of John Piggot, who had died owing half a year's rent. From the inventory, we gather that the cottage consisted of four rooms. The kitchen contained a dresser, two stools and five chairs. The room behind it, two square tables, an old cupboard and a bedstead. The room above that, an old flock bed, a close stool and a screen. The front room above the kitchen, nothing but a deal tester frame. The town crier announced the sale, but there were no bidders. Luke Medwin valued the goods at 27s., and they were bought by Robert Piggott.

In 1775, William Hawes was succeeded as Treasurer by his nephew, Buckle Hawes, who had for some time done all the secretarial work and run as a partner his uncle's drapery business. For some years, he drew up bills for School uniforms, made out to himself and receipted by himself, though occasionally we find the signature of Thomas Emes, who was himself in time to become Treasurer of the School Trust. Buckle Hawes was not the only one of the Feoffees to supply the School with materials. The Lovegroves, the Hammonds and the Lockwoods appear again and again as builders, painters, glaziers, Feoffees, Churchwardens and Overseers of the Poor. Other familiar eighteenth century names are Gray, Hobbs, Clark and Loftin; and all of them had boys at the School at one time or another. One, William Loftin, of Windsor Park, left in 1759 a charitable bequest to apprentice to any trade or business poor children of Marlow. The Oxlades were the agents of the Claytons and lived at Widmere. The Medwins lived at Little Marlow and were possibly the agents of the Borlase Warrens. It was they who undertook any special business transactions on behalf of the Governor and Feoffees. The Sawyers, one after another, represented Medmenham parish.

The Governor, John Borlase Warren, signed only one School document, in 1776, when he objected to certain nominations of Feoffees and insisted on other selections. He was then aged 23 years. He had been educated at Winchester

1.8.1. Admiral Sir John Borlase Warren, 1st Baronet (1753–1822); in his coat of arms, those of Borlase can be seen quartered with those of Warren

1.8.2. Memorial to Sir John Borlase Warren in St Mary & St Edburga's Church, Stratton Audley

and Emmanuel College, Cambridge. In 1775, the Borlase baronetcy was revived in his favour, and in the same year he sat together with William Clayton as MP for Marlow — the last Borlase to represent the town. In 1777, he set off to play his part in the American War as a sailor under Lord Howe. At the end of the war, he was a Captain. During the Revolution and the Napoleonic Wars, he was continually active, capturing a French squadron in 1794, and another in 1799 when he was a Rear Admiral. He was made full Admiral in 1810. He died in 1822 and is buried in Stratton Audley. However, his connection with Borlase had ceased in 1781 when he sold his estates in Little Marlow and Medmenham to William Lee Antonie (1764–1815), of Colworth House, Bedfordshire.

William Heather remained Schoolmaster until 1782 when he resigned, and his nephew, Thomas Heather, took his place. He had been gradually adding to the School's equipment. From 1775 on, he had bought supplies of Dilworth's Spelling Book, price 1s., and occasionally Bond's expositors, dictionaries or spelling books, with words explained. In 1778, he began renting land from the Feoffees, for which he paid an annual rent of £7.

THOMAS HEATHER II (1782–1793)

Thomas Heather, like his uncle, was paid £12 per year, out of which £5 was deducted for the rent of land. The only addition to the School equipment in his time — he died in 1793 — was an *Explanation of the Church Catechism*. He bought 15 copies for 8s. 9d. in 1786 and from time to time renewed his stock. The cost of the two reams of paper soared up to £1 10s. 0d. Among the Feoffees of this time were William and Thomas Wethered. The last of the Medwins resigned in 1790 because he lived at Ealing, and the distance to Marlow to attend meetings was too great. Among the boys at School, one meets with familiar names such as Aldridge, Carr, Gray, Copas, Barney, Townsend (Abraham and Samuel), Langley, Gardner and White. Thomas Emes was now a Feoffee. Buckle Hawes, the Treasurer, had sold his business in 1794 to Greenaway and Lovegrove, who now supplied the material for the School uniforms.

From 1787 onwards, the Feoffees became very active and there was every sign of prosperity. In 1788, they decided to rebuild four tenements in Chapel End, "by the turnpike", at an estimated cost of £330. Harry Barney and Benjamin Gray were to be asked to answer within six days whether they could complete the work in ten weeks. A resolution was passed "to erect as many decent habitations as the money in hand will admit of for the benefit of the Charity". Gray and Barney set to work immediately, Gray being responsible for the brickwork and Barney for the woodwork. William Langley dug a well 20½ feet deep. James Lovegrove put in the windows. The actual cost of the houses was £354 14s. 5d. In the same year, Thomas Heather's washhouse was repaired, and Harry Barney undertook alterations to the property at Bix.

In 1789, Thomas Emes, as agent for the Royal Exchange Assurance, insured against fire all the Borlase property for an annual premium of £1 15d. 6s. The whole estate was valued for insurance purposes at £1,300; "£400 on the Free School and dwelling house under one roof, brick and stone built and tiled, tenant, Thomas Heather; £100 on a House of Correction adjoining, brick built and tiled; £40 on a barn, separate, thatched; £150 on two houses, brick built and tiled near, tenants, the Widow Gray and Thomas Barnes. £60 on three tenements adjoining, brick and plaster built and tiled, situate in Great Marlow, tenants, Collins, Price and Warner; £200 on four tenements under one roof, brick built and tiled, situate in Great Marlow, tenants, William Macey, William Green and others; £140 on a house, brick and plaster built and tiled, situate in Bix in the County of Oxford, tenant Thomas Beckett; £20 on a granary and woodhouse adjoining; £30 on a cowhouse, stable and coalhouse adjoining; £60 on a wheat barn; £20 on a barley barn and stable adjoining; and £30 on a house, tenant Edward Wheeler, all thatched and situate near." As £350 had recently been paid for building the four houses in Chapel End, and as the insurance value is given as £200, perhaps we may almost double the £1,300 to obtain the real value of the buildings. Then there is the value of the land at Marlow and Bix to be added.

During this decade, we first come across hotel bills and printed bill heads. The Feoffees visited Bix and dined at the Catherine Wheel, Henley, kept by Henry Saunders. They paid for dinners 15s., beer 5s., wine 15s. 6d., punch 2s. 6d., tobacco 9d., horse 4s., and coffee 1s. 6d. Other expenses of the trip were: servants 3s. 10d., man showing premises 1s., horse hire "for several of the trustees" 5s. 1d., post chaise and driver to Henley 16s. 2d., at Medmenham 3s.

The keeper of the Crown and Broad Arrow, Marlow, was Nicholas Thomas. The first meeting of the Feoffees here — they had previously met at the School — was on 10 May 1782. There was a bill of £2 18s. 0d. for 12 dinners, beer, tobacco, wine, punch and tips. Later, we meet more frequently with suppers, washed down with four times their value in beer, punch and wine. One bill of 12s. 9d. includes bread, cheese and radish 9d., beer 1s. 6d., wine 4s., punch 6s.

REV. H. H. GOWER (1793–1809)

In 1793, Thomas Heather was succeeded as Master by the Rev. H. H. Gower, who like his predecessors, was paid £12 per year. Out of this, he refunded £7 for the rent of the "closes" and from 1800, £4 for the rent of the cottage next to the School on the town side. As we know that he had an assistant to aid him, it is clear that he had little of his salary to himself. He probably made his living out of his fee-paying pupils. Like his predecessors too, he kept strictly, or was kept, to the school books mentioned in the Founder's will, but he bought copies far more frequently. There is a bill of his for 1799: 20 Testaments £1 10s. 0d.; 19 spelling books £1 2s. 2d.; 19 Psalters £1 3s. 9d.; two reams of paper made into books £2 17s. 6d.; pens and ink £1. Judging by a list of Free Scholars of 1794,

1.10.1. A view of Court Garden and Great Marlow in 1793, the year the Rev. H. H. Gower became Schoolmaster

there seems to have been a full complement of boys on the Foundation at that time, and so there probably was in the year of this bill. This list contains the names of three boys who had been on the Foundation for four years and were qualified to compete for the apprenticeship grant. They were John Clark, Thomas Stacey and Thomas Fox. Ten boys had completed three years: Jeffry Hackshaw, Henry Johnson, Joseph James, John Townsend, William Street, Richard Stevens, Joseph Carr, Thomas Bowles, William Johnson and Frederick Clark. Only three boys had completed their second year: Charles Clark, William Harding and Samuel Adams. That left eight boys in their first year: Richard Smith, Thomas Fletcher, William Warner, William Franklin, Robert Mossenton, John Coleman, William Rose and William Silver. The School was inspected by the Feoffees at Easter, when each boy was given 2d., and the Assistant 2s. 6d. A few years later, the maid also received 1s. on these occasions. It was now that the Feoffees selected the best boys for the apprenticeship grant. Of the 24 boys mentioned, John Clark alone received the £2 in 1794, but during the next three years Stacey, Johnson, Stevens, Hackshaw, Harding, Fletcher, Franklin, Mossenton and Warner all received the bequest — ten of the 24 boys.

During this period, applications for free places at the School had to be made on printed forms. The boy's name and age and the parent's name and occupation had to be stated. These warnings were clearly made: "Boys admitted on the Foundation of Great Marlow Free School must attend regularly. No excuse will be allowed except in case of illness or boys really going to work in time of harvest. The Schoolmaster has strict orders to report all that absent themselves, and all those who have not such substantial reasons for being absent as above will be expelled the said School and receive no benefit therefrom."

An analysis of the ages of the boys admitted shows that the usual age of entry was ten. As several applications often had to be made owing to the number of candidates and lack of vacancies, some applicants were only eight when they first applied.

In 1794, James Field died. He had been Master of the House of Correction since our records began and the tailor who had for over half a century made the School uniforms, or "blew grounds", as he called them. He was succeeded in the House of Correction by Robert Gray, who always called it a "House of Commission". Gray was a bricklayer and general labourer, so the uniforms from now on were made by Edward Stevens, father of the boy Richard Stevens.

Judging by the instructions given to Robert Gray by the Feoffees on his appointment, the Mastership of the House of Correction was almost a sinecure, and the Master was lucky to have the £3 2s. 0d. per year continued. Here are the instructions "for the due execution of his office":

"You are to take care that the state of the premises be preserved to the best of your power. The garden fences are to be done at your own expense, and when the drain and ditch is required, that you keep it clean. You must be very careful not to annoy or do anything to disturb the Master of the Free School or his family, and be ready to distribute letters, to call any extra meeting, or go of an errand when required."

In 1797, Buckle Hawes died, having held the office of Treasurer for twenty-two years. Thomas Emes naturally stepped into his shoes. Emes was a methodical treasurer and kept a regular balance sheet for each year in a book he called his "waste book". Since 1793, three new tenements had been built at Chapel End. This time, the Trust was not rich enough to pay the total cost, so £200 was borrowed from one of the Feoffees, Joseph Bird. This helped the Feoffees to pay Benjamin Gray a bill of £202 9s. 4d. for the brickwork, and James Lovegrove £24 16s. 0d. for painting and glass; but for some years, Harry Barney received interest on his bill of £113 6s. 11d. for the woodwork. Joseph Bird was fully repaid

1.10.3. A view of Marlow from 1799, showing All Saints' Church (with the old spire that collapsed and was replaced in 1832–1835) and the old wooden bridge across the Thames, with five eel traps on the left

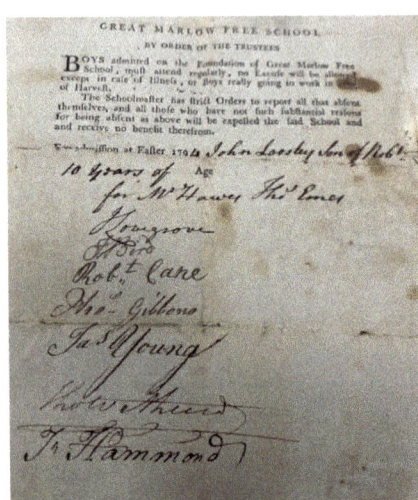

1.10.2. An official warning to boys not to be absent from School without good reason, signed by the Feoffees

1.10.4. The Royal Military College cadets on parade before George III at Remnantz in the early nineteenth century

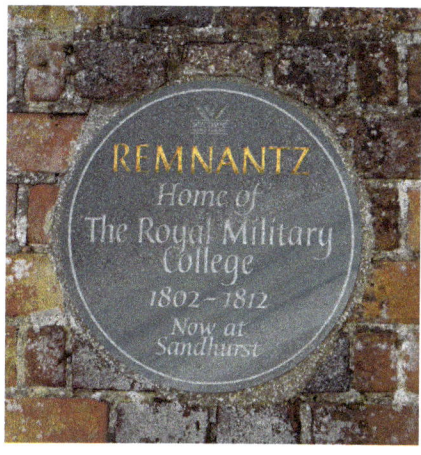

1.10.5. A plaque recording the site of the Royal Military College at Remnantz

by 1810, and Harry Barney by 1812. These alterations increased the Assurance value of the Borlase property to £1,500. The Trust, despite some of their tenants being irregular rent payers, could reckon on an average income of £70, £30 of which was paid by John Beckett for his farm at Bix. The cottagers of Chapel Street paid £3 10s. 0d. per year. In some years, there was an additional income from the sale of trees.

However, with the turn of the century, we begin to see signs of distress. The Industrial Revolution was telling its tale on Marlow, for the bone lace makers were being outbid by the manufacturers of the Midlands. The protracted Revolutionary and Napoleonic wars were sending up the cost of living. The Feoffees found their tenants unable to pay rent, and among the accounts are several notices to quit and lists of tenement holders with long arrears of rent. True, the Royal Military College at Remnantz between 1802 to 1812, located opposite the School, brought trade into the town, and all the big houses were occupied, but even that did not make up for the loss of local industries. New roads were being constructed and improved, and the Thames was no longer the bearer of the goods of the district.

The cost of two reams of paper was £2 17s. 6d. in 1800, £3 17s. 6d. in 1806, and £4 in 1813. The rent of John Beckett was doubled, and in spite of the corn laws, he was given notice to quit for arrears of rent in 1814. He seems to have stayed on, but his arrears were £56 10s. 0d. in 1817.

REV. STEPHEN GAGE (1809–1814)

Rev. H. H. Gower died in the winter of 1809, and for a while his widow, S. E. Gower, tried to manage the School, but was not very successful in controlling the boys. The Feoffees gave her notice to quit, but she wrote to the Governor that the Rev. Stephen Gage had "generously proposed himself as Master of the Free School". Governor Antonie replied that he was willing to appoint him, and the Feoffees allowed Mrs Gower to remain in possession. From now until Christmas 1814, Gage, Vicar of Bisham, and over 70 years of age, conducted the School, but it was Mrs Gower who signed the testimonials of the boys who were leaving. Her testimonials named the trade that the boy was taking up, if that was known. Seven boys were apprenticed to shoemakers, one to a carpenter, one to a bricklayer, one to a cordwainer and one to a tailor. Among the boys of this period are other familiar Marlow names: Davis, East, White, Wellicome, Sparks, Plumridge, and of course, Sawyer, Townsend, Clark and Gray. Among the Feoffees were James Deane, William Townsend, Robert Lunnon and Thomas Rolls (coal merchant). After 1802, Thomas Emes was succeeded as Treasurer by Timothy Tregoe, and he in 1814 by Thomas Wethered.

In 1811, there was a change of Governor. William Lee Antonie had been Governor of the School and owner of the Medmenham and Little Marlow estates since 1781. In 1790–1796, he sat as MP for Great Marlow and in 1802–1812 for Bedford. He sold the Little Marlow estate to the distinguished General, Sir George Nugent GCB (1757–1849). Antonie died a bachelor in 1815.

After the resignation of the Rev. Stephen Gage at Christmas 1814, there was a short period of nine weeks during which a local man, Edward Neighbour, conducted the School, pending the appointment of a new Master. Sir George Nugent was abroad, and his deputy, Sir Scrope Bernard-Morland MP, would not undertake the responsibility during his absence.

1.11.1. Field Marshal Sir George Nugent, Governor of Borlase School

WILLIAM FRANCIS (1814–1835)

When, in 1814, an advertisement for a new Master was inserted in a Reading newspaper, the salary was stated to be £50. There were four applicants. One, J. Witherington, wrote that he had "a knowledge of the French and Latin languages, writing, arithmetic, mathematics, algebra, geography, book keeping and other requisites of a liberal and commercial education".

The post was given to William Francis (1774–1843), the Headmaster of Taplow-Hill Academy, Maidenhead. Together with his application, he sent a printed prospectus of his school. It had "a most salubrious and eligible situation". "Young gentlemen were genteelly Boarded and carefully instructed in Classical and the several Branches of Mathematical Learning by W. Francis and Assistants. Terms: 25 Guineas per Annum, and 1 Guinea Entrance. French, Dancing and Drawing, each 1 Guinea per Quarter and 1 Guinea Entrance." Then follow twelve testimonials, three from professors at the Royal Military College, three from eminent mathematicians and six from clergymen, provided when Francis had applied for his position at Taplow in 1804. These bear evidence of "the great talents and literary acquirements, the extraordinary knowledge of Mathematics, the exemplary moral character" of the new Master. Francis began his duties at Marlow at Easter 1815. Nearly £100 had been spent on repairs to the School House. However, Francis did not take the cottage on the town side of the School, but he retained the land, for which he paid a rent of £9 6s. 0d.

Possibly the Feoffees felt in appointing Francis and paying him a higher salary than his predecessors that Borlase would from now on have to provide a higher type of education than hitherto. A boys' school, under the auspices of the National Society, had been opened in Marlow in 1813. The girls were similarly provided for in the following year. There were approximately 4,000 inhabitants in Marlow at that time, many of whom had become poor since the removal of the Military College to Sandhurst.

The Borlase boys of 1817 must have been amazed at the behaviour of a family who came to live at Albion House in West Street, next door to the Borlase tenements. The head of the household was Percy Bysshe Shelley (1792–1822), then a young man of 24 years, but even then married to his second wife, Mary Wollstonecraft Shelley (1797–1851), the daughter of the philosophers William Godwin and Mary Wollstonecraft. With them was Jane ('Claire') Clairmont, the daughter of Godwin's wife by a former marriage, and her child, Allegra, afterwards proved to be the daughter of Lord Byron. Frequent visitors to the house, besides Godwin and his wife, were Thomas Love Peacock, the novelist, who lived in Marlow; Thomas Jefferson Hogg, who with Shelley had been expelled from Oxford; and Leigh Hunt, then editor of *The Examiner* — all of them eccentric characters. As they sat under the tree covering where the Fives Court used to be, they could hear the noise from the Schoolroom, and possibly Borlase boys listened to some of the learned conversation on literature, philosophy, and schemes for the amelioration of mankind. They may have heard Percy read parts of *The Revolt of Islam*, or Mary read chapters from her novel, *Frankenstein*, or Peacock read scenes from *Nightmare Abbey*, all of which works were written at Marlow at this time, between February 1817 and January 1818, when the Shelleys left Marlow. However, it is more probable that the Borlase boys were amazed to see Percy pacing West Street with his shirt open at the neck and his head covered with a garland of wild flowers or old man's beard. They may have seen him exchange boots or coats with a beggar. He is certain to have visited some of their homes distributing his blankets during the cold winter of 1817.

1.12.2. Mary Wollstonecraft Shelley and Percy Bysshe Shelley

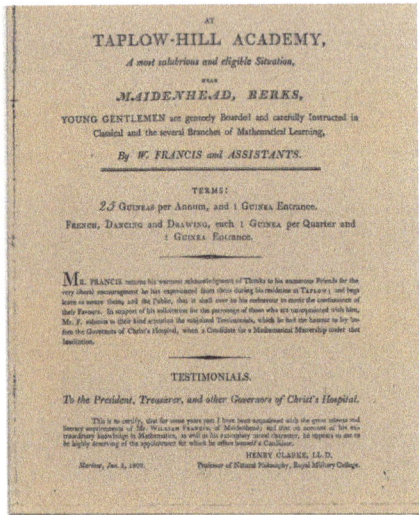

1.12.1. Prospectus of Taplow-Hill Academy, containing testimonials for William Francis

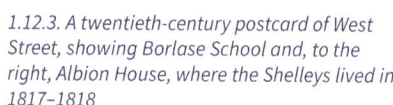

1.12.3. A twentieth-century postcard of West Street, showing Borlase School and, to the right, Albion House, where the Shelleys lived in 1817–1818

Percy Shelley's reference to the School in his beautiful dedication of *The Revolt of Islam* to Mary is hardly complimentary to the tone of the School under Francis. But perhaps little attention should be paid to it as evidence of the conduct of the Master, when it is considered that any form of restraint was tyranny to Shelley.

*I do remember well the hour that burst
My spirit's sleep; a fresh May morn it was,
When I walked forth upon the glittering grass,
And wept, I knew not why; until there rose
From the near schoolroom, voices, that, alas!
Were but one echo from the world of woes—
The harsh and grating strife of tyrants and of foes.*

So far, nothing has been heard of the School for "poor women children" provided for in the Founder's will. In 1822, the Feoffees decided to open this institution in the House of Correction. On 1 May, Miss Lovegrove bought from Thomas Rolls & Son 44¼ yards print, £2 2s. 5d.; 14 yards Irish, £1 2s. 2d.; 2 yards calico, 1s.; 12 pairs gloves, 10s. And later, she added 12 straw bonnets and 26 yards blue serge. In November, Mrs Elizabeth Barney was appointed Mistress of the new School. Apparently, the children were to be taught dressmaking and millinery, and to be encouraged to make their own hats. In 1824, Mrs Barney charged for straw for plaiting, 12s.; for mill, 2s. 6d.; "larning the children", 6s. Occasionally, books were bought for the girls. In 1824, six Bible and Gospel histories were bought for them. In 1828, Francis charged for six spelling books, and in 1829, for eight Testaments, all for the use of the girls. Twelve girls were admitted to the School each year. Mrs Barney was paid £12 per year in quarterly instalments.

There is nothing much to report of the boys' School for some time. Thomas Rolls became Treasurer of the Trust in 1817. In 1819, there was a new Assurance policy for £2,000 with the Royal Exchange, John Ralfs, the draper, being the local agent. In 1827, Ralfs was succeeded both as insurance agent and as School draper by W. H. Ubsdell, the first of the Marlow tradesmen, excluding the hotel keepers, to have a printed bill-head. He called himself a linen and woollen draper, haberdasher, hosier, glover, hatter, etc., and importer of Irish linen, but he did not give the address of his shop. He was also the first tradesman to call the School a Blue Coat School. There were no dinners at the Crown Inn in those days, but in 1828, a gig and horse were hired from R. Westbrook, of the Crown Inn and Posting House (the Broad Arrow had disappeared from the name) to visit the farm at Bix. Poor John Beckett, of Bix Farm, was in worse straits than ever. Thomas Rolls & Son, on behalf of the Feoffees, had to deliver on him a distress warrant for arrears of rent and put a man in possession at the farmhouse.

On 14 May 1829, an Act of Parliament approved the building of a new suspension

1.12.4. In the dedication of The Revolt of Islam, *Shelley mentions the noise from Borlase School next door*

Foundation and the First 250 Years (1624-1874)   CHAPTER 1 | 21

1.12.5. The House of Correction, adjoining the School House, where poor girls were taught lace making

bridge over the River Thames at Great Marlow. This was an important town improvement initiative and involved rebuilding the existing wooden structure in metal and repositioning it to the bottom of the High Street (it had previously run from the bottom of St Peter's Street). However, in a letter to the *Bucks Gazette*, William Francis drew attention to the slow pace and poor quality of the work and the amount of money spent. A heated exchange of letters ensued between Francis and the bridge engineer, John Millington. The newspaper initially sided with Millington, but problems with the bridge became apparent when the magistrates appointed to manage the works met. Shortly afterwards, Millington "left for Mexico" and William Tierney Clark, credited with the successful construction of the bridge, took over. In January 1830, the *Bucks Gazette* humbly acknowledged: "We owe, in common with others, a debt of justice to Mr Francis of Marlow, for his bold and fearless attempt to unmask the pretensions of our Trans-Atlantic engineer (Mr Millington) and showing to the public the value of claims, which had not one atom of sound science to support them."

But if the first fifteen years of Francis's mastership were quiet and uneventful, the remaining five were not so. In 1830, the Feoffees had become so dissatisfied with his conduct that they gave him notice to quit. Francis paid no attention. The Feoffees, knowing Francis, and fearing expensive litigation, let things go on. Then, later that year, Francis was convicted of assault and imprisoned for one week in Aylesbury Jail. In February 1833, legal proceedings in the Court of the King's Bench were instituted against him for libel on the Senior Feoffee, Thomas Wethered. The trial did not take place until June 1834 and, in November 1834, Francis was convicted and sentenced to three months' imprisonment, again at Aylesbury. The judge's comments forced the Feoffees to take notice and act. The case was reported in the *Morning Herald* of Tuesday 25 November. "Such expressions," said the Judge, "showed the deepest rancour in the breast of the defendant. It had been said that the defendant was a Schoolmaster and had been so for twenty years. It was evident he was a most improper man to fill that situation."

More recent research sheds light on Francis's tenure at the School, suggesting his situation was more nuanced than previously thought. In 1830, he was convicted of assault against a local baker named William Hatch. In his summary, the presiding judge said the witnesses on each side were so contradictory that one party must have perjured himself. Although the jury decided that Francis had struck the first blow and had, therefore, disturbed the peace, Hatch

1.12.6. The new Marlow Suspension Bridge, completed in 1832

1.12.7. Plaque on Marlow Bridge commemorating William Tierney Clark, the architect who replaced John Millington after William Francis's intervention

was subsequently found guilty of several violent crimes, including a brutal assault on his wife. So perhaps Francis had not been the guilty party in the altercation, explaining why the School Feoffees decided not to dismiss him, despite his conviction.

In 1833, Thomas Wethered took legal action against William Francis for criminal libel. Once again, it is important to look a little deeper into the matter. From 1688 to 1868, the voters of Great Marlow had the right to elect two MPs, and from 1790, the borough was 'in the pocket' of the Williams family of Bisham. For several years, Francis had been involved in local politics but was on a different side from that of Thomas Wethered, chief Feoffee of the School, who supported the established MPs, Owen and Thomas Peers Williams. In January 1833, the *Windsor & Eton Express* published an anonymous letter from Francis accusing Thomas Wethered of political shenanigans, a spat that was typical of the time. However, Thomas Wethered's son, Captain Edward Wethered, had recently died aged 32 years. So when the letter from Francis unpleasantly concluded, "although the laws of the land cannot reach such odious misconduct the laws of the Almighty will, and relying upon the sacred truths of the Decalogue, I think I already see the iniquity of the Sire has been visited upon the head of the son", the grieving Thomas Wethered instigated legal proceedings against Francis for criminal libel. In June 1834, the case went to court. However, the law at the time meant that Francis's lawyer could not present evidence to substantiate the allegations that he had made in the letter. This restriction that the truth was no defence to a charge of criminal libel removed any possibility of the jury understanding the events that led up to Francis writing the letter. Francis spent three months in Aylesbury jail but, after his release, he became a champion of fair elections. He spent the next six years until his death ensuring that electors were correctly registered to vote.

Immediately after Francis's conviction, the Feoffees decided to hold a meeting at the Crown Hotel and to call in Sir George Nugent, the Governor. On 4 December 1834, the date fixed for the meeting, the Governor was so ill that it was decided to meet at his home, Westhorpe House. Thomas Rolls, the Treasurer, ordered Mrs Francis to send six boys, two from each class — all to bring their School books. At the meeting, it was decided that Francis must be removed and a new master appointed. But the Feoffees knew they were not done with him yet. "The Charity," says Rolls, "through the disrepute of the Master is very nearly ruined in character and utility… Very serious repairs are wanting to the School House, although the Master, by the terms of the Founder's will is bound to keep these premises in good repair… The expenses of proceedings at law or in equity

1.12.8. Westhorpe House, Little Marlow, formerly home to Sir George Nugent

to remove the Master will no doubt be met on his part by the utmost cunning, chicanery and legal procrastination in every possible shape."

No assistance would come from the Charity Commissioners because a new Act had been passed to limit their powers. Meanwhile, while legal proceedings to remove Francis were pending, Francis's son, Frederick, ran the School. In June 1835, Frederick wrote a carefully penned letter to the Feoffees begging them to have compassion on the family and on his father who had served them for twenty years, and who was to be left penniless in his old age. The Feoffees paid no attention to this appeal, and appointed George Gale on one year's probation. The solicitor tried hard to deliver a notice to quit on Francis, but he would not easily be removed. The Sheriff's officer had to be called in. Francis was finally turned out of the School House in June. The Feoffees proceeded to do the necessary repairs, and for safety's sake put Joseph Gray to sleep there. Francis received his full half-year's pay up to April 1835, adding to the receipt, "balance which I receive without prejudice to legal proceedings now pending". He still owed for the rent of his fields, and as he did not answer a demand from Rolls, the Feoffees seized his haystack. The last we hear of him is in a letter to Rolls in April 1836, demanding his salary up to June 1835. The tone is not friendly. "You seem," he writes, "to have overlooked the balance of the salary due to me to the expiration of three months after I received notice to quit. However, as the funds of the School have been very much exhausted since they came under your control, I will waive claim to more than one month's notice." He did not get it! The solicitor's bill for ejecting Francis was £108 11s. 0d. Francis died in Marlow in 1843.

It was in one of Thomas Rolls's letters during this trouble that we first come across the full name of the School, Sir William Borlase's School.

GEORGE GALE (1835–1844)

George Gale started as Schoolmaster under serious disadvantages, for not only was the School in a bad way, but so too were the finances of the Trust. Retrenchment was the motto of the Feoffees. He had started school in the National School Room on 16 February 1835 with four dozen copybooks, two dozen ciphering books and 250 quills as the only equipment for which the Feoffees paid. His salary was only £25, half that of Francis. Elizabeth Barney, too, had her salary cut down from £12 to £10, and it was decided that the girls should no longer be provided with uniforms.

The Feoffees were at their wits' end how to balance their accounts. In 1830, they had borrowed £300 from one of their members, John Cozens, to build two new tenements in West Street and a barn at the farm at Bix. In 1836, Cozens died, and the executors were pressing for the return of the principal. Money, too, had been borrowed from Thomas Wethered — £64, and the Treasurer himself had advanced £30. All this was in addition to the lawyer's bill of £108 11s. 0d. and numerous bills to tradesmen. The total debt of the Trust was £551. The average ordinary annual expenditure from 1830 to 1836 was £132 18s. 2d., made up of £15 interest to Cozens; £5 insurance premium; £50 salary to Francis; £12 to Elizabeth Barney; £3 2s. 0d. to the "whipper", Robert Gray; £1 to the Agnes Friar bequest; £7 for apprenticing boys; £3 commission to the collector of rents; £4 14s. 0d. for boys' uniforms; £2 3s. 0d. for girls' uniforms; £6 18s. 8d. for books, etc.; 6s., annual gift at Easter; 5s., assistant's fee; 1s., master's servant; £20 (average) for repairs; £1 16s. 0d. land tax for Bix; and 13s. quit rent for Bix. To meet this expenditure, there was an annual income of £71 12s. 10d. from the Marlow estate. (As usual, John Beckett, of Bix, was hopelessly in arrears, but had promised to pay £30.) From the Schoolhouse yard and garden in the possession of Francis there was no rent. Nor was there from the cottages and gardens occupied by Robert Gray and Mrs Barney. From the two new tenements on the town side of the School came £6 each. From the slope, the playground and the garden belonging to the Schoolmaster, came £9 6s. 0d. From the barley field, rented by Thomas Wethered, came £12 6s. 10d. Four tenement holders in Chapel Street paid £5 each, and the other three £6 each. Rolls had a scheme to increase the income to £122 6s. 10d. and decrease the expenditure to £99 13s. 8d., and to use the balance for the reduction of the debt. He wrote several letters to the Charity Commissioners and to Betton's Charity to appeal for help.

Betton's Charity was administered by the Ironmongers' Company, and before any of the money could be touched, there was the Court of Chancery to be faced. The officials of the Company occasionally sent round questionnaires to the applicants, and from Rolls's answers to some of these questions, we may glean some interesting information. Marlow in 1840, he says, was partly agricultural and partly manufacturing, and had a population of 3,763; Little Marlow had 860 and Medmenham 385. Reckoning six square feet for each child, the Boys' School could accommodate 43, and the Girls' School 28. The boys had one month's vacation at Christmas, a week at Easter, and a month during harvest. In another letter, dated 6 March 1841, he says, "The children are taught in strict conformity with the tenets of the Church of England, attend the Parish Church regularly, and only yesterday repeated the Church Catechism in the presence of the Congregation."

The active Feoffees of Gale's period were Thomas Wethered; Thomas Rolls, a coal merchant; Joshua Rolls, a draper; William Bond and Thomas Corby, builders, who did much of the repairs at both Marlow and Bix; Joseph Townsend, of Well End, an experienced businessman who was always consulted on matters legal; William Morris; William Grant; John Gibbons; Robert Hammond; and Harry Calcutt. Apart from ordinary routine business and the eternal question of balancing their books, their chief concern at this time was with Bix Farm. Old John Beckett died in 1839, heavily in debt. They wished to get rid of the family, but all persuasion, and even a notice to quit served on his son, John, failed to avail them. John was encouraged in his attitude by the local Vicar, who brought pressure to bear on the Feoffees to repair the farmhouse and the dilapidated out-buildings. The Feoffees submitted to the Vicar, repaired the buildings and trusted to luck for their money. Notices to quit were also served on two Marlow tenants. They, like Francis, shut their doors and windows, but now Marlow had a constable, who eventually succeeded in delivering the notices.

We hear little of the girls except that Mrs Barney still taught them at the House of Correction, and that Mrs Wethered and Miss Wethered, of Remnantz, helped to teach and clothe them.

Gale had eventually restored the prestige of the Boys' School, because the applications for free places were as numerous as ever. Among

1.13.1. A contemporary photograph of the farm at Bix, formerly part of the Borlase estate

24 | CHAPTER 1   Foundation and the First 250 Years (1624-1874)

the boys of this time, we frequently meet with familiar Marlow names: Green, Walker, Gray, Coster, Rose, East, Nicholls, Sawyer, Davis, Cox, Price, Stockbridge and Wellicome. The majority stayed on for four years and were duly apprenticed, several to Marlow tradesmen of High Street, West Street and the Common Slough — tailors, blacksmiths, cordwainers, wheelwrights, builders, butchers; but several also to tradesmen of other towns — Wycombe, Burnham, Thame, Eton, Islington, St. Ives (Huntingdon), Wokingham, Chertsey, Shoreditch and Hoxton.

Gale went into the School House as soon as it was ready after the repairs. In April 1837, he was presented by the Feoffees with an extra £5, and for a while had a salary of £30 per year. In 1843, he wrote a letter of appeal to the Feoffees pointing out that from his salary of £30, he had to pay rates and taxes up to £10 1s. 6½d. — made up of assessed taxes, £4 15s. 1d.; Church rates, 18s. 7d.; incidental rates, 2s. 6d.; way rate 5s.; poor rates, £3 16s. 0d.; and income tax, 4s. 4½d. Only by the strictest economy could he keep up appearances. The Feoffees increased his salary to £35. As a Schoolmaster, he was very economical with School funds, for he bought hardly any textbooks in his time, and his half-yearly bills hardly ever exceeded £2. He died in the autumn of 1844. In the following year, the fixtures in the House, the property of Mrs Gale, were valued by Thomas Wethered at £13 15s. 0d. In the front room were a 30-inch stove, a stone chimneypiece and two bookshelves. In the back bedroom, there was a 27-inch stove. In the parlour, a 28-inch stove, a bell and pull. In the kitchen, a 3-foot range, with oven and boiler, an ironing stove, a deal dresser with three shelves and drawers, a door bell and pull. In the pantry, three shelves. In the Schoolroom, a grate, a double desk, ten feet long, three side desks and one small desk, a master's desk and stool, seven forms and one ten-foot shelf. In the wash-house, a 26-gallon copper and two shelves.

In *The Borlasian* of May 1887, the reminiscences of Robert H. Smith, who went to Borlase in 1836, were published. "The Blue Boys," he says, "wore a uniform at Church parade on Sundays. It was formed of a piece of very rough blue cloth, with two holes cut in it for the arms to pass through, and a piece of red tape to fasten it round the neck. We also wore a round shallow cap of the same material, with a narrow red tape band. Thus attired, we were the sport of all the other boys in the parish.

"One Sunday in each year, about Easter, we boys, during the service (at the Parish Church), had to stand up and give audible evidence of our proficiency by reciting a portion of the Catechism. Although we were thoroughly drilled in the respective answers we were called upon to make, we were so unused to that sort of thing that the ordeal was a very trying one. Our master was a retired Exciseman who sought to add something to the income from his pension by accepting this appointment… Gale was a worthy man of venerable appearance, his hair was silver white, and he had a particularly long nose, from which we called him among ourselves, 'Old Pecker'.

"School opened at 9 am and invariably with a prayer of extraordinary length, read with great fervour. Our daily duties were by no means laborious or trying. On certain days, we did writing, on others ciphering, mostly on slates… We used quill pens. The headlines in our copy-books were the work of our master. Our other studies comprised a little spelling, tables and reading, mostly confined to the Psalms…

"The School Meadow was forbidden ground, hence our sports were confined to marbles, hoops, and tops, in winter; and egg-hat, baseball and a little cricket played under the greatest difficulties in the summer."

CHARLES T. WETHERED (1844–1850)

Charles Wethered was appointed Master in October 1844, at a salary of £30, out of which he paid £5 rent. His salary was raised to £35 in 1846. By now, the finances of the Trust had slightly improved. To clear themselves of all other debts, the Feoffees had borrowed £500 from Thomas Wethered at 4% interest, and from 1846 onwards they were able to pay off annually some part of the principal. Charles Wethered was consequently able to buy more School equipment than his predecessor. It is in his day that we first meet with lead pencils, steel pens and blotting paper. He also bought National School spelling books, Hills' Geographical Slips, Tutor's Assistants and Souter and Law's Spelling Books.

An Old Borlasian, William Walker, of Reading, remembers Charles Wethered. "Mr Charles Wethered was Master when my Father took me to him at Easter 1849, when I was nearly nine years old. There were 24 Borlasians or Blue Boys, and he was allowed to have 24 boys who paid a shilling a week and had to find all the books, etc. The Blue Boys did not find anything except slate pencils. We wrote with a quill pen which he showed us how to make. When we first went to School, we made our own writing books. The big boys would go into the Master's kitchen, and with his housekeeper make the books from great sheets of paper. There were four large desks in the Schoolroom, two for Blue Boys and two for Day Boys. The Head Boy (monitor) sat at the end of the desk, and each class had to learn the same lesson, for which the monitors were responsible, and if we did not do our work, we were 'bumped' by the other boys. We used to line up every morning for Scripture. On Fridays, we had Collects, Gospel and Catechism, and the same on Sundays. On Mid Lent Sunday afternoon, we had to go to Church to be examined by the Vicar and the Trustees."

1.14.1. William Walker (aged 96 years in 1935)

Foundation and the First 250 Years (1624-1874)

CHAPTER 1 | 25

 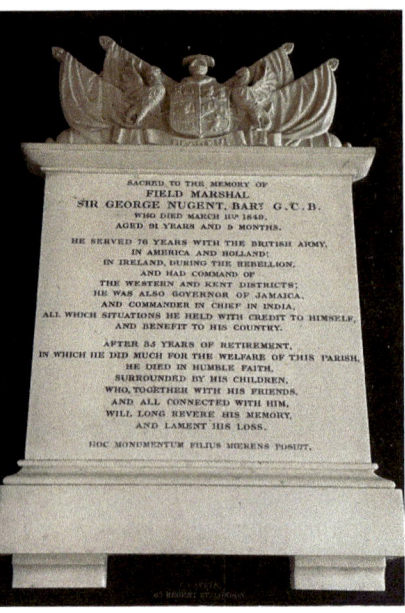

1.14.2. Sir George Nugent, while serving in the Pembroke Cavalry in 1798, and the memorial to him in St John the Baptist Church, Little Marlow.

When the boys were idle, they were sent out to read the old motto of the School, which was carved on a stone in the wall, "If any will not work, neither shall he eat!"

The stationery was mostly bought from a local tradesman, George S. Pearce, who ran a circulating library, a printing office and a hair-dressing establishment in High Street. The blue cloth was supplied by Joshua and Thomas Rolls, High Street, or by William Grant, of West Street. William Stockbridge now did the tailoring and William East did the odd jobs, such as thatching the barn or repairing fences.

The Girls' School was conducted by Elizabeth Barney up to March 1848, when she resigned. For a short while, Phoebe Curtis took her place. In May, a regular Mistress, Catherine Camden, began her duties. But some of the Feoffees, notably Joseph Townsend, were anxious to bring the institution to an end, because parents would no longer let their children become bone lace makers. They talked of establishing an Infant School in Marlow to take its place. In March 1852, the girls were sent off to the National School in Church Passage, and from then on, Mary Anne Simpson, the Treasurer of the School, received the £5. A grant of £2 10s. 0d. was made to the Infants' School in Oxford Lane, and £2 10s. 0d. to the Infant School near the Bridge.

Again quoting William Walker. "When I first went to School, there were 24 girls in the cottages next to our School. In winter, they used to wear blue stiff frocks and blue cloaks, and bonnets with blue and red ribbon. In summer, they had white tippets, very stiff to a point at the back, and fastened with large brass pins. On Sundays, they used to sit just in front of us in the gallery in the Church."

The six years of Charles Wethered saw the passing of several familiar names. At Bix, John Beckett was at long last obliged to go, and the farm was let to James Wheeler, a timber merchant from Henley, who first forced the Feoffees to pay for extensive repairs, and afterwards failed to pay his rent punctually.

Thomas Wethered, the Senior Feoffee, and the founder of the brewery in Marlow, died in 1849. He was a link with the eighteenth century and had stood by the School throughout the trouble with Francis. The Trust still owed him £350 at the time of his death. Charles Wethered died on 28 October 1850.

Sir George Nugent, the Governor, also died in 1849, at the age of 91 years. Born in 1757, he had entered the Army in 1773. He served in the American War of Independence and by the end of it in 1783 was a Lieutenant Colonel. In 1793, he accompanied the Guards to Holland. To meet Napoleon's threatened invasion, he raised a Corps in Buckinghamshire. He represented the County in Parliament from 1790 to 1800. From 1801 to 1806, he was Lieutenant Governor of Jamaica. On his return, he was created a baronet. From 1811 to 1813, he was Commander-in-Chief in India. He was promoted to General in 1813, and given the GCB in 1815.

EDWIN SEGRAVE (1850–1880)

Edwin Segrave had been educated at Newport Free Grammar School, Essex, where he had won prizes for English and Mathematics. After a short period of teaching, he became clerk to W. L. Ward, the Marlow solicitor, whom he served for 14 years. His salary as Master of Borlase was £30, raised to £35 in 1835 and to £40 in 1854. From 1856 onwards, he had an additional bonus of £5. He also collected the cottage rents, for which he was paid a commission.

In 1853, Frederick Parker, of Beech Lodge, one of the Feoffees, considering that unless Borlase could give a higher type of education, parents would send their children elsewhere, urged the Feoffees to provide more textbooks. Accordingly, that year, 12 copies were bought of each of these textbooks — *History of England*, *English Grammar*, the Bible, and the Testament — and 18 copies of Cropman's *Introduction to the Christian Religion*. The Bibles and Testaments were bought for the Trust by Parker himself, and the *Introduction* by W. L. Ward. Two years later, 12 maps were bought from SPCK (the Society for Promoting Christian Knowledge), and mounted by William Mealing. The maps were of England and Wales, the World, Europe, Asia, Africa, America, Scotland, Ireland, the Old Testament, the

New Testament, Palestine, and Jerusalem. Six geography books were added in 1859.

Among the boys of these early days of Segrave were George Meakes, John Samuel Carter, Henry Gill, Alfred Neighbour, Charles Sawyer, Samuel Clark, Thomas Gray, Charles Nicholls, Alfred Davis, William Carter, Charles Blewitt, Thomas Hobbs, Edward Coster, Christian Batting, George East, Joseph Sawyer, Cornelius Clark, William Davis, George Henry Coster, William Batting, Frank East, and Alfred East.

Samuel Clark was apprenticed to a Nottingham tailor, Cornelius Clark to a Maidenhead chemist, Alfred Davis to W. N. Habgood, the draper who supplied the cloth for making the School uniform for the girls — because since the girls had been sent to the National School, the Feoffees had resumed the payment for their clothing. In addition, they gave uniforms to the six infants in the Church Passage School and to six in the Oxford Lane School. Other purchases of cloth were sometimes made from John Morgan, and of bonnets from Samuel King of West House. Joshua and Thomas Rolls still supplied the cloth for the boys' uniforms.

The Feoffees were Thomas Rolls, the Bridge, coal merchant and Treasurer since 1817; John Gibbons, grocer; Joseph Townsend JP, Woodend, Medmenham; Owen Wethered, brewer; Robert Hammond JP; Frederick Parker; William Bond, builder; Thomas Rolls, High Street, wine merchant and auctioneer; Thomas Corby, builder; and Henry Calcutt and William Morris, farmers, of Little Marlow. The Governor was Sir George Edmund Nugent, 2nd Baronet (1802–1892).

In 1853, the Charitable Trust Act had been passed, enforcing trustees to keep their accounts regularly in a book and to make annual returns to the Charity Commissioners. From these returns, we find that the Trust was not only solvent, but capable of paying back some part of the principal to the executors of Thomas Wethered. By 1859, they had repaid altogether £400, and the remaining £100 was cancelled by the executors, Owen and Lawrence William Wethered.

In 1850, the old House of Correction, with the "barn, the yard adjoining and the Court with the pump" had been let to Thomas Brown on a 14-year lease at an annual rent of £5. The Feoffees still paid £2 10s. 0d. for Camel Orchard, which belonged to the Dean and Chapter of Gloucester, and was sublet by them to W. and I. Wright. They sublet it to the Feoffees, and they, as part of a garden, sublet it to Joseph Eagle, and after his death to H. Sawyer.

G. S. Pearce supplied the School stationery until 1868, when he was followed by E. C. Hunter, and he in 1973 by George Cannon, of the Stamp Office. The School uniforms were bought from W. N. Habgood up to 1868, and then from James Roberts, West Street. The yearly ton of "sea coal" was delivered up to 1859 by W. Sparks, of the Old Bridge Wharf, and from 1871 by G. Creswell. Numerous firms from time to time repaired the School property — T. Corby, Alfred Batting & Sons, William Plumridge, William Crake (who also succeeded Segrave as collector of cottage rents), and the Lovegroves (who had almost throughout the School's history done the glazing and plumbing).

In 1863, Thomas Rolls, High Street, succeeded Thomas Rolls, the Bridge, as Treasurer. In 1864, Thomas Summers Cocks; James Carson; Lawrence William Wethered; Robert Foottit, chemist; Rev. Thomas Powys, of Medmenham; John Hewett; and James Fryer, of Little Marlow, were elected Feoffees. In the following year, R. Foottit became Treasurer, and about the same time, J. P. Ellames succeeded Nugent as Governor. By 1872, J. Hewett, T. Rolls (the Bridge), R. Foottit, J. Carson and Rev. T. A. Powys had died, and T. Rolls (High Street) had resigned, and their places were taken by T. O. Wethered MP; Rev. J. A. Cree, Vicar of Marlow; Rev. W. Hill, Vicar of Medmenham; T. King, of Widmere; C. M. Foottit, the new Treasurer (the last to hold the office in the old Trust); and A. Lawrence. By 1878, Morris, Calcutt and Corby had died, and the last men appointed to the old Trust were Rev. J. Baines, Harry Calcutt, son of the old Feoffee from Little Marlow, and E. Hewett, who had for some time been agent of the Royal Exchange Assurance.

The Feoffees were never very long without financial worries. In 1859, a fire destroyed some of the outhouses at Bix Farm, and it cost the Trust £165 to make good the damage. Altogether, this farm was a doubtful asset. The Becketts had allowed the 50 acres that constituted it to deteriorate, and they had been most lax in their rent paying. Wheeler, the next tenant, was hardly more satisfactory. Costly repairs were needed annually, and the cottage attached to the farm had so deteriorated that it was cheaper to remove it than to repair it. In 1862, the Feoffees bought Camel Orchard for £90, most of the Feoffees lending £15 each in order that the purchase might be made. By 1865, all the loans had been repaid. In 1875, it was decided to sell the seven cottages in Chapel Street, and to place an advertisement of sale in the *South Bucks Free Press*. Messrs Rolls and Lawrence undertook the valuation. The following year, the property was sold to Mrs Atkinson for £838 10s. 0d., and the money invested in 3% Consols. The reason given for the sale was that the funds of the Trust would benefit because of the high cost of repairs to such old property.

In 1865, Segrave was given £5 gratuity, which was increased in 1867 to £10, and in 1868 to £20 per year. From 1870, the gratuity was merged into his salary, now £70. In 1874, he was given the meadow, rent free — he had previously paid £20 per year for it.

Until the last few years of Segrave's tenure, the School ran on much as usual. There was a full complement of 24 boys, with 24 girls at the National and Infant Schools, and as much competition for places as formerly. Out of 35 boys apprenticed, 28 may be said to have gone to craftsmen — six to builders, five to carpenters, four to cabinet makers, three to whitesmiths, two to shoemakers, two to wheelwrights, while one became a baker, one a coachbuilder, one a blacksmith, one a tailor, one a florist and gardener, and one a chairmaker. Of the remaining seven, one became an ironmonger; three, drapers with the firm of Joseph Wright Morgan and James William Morgan; two, chemists with the Foottits, and one, G. R. Piggott, a pupil teacher at the National School. Piggott thanked Segrave for the help that he had received at Borlase. After passing an examination at Wycombe, he had been apprenticed for five years with Williams, the National School Master. He had two more examinations to face, but he was pleased with the initial salary of £8 per year!

New textbooks were bought from time to time, but in small parcels, except in 1863, when the sum of £2 18s. 0d. was spent on 12 Bibles, 12 *The World We Live In*, 6 *Walkinghame's Tutor's Assistant*, 6 *Butter's Spelling*, 12 *Catechisms of Geography* and 12 *Catechisms of Grammar*.

Ten years later, the Feoffees began to spend £1 annually on prizes for proficiency.

In 1870, Forster's Elementary Education Act was passed, providing cheap or free education for all. It was, of course, some time before such a comprehensive Act could be put fully into force. Indeed, it was not until 1876 that compulsory attendance at school was made general. By 1878, no child under 10 years could go to work, and no child between 10 and 14 years, unless it had a certificate that it had passed the School Standard at an examination by a Government Inspector or it had a certificate that it had attended school 250 times each year for two years. In 1879, it was to be the Third Standard and three years.

It was becoming more and more evident that the Free School as an institution to teach boys to "read, write and cast accounts" had fulfilled its mission. Segrave, too, was getting old. Boys had to be expelled for absence. From 1875 onwards, parents had to undertake, in the event of their sons being elected by the Feoffees, to guarantee their daily attendance as required by the School regulations, unless illness or unavoidable causes should prevent, when they would present a satisfactory reason to the Master for their absence from School. Trouble also arose over the question of fagging and cleaning out the Schoolroom after School hours. At last, in 1879, Segrave offered to send the boys to the National School at his own expense. The Feoffees thanked him, but stood the expense themselves. So 17 boys — C. East, B. Anthony, E. Spicer, G. Peddle, W. Rose, W. Bradshaw, G. Harvey, J. Taylor, W. Fasey, A. Wye, W. East, F. Fleming, F. Price, A. Higgins, W. F. Plumridge, H. Hawes and H. Tucker were sent off to the National School. But they were still Borlasians, paid for and uniformed by the Trust, examined annually, and given their pence and their prizes. The last of them did not leave the National School until 1883. Four of them were to return to Borlase, as re-organized under the new scheme. So, although the old foundation disappeared, there were always Borlasians.

Segrave remained in the School House until 1881, and after much correspondence with the Charity Commissioners, he was given a pension of £40.

1.15.1. The boys of Borlase School in the 1880s

CHAPTER 2
REVIVAL AND RENEWAL (1874–1974)

THE NEW SCHEME

At a meeting of the Feoffees on 4 February 1879, the question of what was to become of the School on the retirement of Segrave was first discussed. It was decided to get immediately in touch with the Charity Commissioners and to ask their advice. An Assistant Commissioner was sent down from London, and he went into the question of the value of the School property and inspected the School House. By August, the draft scheme of the Charity Commissioners as to the future conduct of the School was ready. During the autumn, the Feoffees met on several occasions to discuss the Scheme clause by clause. On 4 May 1880, they met for the last time and resolved to accept the Scheme as amended.

There were to be twelve Governors. The Lord of the Manor of Danvers was to be on the Board, *ex officio*. One Governor was to represent the Magistrates, and two to be elected by the Vestry of Great Marlow, these three to hold office for five years. For the time being, the Board was to be increased to 14 in order to include all the old Feoffees as Co-operative Governors. They were: L. W. Wethered, T. O. Wethered MP, T. S. Cocks, Rev. J. A. Cree, Rev. W. Hill, A. Lawrence, T. King, J. Frier, H. Calcutt and C. M. Foottit. Vacancies among the Co-operative Governors were to be filled by the general body; Little Marlow was to have two seats and Medmenham one. The Magistrates elected Captain J. S. Carson, and the Vestry elected O. P. Wethered and J. Morgan. The Governors were to keep accounts and to publish them, have the custody of the deeds and other documents, make arrangements for banking, let and manage the property, make investments and take over all duties of the Feoffees. Furthermore, they were to put the new Scheme into operation.

The School was to be a day school for boys and, if the Governors thought fit, room was to be made for boarders. Immediate provision was to be made for fifty day boys, and the new buildings were to be so planned as to allow for convenient extension. The Headmaster and any other members of the Staff to be appointed need not be in Holy Orders. The Headmaster was to live in the residence assigned to him and to have no other employment. Neither he nor any member of the Staff could be a Governor. Nor could he or any Master accept a gratuity or fee from any boy, unless authorized by the Governors. The Governors were to determine the School curriculum, the length of terms and holidays, the employment of more assistant masters and the sanitary arrangements, but the Headmaster's advice was to be considered. The Headmaster was to determine the choice of textbooks, the methods of teaching, the arrangement of classes and school hours, and he was to have the power of appointing the assistant staff. He was to have a fixed yearly salary of £70, together with a capitation fee of £3 per boy per year. Boys, irrespective of place of birth or residence, could be taken in, provided they were of good character and good health. The tuition fees were not to be less than £3 or more than £6 per year. Boarding fees were not to exceed £35 per year.

Boys were not to be taken in under the age of 8 years or to remain beyond the age of 18 years. Applications for admission were to be made to the Headmaster, and the boys were to undergo an entrance examination in reading, writing from dictation, sums in the first four rules of arithmetic and the outlines of the geography of England. There was to be no religious test, and here it may be noted that at no time in the history of Borlase is there any record of religious distinctions.

Instruction was to be given in Reading, Writing and Arithmetic, in Geography and History, in English Grammar, Composition and Literature, Mathematics, Latin, in at least one foreign European language, in Natural Science and in Drawing, Drill and Vocal Music. Once every year, the School was to be examined by a person unconnected with the School, and he was to present a report to the Governors. The Headmaster, too, was to report annually on the general progress of the School. Prizes were to be awarded as marks of distinction to meritorious scholars.

There were to be twelve foundation scholarships: eight for Marlow, three for Little Marlow and one for Medmenham, the method of selection being left to the Governors. They were empowered to offer one or more exhibitions to enable boys to proceed to places

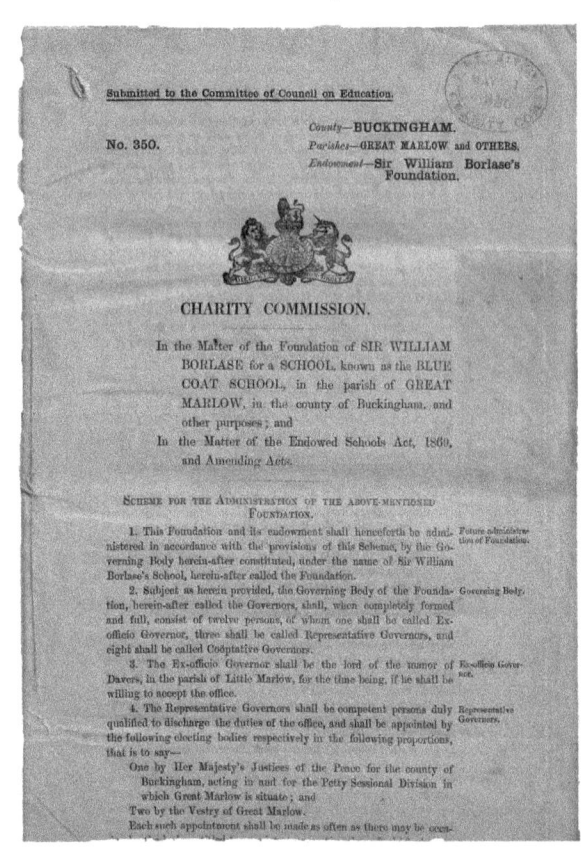

2.1.1. Scheme from the Charity Commission for the administration of Borlase School, dated 1 May 1880

2.1.2. View of West Street and the original School House, before it was extended, and a plan of the proposed School buildings

of higher education. There were also twelve scholarships for girls, entitling them to free education at an elementary school.

The Governors were to transfer £400 Government Stock into the name of the Official Trustees of Charitable Funds, the income from which was to be paid to them for repairing the School property. They could make provision for a pension fund for the Headmaster, both he and the Governors contributing. Any surplus revenue could be used for additions to the School premises or for increased salaries to the Staff. Further donations or endowments could be received.

The School was to be conducted strictly in accordance with the Scheme until such time as the Charity Commissioners should see fit to alter it.

At the first meeting of the Governors on 1 February 1881, Rev. J. A. Cree was elected Chairman, and T. O. Wethered, Vice-Chairman. J. Rawson was appointed Clerk to the Governors, and a subcommittee was chosen to draw up an advertisement for a Master. It was estimated that there would be a sum of £622, made up from the balance in hand from the funds of the Feoffees, together with proceeds of the sale of part of the 3% Consols, which would be available as the nucleus of the building fund.

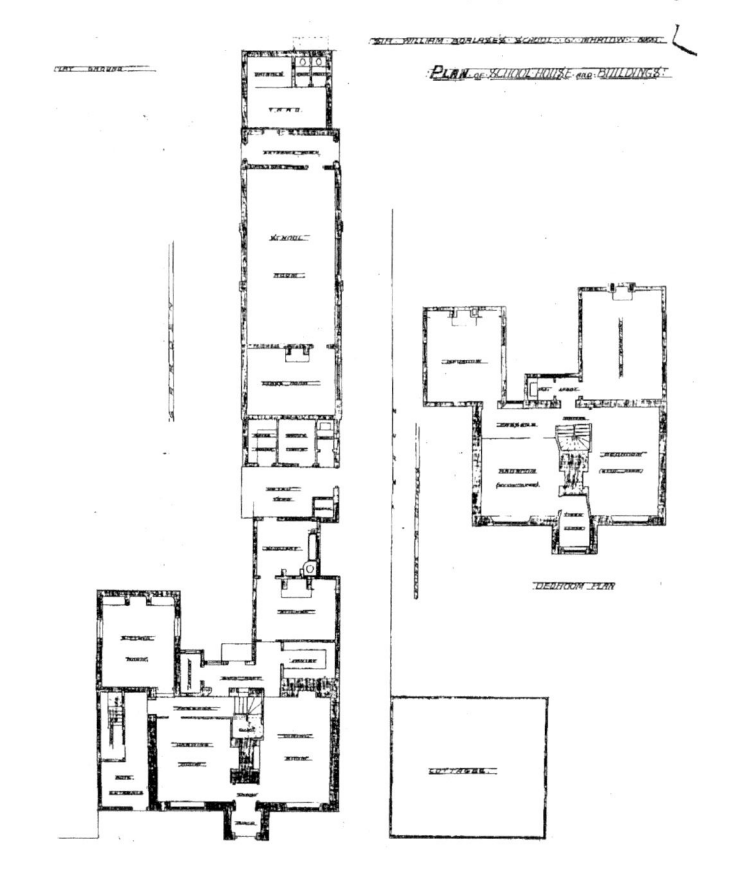

Revival and Renewal (1874-1974)

CHAPTER 2

For two years, income from rents had been steadily coming in, and except for Segrave's pension and the fees for the foundations at the elementary schools, there had been little outlay. Apprenticeship fees, uniforms and the Easter pence had been abolished. The Governors resolved to take out a new insurance policy for £300 on the two West Street cottages, and for £1,000 on the School House. The question of Bix Farm was to be deferred. The twelve girls entitled to scholarships under the new Scheme were to be elected forthwith.

The advertisement for a new Master was put in *The Times* and *The Guardian*. There were at least 56 applications. The Governors selected 14 of them and independently placed them in order of merit. Each one of the subcommittee of seven put the Rev. Michael Graves head of his list, and the Clerk was directed to invite him to meet the Governors at the School House at 10.30 a.m. on Friday 8 April. If he accepted the post after seeing the School premises, he was to be paid his second class railway fare, but if he declined after that inspection, he was to pay his own expenses!

That day, 8 April 1881, saw the beginning of over half a century's association between the Rev. Michael Graves and Sir William Borlase's School — now the recognized official title of the School. Indeed, Borlase School as we know it is mainly his creation. The Governors held a preliminary meeting to discuss a means of increasing the building fund of not less than £500, to be repaid in five years. They called in the candidate and asked him what he considered requisite in the way of accommodation. "He stated that first of all a new schoolroom was essential. He considered there ought to be a drawing room, a study, a dining room (to be for both himself and the boarders), a kitchen and scullery, all, if possible, downstairs, two bedrooms (for himself and his mother), bedrooms for six boarders at least, to begin with, and one for servants.

"After some discussion as to where and how such alteration could be made, the meeting was of opinion that his suggestions were not other than reasonable, and enquired of Mr Graves if he would be willing to undertake the School, provided alterations were made agreeable to his suggestions, and he replied that he would be willing to do so. Mr Graves then left."

One is left with the impression that the Governors were taken by surprise at the insight and quick decision of their new young Headmaster. The minutes do not state whether the second class fare was paid. It was decided to get an estimate of the cost of the alterations, to appoint Charles Carter of West Street as architect, and to get in touch with Hammond Chambers, who lived opposite the School at Heather's, and who now leased the School land where the House of Correction and the old barn used to be. He had pulled down these old erections to improve the view from his house, and might object to extension of the School in this direction.

Four days later, the Governors met again and learned from Charles Carter that the proposed alterations would cost £1,000. They decided that only £450 could be spent, and that this sum was to include the price of an iron schoolroom. The next Governors' meeting was to be on 26 April, but that had to be postponed to the following day owing to the funeral of the Earl of Beaconsfield (Benjamin Disraeli). On 27 April, the Rev. Michael Graves was formally appointed Headmaster and informed of the proposed repairs and alterations. On 12 May, it was decided to push on with the building without waiting for the consent of the Charity Commissioners, and to open the School forthwith. The Headmaster had seen a room, a paint shop off West Street, that would serve temporarily as a schoolroom. He himself would have to live in lodgings. A competitive examination was to be held to decide the award of the twelve scholarships to boys. Those already on the foundation were entitled to compete, but the fact that they were on the old foundation did not automatically qualify them to be on the new one. On 20 May, "Rev. Michael Graves signed the necessary declaration or agreement promising always to the best of his ability to discharge the duties of Headmaster of Sir William Borlase's School at Great Marlow".

REV. MICHAEL GRAVES (1881–1895)

Here, then, was a Headmaster without a Staff, without a School and without a pupil! If he had any boarders, the Governors decided that at first the sum charged should be £32, with £5 tuition fees. There were to be three terms of 13 weeks each, leaving about 13 weeks for holidays. The hours of instruction were to be from 9.00 a.m. to 12.30 p.m. every weekday, and from 2.30 p.m. to 4.30 p.m. on Mondays, Tuesdays, Thursdays and Fridays; Wednesdays and Saturdays were to be half-holidays. The Headmaster would find for the day boys, and the Governors would find for the foundationers, books and stationery up to 7s. 9d. per term for each boy.

On 31 May, the tender of A. Corby for carrying out reconstruction was accepted. The results of the examination of candidates for foundation scholarships were considered, and these boys elected: A. Higgins, W. Rose, J. Green, F. Barnes, H. Rippington, H. James, G. Scown, H. Hawes, all of Marlow; W. Clifford, C. Brown and W. P. Davis, of Little Marlow, and (as there were no satisfactory candidates from Medmenham) H. Bradshaw, of Marlow. Of these, four (A. Higgins, W. Rose, H. Hawes and H. Bradshaw) were on the old foundation, and may be considered as the bridge between the old and the new. In the first term, there were five non-foundationers.

In June, the Governors discussed a suggestion of the Headmaster that while they were building the kitchen, they may as well build a bedroom over it to provide accommodation for eight more boarders. Carter estimated that the extra cost would be £70. It was decided to include the bedroom. In August, it was resolved to erect a permanent schoolroom capable of accommodating 60 boys. In September, it was decided to build outhouses and offices. There was much discussion as to whether the schoolroom should run north to south or east to west. The reason for this rapid increase in expenditure was that it was already becoming clear that the School was going to flourish. In the second term, there were 33 boys, and the question of appointing an assistant master was mooted.

By 3 February 1882, the schoolroom was ready. The Governors invited William Copeland Borlase, MP for East Cornwall and a distant relative of the Founder, to the opening ceremony, and gave notice to quit the paint shop. Messrs Wethered also gave notice that they intended to give up the tenancy of the

2.2.1. The Rev. Michael Graves (Headmaster 1881–1895)

meadow behind the School, as it was now used by the boys as a playing field.

The formal opening of the new schoolroom and the first Speech Day was 10 February 1882, and the ceremony was reported in the *South Bucks Free Press* on 17 February. The report says that the new building was designed by Charles Carter and built by J. S. Carter. It was 34 ft by 18 ft and provided accommodation for 70 or 80 boys. A classroom adjoining could accommodate 25 boys. The height of these rooms was 14 ft. The building had been substantially constructed of red brick and flints, and the floor was of wood blocks, by which all reverberation was avoided.

T. S. Cocks took the chair and explained shortly what had recently happened in Borlase history. Colonel O. P. Wethered was called upon to make a financial statement. He disclosed that the Governors had gone much beyond their original intentions, that the alterations to the house had cost £500 and the new schoolroom £400. The Governors themselves with 18 other ladies and gentlemen had subscribed £317, but the Trust would still be £100 in debt. He appealed for further assistance. The Headmaster then made his first Report.

From 15 boys in the first term, the numbers had shot up to 45 in the third term. The paint shop had become too small. He himself had gone to live at the School House on 13 January.

The boys had made good progress at their studies and had been given an examination. He recommended for prizes in the Third Form, Alfred Davis and Clifford; in the Second Form, Pepper and Scown; and in the First Form, G. E. Davis and Bradshaw. William C. Borlase then delivered the principal speech of the day and recounted the history of the Borlases. He was, he said, the first William Borlase MP who had come to the School since the Founder himself! After the speeches, the Chairman declared the new schoolroom open.

In March, the question of an assistant master was again raised. The Governors failing to see their way to meet the extra expense, T. S. Cocks (now the Chairman) guaranteed to pay a man £50 per year. At the end of the summer term, preparations were made to engage a third master. The School fees were raised to £6. At Easter 1882, the end of the first financial year, the Trust had already paid out £685 for repairs and the new buildings and had a total expenditure of £934. Nevertheless, they were only £266 in debt. School fees had yielded them £98. At Easter 1883, although they had paid out £275 more to builders and contractors, and their total expenses were £824, they were £27 in hand, and fees had yielded them £209. In August, the Rev. Michael Graves was married to Mrs Sophia Fenwick, née Wethered, and for a term resided at Remnantz; Mrs Graves,

2.2.2. William Copeland Borlase MP opened the new schoolroom in 1882

Revival and Renewal (1874–1974)   CHAPTER 2 | 33

2.2.3. View of West Street, showing the extension to the east of the original School House

to Marlow for charitable purposes a field called Martin's Close. This had recently been sold by the Trustees to Captain Carson, and there was a sum of £3,661 invested. The interest on this sum was handed over to the School Governors on condition that they paid annually 20 shillings to twenty poor widows on St Thomas's Day, according to the will of the donor. As the Rev. Arthur Feardon, Vicar of Marlow, was a trustee of this fund, he was now elected as an additional Governor of the School.

In January 1885, the first edition of *The Borlasian* magazine was published. From it, we learn that there was now on the Staff, in addition to the two assistant masters, C. T. Ellis and F. W. Evans, a drill instructor, Colour-Sergeant Mentor. It is evident that the progress of the School was being hampered by lack of space. The Headmaster pointed out that accommodation for the Assistant Staff had had to be found outside, and that it was impossible to teach science until there was a room suitable for the purpose. He had already taken over the tenancy of the Home Meadow in order to provide the boys with a playing field, and he was now prepared to compensate the Governors for the loss of rent, if they would consent to pull down the two cottages in West Street to allow for the expansion of the

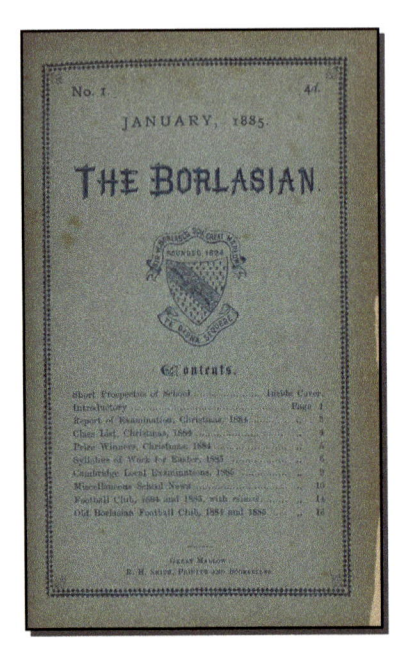

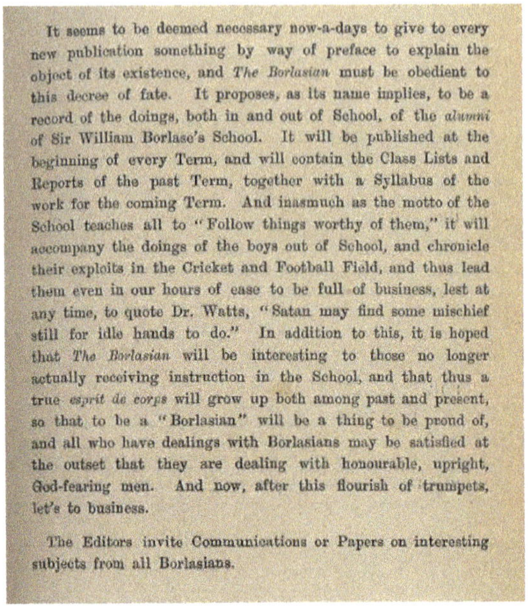

senior, managed the School House with the assistance of the masters. At the end of the term, Mrs Graves, senior, left Marlow and was thanked for her good services by the Governors. It was this Christmas, too, that the first results of public examinations were announced, Rose and Mills having passed the Cambridge Locals Junior examination. In 1884, the Governors acquired a very useful addition to their revenue. Henry Pendleton had sometime bequeathed

*2.2.4. The first edition of **The Borlasian** magazine, published in January 1885*

34 | CHAPTER 2   Revival and Renewal (1874-1974)

2.2.5. The Victorian extension to the School and the inscriptions on the facade; the Latin inscription means: 'Peace to all who enter; health to all who abide; blessings on all who leave'

School House. The Governors were reluctant to move, but by May 1886, they had sanctioned an expenditure of £615 on new buildings. Charles Carter was again to be the architect, and W. R. Loosley of High Wycombe, the builder. £500 stock was sold this year.

In 1887, it was decided to level the School yard and to erect entrance gates. The sale of a further £600 stock was sanctioned for further extensions of the School House. It was evident such expenditure was a sound investment, for while the income from land yielded £107, and that from investments £117, the income from fees had jumped to £326, and there were 68 boys on the register during the summer term. During the next three years, the Governors paid out £1,235 for additional buildings, those still existing between the old School House and the entrance gates, and the large dormitory. Nor must it be supposed the Headmaster was even then satisfied with the expenditure of the Governors, for iron buildings were being erected at his own expense to supply further classrooms. Boarders were flowing in, and one house after another — part of Shelley House, the house in High Street that became the International Stores, and a house in Glade Road — were taken by him for these boys. From 68 boys in 1887, the numbers jumped up to 100 in 1889, 125 in 1890, and 150 in 1892. The income from fees increased from £201 in 1884 (the end of the first year since the Headmaster's marriage) to £363 in 1888 (the first full year

Revival and Renewal (1874-1974)

2.2.6. The Victorian staircase and fireplace (now the School Reception)

after the first extensions) and to £814 in 1893, when all the buildings were in full use. It was in 1893 that the Governors sanctioned the last expenditure on new buildings during this period. The garden, which up to now had been leased by Hammond Chambers, was taken over, and the present School House drawing room, with the dormitory above it, erected. This block was completed by March 1894 and cost £1,044. For all the buildings of this period, Charles Carter was the architect.

We get an idea of what the Headmaster himself had done when he decided, owing to the ill health of Mrs Graves, to retire at Christmas 1895. The temporary iron buildings had cost him £1,170. The Governors paid him £700 for them, and they included a dining hall, a gymnasium, eight boys' studies, a library, a chapel and vestry, a changing room, a laboratory, together with gas fittings, a heating apparatus, desks, forms, seats and gymnastic apparatus.

Some concessions were made from time to time by the Governors. The Headmaster, though he offered, was not called upon to make good the loss of rent from the two cottages. In 1889, he was released from the obligation of paying rent for the playing field and the garden.

Up to 1890, he paid from his own pocket for instructors to give lessons in music, drawing and drill, but from then on the Governors paid these salaries. From 1891, they paid the salary of a third assistant master.

There are a few more interesting points in the accounts of this period. Bix Farm still remained a thorn in the hands of the Governors. There was the usual trouble with the repairs and the arrears of rent from the ever-changing tenants. They several times resolved to sell it, but nothing came of the protracted negotiations. Then there was Gower's Close, the only other property remaining after the cottages in West Street, the playing fields, the Headmaster's garden and the garden of Hammond Chambers had become parts of the School. There was no access to Gower's Close, and plans were drawn up for constructing a road to it. Messrs Wethered once threatened to give up the tenancy, but were prevailed upon to retain it.

Up to 1892, the girls' fees at the National School were paid. When it was no longer necessary to pay the fees, the question arose what to do with the money. It was resolved to pay a cookery mistress £10 per year for a course of lessons, and this arrangement proved such a success that the scheme was renewed year by year. One girl, Emma Truss, applied for and was granted the exhibition for girls mentioned in the foundation scheme. She was given £15 per year for the two years to complete her education at Whitland's College. In 1891, two exhibitions of £30 and £10 per year for three years were granted to G. E. Davis to enable him to proceed to Queens' College, Cambridge. At the end of these three years, he was given an additional £20 for a fourth year.

There were a few changes in the personnel of the Governors. In 1886, H. W. Cripps was elected by the Magistrates, and at his resignation in 1888, Lieutenant General George W. A. Higginson CB took his place. By May 1890, L. W. Wethered, C. M. Foottit and J. Frier had ceased to be Governors, and the number of co-operative members was reduced to eight, Rev. E. J. Haynes being chosen to represent Little Marlow. In 1891, at the death of T. King, W. J. Shone was elected, and in 1893, Rev. A. S. Thompson and R. Hay Murray replaced Rev. E. J. Haynes and Rev. J. A. Cree. T. S. Cocks retained the Chairmanship after the departure of Rev. J. A. Cree from Marlow, and T. O. Wethered acted as Vice-Chairman.

We see from these accounts and minutes of Governors' meetings that Michael Graves

2.2.7. Victorian stained-glass windows incorporating monograms, possibly of Governors and other benefactors

Revival and Renewal (1874–1974) CHAPTER 2 | 37

2.2.8. *The Rev. Michael Graves (standing left), the assistant masters and the boys in 1887 and 1888*

was a Headmaster with vision and enterprise, capable of quick decision and capable, too, of gently leading reluctant Governors along paths they often feared to tread. But was all this planning and building of real value to the neighbourhood? It brought trade into Marlow, of course, and helped to fill its streets with more life than otherwise there would have been. But was the School conducted for the benefit of the locality as the Founder had intended?

To answer that, we must refer to the careers of some of the boys. At the beginning of the second term in the paint shop, an old boy, educated at, and apprenticed from, the Free School, brought with him a new boy, his son. This boy was nearly 15 years, and older than any of the other pupils in the shop. The Headmaster inspired him with his own thoroughness and aspiration. The boy responded and became the Headmaster's right-hand man. He was a born organizer. You turn to the first issue of *The Borlasian*, January 1885, and you learn that he was the first boy from the School to get a certificate at a public examination, for Alfred Davis passed the Cambridge Local Junior in 1882. In 1884, he passed the Senior, and so appears at the head of the School Honours Board. On page 10 of this first issue, we learn that the School had a flourishing Football Club; the Honorary Treasurer was Rev. M. Graves and the Honorary Secretary was A. Davis. On the next page is an account of a trial match, and the umpire was, again, A. Davis. On page 16, there is talk of forming an Old Boys' Football Club: President, Rev. M. Graves; Honorary Secretary, A. Davis. Next term, he was Honorary Secretary of the Athletics Sports, the third term Honorary Secretary of the Cricket Club. In the School list, he appears as Davis Maximus. After four years at Borlase, he left for Aberystwyth University College. After a period of teaching, he was back in Marlow by 1891, having adopted journalism. The Old Boys' notes in *The Borlasian* suddenly become much fuller and more businesslike. Since he had been away, the Old Boys' Football Club had become defunct, "but," we read, "next season will see the O.B.F.C. terminate its period of inactivity". He was to become the organizer of the Berks and Bucks Football Association, a legislator of the National Soccer Board, and local JP, and the first Old Borlasian to be a Governor of his old School.

Or take another Davis, G. E. Davis, the son of a Little Marlow gardener, who came to the paint shop as a Foundationer at the age of 9 years, one month after Alfred Davis. In 1886, when he was 14 years, he took first class honours in the Cambridge Locals Junior examination, and repeated the feat the following year. In 1888, he passed the Senior, with distinction in English and Religious Knowledge, and won the Royal Geographical Society Medal for the best paper in Geography. In 1889, he sat the same examination, came out with first class, four distinctions, and the Royal Geographical Society Medal for the second time. The same year, he was awarded the Marmaduke Levitt Scholarship of £40 a year for three years. In 1890, he obtained an Oxford and Cambridge Higher Schools certificate, with three distinctions, and an open scholarship of £40 at Queens' College, Cambridge. The Governors awarded him another £40, and he went up with £120 per year. In his first year at Queens', he won the Freshman's Greek Testament Prize, and in his second, the Joshua King Prize for Mathematics. In this third year, he graduated with Honours in Mathematics, and the Governors enabled him to stay up for a fourth year by awarding him a further scholarship of £20. G. E. Davis was also Captain of the School Cricket and Football teams during his last year at School, and had had some experience of Rowing. At Cambridge, he rowed in the Queens' Eight in the May Races of 1892 and captained the College Soccer team the following year.

These two instances will perhaps be enough to show that the re-organized Borlase opened up a new world to local boys and gave them opportunities of distinction that the Old Foundation could not possibly give. These boys were the pioneers; other successes were to follow. The first to pass London Matriculation straight from Borlase was E. P. S. Benson, the son of a Chelmsford farmer; and the second, Ll. Shone, the son of a Marlow surgeon. Other successful scholars were J. D. R. Munro and R. M. Munro, the sons of a Cheshire doctor; J. W. Ford, the son of a Marlow bank manager, who matriculated from School and went on to take a London Arts degree; T. W. Munday, a foundationer from Marlow; C. P. Lovell, of Marlow; S. J. Taylor, of Marlow; L. C. P. Milman, L. G. Nash and E. C. Lord.

The Borlasian magazines of this period are neat little blue booklets of 20 to 30 pages and they were published at the beginning of each term. On the inside of the cover is an abridged prospectus, with the names of the assistant masters. As has been mentioned, the first two masters were C. T. Ellis and F. W. Evans, with Colour-Sergeant Mentor as drill instructor. In May 1886, E. Swallow took the place of Evans. In January 1886, W. R. O. Hindle and F. T. Handsombody replaced Ellis and Swallow. A year later, A. W. Pratt succeeded Hindle, but he stayed one term and was followed by E. W. Clark. In September 1886, a third master, W. H. Jeffreys, joined the staff, and the following term came a fourth master, the old boy, E. P. S. Benson. By September 1889, there was a fifth master, A. C. Tearle, and by September 1890, a sixth, B. F. Hardy. In August 1891, Jeffreys, the senior assistant, left, and H. M. Gorham took his place. Alfred Davis also joined the staff as a seventh master, but only for one term, for in January 1892, his place was taken by W. Wotherspoon, and he was followed by C. W. Newton in September. In September 1894, came an eighth assistant master in E. L. Paxley. Tearle left at Easter 1895, and S. L. Sarel joined the Staff. As at no time did the Governors employ more than three masters; the remainder must have been engaged by the Headmaster on his own responsibility to take charge of the numerous boarders.

There follows a School list with the marks of each boy for the previous term and in the examination, because all boys were examined at Christmas by the Staff, and in the summer by an outside examiner. The more satisfactory boys in each form were presented with prizes supplied by the Headmaster at Christmas, and by the Governors at the Summer Speech Day. The full syllabus for the new term was printed in detail, so that it is possible for, say, F. W. Rowe to find out that in the Summer term of 1885, he was in the Third Form, that he studied the history of the Hanoverians and the geography of the Balkans, Italy and the British Isles, that he scored 2,849 marks that term, with 516 in the examination, that he was twice absent and five times late, and that he was given *The Wonders of the Physical World* as a reward for his industry and efficiency.

The School had throughout these fifteen years a vigorous and successful Association

2.2.9. Borlase Football Club, 1887

Football Club. From 1881, they played Wycombe Royal Grammar School and Craufurd College, and from 1882, Henley Grammar School. But they soon proved much too strong for these schools, for they beat Wycombe 11-0 in 1885, and Henley 14-0 in 1886 and 12-1 in 1887. In 1888, they played and defeated the British Orphan Asylum, Slough, and Lord Williams's School, Thame. They gave up playing neighbouring schools and played such teams as Marlow Reserves, Maidenhead Reserves and Wycombe Wanderers Reserves. Later, they went still further afield and engaged Reading School and Magdalen College School, the home games being played on the Crown ground.

There was also a most successful Old Boys' Football Club, from which some boys graduated to higher-class Football. A. Milward, the son of a Marlow banker, and one of the old paint shop boys, played for Everton and for England against Scotland in April 1881. G. H. Creswell also played for Everton. E. Shaw and C. T. A. Walker played for Berks and Bucks. Indeed, Shaw once played for the South of England against the North in 1891, a season when no Football was possible in the South for six weeks owing to severe frost.

Cricket at Borlase has a longer history than Football, for in the first issue of the *Bucks Free Press*, 10 July 1857, there is a report of two matches. "Mr W. Brooks had arranged a series of cricket matches between the schools of the town." In the first match, the Blue Coat School defeated the National School. Borlase made 29 and 28, and the National School 27 and 26! In the return match, the tables were turned, for the National School made 50, and Borlase, represented by Hopkins, W. Batting, Horn, S. Taylor, Barney, Bowgett, T. Plumridge, Stallwood, Way, White and Brough, only 22 and 21. In another match, reported on 2 October 1857, Borlase made only 7 and 16 against Marlow Place Academy, who scored 65 and 32. The match was played on the Town Cricket Ground, and W. L. Ward and M. Matthews "liberally provided abundance of cake, wine and tea for the schools".

Cricket under the new foundation started in 1882 with T. H. B. Rush as Captain. The team played three matches, beat Bisham School by 143 runs, but lost to Wycombe R.G.S. by an innings and 42 runs, and to Medmenham by 36 runs. In the next year, they won five out of eight matches, beating Wycombe R.G.S. home and away. From 1885, the scores were printed

2.2.10. Borlase Cricket Club in the late nineteenth century

in full, with batting and bowling averages. W. W. Rush and W. Richardson were the star batsmen of that year, and Richardson and Creswell were the most destructive bowlers. By 1886, F. T. Handsombody had become the coach. There were several mixed matches (boys and masters), and the Town Ground was used for home matches. The School won ten of its twelve games. In 1887, Handsombody scored 123 against Bisham, and in 1893, 105 against the same club. Another master, A. C. Tearle, made 101 against Wycombe also in 1893, and another, W. Wotherspoon, 103 against Burnham in 1892. The only century made by a boy was 100 against St. Mark's School, Windsor, by L. C. P. Milman in 1895.

The chief event of the Spring Term was the Athletic Sports. In 1885, the events were 100 yards, half-mile, long jump and high jump for seniors; long jump, high jump and quarter-mile for juniors; 120 yards for boys under 11; and as open events, a quarter-mile handicap, place kicking at goal, three-legged race, egg and spoon race, obstruction race, sack race and quarter-mile consolation handicap. From 1884, there was a pole jump, and from 1885, a hurdle race, a tug-of-war, a wheelbarrow race, a jockey race and a sack race (heads inside!). Most of the comic races, it is true, were given only one trial, and bit by bit they were dropped. From 1893, there was a Junior Challenge Cup as well as a Senior Challenge Cup. The mile was first run in 1894, when it was won by F. B. Harman.

The Fives Court was built in 1887, and H. B. Lysons and Ll. Shone won a doubles competition in 1888. From 1890, the annual Fives competition was in singles. In 1889, the Cricket pitch on the Colonel's Meadow was levelled, and Marlow built its bathing pool in the same year. There were also races in 1889 in the backwater behind Marlow Lock. Boys were given instruction from the time the new pool was made.

There was a School Rowing Club in 1889 and, in the following year, a race between Day Boys and Boarders was won by the former.

Revival and Renewal (1874-1974)

E. W. CLARK (1896–1901)

When the Rev. Michael Graves intimated to the Governors that he intended to resign the Headmastership at Christmas 1895, the advertisement for his successor was inserted in *The Guardian*, *The Spectator*, *The Times*, *The South Bucks Standard* and *The South Bucks Free Press*. The post was given to E. W. Clark, who had been on the Staff at Borlase since September 1888 and Senior Assistant Master since September 1891. He was a brilliant scholar, an exhibitioner of Christ Church, Oxford, with Honours in Classics and Mathematics and Final School Modern History. He had already proved himself a most capable teacher of Latin and Greek, and a good cricketer. And it is not surprising that Classics and Cricket were the most successful departments in School life during his five and a half years as Headmaster. Indeed, during the whole time he was at Borlase, from 1888 to 1901, 29 boys won distinction in Latin in the Cambridge Locals examinations, and 6 in the Oxford and Cambridge examinations. In 1898, out of 3,680 candidates, J. A. Robinson obtained 25th place; and in 1899, out of 3,547 candidates, Borlase boys were placed 10th, 43rd, 91st and 127th in Latin. In 1896, there were still at School three boys who held classical scholarships at the Universities. S. J. Taylor, a Marlow foundationer, had won a First Classical Exhibition at Queens' College, Cambridge. The grant of a scholarship by the Governors and the generosity of T. O. Wethered when the funds ran low, enabled him to take in due course a Cambridge Honours degree in Classics. L. C. P. Milman obtained a Sizarship at Sidney Sussex College, Cambridge, and later also took a degree in Classics. A. R. W. Law won the Mayo Scholarship for Classics at Oxford. A year earlier, W. T. Munday had gone up to St. David's College, Lampeter. Munday was another Marlow foundationer who was assisted by the Governors and T. O. Wethered. He, too, took an Honours degree in Classics.

These five and a half years were a period of rapid decline in the fortunes of Borlase, for the number of boys at the school fell from 144 in 1895 to 109 in 1896, and to 77 in 1900. The Headmaster did not have the business capacity of his predecessor, and there was a certain lack of discipline in the School. But it must be admitted that it was becoming more and more difficult to attract boarders from distant parts of the country. Education was making vast strides. Now, all children could be educated for free up to the age of 14 years. There was a big demand for secondary education, partly as a preparation for the professions and partly as a link between the elementary schools and the universities. In 1888, the County Councils had come into being, and local authorities were vying with one another in building or procuring County Schools. Local patriotism was being fostered, and parents were more and more inclined to send their children to their own local schools.

The Governors were much concerned with the decrease in revenue. Fees yielded £730 in 1896, £494 in 1897, and only £396 in 1899, when there was an overdraft in the bank of £121. In 1898, one master paid by the Governors was dispensed with, and the grant for the payment of assistant masters was reduced from £150 to £100. The scholarship holders at the Universities would have had their college careers cut short but for the offer of £50 by T. O. Wethered. The Headmaster, too, was lax in collecting fees. Seeing no prospect of improvement, E. W. Clark resigned at Easter 1901.

Since April 1896, T. S. Cocks had resigned the Chairmanship of the Governors, and General Higginson had been elected in his place. At the same time, the Rev. Michael Graves, the former Headmaster, was elected a Governor. In July, James W. Morgan and F. O. Wethered

2.3.1. Borlase boys in c.1896

2.3.2. Borlase boys outside the School in West Street, c.1896

were elected by the Parish. In October 1897, Dr Shone resigned, and in March 1898, G. R. Ward and Dr J. D. Dickson were appointed. Colonel Bradish-Ellames became an *ex officio* Governor upon his taking up residence at Little Marlow in February 1900.

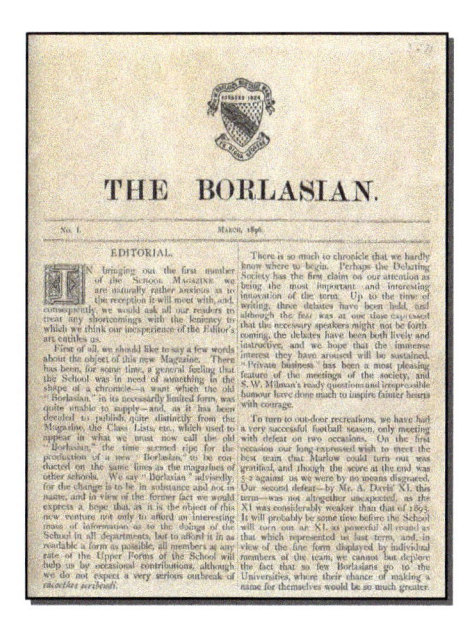

2.3.3. The revised format of The Borlasian *magazine, published in 1896*

The Borlasian had undergone a great change. Instead of the thirty or forty small pages, the magazine now contained only nine or ten large pages. The classlists, marks, etc., disappeared. But although the editor of the first issue considered that "the time seemed ripe for the production of a new "Borlasian," to be conducted on the same lines as the magazines of other schools" and hoped that "all members at any rate of the Upper Forms of the School will help us by occasional contributions", the magazine contained little except School Notes and records of the activities of the Debating Society and the Football and Cricket teams.

From the School Notes, we learn that D. Davis and W. H. Counsell joined the Staff in January 1896. In December, W. F. Stanyon, the Music master, left after five years' service. In March 1897, B. F. Hardy and W. H. Counsell found new posts. In July, F. T. Handsombody, after eleven years at Borlase, departed to be the Headmaster of King's Collegiate School in Windsor, Nova Scotia, Canada, a post that he held until 1914. C. W. Newton left in July 1899. The Rev. M. Graves became Vicar of Turville in 1897. In July 1898, Kentons, the hostel in Glade Road, was given up.

An old boy, W. Pescod, took part in the Jameson Raid. The Debating Society started its activities on 29 February 1896, with a debate on the question "That this House supports the action of Dr Jameson in marching on Johannesburg". This motion was carried by a majority of 17. There were three debates that term, for it was found advisable to devote alternate Saturdays to preparation for the School Concert, to be held on 28 March. The concert opened with the School Orchestra playing the 'March of the Israelites' from the oratorio *Eli*. In addition to songs by boys and masters, there were banjo, violin and mandolin solos.

The Society continued its activities in October, and there were six debates during the autumn term. The House decided that it was possible to evacuate Egypt, that it was impracticable to tax all foreigners entering England, that Home Rule would be beneficial to Ireland, and that the Cubans were wrong to attempt to gain their freedom. There was another concert on 14 November, with the School Band and the School Choir contributing items.

After the departure of W. F. Stanyon, the Debating Society languished, although in the spring of 1898, it had sufficient energy to reject the motion "That the proposed railway to Henley would not be beneficial to the county"! The decrease in the numbers in the School told its tale on the Football teams, for whereas in 1895–1896, under the captaincy of S. W. Milman, the School still held its own with Reading School and St. Mark's School, by 1900, the only school played was Magdalen College School.

2.3.4. Fred T. Handsombody (Staff 1886–1897)

Revival and Renewal (1874-1974)   CHAPTER 2 | 43

The Cricket team of 1896, captained by O. H. P. Cox, were beaten by one run by Reading School. They defeated Marlow, and put up a good show against a scratch team 225 for 7. Warner was caught and bowled by Finnis for 15, but Bardswell made 73 before he was caught. W. H. Haly was Captain in 1897. The School defeated Magdalen College School twice, but lost their other five matches. Haly was also Captain in 1898, when the School won three matches and lost six. Under F. Ellerton in 1899, the School won three matches out of seven. In 1900, under M. Ellerton, the team won five matches and lost eight.

E. H. BLAKENEY (1901–1904)

In March 1901, the Governors appointed E. H. Blakeney as successor to E. W. Clark. Blakeney had been educated at Westminster School and Trinity College, Cambridge, and had been the Headmaster of Sandwich Grammar School since 1895. He was already known as a poet and editor of Latin and English Classics.

The Governors were face to face with still another financial crisis. The number of boys in the School had decreased to about fifty, of whom twelve were scholarship boys who did not pay fees. The School did not pay its way, and there was already an overdraft in the bank of £150. Nothing but a great effort on the part of the Governors themselves and friends of the School would save the situation. A subscription list was opened, and the sum of £476 13s. collected. All but three or four of the subscribers were then or later Governors.

Col. O. P. Wethered	£100
T. O. Wethered	£100
Gen. Sir George Higginson	£50
Hon. W. F. D. Smith	£50
R. W. Hudson	£50
F. O. Wethered	£25
Lt-Col. Bradish-Ellames	£25
Rev. M. Graves	£25
Sir William Clayton	£10 10s.
R. Griffin	£10
R. Hay Murray	£10
W. W. Astor	£5
Earl Howe	£5
A. D. Cripps	£5
Rev. A. S. Thompson	£3
Rev. H. O. F. Whittingstall	£2 2s.
W. H. Grenfell	£1 1s.

With this sum in hand and the Trust solvent once more, the Governors were able to take into consideration a scheme of the County Council to provide technical education in the town. The Council were prepared to pay half the cost of erecting a new building with laboratories for Physics and Chemistry, a lecture room and an Art room. A site between the School House and Shelley House was chosen. R. Wellicome was appointed architect, and W. and T. Sellman contractors. The estimated cost was £1,400 and the County Council guaranteed £700, with £100 a year towards the salary of a Science master. They would also provide a peripatetic master to visit Marlow once per week to give instruction in Art.

About this time, the two remaining parts of Sir William Borlase's estate that were not needed for extensions of the School were sold. Bix Farm brought in £1,200, and the Barley Field (or Gower's Close, as it was called in the old documents) was sold for £900.

The situation was further improved by the erection of the workshop, a gift to the School by Edward Riley and his half sister, Miss Wilson Mitchell. Friends of the School equipped the new workshop with tools, and a lathe was given by Mrs Hudson. Colonel O. P. Wethered gave £100 towards equipping the Science laboratories. Dr Nicholson gave the standard barometer that is still in the Physics laboratory. The County Council fitted out the Art room, and the Marlow Institute sent up the plaster casts. Above all, two anonymous donors guaranteed to the School funds £200 per year for three years. All of this benefaction goes to show that the spirit of Sir William Borlase was by no means dead at the beginning of the twentieth century.

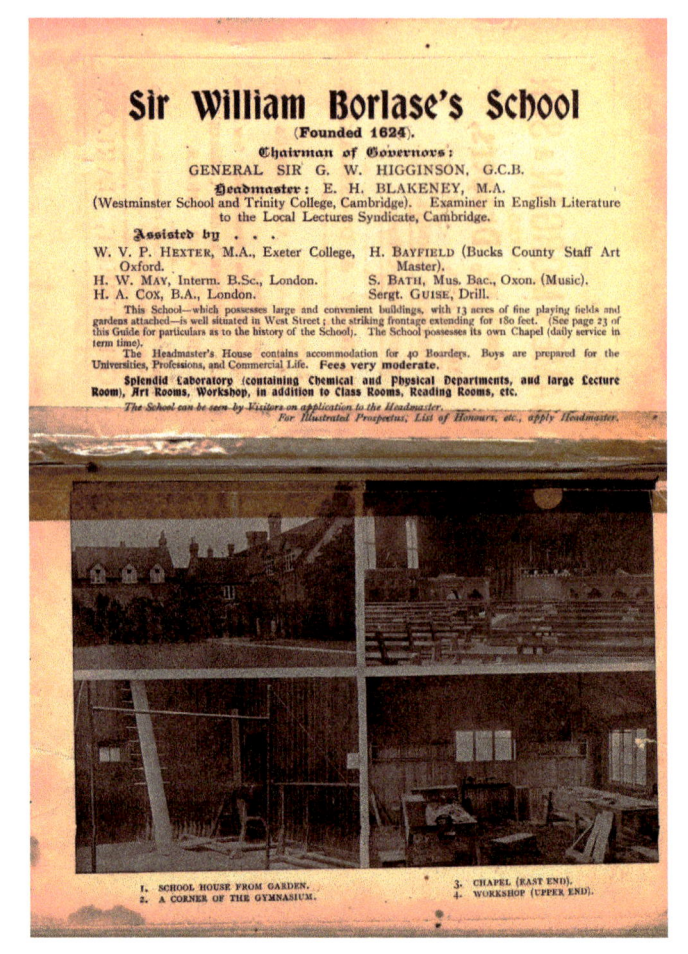

2.4.1. An advertisement for the School under the Headmastership of E. H. Blakeney

2.4.2. The new buildings, incorporating the entry archway, completed in 1903

Revival and Renewal (1874-1974) CHAPTER 2 | 45

2.4.3. Borlase boys on Church Parade, c.1903; the tall figure fifth from left is Basil Arthur Horsfall who was awarded the Victoria Cross in World War I

2.4.4. The Quadrangle and archway to West Street; the interior of the wood workshop, a gift of Edward Riley and Miss Mitchell; the interior of the Art room, with plaster casts supplied by the Marlow Institute; the interior of the Chemistry laboratory; and the interior of the Physics laboratory

46 | CHAPTER 2

Revival and Renewal (1874-1974)

All these changes involved alterations in the scheme of government. The Board of Education took over the function of the Charity Commissioners. The County Council and the Marlow Urban District Council were to have two representatives each on the Board of Governors. Access was to be given after School hours to classes organized by the Bucks County Council. The School was to be qualified to earn grants from the Board of Education and the County Council. The tuition fees of the School were to be increased to £12 per year, and the boarding fees to £42, and in addition to the annual inspection of the School by an examiner appointed by the Governors, there was periodically to be an inspection by the Board of Education Inspectors.

The new Governors representing the Council were John Thomas and Robert Griffin. F. O. Wethered was chosen to represent the Oxford University Hebdomadal Council, and Alfred Davis to represent the Marlow Urban District Council, along with an old Governor, J. W. Morgan, who, however, died in 1903, and was succeeded by his son, W. J. Morgan. At the resignation of Rev. H. O. F. Whittingstall, his successor as Vicar of Marlow, Rev. J. H. Light, took his place. Edward Riley became a Governor on the resignation of A. Lawrence in 1903. In 1904, the Clerk to the Governors, A. D. Cripps, died and Ll. Shone was elected in his place.

The only two masters who remained any length of time were W. V. P. Hexter, the senior assistant, and H. W. May. The outstanding scholastic successes of the three years were the gaining by W. H. C. Prideaux of an £84 Science and Mathematics Scholarship to Faraday House, and the winning by W. M. Peacock of a £30 Open Classical Scholarship to Marlborough College. In 1904, J. C. B. Constable obtained a 1st Class College of Preceptors Certificate, and was top of all England in Latin.

In 1902, an Old Boys' Club was founded, with the Rev. M. Graves as President, A. Davis as Honorary Secretary, and W. V. P. Hexter as Honorary Treasurer. One of their first activities was to wind up the accounts of the Old Borlasian Football Club of earlier days and with the balance to buy the Old Boys' Shield, which was competed for on Sports Day.

REV. ALBERT J. SKINNER (1904–1927)

E. H. Blakeney left suddenly in the summer holidays of 1904 on his appointment as Headmaster of King's School, Ely. The Governors had 33 applicants for the vacancy and out of them chose the Rev. Albert James Skinner, an old Oundle boy, who had at one time been on the staff of Reading School. He came to Borlase from Hereford, where he had been Headmaster of the County School. As E. H. Blakeney had taken some of his boarders with him to Ely, and other boys had left in July, there were only 28 pupils on the School books. As ten of these were foundationers (there were two vacancies), it can be gathered that, despite the grants from the Board of Education and the County Council towards the expenses of the new Science department, the financial crisis of the past few years was not over. The new Headmaster, however, was an excellent organizer, and being himself a scientist, he was able to make full use of the new buildings. In

2.5.1. The Rev. A. J. Skinner (Headmaster 1904–1927) and his entry in the Staff register

Revival and Renewal (1874-1974)   CHAPTER 2 | 47

2.5.2. The staff and prefects in 1904–1905. Seated: Mr Hexter, Rev. A. J. Skinner (Headmaster) and Mr Dodd; standing: Briscoe, Mrs Skinner and Constable

his first Speech Day in July 1905, he was able to announce that the numbers had increased to 50. So far, the Staff consisted of the Headmaster, two regular assistant masters, a visiting teacher of drawing and a drill instructor. An additional assistant master was appointed in September 1905.

By July 1906, the numbers had reached 54. Two boys had been sent up for London Matriculation. J. C. B. Constable had passed in the First Division and R. A. Clifford in the Second. This year saw the endowment of the first of the School's scholarships, which enabled many Borlasians to stay on at School or to proceed to the Universities. T. O. Wethered endowed the School with an annual scholarship of £30, tenable at any place of higher education. It could be held for two years, but might be renewed for a third if the student's report was satisfactory. It was open to any boys who had been at Borlase for two years and who were over 16 years of age.

By 1907, the numbers had reached 70, of whom 21 were boarders and 7 pupil teachers, admitted under a new scheme of the County Council. Despite the closing of the School for three weeks in February owing to an outbreak of scarlet fever in the town, there were two more Matriculation successes and two Oxford Locals Senior certificates gained. The finances of the School were now on a firmer foundation, because there was an income from fees of over £500. This, together with increased grants from the Board of Education and the County Council and the revenue from Consols, left the Trust with a surplus for the year of £85.

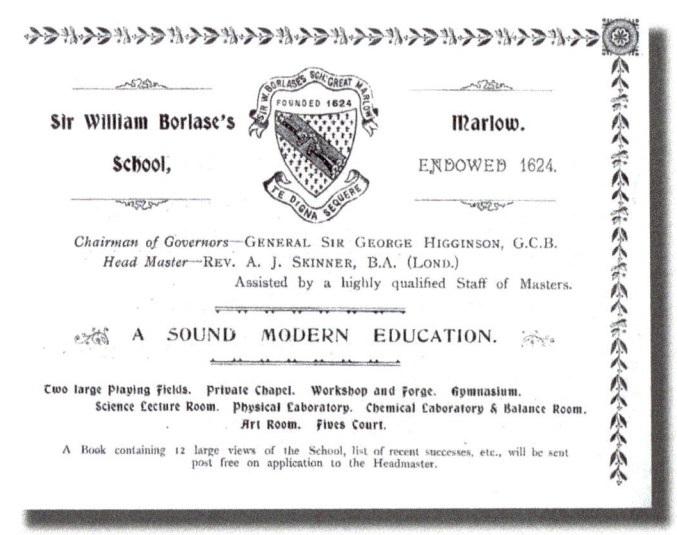

2.5.3. A School advertisement from the Headmastership of the Rev. A. J. Skinner

2.5.4. The foundation stone of the new Assembly Hall, laid in 1909

In 1908, the Board of Education required that free place scholarships should be given to 25% of the pupils at the School. This was rather hard on the Governors, because they already had to provide by the Scheme of 1881 for twelve free places for foundationers from three local parishes, but they complied with the new regulations, and held the necessary examination. But it was becoming more and more apparent that if the numbers in the School continued to increase, there would be a need for more permanent buildings. It was estimated that £500 would have to be spent on the old iron buildings if they were to be repaired. The Governors decided that under the circumstances it was best to consult an architect as to the estimated cost of building an Assembly Hall that could be divided into two classrooms. Accordingly, they got in touch with W. A. Forsyth, a London architect. Plans and negotiations were completed early in 1909, the tender of Y. J. Lovell and Son accepted, and building began in the summer. The foundation stone of the Assembly Hall was laid with Masonic ceremonial by the Earl of Orkney on 13 October 1909.

Here is a description of the ceremony taken from *The South Bucks Standard*:

"The Brethren assembled in the School at the appointed time, and shortly before four o'clock the first notes of the American organ announced that the grand ceremonial had begun. Soon the voices of the choir and brethren were heard in the hymn 'Through the night of doubt and sorrow', and a moment or two later the choristers, lads in surplices, and members of the Royal Windsor Glee Party, in Masonic regalia, were observed approaching at the head of the procession, which was formed in the following order:

Choir Boys,
Tyler,
Visiting Brethren and Brethren of Marlow Lodge,
Officers of Marlow Lodge,
Banners of Marlow Lodge,
J.W. of Marlow Lodge, S.W. of Marlow Lodge,
W.M. of Marlow Lodge,
Past Provincial Officers,
The Provincial Assistant Grand Director of Ceremonies,
Three Masters of Lodges, bearing the Cornucopia and ewers with wine and oil,
The Provincial Grand Superintendent of Works with the mallet,
The Provincial Grand Secretary with the plate,
The Provincial Grand Registrar, bearing the seal,
The Provincial Grand Treasurer, bearing the phial containing the coin to be deposited on the stone,
The Provincial Junior Grand Warden with the plumb rule,
Four Lewises, bearing the Sacred Law on a cushion,
The Provincial Grand Chaplains,
The Deputy Provincial Grand Master with a square,
The Deputy Grand Sword Bearer,
The Right Worshipful the Provincial Grand Master,
The Right Hon. Earl of Orkney,
Two Provincial Grand Deacons,
Grand Officers

2.5.5. The Masonic procession at the laying of the foundation stone of the Assembly Hall, 1909

Revival and Renewal (1874–1974)

2.5.6. The ceremonial laying of the foundation stone of the Assembly Hall, 1909

The Right Worshipful Provincial Grand Master proceeded to the table, where General Sir George Higginson was already seated in the place of honour, in the chair, the Earl being accompanied by the Provincial Grand Director of Ceremonies and other Officers of the Craft. The Sacred Law (an open Bible), which had been borne on a cushion by four Lewises, was placed on the pedestal in front of the Chairman's table."

General Sir George Higgonson, as Chairman of the Governors, welcomed the Masons and other guests, and Lord Orkney, on behalf of the Masons, replied. The Provincial Grand Chaplain offered a prayer, the Provincial Grand Secretary read the inscription on the stone, the Provincial Grand Treasurer deposited the phial containing the coins, and the Provincial Grand Secretary placed the plate on the lower stone. The cement was next spread, and the Right Worshipful Provincial Grand Master adjusted the same with a silver trowel, handed to him by the Provincial Grand Chaplain (Rev. A. J. Skinner).

The anthem 'O, give thanks unto the Lord' having been sung, the Right Worshipful Grand Master proceeded to prove the just position and form of the stone by the plumb rule, level and square, which were successively delivered to him by the Junior Provincial Grand Warden, the Senior Provincial Grand Warden and the Provincial Deputy-Grand Master. Being satisfied in these particulars, the Provincial Grand Master gave the stone three knocks with the mallet and said: "I declare this stone well and truly laid."

The Cornucopia containing the corn, and the ewers with the wine and oil, were then handed to the Provincial Grand Master. Having strewn the corn on the stone, he said: "I scatter this corn as a sign of productiveness", and then the voice of the Provincial Grand Chaplain was heard intoning the words: "There shall be a handful of corn in the earth upon the top of the mountains; the fruit thereof shall shake like Lebanon; and they of the city shall flourish like the grass of the earth."

The Provincial Grand Master, having poured wine on the stone, said: "I pour this wine as a sign of hospitality", and the Provincial Grand Chaplain responded: "And for a drink offering thou shalt offer the third part of a hin of wine, for a sweet savour unto the Lord."

The oil was poured on the stone, the Provincial Grand Master saying: "I pour this oil as a token of peace." The Provincial Grand Chaplain answered: "And thou shalt make it an oil of holy ointment, an ointment compound after the art of the apothecary; it shall be a holy anointing oil. And thou shalt anoint the tabernacle of the congregation therewith, and the ark of the testimony."

Then followed a hymn and a concluding prayer, offered by the Provincial Grand Chaplain.

2.5.7. Exterior and interior of the new Assembly Hall in 1909 and the exterior in 2023

The estimated cost of the Assembly Hall was £1,522. The sale of Consols to meet this expense left the Trust only £2,800 still invested. In October 1909, it was suggested that this money should be spent on providing the School with three permanent additional classrooms, joining up the new Assembly Hall with the old buildings, and forming the north side of the Quadrangle. As Edward Riley suggested: "It was better to have the money in a productive form of education such as new buildings, rather than in Consols as at present." The architect estimated the new buildings to cost £2,645, and the additional cost of fittings and furniture would leave the Trust with a debit balance of around £600. To supply the sum, there was still another whip-round among the Governors, which produced £563 3s., made up as follows:

T. O. Wethered	£140
E. Riley	£100
Miss Mitchell	£100
Gen. Sir George Higginson	£50
Rev. M. Graves	£50
Sir William M. Clayton	£50
Baron Kearley	£50
Robert Griffin	£20
Dr Dickson	£3 3s.

Revival and Renewal (1874-1974) CHAPTER 2 | 51

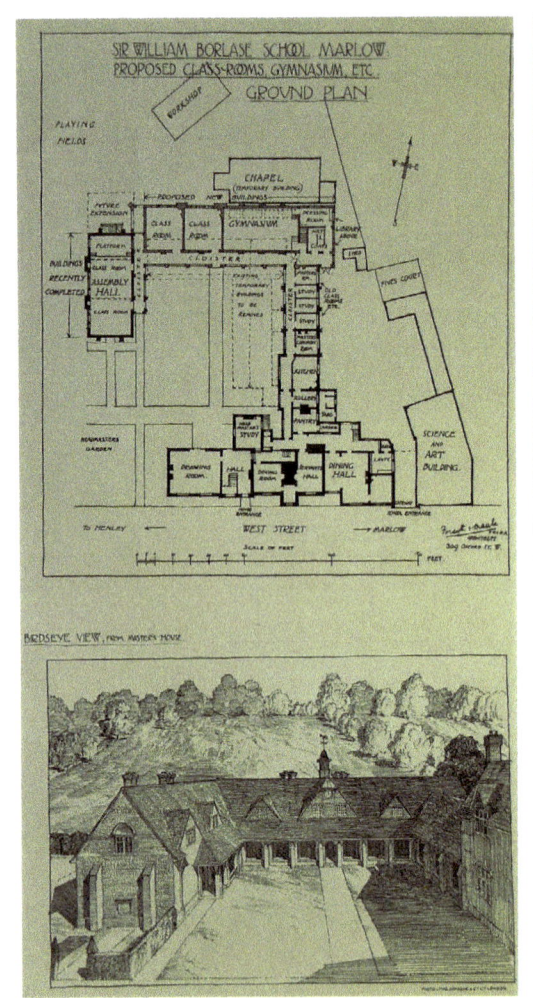

2.5.8. A plan to complete the north side of the Cloisters with classrooms and a gymnasium

2.5.9. Interior of the new Swedish gymnasium in the Cloisters (now the Stuart Lever Room)

Before building could be started, it was necessary to apply to the Board of Education for sanction to sell the remainder of the endowment. The Board refused their sanction unless the School were from then on to be controlled by the County Council. Once again, there were protracted negotiations, ending in September 1910, in an agreement that the School should from then on come under the management of the County, provided the Board of Education and the County Council guaranteed that there should be no radical change in the nature of the School.

The Speech Day of 1910 was held in the new Assembly Hall. The numbers in the School were approaching one hundred, and the Honours List was growing year by year. In the year 1909–1910, D. H. Dickson had won a County Major Scholarship of £50 per year. L. A. Gaffney and F. W. Greenaway had won Intermediate County Scholarships of £25 per year. There were two successes in London Matriculation: J. W. Shaw and F. A. Sloan. There were five passes in the Oxford Locals Senior, and seven in the Junior.

In November 1910, the County Council accepted their appointment as Trustees. The value of Consols was falling at this time, and there was still a danger that the new classrooms could not be built. These further donations enabled the Governors to accept the tender of W. and T. Sellman, and the building of the new block began in March 1911:

T. O. Wethered	£100
Haden Crawford	£25
Sir John Thomas	£25
Dr T. G. Nicholson	£21
Rev. A. J. Skinner	£10
Rev. J. H. Light	£2 2s.

By July, the total subscriptions had reached £693 15s. The sale of the remaining Consols was authorized by the Board of Education. The two classrooms and the Gymnasium were ready for use by the opening of the September term. Meanwhile, donations from C. A. Cripps, A. H. Hornby Lewis, Sir George Higginson and the Old Borlasian Club enabled the Governors

2.5.10. The Cloisters clocktower today, paid for by donations in 1911, and the old School bell, at the north-east corner of the Cloisters

to crown the new block of buildings with the electric clock. The new buildings and the old were made more attractive by the addition of the Cloisters.

In December 1911, the School received the second of its valuable internal scholarships. Miss Mitchell and her half-brother Edward Riley invested £1,000, to produce an annual sum of £40. This scholarship was open to any boy who had been educated at Borlase for three years. It could be used to enable the boy to proceed to any place of higher education or to stay on at School. In the first place, it could be granted for one year only, but it could be renewed for two more years at the discretion of the Governors.

Although the County Council had accepted the trusteeship of the School in November 1910, negotiations went on between the various parties interested in the new scheme of government up to March 1912, when the scheme was definitely adopted by the County Council. Consequently, this date may be taken as the end of the old foundation, when the School was entirely governed by local gentlemen, as arranged by the will of Sir William Borlase.

In 1912, there were once more a hundred boys in the School. L. A. Gaffney had won a Major Scholarship of £50 a year, and had obtained a First Division pass in the London Matriculation. W. D. Boyt had gained an Intermediate Scholarship of £25, and there were four more Matriculation successes.

Between 1904 and 1912, old Governors who died or resigned were: Colonel Bradish-Ellames (died 1905), Rev. A. S. Thompson (resigned 1905), G. R. Ward (died 1907) and R. W. Hudson (resigned 1909). Their places were taken by Sir William Clayton (1907), Rev. P. Lambert (1907) and Baron Kearley (1909). Sir John Thomas was knighted in 1907.

The following members of the Staff came and went during that period: G. Milner (1904–1905), E. Dodd (1904–1906), G. M. Gaskell (1905–1907), B. M. R. Denny (1905–1907), W. Cottrell (1906–1909), C. A. Woodger (1906–1910), T. Mardon (1907–1908), Miss V. Cooper, appointed to take charge of the preparatory department (1908–1910), A. T. Bennett (1907–1909) and W. J. Scott (1910–1911). There remained on the staff E. L. Wells (1908), Rev. R. W. Clarke (1909), A. T. Eggington (1910), A. L. Hardy (1910) and F. A. Sloan, an old boy, in charge of the preparatory department (1910).

Among out-of-class activities may be mentioned the performances on the Headmaster's lawn of *As You Like It* in 1905 and of *A Midsummer Night's Dream* in 1909. There were several concerts, and each year an entertainment on Speech Day. A National History Museum was started, and efforts were made to add to the Library.

Revival and Renewal (1874-1974)

CHAPTER 2 | 53

2.5.11. The cast of the 1905 production of As You Like It

There was a rifle range, the boys competing each year for a cup presented by Mrs Henderson. In the spring term, the Fives competition was held annually. In this term, the Sixes battles (six-a-side Soccer competitions) were also fought. At first, six teams, named after six captains, competed in a league. Later, the teams were named after the principal professional teams. In 1911 is the first record of the original four of the current School Houses: Britons, Danes, Normans and Saxons.

2.5.12. The miniature rifle range

The Cricket and Football teams improved as the number of pupils increased. The fixtures with Wycombe R.G.S. and Henley Grammar School were revived. From 1908, games were played with Windsor County School; King Alfred's School, Wantage; and Alleyn's School, Dulwich, who were beaten in that year on their own ground at Football. Indeed, the prestige of Borlase Football was fully restored in the years 1908 and 1909, when the School team was led by Harry E. Stranger. Stranger went on to serve in World War I as a Captain with the Royal Guernsey Light Infantry and was awarded the Military Cross. Harry's two brothers, George and Frank, both keen cricketers at Borlase, also served. Tragically, all three were killed within seven weeks of each other in the early summer of 1918. George died at Lys, where only 58 men out of 503 survived a German offensive; Harry was wounded in the same battle and died a month later. Frank had been killed while fighting for the Australian infantry two weeks before George. The Harry Stranger Prize for PE is still awarded annually at Speech Day in his memory.

In 1907, the Old Borlasian Club got on to a permanent footing. The first of its annual dinners was held at the Holborn Restaurant in May 1908. The Rev. Michael Graves was President, F. B. Harman was Honorary Secretary and Alfred Davis JP was Honorary Treasurer.

2.5.13. The Cricket and Football 1st XIs of 1907 to 1909, captained by H. E. Stranger, and (above) the sports shields bearing his name that still hang in the Cloisters

2.5.14. The second Annual Dinner of the Old Borlasian Club, held at the Holborn Restaurant in 1909

Revival and Renewal (1874-1974)   CHAPTER 2   55

WORLD WAR I (1914–1918)

The Governors probably did wisely to surrender the School to the County Council. Poorly provided as it was with capital to hold its own in the twentieth century with public schools, it could only degenerate into a private school, dependent on its ability to attract boarders, and of little value to the locality. The boys of the three parishes — all except the twelve foundationers, who would have been regarded as necessary evils — would, if they required secondary education at all, have had to seek it in Wycombe or Maidenhead. Under the County Council, the Governors were still able to exercise their influence and maintain the traditions of the School. Sir William Borlase in the seventeenth century could hardly have expected boys outside the three parishes to be able to attend school at Marlow. The advent of trains and motor cars entirely altered the situation.

The change did not diminish the interest of the Governors in the School. In October 1913, Edward Riley and Miss Mitchell offered to build a Chapel. The Riley family were great Marlow philanthropists — they founded the Riley Park Trust particularly for the enjoyment of young children to play, thereby avoiding the danger of children being on the streets. W. A. Forsyth submitted plans for a Chapel on alternative sites around the School. Riley chose the unorthodox north-to-south orientation, and W. and T. Sellman began building. The foundation, with this inscription, was laid by Miss Mitchell: "This stone was laid by Mary Wilson Mitchell, who, in conjunction with her brother, Edward Riley, of Marlow, erected this Chapel for the benefit of Sir William Borlase's School, MCMXIV."

The Chapel was ready for use by the summer of 1914. The Vicar promised a lectern, the Rev. Michael Graves gave the oak altar and the stone pulpit, and General Sir George Higginson gave £25 towards providing seats. Lord Devonport gave the choir stalls, and Lady Clayton the American organ.

Hardly had the Chapel been completed when the School suffered a great loss in the death of the donor. In memory of him, his widow,

2.5.15. The School Chapel, completed in 1914

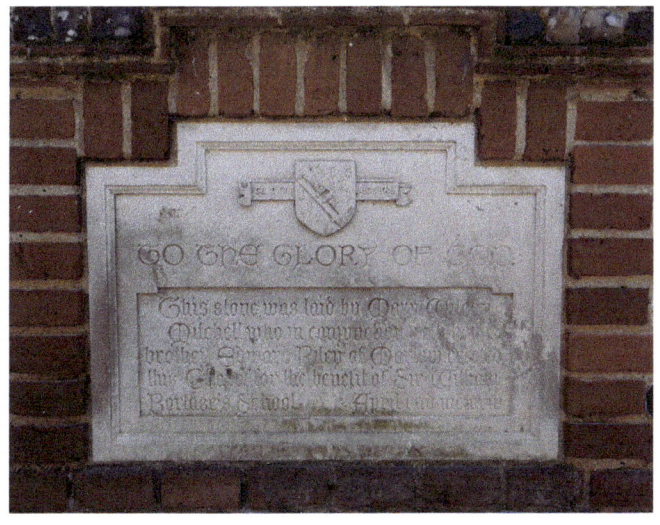

2.5.16. School Chapel foundation stone and the ceremonial trowel presented to Miss Mitchell

Mrs Riley, gave the centre window, under which is a brass tablet with this inscription: "This window was given by Emma Riley in memory of her husband, Edward Riley, F.I.C., for many years a Governor of Borlase School who died 12th September, 1914."

T. O. Wethered gave the window to the east of the altar about the same time. The window to the west of the altar was given in 1918 as a War Memorial. The east window in the nave was a legacy bequest from Thomas Stanmore (OB 1883–1888), a treasurer of the Old Borlasian Club, and was unveiled at Speech Day 1957. The tablet on the east wall was placed by Dr Dickson, in memory of his son, David Angus Dickson (OB 1906–1911), who was drowned when serving on HMS Hawke on 15 October 1914. To the left of the altar hangs a reproduction of the Madonna of the Goldfinch from the School of Raphael, donated by Dr Peter Phillips (Chairman of Governors) and his wife in December 1995.

Two other Governors and benefactors of the School died during the War: Sir William Clayton, in 1914, and Rev. J. H. Light, Vicar of Marlow, in 1916. Among those who became Governors between 1912 and 1918 were W. R. D. Mackenzie, W. Niven, H. H. Worthington, James Boyton MP, Lt-Col. Sir A. H. Hine, Rev. O. F. Spearing, Rev. J. H. Best and Rev. G. H. Jones.

The numbers in the School continued to grow up to the outbreak of the War. In 1903,

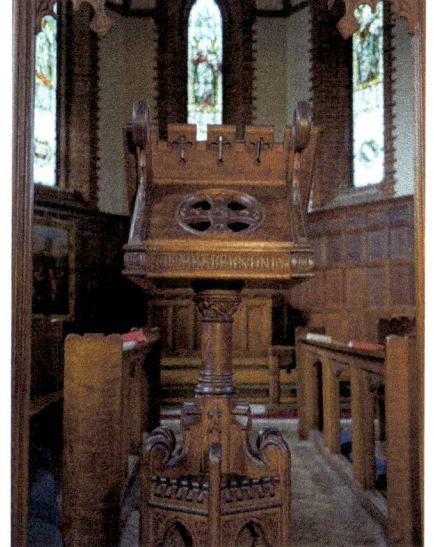

2.5.17. Interior of the Chapel and the lectern

Revival and Renewal (1874-1974)   CHAPTER 2 | 57

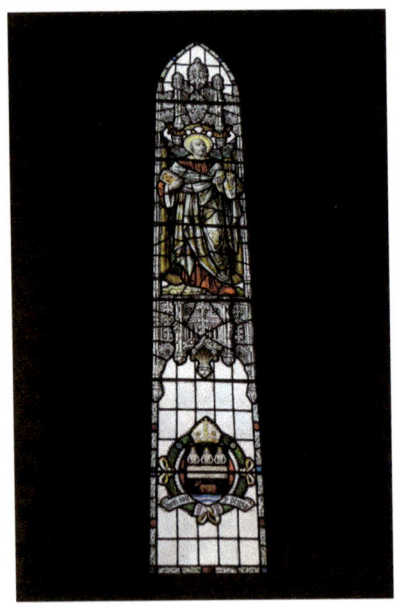

2.5.18. The stained-glass windows at the north end of the Chapel given, respectively, as a War Memorial, in memory of Edward Riley (pictured below) and by T. O. Wethered; the last contains the Borlase coat of arms at the bottom

2.5.19. The east window of the Chapel, given by Thomas Stanmore

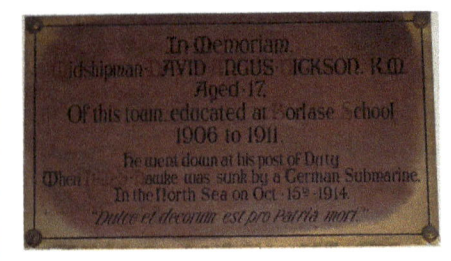

2.5.20. Memorial to David Angus Dickson in the Chapel

there were 107 pupils; in 1914, there were 114. In common with all schools, Borlase suffered a rapid decline in numbers during the early War years. At first, parents found it difficult to pay tuition and boarding fees. Later, the senior boys were taken into the Army, and boys of 14 and 15 years were withdrawn from School owing to the high wages paid in offices and elsewhere. In addition, parents often needed the boys at home. By 1916, the number of pupils had declined to 64. Then came the air-raids and the flight of families from London to the relative safety of the Home Counties and, from 1917 onwards, the numbers steadily increased.

In common with all other Schools, Borlase suffered from numerous changes in the Staff, but unlike most Schools did not engage female teachers at this time. In 1912, the assistant staff consisted of Rev. R. W. Clarke, E. L. Wells, A. T. Eggington, A. L. Harding and F. A. Sloan. Wells left in 1913, after 6 years in Marlow, and was replaced by L. W. Whitty. Clarke left in 1914. Eggington, Whitty and Sloan joined the Army in 1914. Among the masters who served some time on the Staff during the War were two old boys, W. D. Boyt and R. A. Clifford.

In 1913, L. A. Gaffney gained an open Science Scholarship at New College, Oxford.

58 | CHAPTER 2 — Revival and Renewal (1874-1974)

This, together with the Major Scholarship he had gained the previous year, enabled him to go up to Oxford in the autumn of that year. The principal scholastic success of 1914 was the winning of a £25 County Intermediate Scholarship by A. E. Baldwin, who also passed the London Matriculation in the First Division. In 1915, he won a County Major Scholarship, but stayed on in School and took his Intermediate London. Two years later, he performed the astounding feat of taking a London Honours Degree direct from School. Another War-time success was the winning of a Major Scholarship in 1916 by F. G. Hill.

In Football and Cricket, the School continued to hold its own very well. Games were regularly played with Alleyn's School, Dulwich, Westminster City School and Reading School, until War-time restrictions and high fares put, for a time, an end to these contests. Most of the games with Wycombe, Henley, Windsor and Maidenhead were won. The Sports, the Sixes and the Fives were as keenly contested as ever.

2.5.21. Painting of the Madonna of the Goldfinch, donated by Dr Peter Phillips in 1995

2.5.22. The Football 1st XI of 1913–1914

Revival and Renewal (1874-1974)   CHAPTER 2 | 59

Many Borlasians fought and died in World War I. Up to the outbreak of war, the entire School list of boys who had entered since the reconstruction in 1881 was only 908. By 1914, many of these were over military age, many dead, many unfit, and the boys still in School too young to join the forces. Many, too, had been lost sight of. However, more than 400 Old Borlasians and 11 members of the Staff are known to have served. They were to be found in all branches of the Navy, Army and Air Force and in British, Australian, Canadian, Indian and New Zealand regiments. At least 192 of them were officers. They served in all parts of the globe, and between them won almost every kind of honour.

Victoria Cross
Horsfall, Second Lieutenant B. A., East Lancashire Regiment (killed in action)

Distinguished Service Order
Belgrave, Major H. D., West Kent Regiment
Belgrave, Major J. D., Royal Artillery
Chenevix-Trench, Major J. F., Northumberland Fusiliers
Croft, Lieutenant-Colonel W. D., Royal Scots (also three Bars to D.S.O.)
Fitzgerald, Lieutenant-Colonel A. S., Royal Warwickshire Regiment
Franklin, Major R. N., Australian Light Horse
Harington, Lieutenant-Colonel J., Rifle Brigade
Kirby, Lieutenant-Colonel H. A., Royal Garrison Artillery (also M.C.)
Newton-Clare, Squadron-Commander E. T., Royal Naval Air Force
Reid, Captain N. S., Oxford and Bucks Light Infantry (also M.C.)
Woodgate, Captain A. B., East Lancashire Regiment (also M.C.)

Military Cross
Clarke, Lieutenant F. L., London Regiment
Deane, Lieutenant S. L., Rifle Brigade
Dickson, Captain I. D., Royal Army Medical Corps
Durnford, Rev. F. H., Chaplain to the Forces
Edge-Partington, Rev. E. F., Chaplain to the Forces
Fitzherbert, Captain A. V., South Irish Horse
Fitzherbert, Flight-Lieutenant C. H., Royal Naval Air Service
Flint, Captain N. S., Oxford and Bucks Light Infantry
Forbes, Lieutenant G. F. M., Gloucester Regiment
Fulljames, Captain R. M., Durham Light Infantry (also Bar to M.C.)
Hazelrigg, Captain G. M., Army Service Corps
Hepworth, Captain A. M., The Queen's Regiment (killed in action)
Kirby, Captain H. A., Royal Garrison Artillery (also D.S.O.)
Lochner, Captain R. G., South Wales Borderers
Milson, Second-Lieutenant M. G., Royal Fusiliers
Nash, Captain F. H., North Staffordshire Regiment (killed in action)
Reeves, Second-Lieutenant G. G., Oxford and Bucks Light Infantry
Reid, Second-Lieutenant G. P. S., Seaforth Highlands and R.F.C. (killed)
Reid, Captain N. S., Oxford and Bucks Light Infantry (also D.S.O.)
Robertson, Captain C. J. T., Army Ordnance Corps
Selby-Lowndes, Second-Lieutenant J. W. F., Grenadier Guards
Sloan, Captain F. A., Bedfordshire Regiment
Stewart, Second-Lieutenant C. H. I., London Regiment (also D.C.M.)
Stranger, Captain H. E. K., Royal Guernsey Light Infantry (died of wounds)
Woodgate, Captain A. B., East Lancashire Regiment (also D.S.O.)
Young, Captain E. W. G., Royal Army Medical Corps

Distinguished Service Cross
Smith, Lieutenant F. C., Royal Air Force (killed)

Companion of the Order of St Michael and St George
Milman, Lieutenant-Colonel L. C. P., Royal Artillery, Assistant Director at the Ministry of Munitions

French Croix de Guerre
Dickson, Captain B. T., South Lancashire Regiment
Woodroffe, Captain W. G., Middlesex Regiment (killed in action)

Italian Bronze Medal
Flint, Captain N. S., Oxford and Bucks Light Infantry

Order of the Nile
Fairbairn, Captain D. A., Duke of Wellington's Regiment, attached to the Egyptian Army
Hobbs, Captain H. C. F., West Yorkshire Regiment, attached to the Egyptian Army

Belgian Croix de Guerre
Lawton, Sapper H., Royal Engineers

Distinguished Conduct Medal
Stewart, Private C. H. I., London Regiment (also M.C.)

Military Medal
Matthews, Rifleman R. D., London Regiment
Shaw, Lance-Corporal F. T., Oxford and Bucks Light Infantry
Snodgrass, Gunner, C. A., Royal Field Artillery

Meritorious Service Medal
Baldwin, Q. M. Sergeant B. A., Duke of Cornwall's Light Infantry

Russian Medal of St George
Walpole, Hugh, Russian Red Cross

But if the Honours list is long, so also is that of the Borlasians who made the supreme sacrifice and laid down their lives for King and Country.

Ayliffe, Rifleman Ronald Glisbey (OB 1906–1909), Queen's Westminster Rifles
Bartlett, Private Gilbert (OB 1901–1905), 3rd South African Infantry
Bath, Captain John Euel Witherden (OB 1903–1905), 5th Royal Berks Regiment
Bradford, Captain Cecil Aubrey (OB 1895–1897), Yorkshire Regiment
Bridges, Captain Walter (OB 1889–1892), Army Service Corps
Brown-Constable, Lieutenant John Cecil (OB 1902–1906), London Regiment
Buckell, Trooper Reginald George (OB 1904–1910), Royal Bucks Hussars
Carey, Second-Lieutenant Lloyd Carleton (OB 1910–1912), East Surrey Regiment
Carter, Private Alfred James (OB 1888–1892), 174th Labour Company
Coldwell, Captain Vincent (OB 1892–1898), 4th Indian Cavalry
Corscaden, Second-Lieutenant James Noel (OB 1911), 6th Royal Inniskilling Fusiliers
Couchman, Sergeant Mechanic Thomas (OB 1891–1895), Royal Marine Artillery

Creswell, Sergeant George Henry (OB 1910–1914), 4th Oxford and Bucks Light Infantry
Curtis, Lieutenant Hubert James (OB 1911–1915), Royal Air Force
Davis, Second-Lieutenant Anthony Hugh (OB 1894), 1st Oxford and Bucks Light Infantry
Dean, Private Harry W. (OB 1901–1904), 9th Norfolk Regiment
Dickson, Midshipman David Angus (OB 1906–1910), HMS Hawke
Douglas-Crompton, Second-Lieutenant Sidney Harold Lionel (OB 1908–1913), 1st Royal Fusiliers
Dye, Rifleman Percy Rignall (OB 1898–1902), Queen's Westminster Rifles
Foster, Captain Hedley Roy (OB 1902–1908), Oxford and Bucks Light Infantry
Franklin, Major Reginald Norris (OB 1893–1899), Australian Imperial Force
Gaffney, Second-Lieutenant Leon Arthur (OB 1907–1913), Royal Munster Fusiliers
Good, Lieutenant Herbert Barrett (OB 1912–1915), Royal Air Force
Guthrie, Captain John Neil (OB 1895–1896), Irish Guards
Haly, Second-Lieutenant William Heli (OB 1892–1898), Hampshire Regiment
Hardy, Captain Harold (OB 1898–1900), Royal Irish Rifles
Harris, Rifleman Philip Francis (OB 1907–1910), King's Royal Rifles
Hepworth, Captain Arthur Montagu (OB 1897–1899), Queen's Regiment
Horsfall, Second-Lieutenant Basil Arthur (OB 1903–1905), East Lancashire Regiment
Howard, Major Bernard Henry (OB 1889–1991), 47th Sikhs, Indian Army
Kent, Lieutenant Ernest (OB 1907–1914), Essex Regiment
Kershaw, Second-Lieutenant Kenneth Robert Beresford (OB 1901–1906), Gordon Highlanders
King, Second-Lieutenant Maurice (OB 1907–1914), Egyptian Labour Corps
Langdon, Sapper Albert (OB 1898–1901), Royal Engineers (Signals)
Langley, Trooper Jack (Jnr) (OB 1889–1894), Royal Bucks Hussars
Lewis, Second-Lieutenant Arthur Glanmor (OB 1911–1912), South Wales Borderers
Morgan, Second-Lieutenant Sidney Herbert (OB 1900–1902), East Surrey Regiment
Nash, Captain Francis Henry (OB 1894–1896), North Staffordshire Regiment
Peddle, Private Alfred Harry (OB 1907–1910), King's Own Yorkshire Light Infantry
Pescod, Private Lewis George (OB 1893–1895), 9th Australian Infantry
Pescod, Sergeant Major William Thomas (OB 1884–1888), South African Imperial Light Horse
Pullin, Private Hubert Victor (OB 1911–1913), Royal West Kent Regiment
Reading, Lance-Corporal James William Charles (OB 1901–1907), London Rifle Brigade
Reid, Captain Guy Patrick Spence (OB 1907–1914), Seaforth Highlanders
Roberts, Lieutenant Ralph Jennings (OB 1890–1896), Machine Gun Corps
Robertson, Lance-Corporal Ronald Hugh Wilson (OB 1892–1896), Canadian Infantry
Smith, Lieutenant Frederick Charles (OB 1908–1912), Royal Air Force
Starnes, Private Sydney Alfred (OB 1911–1913), Oxford and Bucks Light Infantry
Stranger, Second-Lieutenant George J. (OB 1905–1910), Royal Guernsey Light Infantry
Stranger, Captain Harry Easterbrook Knollys (OB 1905–1910), Royal Guernsey Light Infantry
Street, Private Thomas (OB 1884–1888), South African Infantry
Taylor, Second-Lieutenant Frederick Charles (OB 1911–1914), Royal Air Force
Trefusis, Captain Arthur Owen (OB 1893–1899), Loyal North Lancashire Regiment
Trefusis, Captain Haworth Walter (OB 1891–1898), Northamptonshire Regiment
Ward, Lance-Corporal Harry Marsh Alfred Gregson (OB 1910–1914), Royal Fusiliers
Wellicome, Sergeant Maurice (OB 1895–1899), Royal Horse Artillery
Wellicome, Sergeant Willie Cecil (OB 1893–1899), Seaforth Highlanders
Woodroffe, Captain Walter Gordon (OB 1904), Middlesex Regiment

Borlase staff

Denny, Second-Lieutenant Barry Maynard Rynd, The King's Liverpool Regiment
Lawson, Sergeant Herbert (May 1910 – April 1916), 2nd Lincoln Regiment
Scott, Second-Lieutenant William James De Vere (May 1911 – December 1911), Manchester Regiment
Wells, Second-Lieutenant Ewart Linley (September 1909 – April 1914), New Zealand Infantry

THE POST-WAR PERIOD

One of the chief concerns of the Governors, Staff and Old Borlasians after the War ended was to erect a suitable memorial for the fallen. The Chapel still needed furnishing and decorating. It was decided to invite subscriptions towards erecting chancel and vestry screens, and oak-panelling the chancel. About £500 was collected, enough to carry on the design and to inscribe on the oak-panelling behind the choir stalls the names of those who had lost their lives in the War, together with their units and the years they were at Borlase. The result of this work was to leave the body of the Chapel looking bare and out of sympathy with the chancel. Further subscriptions were invited to complete the panelling of the rest of the Chapel and provide oak pews like those in the choir stalls. Another £500 was raised, and the work completed by the tercentenary celebrations in 1924. L. H. Smith inscribed the names of over four hundred Old Boys and Masters who had served in the War in an illuminated Book of Remembrance, which is kept in the Chapel.

Between the end of the War and the resignation of the Rev. A. J. Skinner in 1927, the School lost several of its best friends. Sir John Thomas, for many years a Governor, died in 1920. The following year, the School lost T. O. Wethered, who had generously contributed to School funds on so many occasions. Lord Devonport resigned from the Board of Governors

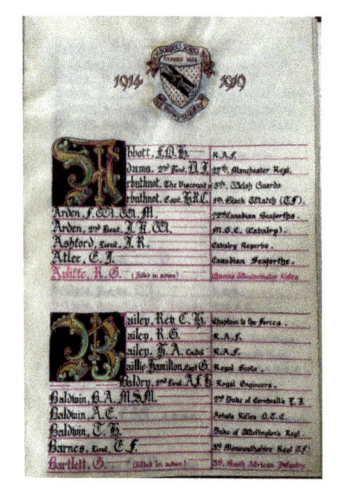

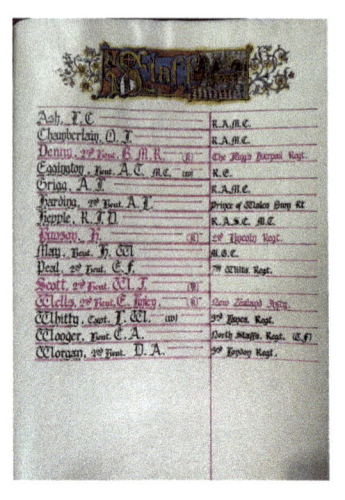

2.5.23. World War I memorial in the School Chapel and pages from the illuminated Book of Remembrance

in the same year. In 1923, Dr J. D. Dickson died, another Governor whose services were greatly missed. Alfred Davis, whom we have so often mentioned, died in 1924. General Sir George Higginson, Chairman of Governors for many years, died soon after celebrating his hundredth birthday in 1927. He was succeeded as Chairman by Canon Michael Graves, now resident in Marlow, Rural Dean and Canon of Christ Church, Oxford, since 1922. Among the new Governors were T. C. J. Williams and F. Jackson, of Bourne End; Major G. F. Clayton-East, Dr G. E. Downs, W. H. Healey and C. H. K. Marten, of Eton College.

The numbers in the School rapidly jumped up from 64 in 1916 to 122 in 1920, and 132 in 1923. An additional master was appointed in 1919, and another in 1921. Graves came twice per week to Borlase to take the School Certificate form in Scripture. One of his last pupils, George McCorquodale, gave this picture of him: "His habits in class were somewhat quaint. He used to raise and lower his eyebrows when he put on his spectacles, the sole reason

---

62 | CHAPTER 2   Revival and Renewal (1874-1974)

2.5.24. Memorial to Thomas Owen Wethered in All Saints' Church, Marlow

being to ascertain whether they were the correct way up. He was apparently fascinated by the clock apparatus, and he would stare at it every Friday during our weekly test. He also paid special attention to the historical pictures which decorate the Fifth Form room. We were well aware of the fact that both these attractions possessed a certain amount of glass. He had an irritating habit of walking up and down the gangways. He constantly took out his watch and apparently checked its correctness by means of the room clock, which, either through lack of sufficient voltage or some electrical defect, remained inactive. In spite of all these queer characteristics, which at the time amused us, I perceived in him a strength of will, a determination, a feeling of hardness, shrewdness, and that he always would be a schoolmaster."

Perhaps the most notable event of this period was the celebration of the tercentenary of the School in 1924. The Speech Day celebrations were held on the lawn. General Sir George Higginson, then 98 years old, was in the chair, and was supported by Morgan Jones, then Parliamentary Secretary to the Board of Education, the Provost of Eton, the Bishop of Buckingham, Major Coningsby Disraeli, and all the School Governors. General Higginson was to appear at two more Speech Days, and to address the School for half an hour when he was a hundred years old. It was always his habit when distributing the prizes to throw the ball to the best bowler of the year. Higginson was a veteran of the Crimean War and afterwards *aide-de-camp* to various members of the Royal family; King George V and Queen Mary were regular visitors to Gyldernscroft, his home in Marlow. When he was well over 90 years of age, he delivered to students a course of lectures on Paris and Rome, on the Duke of Marlborough,

2.5.25. Borlase School Governors in 1923

Revival and Renewal (1874-1974)   CHAPTER 2 | 63

2.5.26. School photographs from 1920 and 1923, when there were 120 and 132 boys, respectively

his military hero, and on his recollections of military celebrities of the nineteenth century.

One of the difficulties of Borlase up to the end of the War was to retain anything like a permanent Staff. The salaries were so low that only inexperienced masters could be engaged, and they very naturally regarded Borlase merely as a stepping-stone to better posts. As it takes five or six years to see a boy through the School, the constant changing of masters, all of whom knew that they had only a passing interest in him, was detrimental to his education. The adoption by the County Council of a better and more uniform scale of salaries after the War led to better results in examinations and a general improvement in the tone of the School. The Staff in 1919 consisted of the Rev. A. J. Skinner, who took the Upper

2.5.27. General Sir George Higginson depicted in Vanity Fair (1884), was Chairman of Governors and a benefactor of the School. King George V regularly visited Higginson's home in Marlow. On 29 July 1924, Higginson presented the Gold Medal to M. R. Rose during the School's tercentenary celebrations

Form French; A. J. Grigg, who had left Borlase in 1917 to join the Army, but who returned in 1919 (Mathematics and Science); J. C. Davies (English and History); J. McGrath (lower forms, French and Spanish); B. Birkett (Art and Woodwork), and T. R. Foreman (Gymnastics). J. McGrath left in 1920 and A. J. Grigg in 1921. Among those who served on the Staff in this period were A. E. Baldwin (1919–1920), A. L. Green, R. G. Stedman, who came in 1921, A. B. Stokes (1921–1926), W. A. Barnes, E. O. Jones and H. J. Ellis.

From the time (1918) when the Board of Education prohibited boys in their schools from sitting for junior examinations, boys at Borlase sat each year for the Oxford Senior Certificate (or School Certificate), the London Matriculation, and, if there were any advanced pupils, for the County Major Scholarship and the London Intermediate. In 1926, M. F. Rose gained a Board of Education Agricultural Scholarship of £300 for three years at St John's College, Cambridge.

The Football and Cricket teams continued to uphold the prestige of Borlase. When road transport replaced tedious train journeys, many old fixtures were renewed. The School played Alleyn's School, Dulwich, Reading School, Westminster City School and Lord Williams's School, Thame, in addition to less distant schools like Amersham, Wycombe, Slough, Windsor, Henley and Maidenhead. Indeed, the fixture lists tended to become overcrowded. The most successful year was 1923, when the Cricket team, led by F. E. R. Hogg, won all its matches except the one with Dulwich,

Revival and Renewal (1874-1974)   CHAPTER 2 | 65

2.5.28. Long-serving Borlase staff: J. C. Davies (Senior Assistant Master 1917–1956), B. Birkett (Art Master 1919–1941) and R. G. Stedman (Science Master 1921–1941)

and the Football team, led by M. R. Rose, was undefeated.

In 1921, Borlase entered for the first time a boat in the Public Schools' race at Marlow Regatta. The venture was a daring one, because most of the best Public Schools contest in this race, and Borlase had a limited number of boys from whom to draw. The School can well be proud of the fact that three times between 1921 and 1927, its crew reached the final, and once, at least, was unlucky not to win the cup.

At Christmas each year, there was a competition in gymnastics between the four houses (Britons, Danes, Normans and Saxons) and a gymnastic display on Speech Day. Boxing was encouraged, a competition held at Christmas, and the best boxers entered for the Public Schools' Boxing Championships. In the spring term, teams were regularly entered for the Desborough and Sainsbury Cross Country races. All year round, shooting was taught and competitions were held.

2.5.29. The Football team of 1923–1924, captained by M. R. Rose (seated centre), was undefeated

66 | CHAPTER 2   Revival and Renewal (1874-1974)

2.5.30. The Borlase Coxed Four of 1932: Cooper (cox), Compton (stroke), Babey (3), Jackson (2), Mitchell (bow) and Dr A. H. West (coach)

2.5.31. The gymnastics team of 1920; Sgt T. R. Foreman is seated in the centre

Running hobby societies at Borlase was difficult because local boys were not available during the dinner hour, and boys who lived at a distance had to reach home at a reasonable hour. What could be done, however, was done. Thanks chiefly to Walter Langley, two performances of The Private Secretary were given in 1919, and every year a scene from Shakespeare or Sheridan formed part of the Speech Day entertainment. From 1925 onwards, the National Savings Association had a branch at Borlase. Boys, under the instructions of B. Birkett, turned out small furniture, wireless sets, and implements in wood and iron. He, too, encouraged sketching as a hobby. A library of local history and lore, which proved very useful in making these notes, gradually accumulated. Many boys combined their search for local history with their sketching and photography.

In the summer of 1927, after 23 years at Borlase, the Rev. A. J. Skinner retired, and he and Mrs Skinner left for Hove. They took with them another old Borlase institution in 'Kate', the good angel of many generations of boarders. A. J. Skinner by no means severed his connection with Borlase, and seldom missed a Sports Day, a Speech Day or an Old Borlasian Dinner.

2.5.32. A scene from The Rivals performed at Speech Day in 1925

2.5.33. Borlase School in 1927, the year of the Rev. A. J. Skinner's retirement

Revival and Renewal (1874-1974)

CHAPTER 2

WILLIAM S. BOOTH (1927–1956)

2.6.1. William S. Booth (Headmaster 1927–1956)

The new Headmaster was William Sykes Booth, a 31-year-old Yorkshireman who had been educated at Manchester Grammar School and held a First Class Honours degree in Classics from Manchester University. In 1930, he was elected a Member of Council of the Classical Association at a meeting of that body held at Hull, under the presidency of the Archbishop of York. So, after 23 years, Borlase returned to its Classical traditions, and Latin was restored as a principal subject in the curriculum.

For some years, it had been evident that the number of boarders at Borlase was dwindling. Parents demanded sea air for their children, and so well advertised had seaside resorts become that riverside towns lost their popularity with dwellers in the larger towns. The rapid growth of road transport meant that country boys, even from remote areas, could get home every night. In 1929, the Governors decided to discontinue the development of the boarding side of the School.

The School House was divided into two. The western half was converted into a private residence for the Headmaster, and the eastern half into a house for Sergeant Foreman. For many years, those boys who wished had dined at the School House, but the question of providing adequate accommodation for the other day boys had never been satisfactorily settled. The Cricket Pavilion had at one time been turned into a Buttery, but it was rather distant in wet weather. However, after the departure of the boarders, there was ample room in their old dining room, meaning that all day boys could be supplied with whatever they needed, and take their midday meal in comfort.

In 1931, the largest of the dormitories (on the first floor on the east side of the Cloisters) was converted into a beautiful library. The access to it was from one of the old studies. There was an oak door and a wide stately Austrian oak staircase leading to another oak door at the top. To quote from the Headmaster's own description of the Library:

"The room itself is large, light and airy, quiet and free from distraction, though it is possible to look through the large central window over the gardens. The view from this window is charming, especially in summer. The room is lit by electricity and efficiently heated. The woodwork is of Austrian oak, except for the floor, which is of polished Oregon pine. The furniture consists of one very massive old oak table, round which the Governors now sit for their meetings, and a smaller table, chairs, and three dark oak bookcases, formerly in Court Gardens, Marlow, but purchased from the Higginson Park trustees out of a bequest made by Lady Clayton. Among the pictures hung in the Library are portraits of Governors and benefactors of the School. There is a very interesting copy, presented by the High Sheriff of Bucks, Major Coningsby Disraeli DL, of a picture which he possesses, depicting a Review of the Gentlemen Cadets of the Royal Military College, Remnantz, Marlow, 1810; also a portrait

2.6.2. Mr Booth with the Staff and senior pupils in 1930

2.6.3. The former Senior Dormitory was converted into a Library (now the Staff Common Room) in 1931; it is accessed by an oak staircase and has views over the Cloister lawn

of Pascoe Grenfell, who was an eighteenth century industrialist from Fawley and MP for Great Marlow from 1802 to 1820, presented by Miss Grenfell." Two pictures too large for the Library walls were gifts to the School. One, a seascape, was a gift from Mr Garfield Weston, whose two boys were at the school, and the other an oil painting of Sir John Borlase, the third of the Knights, and squire of Brockmer.

The County Architect, C. H. Riley, designed the work. Messrs Lovell, of Marlow, were the contractors, and Parker and Sons, of High Wycombe, made the furniture. But the fact that we have such a beautiful library is due to the initiative and enterprise of the Headmaster.

Thanks to the generosity of Governors and Old Boys, and to an annual grant from the County Council, the Library was soon stocked with books. For some years, part of the library of T. O. Wethered, which he had left to the School, had been stored away. Canon Graves gave not only a large number of valuable books, but an additional bookcase. Old Borlasians, especially Tom Lever, A. L. Wood and W. H. Morris, also made very useful contributions.

The view from the Library window referred to was greatly improved by the laying down

Revival and Renewal (1874-1974)　　　　CHAPTER 2　|　69

2.6.4. In addition to funding bookcases for the Library, Lady Clayton presented the School with the House Challenge Cup for Scholastic Work in July 1927

died, and as there was no provision in the will and the heiress was a minor, this much desired improvement had to be abandoned.

It was Mrs Hornby Lewis, too, who gave the School its third scholarship. In memory of her husband, A. H. Hornby Lewis, a former Governor of the School, she invested £1,715 in 3½ percent Conversion Stock, estimated to yield an annual income of £60. The scholarships could be held by three boys from the parishes of Hambledon, Fawley, Bisham, Little Marlow, Wooburn or Great Marlow. It was the practice to grant £10 to the boy who did best in the Oxford School Certificate examination in July each year. The scholarships are for boys still at the school, and may be held in the first place for one year, but may be renewed for one or two more years.

The biggest undertaking of the 1930s was the levelling of the Home Meadow. It had always been felt that the School should never have a satisfactory Cricket pitch while they had to play Football across it. But the Home Meadow had a great slope, and to level it meant the removal of 32,000 tons of earth on some rails and two trucks, a task that took four years. Credit must be given to the Headmaster, who initiated the scheme; next, to James Gray, the gardener and Afghan War veteran, who carried on week in week out; and last, but not least, to the boys, many of whom knew they were working for others and would perhaps never play on the

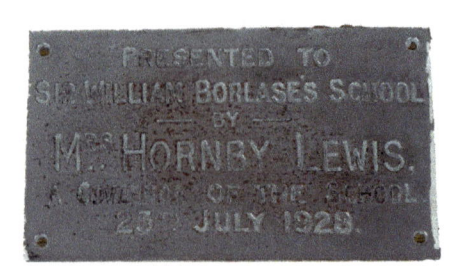

2.6.5. Plaque from the flag-staff given by Mrs Hornby Lewis in 1928

levelled pitch themselves. It was now possible to nurse the Cricket pitch during the winter and to make Rugby Football a School game. An old dogshed was converted into shower baths. Old Borlasians deplored the change from Soccer to Rugby but, as the School grew in numbers, the change became really necessary. Thirty could play instead of twenty-two, all the local Grammar Schools had changed games, and Rugby needed less ball control.

Would Borlase keep up its numbers after the departure of the boarders? There were slightly over 100 boys in 1927. Subsequently, the numbers gradually increased to more than 130, and there were more pupils coming from Maidenhead, Wycombe, Slough and Taplow than ever there were.

of grass lawns in front of the Chapel. At the far end was a flag-staff, given by Mrs Hornby Lewis. One of the drawbacks of Borlase was that its beauty could not be seen from the road. Mrs Hornby Lewis had intended to erect suitable gates in from the Chapel. The plans had been passed, and the County Council had undertaken to widen the road, when the sad news came through that Mrs Hornby Lewis had

2.6.6. James Gray, the gardener, who worked together with boys to level the Home Meadow in the 1930s

70 | CHAPTER 2   Revival and Renewal (1874-1974)

2.6.7. (Right) The levelling of the Home Meadow allowed the introduction of Rugby: the 1st XV in 1936

2.6.8. (Below) A reunion of former boarders, held in 1933. Back row: K. Rouse, G. Bidwell, Marshall, James, M. Dixey, C. Bidwell, Speer, Taylor, De Brunner, Andrew, C. Dixey, Beechey. Front row: Mr Birkett, Mr Grigg, Mr Davies, Mrs Booth, Mr Booth, Mr Stedman, Sgt Foreman, Matthews

2.6.9. School photograph from 1936

Revival and Renewal (1874-1974)   CHAPTER 2 | 71

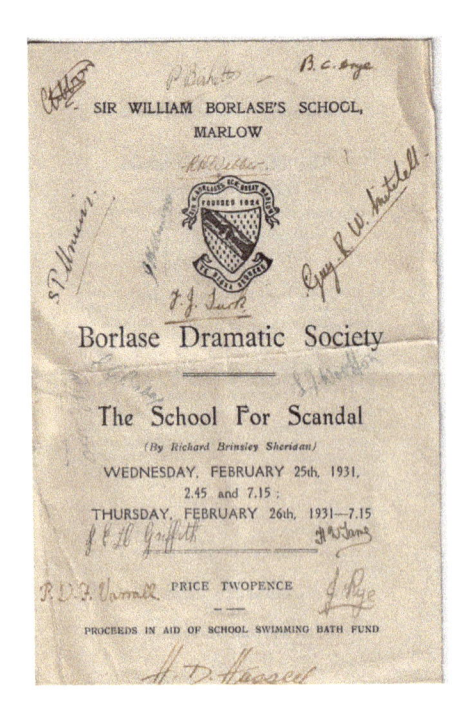

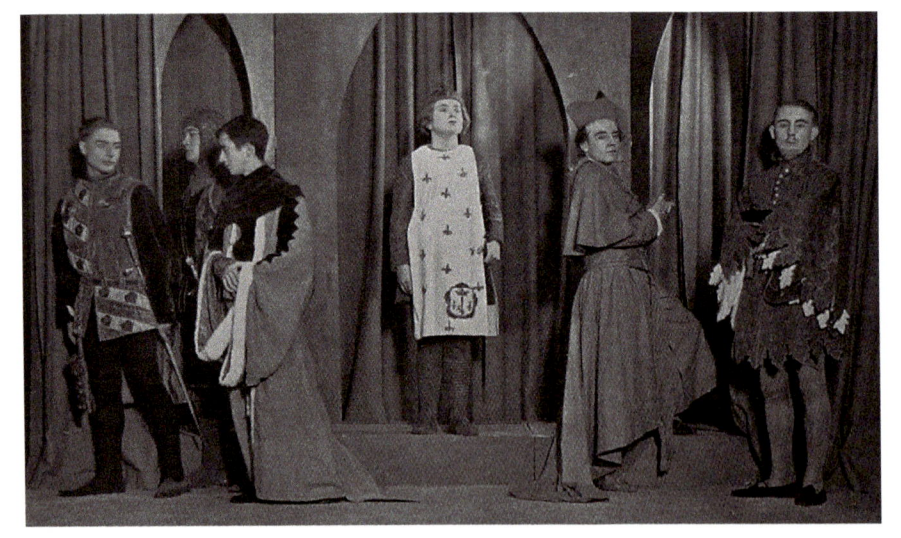

2.6.10. Programme signed by the cast of *The School For Scandal*, performed in 1931; the cast of *Bird in Hand*, produced in 1934; and a scene from *Saint Joan*, staged in 1936

From 1928, Borlase produced an annual play. Thanks chiefly to the Headmaster, Mrs Booth and B. Birkett, the stage in the Assembly Hall was improved, props were designed, and costumes were made. These plays helped to make many boys more confident when appearing in public and to speak more clearly. They also added to the School funds. In 1928, Goldsmith's *She Stoops to Conquer* was produced by W. A. Barnes. In 1929, three short plays were given, *Rory Aforesaid*, produced by R. B. Darby; *Thread o' Scarlet*, produced by the Headmaster; and *Shivering Shocks*, produced by H. I. Nelson. In 1930, *The Merchant of Venice* was chosen. In the summer, *The Knight of the Burning Pestle* was acted on the lawn. In 1931, Sheridan's *The School for Scandal* was presented in February and Sheridan's *The Rivals* in December. The Headmaster produced the last three plays.

Sports were carefully arranged so as to bring out the best in every boy. In the winter term, not only was there Football for the first and second terms, but there was a House competition for the younger boys, run on league lines. At Christmas, there was a Gymnastics competition between the Houses and a Boxing tournament. In the spring term, there was Hockey up to the end of February, followed by Cross Country running, and finally the Athletic Sports. The Headmaster introduced a system of 'limits'. Every boy who started a race had a chance to contribute some points to his House. Good athletes were well catered for and had their reward on Sports Day. Two other popular competitions in the spring term were the Sixes (a six-a-side Soccer competition between the Houses) and Fives. In the summer term came Cricket. Here again, two teams were run, and younger boys competed in a league between the Houses. The competition between the

72 | CHAPTER 2   Revival and Renewal (1874-1974)

2.6.11. Borlase sport in the 1930s: a Cross Country race in 1935, the 1st XI Football team in 1932–1933; the 1st XI Cricket team in 1934, and Rowing in the new School Fours in 1938

Senior House teams for the Cricket Cup was always keenly contested.

By this time, Borlase was entering a Four in the Public Schools' race at Marlow Regatta. They had yet to win the Cup, but the training given at the School helped Marlow Rowing Club to put some promising crews on the river. Indeed, Marlow's Eight in 1932 was composed entirely of Old Borlasians.

In the summer term came swimming. As soon as the weather was fit, time was given to the Lower Forms for instructions in the Marlow swimming baths. So successful was the tuition of Sergeant Foreman and B. Birkett that more than 80% of the boys could swim! In addition to these sports, the rifle range was used on Wednesdays all year round.

The House system helped to develop team spirit. A boy learned to do all he could for his House and for his School. Nor was competition confined to sport. There was also a House Competition for work, and a Cup to be won each year. Captains of Houses learned to lead and to take responsibility, and in time hoped to attain the rank and dignity of prefect.

The Old Borlasian Club continued as active as ever, with the Rev. Canon Graves as President, T. Stanmore as Treasurer, and T. V. Dunham and W. J. Hobbs as Secretaries. At this time, there were more than two hundred active members, and the annual meeting and dinner held in London in November was always well attended. W. Davis, Sports Captain for many years, had given up office, but his place had been well filled by J. R. Laird. The Old Borlasian Club raised a fund to celebrate the half-century's

Revival and Renewal (1874-1974) CHAPTER 2 | 73

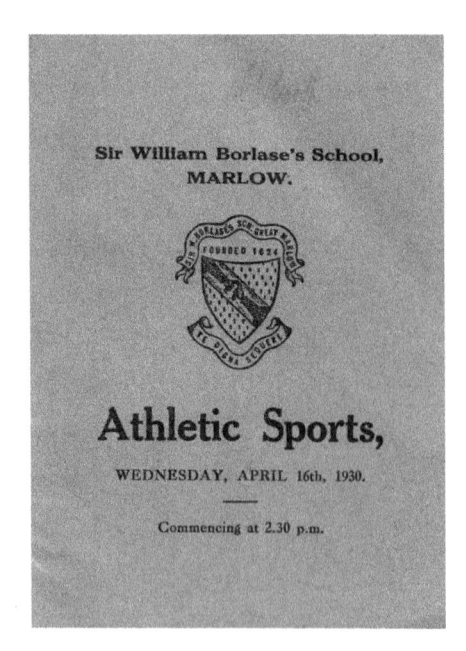

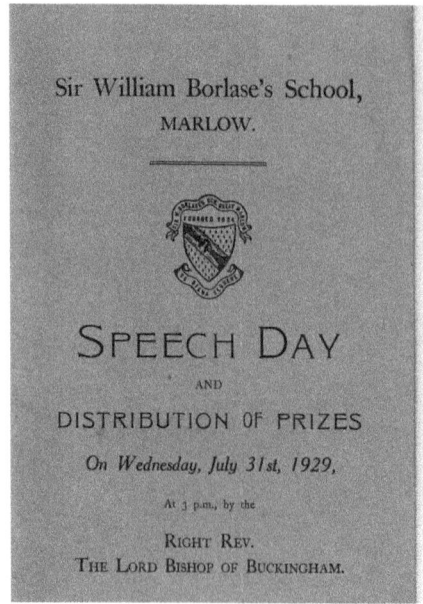

2.6.12. The annual Sports Day and Speech Day were fixtures in the School calendar; Mr Booth distributing the prizes

2.6.13. Annual Dinner of the Old Borlasian Club, 30 November 1933

work of their president, Canon Graves, first as Headmaster, then as Governor, and finally as Chairman of the Governors. The interest from the Michael and Sophia Graves Fund provided the School with an annual prize.

In 1926, Canon Graves conducted the ceremony when Princess Mary and General Sir George Higginson presented the deeds of Court Garden and its estate to the people of Marlow.

In November 1933, at the age of 78 years, Canon Graves announced his engagement to Miss Winifred Emily Baker, whom he had known for many years (Mrs Sophia Graves had died 20 years previously). Sadly, he died only a couple of months later on 16 January 1934. His funeral at All Saints' Church, Marlow, was conducted by the Bishop of Buckingham.

The last big structural change before the outbreak of World War II was the conversion of the east wing of the School House into a Physics laboratory above a dining room below (subsequently also converted into a laboratory). The wall between the old Physics and Chemistry laboratories was knocked down, and the two old laboratories made into an enlarged Chemistry laboratory.

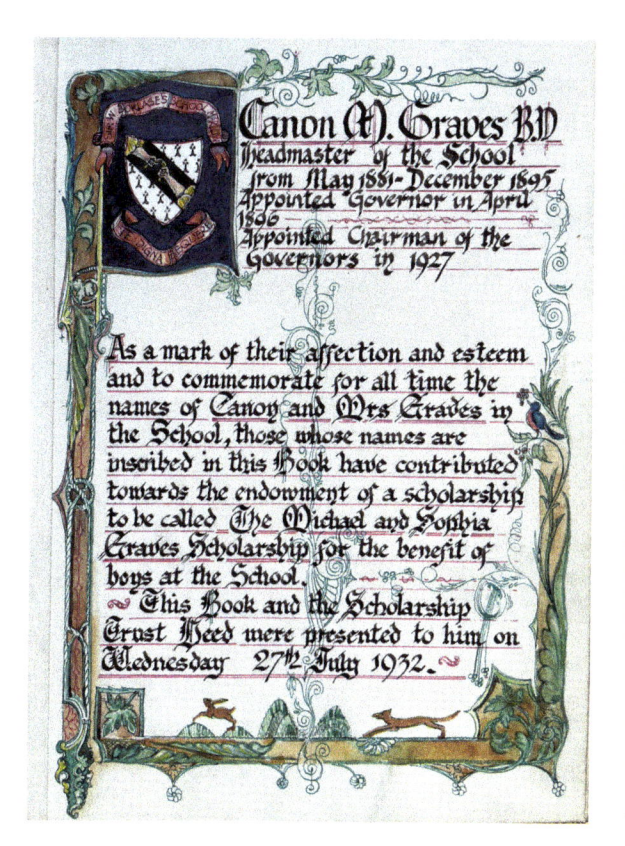

2.6.14. Endowment of The Michael and Sophia Graves Scholarship, July 1932; and Canon Graves escorting Princess Mary in 1926

2.6.15. The burial of Canon Graves at All Saints' Church, Marlow, in 1933

Revival and Renewal (1874-1974) CHAPTER 2 | 75

WORLD WAR II (1939–1945)

There followed six years of war and the end of dreams of structural changes for a decade. The blocked up Cloisters made the School dark and gloomy. The air raid shelter was an eyesore for sixteen years, until it was removed in 1956. It was never used except by small boys to play hide and seek. Plays and concerts went on as usual, the proceeds patriotically invested in Government bonds to await better times.

War Memorials were low down on the list of post-war priorities. However, by 1947, the names of the Old Borlasians who had fallen in World War II were carved under the middle window of the nave, surmounted by a new stained-glass window with depictions of the Navy, Army and Air Force and of Borlase in the appropriate colours. Mr Booth was determined there should be a second war memorial, a pipe organ worthy of the School. In one way and another, he raised a sum of £2,372, and had the organ installed in 1953 and dedicated by the Bishop of Buckingham.

2.6.16. *The west window of the Chapel, depicting the three branches of the armed forces and the Borlase coat of arms, was given as a World War II memorial*

Borlasians who died in World War II

Banks, R. A. (OB 1933–1934), Royal Navy
Barnshaw, J. (OB 1925–1931), Royal Army Pay Corps
Beechey, E. H. R. (OB 1925–1929), Royal Artillery
Bloyce, W. R. (OB 1932–1938), Royal Air Force
Brunton, A. F. (OB 1935–1940), Royal Air Force
Buckingham, E. M. (OB 1931–1934), Royal Air Force
Cave, F. (OB 1930–1934), Royal Air Force
Chubb, D. S. H. (OB 1937–1942), Royal Army Service Corps
Coleman, P. F. (OB 1909–1914), King's African Rifles
Dance, N. B. (OB 1926–1927), Royal Air Force
Drayson, A. W. B. (OB 1927–1929), Anti Aircraft Fleet
Hayton, C. H. N. (OB 1929–1932), Devon Regiment
Howard, A. (OB 1936–1939), Royal Air Force
Johnson, K. R. H. (OB 1929–1931)
Jones, C. W. F. (OB 1910–1915), Royal Artillery
Lee, D. G. (OB 1932–1937), Royal Navy
Lunnon, R. H. W. (OB 1934–1938), Royal Armoured Corps
Mackey, D. J. (OB 1934–1937), Royal Air Force
Malyon, J. A. (OB 1933–1939), Royal Armoured Corps
Martin, D. J. M. (OB 1933–1937), Royal Air Force
Meadows, H. E. (OB 1930–1936), Royal Air Force
Morton, S. E. P. (OB 1928–1932), Royal Artillery
Oxlade, F. A. (OB 1936–1938), Royal Air Force
Randall, M. E. (OB 1934–1937), Royal Air Force
Ranscombe, A. W. F. (OB 1926–1932), Royal Army Medical Corps
Rex, A. H. (OB 1931–1933), Royal Air Force
Savill, D. J. (OB 1940–1942), Merchant Navy
Sellman, D. T. M. (OB 1920–1928), Royal Artillery
Shipton, J. P. (OB 1929–1934), Royal Air Force
Shortland, G. W. (OB 1934–1939), Royal Armoured Corps
Smith, P. R. (OB 1929–1934), Royal Air Force
Speller, T. H. (OB 1930–1935), Royal Air Force
Stone, R. (OB 1932–1938), Royal Air Force
Tadgell, W. L. (OB 1932–1935), Royal Navy
Wethered, I. L. (OB 1932–1937), Royal Air Force
White, D. H. (OB 1919–1925), Royal Armoured Corps
Winterton, M. W. G. (OB 1935–1940), Royal Navy
Woodbridge, P. H. (OB 1932–1933), Royal Air Force

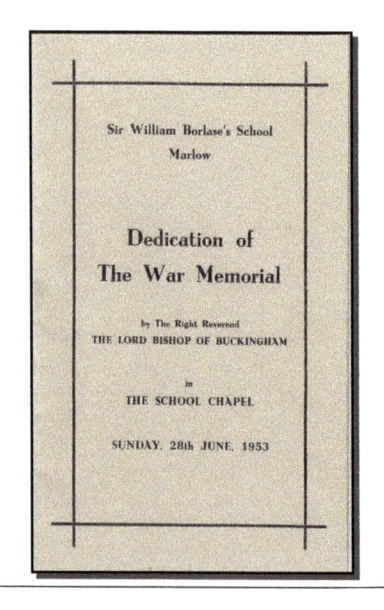

2.6.17 *The service booklet for the Dedication of the War Memorial by the Bishop of Buckingham on 28 June 1953*

2.6.18. World War II memorial in the School Chapel

2.6.19. Borlase boys outside Ye Olde Tuck Shoppe at the end of the war in 1945 and the building in 2023

Revival and Renewal (1874-1974) CHAPTER 2 | 77

2.6.20. W. S. Booth, Headmaster, with his wife and the School Staff in 1948. Back row: G. A. Dewhurst, G. E. Rands, F. J. Davies, C. B. Davenport, F. W. M. Peirce, A. K. Thomas, R. Pitman. Front row: W. O. Robertson, J. C. Davies, W. S. Booth, Mrs Booth, W. F. Jones, R. H. Sage.

Among the Staff, Mr Booth appointed men (for they were still all men) whom he liked, realizing that a happy Staffroom was the greatest asset that a School could have. In his first choice, W. F. Jones (1929), he found not only a born Mathematics teacher but also a man who was devoted to the welfare of the School in innumerable ways. Two years later came W. O. Robertson (1931), who not only taught French and German, but also became the School secretary and knew more of the School and its component parts than any man. R. H. Sage (1934) not only built up the French department to be of the highest standard, but also made the annual School autumn play a famous institution and gained remarkable results in the Thames Regatta with his Fours and Eights. C. B. Davenport (1935) was similarly successful with his English department. He produced summer plays in the open air theatre until that theatre was put out of action by the new buildings. G. A. Dewhurst (1938), a Geographer and keen Footballer, bore the brunt of making Rugby a School game

2.6.21. School Prefects in 1953–1954. Back row: A. A. N. Cruttenden, D. J. Allaway, C. T. Wicks, K. E. Williams, A. A. Edwards. Front row: M. R. Weller, B. J. Bond (School Captain), J. F. Emmons, S. J. Walter.

2.6.22. Mr and Mrs Booth on his retirement as Headmaster in 1956

and coached Cricket and Tennis. R. Pitman (1942) transformed the teaching of Art in the School. F. J. Davies (1942), former Headmaster of Beaconsfield School, did the same with Chemistry. He was the Tennis and box-office expert. F. W. M. Peirce (1940) was not only a most successful teacher of English and Scripture, but also gave up much of his spare time to creating a School orchestra and a School choir. His spring term concerts rival even Mr Sage's autumn plays.

Younger heads of department are D. C. Banner (1951), Latin and expert on Rugby Football; D. C. Paton (1953), Physics and a county Rugby player; and B. Welch, History, who has made Borlase Cricket once again formidable.

When Mr Booth became Headmaster, the Sixth Form was small. If a boy desired to proceed to a university, he had to gain either an Open Scholarship or one of the limited number of awards granted annually by the County Council. In the pre-war period, four open scholarships and seven County awards were won.

War showed how far we lagged behind other nations academically. Far greater opportunities opened up to boys of ability. Between 1940 and 1946, a dozen boys proceeded to universities, mainly to read Science. One went to Bangor to read Forestry, one to London to read Law, and three to Oxford for English and History. From 1947 to 1957, the Sixth Form grew from a handful to 86. Nine boys gained State Scholarships, while no fewer than 47 passed through universities, almost equally divided between Arts and Science. But Grammar School was not merely a preparation for universities; a certain number of boys left after taking the Ordinary level. In 1956, the number of successful candidates was twice that of 1927.

Throughout his 29 years, Mr Booth freely admitted that he could not have carried on without the sustained assistance of Mrs Booth, who always took a most active interest in all the School activities. Both Mr and Mrs Booth helped to shape the Borlase of 1956, from where they retired to Penzance.

ERNEST M. HAZELTON (1956–1974)

The new Headmaster, after taking his degree in Natural Sciences and Physics at Fitzwilliam House, Cambridge, took a post at Portsmouth Grammar School, where he helped to start a Scout Troop and inaugurated the Field Club. In 1936, he went to Epsom College, where he instituted a second day-boy house. In 1938, he led an expedition of university men and senior public school boys to Sörsjön, Sweden, to collect specimens for the Natural History department of the British Museum. In 1943, he became head of the Physics department and resident House Tutor at Clifton College and later House Master of one of the day-boy houses. His recreations included cross country running, field athletics, rock climbing, skiing and sailing. He was married, had three children, including twins, was the first Headmaster of Borlase with a family since 1880, and was the first to live away from the School.

Mr Ernest Mears Hazelton started with virtually a new School. Where once stood the Old Barn, where eighteenth-century masters kept their ponies and stored their crops from the Barley Field, the South Block had been built, with classrooms below and a large Art room above. On the site of the old cricket nets pitch or, subsequently, of the tennis courts, the North Block had been built. An Assembly Hall, which could become a Gymnasium when Mr Trevor Williams took Physical Training or a theatre for Mr Sage or a concert hall for Mr Peirce, took up about half the space. The rest was more classrooms and an up-to-date Geography room. The old gym in the Cloisters became a cloakroom, the old Art Room a Chemistry laboratory, and the old dining room a Physics

2.7.1. Ernest M. Hazelton (Headmaster 1956–1974)

Revival and Renewal (1874-1974)   CHAPTER 2 | 79

laboratory. The reinstatement of the grounds after the building operations included the provision of tennis courts at the top of Home Meadow, to replace those laid down in 1936.

In the next two or three years, the former Headmaster's house was completely taken over, partly as a caretaker's residence, partly as the Headmaster's study, the Deputy Head's room and the School Office, all located in what had been Mr Booth's dining room in the oldest part of the School buildings. As the School Staff grew larger, the old Staff Common Room, near to the old Gymnasium (which had its floor raised to the level of the Cloisters and become the Small Hall), was far too small and a new Staff Room was provided in what had been a dormitory above the Drawing Room, which now became a classroom for the Arts Sixth Form.

In 1956, there were 338 boys in the School, in 1957 there were 366, and in 1958 there were 392, together with a Staff of 22, far more of both than ever before in the history of the School. And that raised problems because, owing to the encroachment of the new buildings, the playing fields were smaller, and the Chapel could hold only half the pupils at a time. Moreover, the larger the School became, the less was the opportunity to play for the School's sports teams, to get a part in a play or a place in the orchestra.

These developments brought about some notable changes in the character of the School. In Mr Booth's time, the School had been small enough to be run as a large family. In 1934, there were 146 boys on the roll. In an emergency, the Headmaster could (and did!) gather the boys around him in an impromptu assembly at a clap of his hands. As the Editorial of the 1956 edition of *The Borlasian* magazine puts it: "A new epoch has begun in the history of Borlase". Close personal contact between the boys and the Headmaster was replaced by delegated authority extending downwards to prefects and House prefects, but with the Headmaster as a focal point. For the first time, a School Office, with a full-time secretary came into being and played a key part in the processing and storing

2.7.2. The School grounds in c.1956, with the newly built South Block and North Block

2.7.3. The North Block, containing classrooms and the School Hall, which could be used as a Gymnasium

2.7.4. School photograph in 1955

of information on every aspect of the life of the School. Miss Elsie Horrox, was appointed as the School Secretary in 1958 and remained in the post until 1985, aided by various assistants.

With his experience of larger schools, Mr Hazelton was particularly suited to this major task of organization. An indefatigable worker, he devoted himself to the School with great energy, overcoming by his example the inertia of those looking back to the 'good old days', and building a new image of assurance and confidence, symbolized by the lavish (by Borlase standards) arrangements for his first Speech Day, with a marquee seating 800 guests as the central point of a programme lasting from 11 a.m. to teatime. This was to be the style throughout Mr Hazelton's term of office and it brought much material benefit to the School. In all spheres, Mr Hazelton's headship was a time of growth: more boys, more Staff, a wider choice of subjects for study, more varied

2.7.5. The hedge along West Street was replaced with a new wall, and a new gateway to the Chapel bearing the School shield (now on display in the Lever Room) was ceremonially opened by Mr Hazelton and guests

Revival and Renewal (1874-1974)

CHAPTER 2 | 81

opportunities for sport. His stewardship also left its mark on the buildings: the Chapel gateway with the School shield and the adjoining brick boundary wall (the Headmaster worked like a Trojan at grubbing out the old hedge that it replaced!); the swimming pool, for which he devised an elaborate scheme of loans and gifts in order to encourage the generous efforts of parents and Old Borlasians; the re-introduction of boarding by the opening of Sentry Hill and the Heights (about which we shall say more later); the acquisition of Colonel's Meadow and Quoitings Piece, and the gilded railings in West Street!

To assist him in these endeavours, Mr Hazelton found many friends and allies. He found them in the Governing Body, on the teaching Staff, among Old Borlasians and in the townsfolk of Marlow. The Senior Master (the title of Deputy Head had not been invented), J. C. Davies, retired in 1956 after 33 years of devoted service to the School. His name must surely be inscribed among the legendary heroes of Borlase history, along with Canon Graves, Sir George Higginson, Commander Owen Wethered and Sergeant Foreman. As a mark of affection, the Old Borlasian Club did him the great honour of electing him as their President. Other members of the Staff, some appointed before World War II, all well indoctrinated by Mr Booth with the 'Borlase spirit', were closely involved in this period of transition. W. O. Robertson, who for many years helped the Headmaster with secretarial work, now became Deputy Headmaster, responsible for much of the discipline and day-to-day running of the School. W. F. Jones (Mathematics), C. B. Davenport (English), G. A. Dewhurst (Geography), F. J. Davies (Chemistry), F. W. M. Peirce (Scripture and English) and R. H. Sage (Modern Languages) were among these established members of the Staff.

The School Governors had always been supportive and loyal to the Headmasters they appointed, and Mr Hazelton received much friendly advice from such men as Robin Laird, who was Chairman of Governors when he came, and Commander O. F. M. Wethered, who was Chairman from 1962 until 1977. Like Robin Laird, the latter was an Old Boy of the School and one of its staunchest friends whose death in 1981 was a great sorrow to all Borlasians. He worthily maintained the long tradition of his family as benefactors of the School. Sir Aubrey Ward gave the School a link with the County Council, as did Mr E. J. Routley, who was particularly helpful at the time when the existence of the School was threatened by the move to comprehensive education. Clifford Jefkins, an Old Borlasian and enthusiastic friend of the School; Freddie Cleare, who was a boarder in the days of the Rev. Skinner, for years Chairman of the Old Borlasian Club Committee, whose death in 1982 was a great loss to the School — these are typical of a host of Old Borlasians ready to give generously of their time and efforts.

In 1959, in order to raise money to buy a new Eight, the School Boat Club, under the leadership of one of the rowing masters, Mr A. W. Malin, organized a committee of parents to run a fete as a fundraising device. It was such a success that its potential as a source of funds for the School as a whole was quickly realized and the Fete became an annual event in the School calendar. The immediate target was the provision of a swimming pool, urgently needed since the old Marlow bathing place could no longer be used owing to water pollution in the Thames, and the School was obliged to transport boys to Burnham Beeches pool for classes. Mr D. T. Williams, the Games master, became the driving force in the School, while the Fete was organized and run by a strong committee of parents, led by its Secretary Mr E. Stanley, the first of a series of devoted workers who held that office.

By 1963, the swimming pool was built, the money raised by the fetes being supplemented by generous contributions from parents and the Old Borlasian Club. Built on the site of the Headmaster's vegetable plot, it was 25 metres long and 3 metres deep at the deep end.

The Fete Committee went on to provide funds for many amenities that could not be provided by the County authorities, the most useful, possibly, being a minibus, a red Transit van bought in 1971. The Fete Committee, as we shall see, was also important in a new development that occurred after the arrival of Mr R. R. Smith.

In 1965, Colonel's Meadow, which had been leased to the School at a peppercorn rent since 1890, was purchased by the County. In 1966, the land to the north of Colonel's Meadow, known as Quoitings Piece, was also bought to provide a pitch for Hockey and junior Rugby and Cricket. These acquisitions of playing fields, besides their obvious value to School games, had the

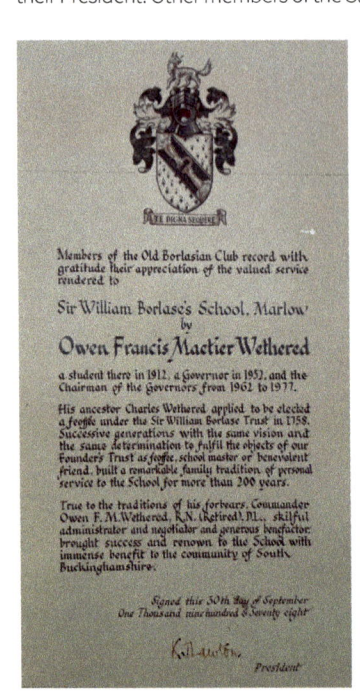

2.7.6. Presentation to Commander Owen F. M. Wethered in 1978, after his retirement as Chairman of Governors

2.7.7. The Borlase swimming pool, shortly after it was completed in 1963

additional benefit of permitting an increase in the number of pupils on the roll.

Colonel's Meadow is named after Colonel Sir William Robert Clayton, 5th Baronet (1786–1866), commander of the Buckinghamshire Yeomanry Cavalry. He rode a charger named Skirmisher throughout the Peninsula War and in subsequent campaigns in The Netherlands. The great black horse was at Waterloo in 1815 but was fatally wounded in the advance on Paris. So attached was Sir William to his horse that he had the body of the charger brought back to Marlow, where it was laid to rest in Colonel's Meadow. A tablet commemorating Skirmisher and his exploits was set in the garden wall of a neighbouring cottage. This stone was later removed to Harleyford Manor, the Clayton family seat, but a replacement stone with the original text was placed on the wall of the cottage. In addition to the text shown in the photograph, the tablet also contains the following verses, written by Sir William:

Sleep on, Sleep on, Thou faithful one,
Light lie the turf upon thy Breast,
Thy toil is o'er thy race is run,
Sleep on and take thy rest.

In vain for thee were the 'Larum Note,
Pour'd from the bugle's brazen throat,
The rolling drum thou heedest not,
Nor noise of signal gun.

Let Charger tramp and Warrior tread
Over the place of thy narrow bed,
They will not wake thee from the dead,
Thy Mortal Strife is Done.

Sleep on, Sleep on, No morrow's sun
Shall light thee to the battle back,
The fight is closed, thy Laurels won,
And this thy Bivouac.

On tented field, or Bloody Plain,
For thee the watch fire flares in vain,
Thou wilt not share its warmth again,
With him who loved thee well.

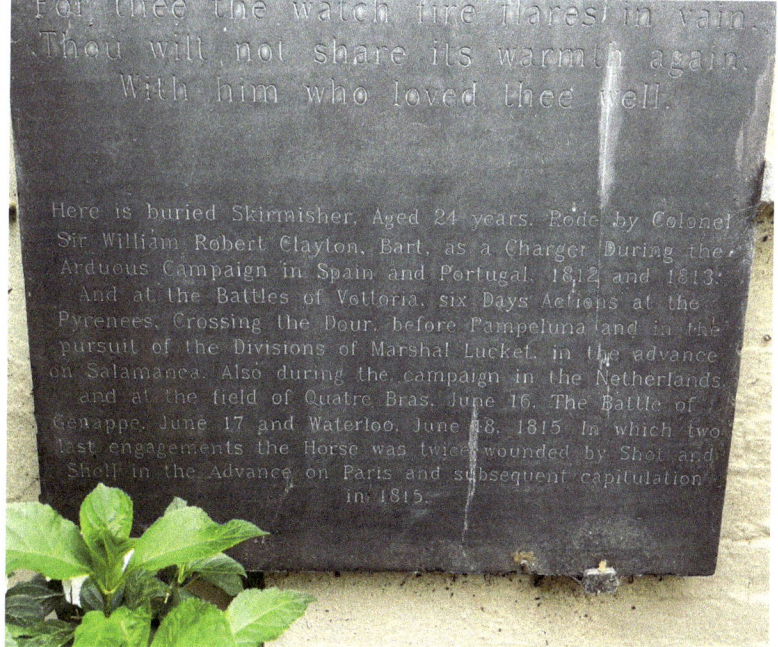

2.7.8. Colonel Sir William Robert Clayton, 5th Baronet, after whom Colonel's Meadow is named and whose horse 'Skirmisher' is buried there; a memorial plaque is on the wall of a neighbour's cottage

Revival and Renewal (1874-1974)

CHAPTER 2 | 83

2.7.9. Productions of The Beggar's Opera *in 1952 and* The Merchant of Venice *in c.1957*

From the start of Mr Booth's Headship, he and Mrs Booth had been very keen on drama in the School and had produced plays on the small platform in the original Assembly Hall. When Russell Sage joined the Staff, he continued to use this inadequate stage and eagerly looked forward to using the new stage on which the first production was *The Merry Wives of Windsor* in February 1957. After some obvious defects in the design and equipment had been corrected, many successful productions followed, including *The Critic* (at which the well-known actor Paul Daneman, who had played the Prince in the School production of *Hamlet* in 1940, was an enthusiastic member of the audience), *Oedipus Rex*, *The Lark*, *The Importance of Being Earnest* and *Rosencrantz and Guildenstern Are Dead*.

After a period of uncertainty, the annual play once again flourished, thanks to the enthusiasm of Mr Andrew Stafford, who successfully directed *The Miser*, *She Stoops to Conquer* and *A Midsummer Night's Dream*. The stage curtains and lighting set installed in 1957 had a much-needed overhaul, thanks largely to the Parents' Association. The new Hall (as drama enthusiasts called the new Gymnasium) was also welcomed by Mr F. W. M. Peirce and later Mr D. J. Colthup who worked hard to organize School orchestras and choirs, despite the poor provision for Music in the crowded timetable. Mr N. H. Bateman also organized many concerts, and musical talent was always well in evidence in the School.

To encourage these activities, Mr Hazelton started, in the Christmas Term of 1957, House Competitions in Music and Drama in which competing teams were trained and directed by senior boys of the Houses, without intervention by members of the Staff. The result was not without its minor disasters, but there were successes as well, and the performers, and especially their instructors, undoubtedly learned a lot from their experiences.

The history of the School Boat Club during the Hazelton period is one of the brave endeavours of a small school to get on terms with much bigger and more experienced clubs. Unlike most School games, Rowing took place at a national level, and success did not come easily. But first there was a problem to resolve. Ever since the School had its own boats (1938), they had been housed in a building on the Bucks bank. In 1956, Messrs J. G. Meakes Limited needed this building for redevelopment and the Boat Club was homeless. Mr Hazelton started lengthy negotiations that led to an arrangement by which racks were made available in Marlow Rowing Club boathouse in return for financial assistance in the construction of a sculling boathouse for the Club. The School therefore renewed its association with Marlow Rowing Club, where its boats, now greatly increased in numbers, remained until the twenty-first century. The most successful year of this period was 1959, when the School won two cups for Eights at Reading Clinker Regatta and Junior Eights at Marlow. In 1960, Borlase sent an Eight to Henley Royal Regatta for the first time. This was repeated in 1974. In 1964, Michael Muir-Smith became Borlase's first Oxbridge Blue, being in the winning Cambridge boat in the University Boat Race. In 1975, this distinction was also gained by Chris Langridge. In 1972, Russell Sage was honoured by having a School Eight named after him. In 1964, a School Regatta was held for the first time and endured as a feature of the end of the Summer Term.

By 1956, Rugby Football was firmly established at Borlase as the main winter game. In that year, Mr D. T. Williams joined the School as the first full-time Games and PE master, which undoubtedly raised the standard of

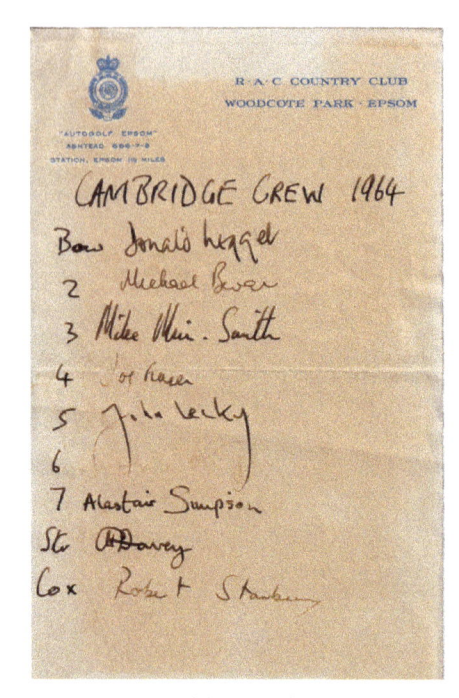

2.7.10. Signatures of the crew of the winning Cambridge Eight in the 1964 University Boat Race (Old Borlasian Michael Muir-Smith sitting at 3)

84 | CHAPTER 2 — Revival and Renewal (1874-1974)

2.7.11. The 1st XV Rugby team of 1962–1963, with Mr D. T. Williams on the left, and the 1st XI Cricket team of 1962, with Mr B. Welch on the left

fitness and skill. The Rugby fixture list gradually improved as the School became able to hold its own with larger schools. An Easter tour to Wales took place in 1959 and was followed by others to Wales and Yorkshire. In 1963, a match with the Lycée Michelet in Paris started a series of games against the French boys. The fact that all the PE masters during this period were themselves keen Rugger men helped in the production of good sides.

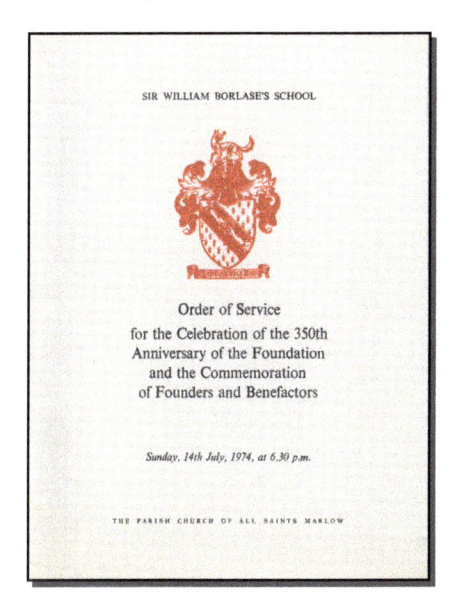

2.7.12. Order of service for a celebration of the 350th anniversary of the School's foundation, July 1974

It might be thought that Cricket suffered by having to compete with the growing popularity of Rowing during the period concerned, but in fact schoolboys seemed to be divided by Nature into 'Wet-bobs' and 'Dry-bobs' and only exceptional individuals were equally good at both. Indeed, the record throughout the period is one of hard work and enthusiasm by teams and coaches (notably Mr B. Welch), producing a very praiseworthy record of results against schools with many more players on whom to draw. A special feature of these years was the steady improvement of the Cricket square in the Colonel's Meadow, particularly during the time that Mr Bruce Campbell was groundsman.

One notable development in the athletic life of the School at this time was the growth of Hockey from a rather minor sporting activity to a popular and highly successful School game. This was largely due to the arrival on the Staff of Mr D. J. Wedd who, as well as teaching English and taking charge of The Heights boarding house, was a Hockey enthusiast. By 1974, the School Hockey teams were not only winning most of their matches, but boys were selected to play for the County at Schoolboy and Under 22 levels, and individuals won national awards, which were presented to them at the School by John Cadman, the England coach.

Many other sports were well represented: Tennis, Cross Country, Badminton, Sailing, Swimming, Athletics… There was indeed something for everyone, and in competition with other Schools, Borlase teams always seemed to give a good account of themselves despite the lack of numbers.

The Annual Sports Day, which had always suffered from being held so early in the year, was nonetheless quite a social occasion in Mr Booth's day, with the House flags flying and the Town Band playing. The proceedings became more utilitarian as the School grew larger. Mr Booth could look at the weather and say, "It's a lovely day. Let's have the mile and half-mile heats!" Such disregard for forward planning did not fit in with the new image and the increased numbers. Several times, the races were spread over two days. Nevertheless, continuity was maintained; Sports Day took place every year, and the events were every bit as keenly contested. It is a surprising fact that Mr Hazelton's last Sports Day in 1974 was the 94th in the series.

With the death of Mr Birkett, the close link between Art and Woodwork was broken, and the appointment of a full-time Art Master opened up the way to progress in Artwork of all kinds (and incidentally to the temporary demise of Woodwork as a School subject). The provision of a well-equipped Art room in the new buildings also helped this development, but it was the personality of Mr Robin Pitman that dominated the revival of Art at the School. So successful was his teaching that, in 1962, the School was invaded by a team from BBC Television who made a programme for the *Monitor* series, illustrating the imaginative and

Revival and Renewal (1874-1974) — CHAPTER 2 | 85

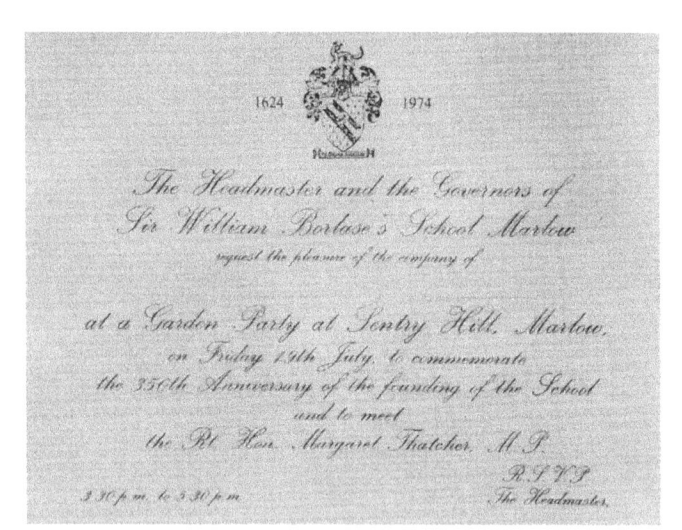

2.7.13. Invitation to a Garden Party at Sentry Hill in 1974 to commemorate the 350th anniversary of the founding of the School; the guest of honour was the Rt Hon. Mrs Margaret Thatcher, pictured with Mr E. M. Hazelton, Mr J. R. Laird, Commander O. F. M. Wethered and Lady Hall

stimulating teaching of Art going on in British schools at that time.

By a happy coincidence, the year of Mr Hazelton's retirement was also the 350th anniversary of the foundation of the School, and these two events combined to build up an atmosphere of excitement in the last week of the Summer Term in 1974. The week started with a Commemoration Service in the Parish Church (heralded by a quarter of Grandsire Triples, with several Old Borlasians among the bellringers). On Monday and Tuesday, a revue entitled *1624 and All That* dealt with the occasion in a more light-hearted manner, with a collection of sketches and musical items performed by boys and Staff. For the more athletic, there was a 'Jeux Sans Frontières' contest between teams drawn from the four Houses, the Staff and the Old Borlasian Club in events fiendishly devised by Mr Alan Black, the Games Master.

The highlight of the week was a Garden Party at the boarding house, Sentry Hill. The guest of honour was to be the Secretary of State for Education who, at the planning stage, was the Rt Hon. Mrs Margaret Thatcher. By July, the Conservative government was no longer in office, but Mrs Thatcher was nonetheless a very welcome guest and, in her speech, made a strong plea for the retention of successful grammar schools like Borlase — a subject very much in the thoughts of all those concerned about the future of the School at that time. The occasion was marred by a violent rainstorm that made it impossible for the 300 guests to walk in the grounds of Sentry Hill. In 1979, Mrs Thatcher became the UK's first female Prime Minister. This memorable week concluded with a Commemoration Dance in the School Hall attended by members of the Staff, Old Borlasians and Sixth Formers.

In 1974, Speech Day — the last of Mr Hazelton's career as Headmaster — was expected to be a rather special occasion. Fate decreed that it was to be more unusual than was planned. The marquee that had been erected on the Home Meadow some days earlier was destroyed by fire in the early hours of the morning, and when this disaster was followed by heavy rain that made an outdoor function impossible, it seemed that there would be nowhere to hold the event. However, the Rev. Dr Day, the Vicar of Marlow, came to the rescue, and Speech Day took place in the Parish Church.

In his Report, Mr Hazelton could justly say that during his stewardship, the School had increased in size (from 338 boys in 1956 to 457 boys in 1974) and progressed on all fronts: academic, cultural and athletic.

To quote R. H. Sage, writing in *The Borlasian* magazine at the time, Mr Hazelton was a "shy and retiring man at heart, suspicious of all that is shallow or sentimental in human relationships. He put his duty to parents and boys before all thought of personal convenience. He scorned cheap popularity. He will be remembered for an era of solid achievement in developing a well-integrated organisation geared to give full opportunity to the talents entrusted to him and to guide them on their proper course for success in the modern world."

2.7.14. Mr E. M. Hazelton on his retirement as Headmaster in 1974

BOARDERS AT SENTRY HILL

2.7.15. The boarders with Mr E. M. Hazelton in 1961, when Sentry Hill opened

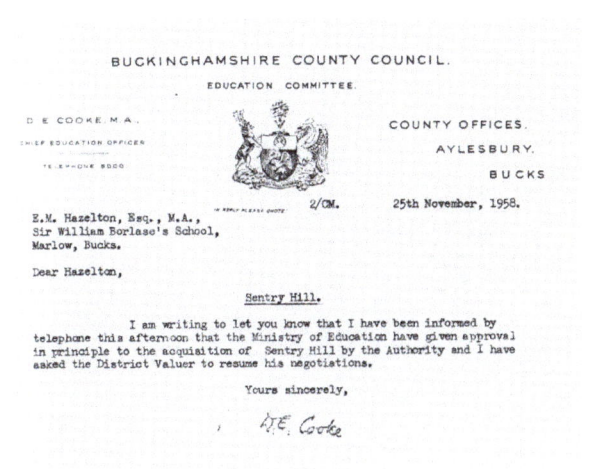

2.7.16. Letter from the County Council confirming their intention to purchase Sentry Hill

For Borlasians today, it might be surprising to think that 50 years ago, one in seven of Borlase's pupils were boarders. Prior to his appointment as Headmaster in 1956, E. M. Hazelton had been a Housemaster at Clifton College (a public school near Bristol). He soon realized that local boys were being prevented from attending Borlase when their fathers were posted overseas with the armed forces, particularly from RAF Medmenham (at that time, the UK still had armed forces stationed around the world, including in Germany). He sold the idea of having a boarding house to the County Council and promised them that it would break even. At the same time, a country house came on the market, standing in its own beautiful grounds of eleven acres sloping down towards the river, situated half a mile from the School along the Henley Road. This house, known as Sentry Hill, was ideal in every way for conversion to a boarding house, and the County authorities acquired it for £11,000, converted it and furnished it in a style worthy of the building. (During World War II, Winston Churchill stayed at Sentry Hill when visiting RAF Medmenham; it was at this RAF station that the V1 and V2 launch sites were identified through stereoscopic photography, and the former officers' mess is now Danesfield House Hotel.) The Council also added a residence (since demolished) for the

2.7.17. Sentry Hill boarding house from the rear and the Entrance Hall

Revival and Renewal (1874-1974) | CHAPTER 2 | 87

2.7.18. The boarders at Sentry Hill in 1973, when numbers peaked

Headmaster and his family because, as we have heard, the old Headmaster's house had been taken over for teaching and administration.

For the summer term of 1961, 29 boys stayed with the families of teaching Staff (such as Mr and Mrs G. A. Dewhurst), before moving to Sentry Hill for the autumn term. Thus, the option of boarding at Borlase, which had been in abeyance since 1929, was reinstated. The boarding house was popular with parents and, at its peak in 1973, there were 65 boarders who made up 15% of the School.

In the autumn of 1963, a large area in the grounds of Sentry Hill was levelled to provide a much-needed Rugby Football pitch, because the Home Meadow was insufficient, and the School had been dependent for some time on Marlow Rugby Football Club for additional pitches.

With Sentry Hill filled to capacity, more boarding accommodation was urgently needed. Soon, another unbelievable piece of good luck occurred when The Heights, a large house standing next door to Sentry Hill, became vacant and was acquired as a Junior Boarding House.

A person whom every boarder will remember is Miss Eleanor D. Smith or 'Matron', who was at Sentry Hill for the whole 25 years. Soon after her appointment, there was a huge storm and a tree just outside her window was struck by lightning and it broke in half. Boys arriving at the age of 11 years naturally felt fairly disorientated and homesick at first. Their dormitory was next to Matron's room and they sat at her table at meal times. The provision of an aspirin was a frequent result of visits to her surgery!

By today's standards, life at Sentry Hill was quite a Spartan existence. There was no television or telephone in the boarding house. Boys wrote a letter home once per week. Each day started with a junior walking round with a hand bell and finished with a roll call to make sure everyone was still there. 'Prep' was from 6.30 to 8.00 p.m. each day. An exception to this routine was Friday evenings, when the seniors had ballroom dancing classes with girls from Wycombe High School. Boys slept on steel beds in dormitories.

Lights out in the dormitories was at 9.15 p.m. for juniors and 9.45 p.m. for seniors.

2.7.19. The Rugby Football pitch at Sentry Hill

2.7.20. The Heights junior boarding house in c.1974

After lights out, there was meant to be no talking, but of course there was. There were also some nocturnal expeditions after lights out — one boy even hitchhiked to Trafalgar Square! Michael Symons (OB 1961–1965) recalls that, towards the end of his time as a boarder, he was in charge of a dormitory of eight and he had a slipper tied to the end of some string for easy retrieval that he threw at anyone who snored. Symons remembers reading avidly about the goings on involving Christine Keeler and Mandy Rice-Davies at Cliveden House, only a few miles away.

Although his wife and three smallish children (the two boys, William and James, later went to Borlase) lived at the Headmaster's residence next door, Mr Hazelton attended most of the meals with the boarders. His family might have felt neglected, but the boarding house was his idea and he was determined for it to be run the way he wanted it to be. Boarders did not stay at School for lunch, but instead cycled the mile or so back to the Dining Room at Sentry Hill.

On Saturday mornings, the boarders had jobs, which essentially meant maintenance work around the estate. The worst job was stone picking, which involved picking up the flints from the surface of the Rugby pitch below the house. On Saturday afternoons, everyone had to participate in some form of sporting activity, for example a Cross Country run, which included 2 miles up the main road from Henley.

Nearly all the boys at Sentry Hill were assigned to the Normans and, because of their higher levels of fitness, Normans tended to dominate School sport in those days. However, it was not just the boys' physical fitness that was

2.7.21. The Senior Day Room at Sentry Hill

Revival and Renewal (1874-1974)   CHAPTER 2 | 89

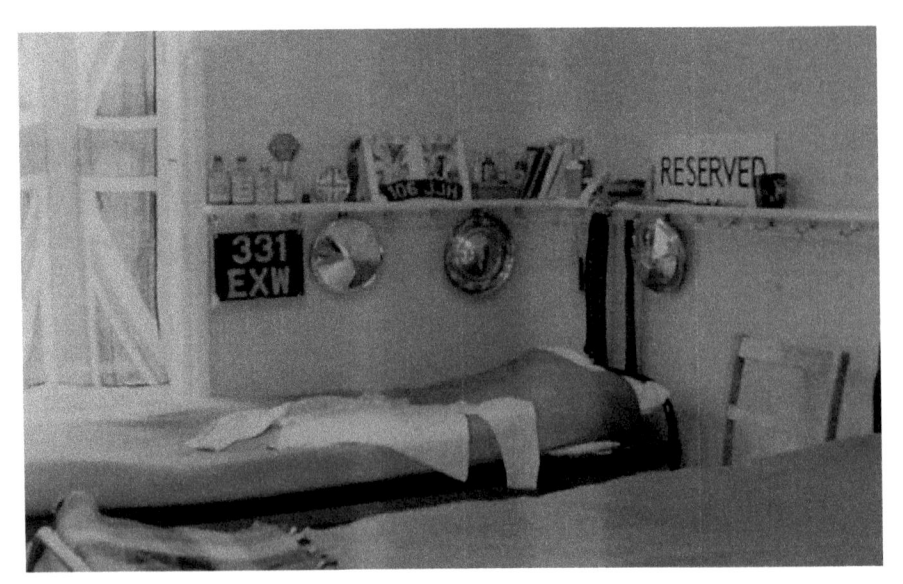

2.7.22. Steel beds in the dormitories at Sentry Hill

looked after. Michael Symons recalls going to a concert where Jacqueline du Pré was playing, a talk by Sir Barnes Wallis (who invented the bouncing bomb) and a series of lectures on film appreciation in High Wycombe. Evening outings to cultural events at Wycombe Abbey were particularly popular with older boys. When going into a large hall there, with the girls on banks of seats around the walls, it felt like an amphitheatre. Once per term, there were trips to London when the boys were allowed to go off on their own and do whatever they wanted — they just had to get back to where the coach was parked!

On most Sundays, boarders went to Matins in the Parish Church and sat where their predecessors had sat fifty years before. The annual Christmas Dinner was a grand occasion, with toasts and formal speeches from invited guests. In this microcosm of the main School, one had the impression that the Headmaster, at home with his family and other, larger family, was really happy and closest to his boys.

Mr Hazelton retired in 1974, and Mr Roy R. Smith succeeded him as Headmaster. He brought in some changes to bring the place up to date but, by the 1980s, numbers had declined and, in 1985, the boarding house was finally closed. A party was held, and Mr Hazelton attended. Sadly, only two months later, he died suddenly from a heart attack at the age of 76 years.

On 17 July 2010, a reunion for Sentry Hill boarders was organized by Michael Symons. A souvenir book (*Sentry Hill: The Boarding House Years 1961-1985*) was published and distributed, containing, among other things, anecdotes about what the boarders had gone on to do, some of which are reproduced below.

Peter van Cuylenburg (OB 1961–1964) now lives in California and really hit the big time: "Steve Jobs, famous for founding Apple Computers, wanted someone to help him to make a success of his struggling next venture, aptly named NeXT Computer. He felt that the work I had done with Texas Industries' computer business was directly relevant to NeXT because of technology similarities. I was concerned that the company was not really viable and that Steve would be hard to work with. Both concerns were well founded!"

Clive Wood (OB 1970–1972) was in the Falkland Islands in 1982 onboard HMS Sheffield when she was hit by an Exocet missile: "Waiting on the foredeck as the ship burned around them, the survivors started going into shock. I remembered my first aid training and the film *The Cruel Sea*. I started a sing-song and had about one hundred men singing Monty Python's *Always Look on the Bright Side of Life*."

Robin Elias (OB 1962–1970) went on tour with the Rolling Stones, Pink Floyd, Genesis, Phil Collins and Tina Turner and, when Liverpool was the European City of Culture, he designed and operated a 15-metre diameter mechanical spider that weighed 32 tons and 'walked' up the side of a building.

Jolyon Macfie (OB 1962–1965), Mike Jones (OB 1962–1970) and Guy Cogan (OB 1970–1975)

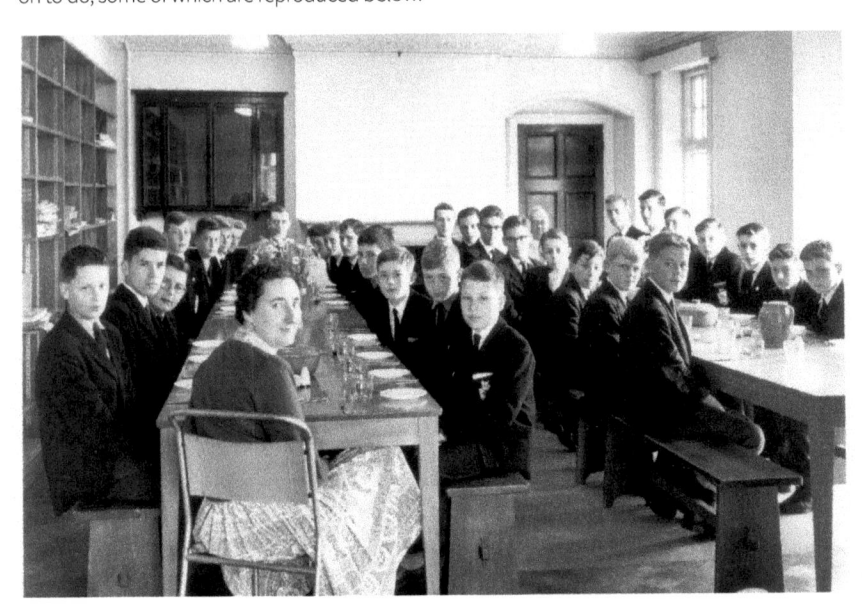

2.7.23. The Dining Room at Sentry Hill

2.7.24. Cross Country at Sentry Hill

were all in New York when planes were crashed into the World Trade Center on 9/11.

Ross Belding (OB 1961–1969), David Milsom (OB 1964–1971) and Charles Allen (OB 1970–1975) have all sailed across the Atlantic, but that was too easy for Phil Scantlebury (OB 1972–1978) — he rowed across!

Garry McElwain (OB 1964–1967) travelled 12,000 miles around Africa in a converted fire engine, crossing 16 countries, after spending his honeymoon hitchhiking round Algeria and Tunisia.

Mark Child (OB 1975–1979) broke the civilian World Freefall Record (over 6 miles) in 1986, jumping out of a hot-air balloon at 36,500 feet.

Matthew Searle (OB 1974–1977), who left Borlase with only five O Levels, has one of his inventions (a self-heating can) on display in the Science Museum.

Simon Taylor (OB 1962–1969) was in the world stage premiere of *Joseph and the Amazing Technicolor Dreamcoat* and subsequently (as Mason Taylor) went on to appear in eight major productions in the West End.

Peter Hitchcock (OB 1958–1965) landed an F4 Phantom on the USS Kittyhawk in the Pacific and flew 8,500 miles non-stop from the UK to the Falkland Islands (with in-flight refuelling twelve times). His flying was not all plain sailing — he had to eject from a Lightning F2A jet in January 1971 and lost an inch in height as well as the aircraft! Nevertheless, he went on to command a 23-aircraft Tornado F3 fighter squadron.

2.7.25. The boarders with Mr R. R. Smith at Sentry Hill in 1984, the year before its closure

Revival and Renewal (1874-1974)

2.7.26. Boarders reunited at Sentry Hill in 2010.
TOP: Back row: Andrew Milsom, Andrew Abbott, Graham Allen, Rupert Scrivener, Chris Elias, William Hazelton, Peter Jones, David Milsom, James Tilley, James Hood.
Standing: Simon Taylor, John Green, Murray Selwyn, John Conry, Adrian Hollingworth, Paul Stanley, Dave Bury, Mick Clark, Ian Ferguson, Garry McElwain, Richard Dunn, Arnis Blumentals, Mike Jones, Phil Woodward, Tim Peacock.
Seated: Pieter Wing, Andrew Hill, Paul Belding, John Clark, Rick Bury, Stan Darling, Philip Jackson, David Hitchcock, Peter Hitchcock, Michael Symons, Neil Edwards, Mike Tolley.
Front row: Paul Ginman, Tony Leach, Rob Crook, Phil Turner, Stuart Le Cornu, Steve Hawker, James Hazelton, Nick Pike, Simon Leach, Steve Watson, David Rosser, Mike Sullivan, Andrew Main, Paul Lee.

92 | CHAPTER 2   Revival and Renewal (1874-1974)

BOTTOM: Back row: Richard Neathey, Robin Walmsley, Phil Scantlebury, Peter Cape, Adam Smith, Mark Hutton, Doug Sheffield, Matthew Searle, Dave Funnell, Colin Funnell, Tom Chapman, Graeme Titchener.
Standing: Ian Vinnicombe, Hugh Fraser, Martyn Wilks, Charles Allen, James Clark, Keith Cogan, Ian Corke, Gary Hammond, John Pothecary, Tim Janman, Hugh Field, Bob Weeks, Will Jackson, Neill Mullinger, Ian Paton, Mark Herbert.
Seated: Paul Ginman, Steve Watson, Rob Crook, Stuart Le Cornu, Steve Hawker, Nick Pike, Chris Wright, Phil Turner, James Hazelton, Simon Leach, Tony Leach, David Rosser, Mike Sullivan, Andrew Main, Paul Lee.
Front row: Michael Liebrecht, Rob Baker, Richard Walton, Phil Paton, Adrian Matthews, Simon Marsden, Paul Craven, Andrew Boyle, Mark Ringrose, Ian Neal, John Adcock, Marc Liebrecht.

Revival and Renewal (1874-1974) | CHAPTER 2 | 93

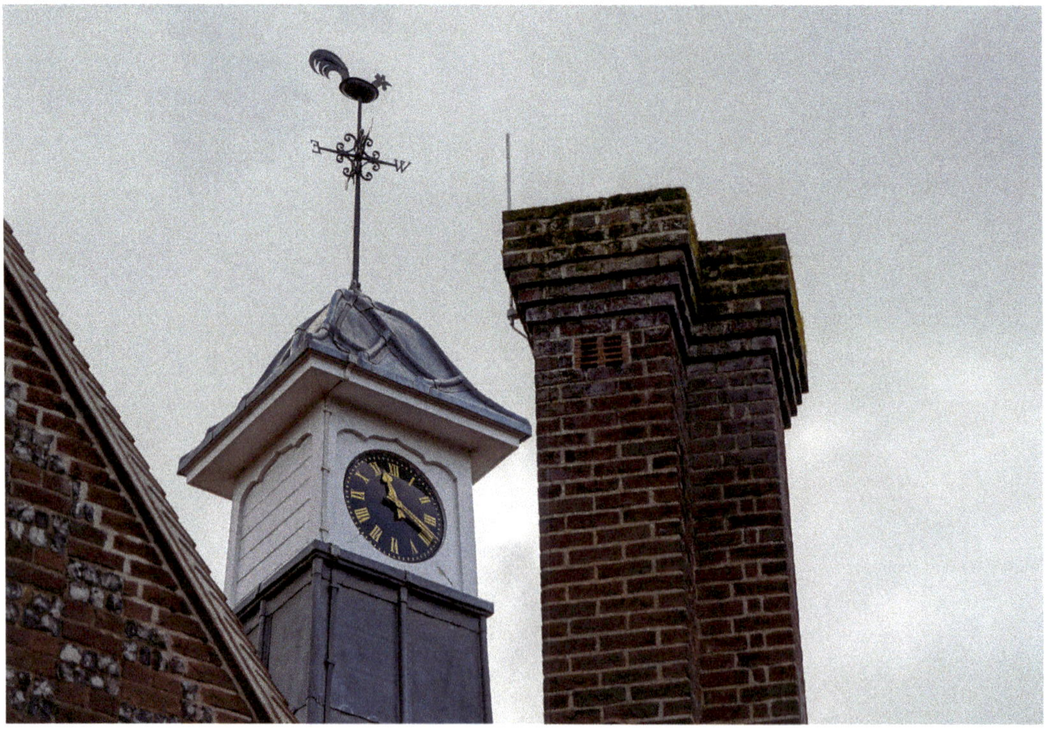

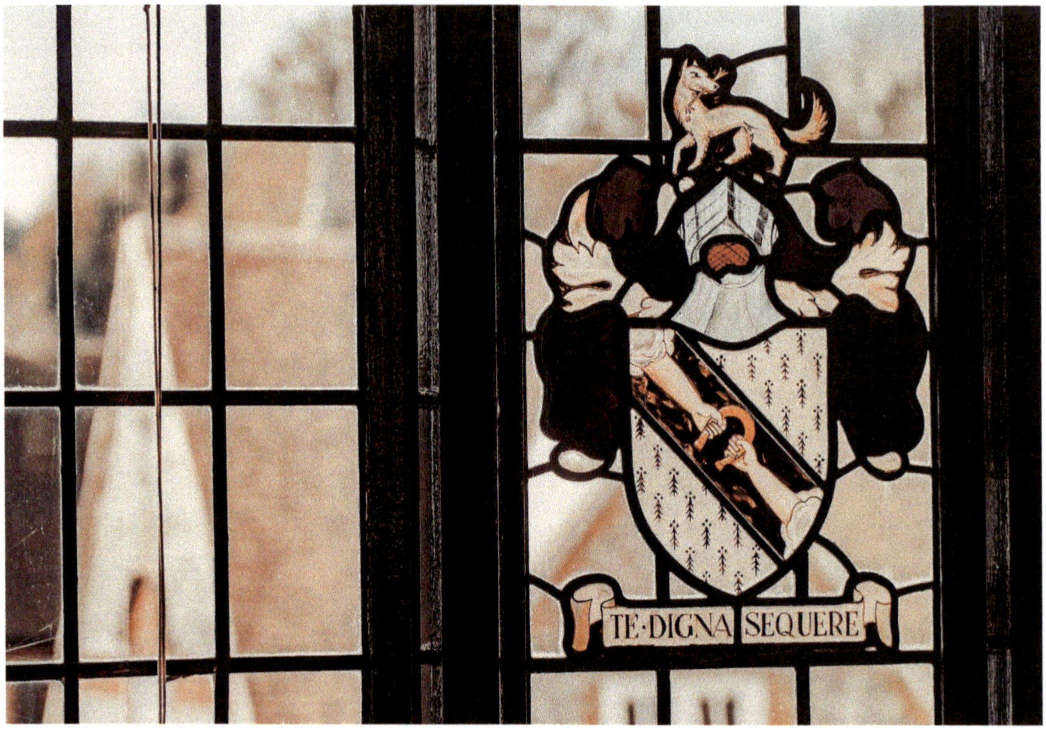
TE·DIGNA SEQUERE

CHAPTER 3
THE MODERN ERA (1974–2024)

ROY R. SMITH (1974–1988)

3.1.1. Mr Roy R. Smith (Headmaster 1974–1988)

Mr Hazelton's successor in 1974 was Mr Roy R. Smith, a graduate of London University and a barrister, a bachelor and formerly headmaster of the Davenant Foundation Grammar School at Loughton, Essex.

Once again, the change of Headmaster had its effect on the School — not of course a revolution, but a gradual modification of the ways things were done. Other factors contributed to this change. The 'permissive society' of the 'swinging sixties' had reached even the placid educational world of South Bucks. Young people wanted more of a say in their own affairs, and discipline became more a matter of consensus. This new spirit found sympathetic understanding in the new Headmaster. He had a clear idea of what kind of a School he wanted and was quietly resolute in putting his views into practice, although was always ready to give reasons for his actions or to listen sympathetically to objections.

The previous change of Headmaster had been accompanied by the new buildings and the increased intake of 1956. The 1974 change coincided with the new trends in education expressed by the growth of comprehensive schools over most of the country. Areas such as Buckinghamshire, where selection had been retained, were nonetheless affected by this movement. During the late 1960s and early 1970s, the fate of Borlase hung precariously in the balance. Various schemes were proposed and discussed in the Wycombe Division of Buckinghamshire County Council Education Department and in none of them was the role assigned to Borlase acceptable to those who wanted to preserve the School as they knew and loved it. The compact nature of the School buildings and the limited area of the site on which they stood precluded a change to a fully comprehensive school. Borlase ran the risk of becoming a part of a larger institution, separate only in its geographical location. The Headmaster, with the enthusiastic support of the governors, the Old Borlasian Club, the Staff and the parents, campaigned strenuously to maintain the School's existence. Finally, the advent of Mrs Thatcher's Conservative government meant that, for the time being at least, the School was preserved.

The 'victory', as some would like to call it, was accompanied by a change of emphasis that was in line with the new Headmaster's view of his task. While continuing to pursue the ideal of academic excellence (and the record of examination successes and awards is proof enough of this), the School began to show small but important examples of a change in attitude towards boys who were not academic high-flyers but whose abilities lay elsewhere. Borlase became a team, or even a family, in which each member had responsibility for the success of the whole undertaking and contributed his share to the best of his ability.

In common with other schools, Borlase had to include on its Governing Body representatives of both Staff and parents and, with several Old Borlasians among the Governors, there was a deeper feeling of involvement with the progress and development of the School.

The so-called 11+ test for the selection of pupils became the 12+, enabling the School to take a three-form entry and giving greater scope for setting by ability and a more flexible choice of subjects for study. Biology, which had been introduced as a class subject in 1960 was given better facilities, whereas Latin was taught to a restricted number of boys, and Greek practically disappeared. With no fuss or

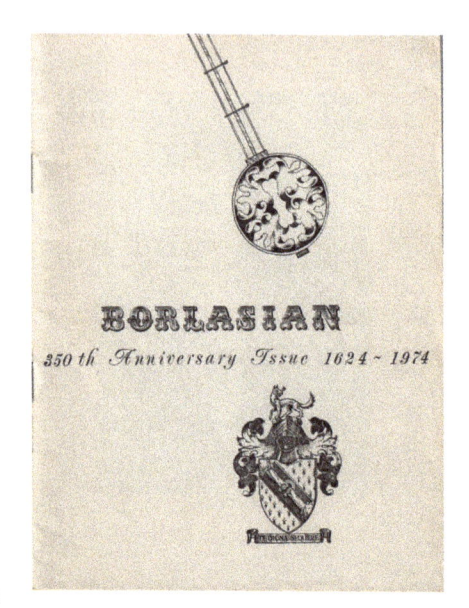

3.1.2. The Borlasian temporarily ceased publication in 1974, but resumed in 1982 with a less formal format

official announcement, corporal punishment fell into disuse, with no apparent detrimental effect on School discipline. Around this time, arrangements were made for the introduction of Design and Technology as a regular School subject.

Economies imposed by the local authority enforced certain changes. *The Borlasian* magazine ceased publication in 1974, having appeared annually since 1882. For some years, it was replaced by a photocopied publication that appeared at irregular intervals. However, regular publication of the magazine resumed in 1982. While giving full cover to the many activities taking place in the School, it also reflected the change in attitude that had taken place. Instead of the routine reporting of official events and statistics, with a small and carefully selected handful of 'original contributions', the new magazine was bright and breezy, unselfconscious and young at heart. Even the cover carried a caricature of the School coat of arms that dignified early editions.

Speech Day, which had progressed from a simple, open-air occasion to a grand social event for a thousand guests in a vast marquee, became an expensive luxury that could not be justified. It was replaced in 1982 by an Open Day, when parents and friends could visit the School and see the work done there. However, this change caused some misgivings among the Governors and Old Borlasians, and Speech Day in the marquee was reintroduced in 1984.

An important development that took place shortly after Mr Smith's arrival was the formation of a Parents' Association. Although Parents' Meetings had taken place regularly in the past, they merely provided an opportunity for parents to discuss their sons' progress with the Staff. The Fete Committee was the nearest thing to parent participation in School activities. In 1974, this committee became the constituent body for the formation of a Parents' Association. This new organization not only continued the fundraising efforts of the School Fete (which remained the main money-making activity of the year), but also arranged social events that brought parents together in meetings and entertainment events of all kinds. In countless ways, the parents, through their Association, contributed to the facilities offered by the School, donating every kind of article from a micro-computer to new curtains and lighting equipment for the stage. The Association also organized such useful events as Careers Evenings, when local business leaders and professionals gave advice and information about careers in their own field. With parents of every age group in the School represented on its committee, together with the Headmaster and members of the Staff, the Association became an important element in the life of the School.

The mention of a micro-computer draws attention to the fact that Borlase was not left behind in the introduction of new technology. As far back as 1967, Borlase, Christ's Hospital and Dover Grammar School initiated a pilot scheme for school computer programming, using the IBM computer at Imperial College London. The process involved coding programmes on punched cards, which were sent to Imperial College by post. The College then returned the print-outs. This system, with minor improvements, continued until 1976, when Buckinghamshire made the County computer available to schools. By this time, computer programming and computer science were taught in the Sixth Form. In 1979, the Parents' Association bought an RML 380Z micro-computer for the school, which greatly increased interest in the subject. Instead of a week's wait for the print-out, there was an instant display on a screen. At first, only the Sixth Form was involved, but soon the Fifth and then the Fourth Forms were introduced to Computing, and many boys emerged with considerable expertise in programming. In 1982, aided by a government grant, the School bought a second RML 380Z micro-computer and, in 1983, the Physics department acquired a BBC micro-computer of its own. With this equipment, there were facilities for boys to make their own programmes, while teachers, especially in the Mathematics, Physics and Economics departments, could make great use of these machines. Several masters were involved in this development, but Mr B. H. Teasdill, who first became involved with it in 1968, was largely responsible for its success.

For many years, the Science department was hampered by lack of proper accommodation. For decades, Science masters despaired at the meagre facilities available for teaching their subjects. When Biology was introduced in 1960, all kinds of makeshift arrangements were made, in cupboards, cloakrooms and at the back of the Physics laboratory. Promises of something

3.1.3. The new Science block built in 1981

better were regularly given, but Chemistry and Physics still soldiered on in premises designed for the Science teaching methods of 1902. In 1981, the unbelievable happened, and a new Science centre was built behind North Block, where two 'temporary' classrooms had stood for many years. The new building contained two Chemistry and two Physics laboratories and a dark-room, all equipped with modern installations. There are also two classrooms and a Sixth Form common room and coffee bar. This too was an overdue amenity. For a time in Mr Hazelton's day, the old Church of England Infants' School in Oxford Road (known as the Booth Building) was a kind of Sixth Form centre, at least for scientists, but its remoteness from the main buildings led to some abuse of privilege. The new accommodation in such a central position proved more successful.

A multiplicity of clubs and societies flourished over the years, all guided and supported by members of Staff no less enthusiastic than the boys. An aphorism well known to teachers is: "If you want them to burn, you must blaze". Borlase has never been short of teachers ready to give generously of their time and energy in so-called out-of-School activities, where in fact some of the most important work of the School is done.

Drama, for many years a very popular and successful activity, reached new heights under the leadership of Mr Andrew Stafford who introduced girls from Wycombe High School into his productions — a procedure that would have been frowned on in less permissive days.

Music, which has always been difficult to fit into the regular curriculum, depended on the energy and enthusiasm of masters such as Fred Peirce, David Colthup, Normal Bateman and their successors. The School orchestra and choir flourished and displayed their skills in many concerts, thereby effectively answering the criticism that Borlase was not a musical School.

Mr J. R. Hamer, the Art master, who had had some experience as a jazz musician, introduced Jazz as a subject in the Sixth Form general studies course. From this beginning, there developed some very successful jazz concerts. Various well-known personalities from the world of jazz have made guest

3.1.4. A selection of School plays in the 1980s: **The Miser** *(1981),* **She Stoops to Conquer** *(1982),* **Julius Caesar** *(1984) and* **The Importance of Being Earnest** *(1987)*

3.1.5. Borlase Four from 1984: Billy Gray (bow), Chris Chinn (2), Paddy Blake (3) and Chris Lane (stroke); the crew also represented England that year

3.1.6. Borlase Four at the qualifying for the Visitors' Challenge Cup at Henley in 1989 : G. J. Roy (bow), S. W. May (2), A. D. Campbell (3), A. A. Temple (stroke), coached by A. C. Craig

appearances at the School, including Humphrey Lyttleton, the trumpeter Kenny Baker and the American 'Wild Bill' Davison.

For its size, Borlase always had a splendid record of achievement in Sport, often matched with far larger schools. From 1974, this record was not only maintained but in some cases notably improved.

As a riverside School, Borlase might be expected to have a successful Boat Club, although the limited number of pupils from whom rowing boys were drawn often meant it was difficult to find good crews every year. As the School numbers rose, this problem became less serious. After 1976, there were only two coaches available from the Staff, but the Boat Club continued to grow. Help from the Parents' Association and organized fundraising by the Club itself, with the enthusiastic help of 'rowing parents', enabled the School to increase substantially the stock of boats and equipment, including a new Four, named 'Owen Wethered' in memory of the well-loved Old Borlasian, ex-chairman of Governors, and friend and benefactor of the School, Commander O. F. M. Wethered.

Among many successes in the 1974–1984 period were the first win in a heat of the Princess Elizabeth Cup at Henley in 1975 and the winning of the Fours Cup at the National Schools' Regatta and the Senior Coxless Fours Cup at Marlow Regatta, both in 1983. This splendid crew competed for the Visitors' Challenge Cup at Henley and was beaten by Harvard (no less!) on the Friday. An even more rewarding year was 1984, when a long list of successes included three wins at the National Schools' Regatta and a win for a composite crew from Borlase and Shiplake College in the Visitors' Cup at Henley. This crew, stroked by Lance Robinson from Borlase, was selected to represent Great Britain in Coxless Fours at the Junior National Championships in Sweden. Another School crew became the Junior Coxless Fours champions at the National Championships at Nottingham, where an Old Borlasian, Mark Buckingham, was stroking the Leander Elite Eight. Truly a record of which the two dedicated coaches, Tony Craig and David Ravens, can be proud.

Rugby Football has been equally successful, especially since 1978 when the 1st XV pitch was transferred to the Colonel's Meadow. The drier, wider pitch encouraged a more open and fluid game. In 1979–1980, the wingers R. Valentine and J. Elliott scored fifty tries between them. In the 1982–1983 season, the School 1st team was unbeaten in 24 matches. At the end of the season, the team represented Wasps Colts and beat London Welsh 25–0 at Twickenham. Several tours abroad were undertaken, including one to Yugoslavia in 1978, and foreign sides were entertained at home. Besides the 1st XV, other sides regularly fielded were 2nd, 3rd, under 15, under 14 and under 13 teams, so that, on a typical Saturday, a hundred boys were playing Rugby for the School.

Cricket has maintained a strong position, favoured by the excellent square already mentioned. The good work done by Bruce Campbell has been continued since 1977 by the present groundsman, Mr Swadling, and at a time when grass wickets are disappearing, the School has easily the best square of all the schools in Buckinghamshire. Besides doing well in its regular 1st XI fixtures, since 1981, the School has participated in the Barclays Bank Competition, being runners-up to Mill Hill School in the area final in 1983.

Another sport that has brought more than local fame to Borlase is Hockey, under the outstanding leadership of David Wedd. The successes of the School teams during the past ten years are too many to be listed. To consider only the 1983–1984 season, out of more than forty School matches in various

3.1.7. The Borlase 1st XV Rugby team were unbeaten in the 1982–1983 season; back row: Harvey, Walker, Barnes, Spicer, Elliott, Maskery, Smith, Evans, Webb; front row: Carter, Coll, Douneen (captain), Gamble, Jayes, Aylward (not in picture: Nicholas)

3.1.8. Borlase's U16 Hockey team were National U16 Champions in 1987

age groups, only two were lost. Twenty-eight boys played for Buckinghamshire and eight for the south-east of England. Ten boys in the past 10 years have played for England. The under 14 team won all their matches and were runners-up in the National Seven-a-Side Competition, and the under 16 team were Bucks champions, South-East winners and finally won the National title. Not surprisingly, Borlase Hockey teams have been offered many fixtures abroad, especially in Holland.

In addition to these major games, boys can take part in Cross Country, Orienteering, Basketball, Golf, Squash, Sailing, Tennis, Badminton, Rock-climbing, Volleyball and Swimming. In 1982, a new liner was fitted to the Swimming pool, which continues to provide an excellent summer facility for Swimming and Life-saving. There has been for some time an annual trip to the Wye Valley for an adventure holiday, with experience in camping, pony trekking, canoeing, fell-walking and orienteering. Thanks to Alan Black and the members of Staff who have helped in this work, the School has been able

100 | CHAPTER 3

The Modern Era (1974-2024)

3.1.9. Borlase Senior Tennis team, 1986

to offer this wide choice of sporting activities at a consistently high level of achievement.

Amid all this activity, what happened to what many would consider (perhaps wrongly) to be the main purpose of a School, the acquisition of knowledge? Far from suffering from this diversion of energy, academic standards remained high. We may judge the level of achievement in a typical year from the Headmaster's report at the 1984 Speech Day. Among the successes mentioned was an exhibition in History at Christ's College, Cambridge, and an exhibition in Modern Languages at Worcester College, Oxford; forty grade A passes at A level; ten boys gaining places at Oxford or Cambridge and 54 at other universities and polytechnics; two Outward Bound scholarships… "I could go on for a long time; the list is very long," said the Headmaster.

But academic success is not the sole objective of education at Borlase. To quote Mr Smith again: "We do not hope to produce cultural conformists, but people willing and able to recognize the tremendous debt which they owe to the past while possessing both the capacity and the desire to move on in the future".

In 1986, *The Sunday Times* ran a competition to mark the 900th anniversary of the Domesday Book. Entrants were asked to submit an exhibit on a Domesday theme, and Borlase's entry, which compared the Norman period with the current day, won first prize. The exhibit was displayed at the Domesday 900 Exhibition in the Great Hall, Winchester, and Her Majesty Queen Elizabeth The Queen Mother presented the prizes.

One of the noticeable features of this era of Borlase's history is the number of masters who have remained at the School for most of their teaching career. A list of the longest-serving members of Staff appears at the end of this book. The stability accruing from this nucleus of devoted servants was invaluable. It would be difficult to exaggerate the debt owed by the School to such men as D. C. W. Banner, N. H. Bateman, A. Black, D. J. Colthup, C. B. Davenport, J. C. Davies, G. A. Dewhurst, W. F. Jones, R. E. Ogden, D. C. Paton, F. W. M. Peirce, W. O. Robertson, B. H. Teasdill and B. Welch. And not only men! Mrs M. Joy Halton not only brought the feminine touch to many School activities (one thinks of the School play and the School regatta) but also applied her sound judgement to the task of School Governor at a time when the Governing Body assumed a

3.1.10. HM Queen Elizabeth The Queen Mother presents 1st prize at the Domesday 900 Exhibition to Borlase students Charles Richardson and Paul Forbes, pictured with Mr Kerr; the School was presented with a mobile film unit

The Modern Era (1974-2024)

CHAPTER 3 | 101

3.1.11. Charles B. Davenport, teacher at Borlase from 1935 to 1973

more influential role in the life of the School. The School has always been fortunate in its Governors who have been ready to help with their advice, guidance and encouragement, both in routine matters and in moments of crisis.

The Old Borlasian Club continues faithfully to fulfil its stated objective: to promote the interests of the School in every possible way. During this period, they gave their strong support in the campaign to resist the introduction of comprehensive schools in the Marlow area. They contributed generously to the plaques in the School Chapel commemorating those well-respected members of Staff who had died: W. S. Booth, J. C. Davies, W. F. Jones and W. O. Robertson. They gave the School's first Rowing Eight, appropriately named 'Baggy'. In 1971, they donated the new gateway in the boundary wall in West Street, with its handsome heraldic shield. In 1973, they were responsible for commissioning a portrait in oils of Mr W. S. Booth. They helped to buy the School's first minibus and even financed the gilding of the Colonel's Meadow railings.

Admission of Girls

Although students at Borlase were thriving, falling numbers in the school-age population brought problems to the School. It is also possible that the Headmaster and Staff did not recognize the aggressive recruitment of competing schools via 'Open Days' that had emerged; such events were anathema to Mr Smith, who was a naturally shy man. As we have heard, the number of boarders dwindled, and Sentry Hill closed in 1985. A School for fewer than 500 boys was deemed not to be viable, and the very survival of the School once again became threatened. The options presented were either closure or amalgamation with another school.

The continued existence of Borlase School in Marlow is perhaps thanks to the then Vicar of Marlow, the Rev. Canon Dr Sam R. Day, who taught Religious Education at the School in the early 1980s. At the end of one academic year, a meeting of local officials was held in the marquee on the School field to explain that the School could not survive on such small numbers of students and to propose that the School be transferred to buildings in High Wycombe previously occupied by Lady Verney High School. Canon Day made a magnificent speech that so roused the parents who were there that the decision was made to "Keep Borlase in Marlow" (the slogan appeared on a banner across the High Street and on the front of the School buildings) and that the School would become co-educational to increase student numbers.

The introduction of girls began with admission to the Sixth Form in 1987 and at the age of 12 years in 1988. There was also a change in the designated catchment area, which meant that suddenly the School was admitting students from Maidenhead, across the county boundary. In addition, Rowland Brown, the Headmaster of the Royal Grammar School in High Wycombe, retired, and gradually that School began to lose the monopoly of recruiting very bright boys at the expense of Borlase. These changes meant that many pupils arrived from non-selective schools into the Sixth Form, and certain subjects found that they had A level candidates who perhaps had not had the preparation that Borlase gave.

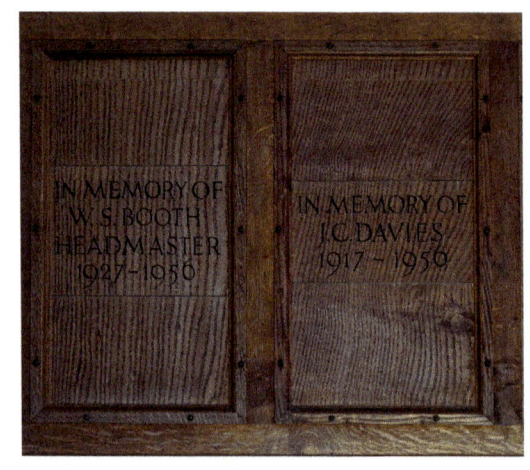

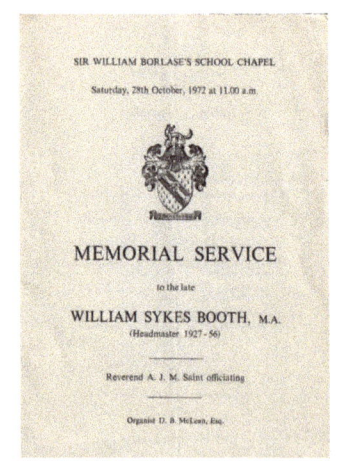

3.1.12. Oil painting of Mr Booth, commissioned by the Old Borlasian Club; Chapel plaques in memory of W. S. Booth and J. C. Davies; and a pew sheet for a Memorial Service for W. S. Booth held in the School Chapel on 28 October 1972

With the arrival of girls, greater numbers of female teachers were appointed to the Staff, as well as a School Matron. A second Deputy Head, Mrs Adrienne Crittenden, was recruited from Wellesbourne School in 1987 to manage the School's transition to being co-educational. In 1988, Mr Smith retired owing to ill health, and Mr Donald C. W. Banner, who had taught Classics at the School since 1951, became the acting Headmaster for one term.

Mrs Crittenden recalled that there was some resentment to the School becoming co-educational. "Not everybody wanted [the change]. I think it's a struggle that's repeated throughout schools, and history as well. The local population will step in as soon as something violates the town's tradition, even if it doesn't really affect them. So that was certainly the challenge when the girls came in at the beginning. The girls were under scrutiny from the community for turning a boys' school into a co-educational one.

"At the end of the first day, the secretary ran to me and said, 'Can you come to the office? There's a woman on the phone wanting to talk to you and she's very indignant.' So I went to the office, picked up the phone and introduced myself. The caller said in a very imperious tone, 'I want to complain about one of your girls.' I said, 'What on earth's the problem?' She said, 'I was standing in the queue in Waitrose this morning. One of your girls was in front of me. And she had a hole in her tights!'"

Any resistance to the change was soon overcome, and it was generally accepted that the presence of students of the opposite sex had a civilizing influence and made for a well-rounded School environment and classroom discussions.

3.1.13. The first cohort of Borlase girls to enter the Sixth Form in 1987

3.1.14. Mrs Adrienne Crittenden, who was appointed Deputy Headmistress to manage the School's transition to being co-educational, and the Sixth Form girls with Mr Banner (Acting Headmaster) and Mrs Crittenden (Deputy Headmistress) in 1988

The Modern Era (1974-2024)

LAURENCE A. SMY (1989–1996)

3.2.1. Laurence A. Smy (Headmaster 1989–1996)

Laurence Smy graduated in History and Theology from the University of Cambridge. He was appointed to the Headship of Borlase in the summer term of 1988 but, although he visited the School every week in the autumn term, it was not until January 1989 that he took up his post. He realized that the choice to take the School co-educational came from necessity not from conviction. He had previously been the Headmaster of Coopers School, a co-educational grammar school in Chislehurst, and was convinced that co-education was the best way to educate both boys and girls. At his first Speech Day, he reported being asked how the new Second Form (Year 8) girls had settled in. He rejoined that both they and he found it a strange question. They had come from co-educational middle schools and from the start were happy to continue their education alongside boys. They accepted every challenge and enjoyed giving the boys a high standard to live up to.

The new Headmaster was concerned that discussion of whether the School should close and the very small intake (39 boys) that had arrived into the Second Form in 1988 had damaged the image of the School in the community and morale in the School. He judged that the School needed to believe in itself again and to proclaim its virtues and achievements. With the support of the new Rector of Marlow, the Rev. Nicholas Moloney, he arranged that the assembly at the beginning and end of each term should take place in the Parish Church of All Saints and should include hymns, readings and prayers and frequently a visiting preacher. This arrangement provided a dignified conclusion to each term and a rousing start to the next. It was fortunate that the local Rabbi supported the attendance of Jewish pupils, who were able to take a full part in Chapel and Church assemblies. In the daily Chapel assemblies, it was possible to sing a hymn, read a prayer together and listen to the parable for the day. In this way, each day began with a perspective larger than the daily life of School and home.

The curriculum grew with the introduction of new GCSE courses. In 1989, a new block to the north and west of the School Hall was completed, designed to provide facilities for Art, Computer Studies and Home Economics. Courses in Personal and Social Education provided the basis for an extension of Pastoral Care, which became a hallmark of the School. The new Deputy Headmistress, Mrs Crittenden, gave a strong lead, and the all-boys culture of the School began to change into a more civilized and caring one.

Many long-serving members of Staff who have already been mentioned in this book retired at the end of the summer term of 1989: Mr D. C. W. Banner, Mr K. G. W. Pappin, Mr D. C. Paton and Mr B. H. Teasdill. In September 1989, Dr Martin Isles joined the School as a second Deputy Head, alongside Mrs Crittenden.

The very small intake in 1988 made the expansion of numbers in the School an imperative for the new Headmaster. Unless this happened, the Sixth Form in 4 years' time would be too small to be viable. At his second Speech Day in 1990, he was able to report that the Second Form intake in 1989 of 113 pupils (53 boys and 60 girls) had been the largest ever. He, together with the Deputy Headmistress, had visited every School that sent children to Borlase to welcome them and answer their questions. The recruitment of 64 new students from other schools to the Sixth Form resulted in a total of 225 pupils in the Sixth Form. The tide was beginning to turn.

A second phase of the building works, formally opened in March 1990, was a new Sports gymnasium and Music suite, adjacent to the swimming pool. The architect was Mr Jeremy Wagge. A new post of Director of Music was created.

3.2.2. Mr K. G. W. Pappin, Mr B. H. Teasdill, Mrs M. J. Halton, Mr D. C. W. Banner and Mr D. C. Paton in 1989

104 | CHAPTER 3 — The Modern Era (1974–2024)

3.2.3. The new Gymnasium and Music suite, opened in March 1990, and an aerial photograph of the School grounds from 1993

An innovation during that year included the introduction of local management of schools and the appointment of a Bursar. The Governors set as their first priority an increase in teaching Staff posts to ensure that class sizes at all levels could be kept as low as possible. They also established the fundamental aims of the School to be:

1) A happy, caring community of young people striving to achieve excellence in all fields;
2) A community which fosters the love of learning and is committed to the extension of knowledge, skills and human potential;
3) A community which develops the self-respect and confidence of its pupils and helps them to take pride in their achievements and those of others;
4) A community which prepares young people for the opportunities, responsibilities and experiences of adult life, helping them to develop their own spiritual and moral values.

The review of the curriculum required by the introduction of the National Curriculum led to the adoption of a compulsory core of subjects for the education of students aged 14–16 years in the School, which included the three Sciences, both History and Geography, and one or two Modern Foreign Languages, in addition to the elective subjects, which included Art, Latin, Music and Technology.

In his 1991 Speech Day address, the Headmaster quoted the guest of honour at a Speech Day 50 years before, Mr Garfield Weston MP, who had taken as his motif "It isn't the gale, but the set of the sails, that determines the way you go". This quotation inspired the magnificent seascape painting that still hangs in the Wethered Room today. The turbulence that all Schools had suffered in 1990–1991 did not prevent Borlase from checking its direction of travel. A team of local authority advisers visited the School to conduct a thorough review (32 working days) of the educational provision that the School was making for its pupils. There were four sections to their report. Under the first (relationships), they reported that "relationships within the school are excellent both between staff and pupils and also within both groups". In a second paragraph they reported: "Teachers stressed the caring nature of the School and their commitment to achieving the best for all the pupils. This commitment shows within classrooms, and also beyond them, where an enormous amount of time is spent developing excellence in extracurricular activities." Under curriculum planning, they reported that it was "of a high quality". On teaching and learning, the advisers reported "the pace and rigour of the lessons observed were impressive — the pace was well judged by teachers and the pupils were kept to task without being unduly stressed". The range of teaching approaches used was "extremely varied". They observed pupils "listening, talking, writing, discussing, reading, predicting, interpreting, explaining, recalling, recording, problem solving, describing, collecting evidence, selecting evidence, hypothesising, experimenting, exploring views, comparing, making and drawing, and being involved in drama and role play and instructing and memorising". They observed that "differentiated learning was present in 94% of lessons and that the School ensured that there is equality of opportunity". In 1990, 87.5% of entries for the GCSE resulted in pupils achieving A, B or C grades and, at A level, the pass rate was 79.0%, with 27.6% of all entries reaching either an A or a B grade. The School felt vindicated in the set of its sails!

Of course, no record of the School at this time would be complete without a reference to outstanding sporting achievements. In his Speech Day address, the Headmaster reported that, on the Rugby field, the 1st XV won all their matches bar one; on the Soccer field, the same was true of the 1st XI. The Hockey 1st XI played in the European championships in Holland and received the award for the best sportsmen in the contest. In Rowing, girls outnumbered boys in terms of participation and victories.

In September 1991, a total of 150 pupils joined the Second Form and the *Good State School Guide* wrote a 'tongue-in-cheek' comment on the parental contribution of £5 at Borlase: "Well worth £5 to get a quality public school education at 0.05% of the cost". On 1 January 1992, the School changed its status,

3.2.4. The newly established Board of Trustees in 1992

3.2.5. The last all-boys Fifth Form in the summer of 1991

with the support of the County Council and registered with the Department for Education. Sir William Borlase's Grammar School became a voluntary controlled school with its own board of trustees. The trust that had existed since before 1912 was re-established with a new body of trustees. The trustees (from left to right in the photograph) were: Lady Margaret Popplewell (former Chair of the Education Committee), Dame Rosemary Rue (President of the British Medical Association), Dr Ewan Page (Vice-Chancellor of the University of Reading), Mr Laurence Smy (Headmaster), Mr Ray Whitney (MP for Wycombe), Dr Peter Phillips (Chair of Governors), Commander The Honourable John Fremantle RN (Lord Lieutenant of Buckinghamshire), Mrs Gail Redwood (Company Secretary, British Airways), Mrs Rosalind Wingrove (Chair of the Education Committee), Baroness Shreela Flather (House of Lords) and Mr Gary Weston (Chair of Associated Foods; absent). At the same time, a new Governing Body was also established.

During that academic year, the emphasis seemed European and international. In 1992, Margaret Thatcher's great project, the European single market, became established. Borlase, which had always prided itself on its teaching of Modern Foreign Languages, created an exchange with the lycée in Marly-le-Roi (Marlow's twin town). Members of the Lower Sixth spent a fortnight there attending classes that related to their A levels, and a group of French Sixth Form students subsequently spent time in Marlow studying their Baccalaureate subjects. The collège in Marly, not to be outdone, participated in an exchange when Third Form (Year 9) students from Borlase spent a week with their opposite numbers at Marly's holiday village in the Jura. A further event involving Fourth Formers (Year 10s) led them to be lodged with families in Provence for a week while they spent their days exploring Orange and Arles. The headmaster of the lycée and the deputy mayor of Marly attended Speech Day in 1992 and paid a tribute to the "generous hospitality" that their students had received in Marlow and reported that they had found "Marlow full of charm, which stole their hearts".

The growth in pupil numbers was putting a strain on classroom space, which the County Council recognized. Student numbers had increased to 360 boys and 211 girls in 1990–1991, and to 363 boys and 286 girls in 1991–1992. In September 1992, the popularity of the School had become such that the Governors agreed to increase the intake number at Second Form level to 150 for the second year running. This intake was also the academically strongest that the School had received. Indeed, it was stronger than that of any other Buckinghamshire grammar school. The first girls to join the Second Form in 1988 moved up to the Sixth Form in September 1992. Consequently, the Fifth Form of 1990–1991 had the distinction of being the last all-boys year group. In 1993, with more than 750 pupils on the School roll, the Governors took the decision not to exceed the standard admission number of 120 for a four-form entry, to prevent the School from becoming too large. Nevertheless, student numbers continued to increase to more than 800 in 1994.

The County Council responded by including the School in a major building programme for 1993–1994. Mr Jeremy Wagge, the architect who had designed the Gymnasium and Music block, was re-engaged. The public consultation began in September 1994 for a set of buildings designed not only to enhance the beautiful and historic School, but also to be a worthy addition to the architecture of West Street and the town itself. The exhibition and consultation proved a great success, and visitors agreed that, by continuing the gabled front of the building with its knapped flint and brickwork and continuing the cloister motif of the School, the architect had excelled himself. The block of buildings was completed in 1995 and provided a new Sixth Form centre with common rooms and study rooms (now the School Library), a fully equipped Computer Studies suite, and many classrooms, used mainly to teach Modern Foreign Languages. The Chapel quadrangle, mirroring the Cloisters to the east, was created. Also in 1995, Mr Ray Kipping joined the Staff as the new Site Manager, a position he still holds nearly 30 years later.

Academically, the School was thriving. The Lower Sixth extended their studies to include a fourth subject, alongside their three A Levels, to be studied at A or AS level. As a result, the range of subject options for the Sixth Form was expanded, which in turn supported a broadening of Sixth Form education. *The Independent* published its list of 100 best schools in Britain, including state and independent schools, and included Borlase among them. However, the School was not to be an 'academic sweatshop'. The

3.2.6. Plan for the new buildings along West Street, the buildings under construction, and the buildings that were completed in 1995 (pictured in 2023)

3.2.7. Laurence Smy with Deputy Headteachers Mrs Adrienne Crittenden and Dr Martin Isles and the Senior Prefects

four fundamental aims were still the way that the 'sails' were set. Sport, Music and Drama were as important as ever. Sport expanded, and teams in Soccer, Netball, Hockey, Rowing, Athletics, Tennis and Cricket flourished. The Young Consumer Quiz Team, having won the national championship, took on the USA champions, Chicago High School, and beat them.

In 1994, the School celebrated the achievement of becoming fully co-educational, with equal numbers of boys and girls. The culture change had been huge. The concept of equality had become well rooted, and when students competed on a single-sex basis, the mutual support was tangible. Boys' Hockey teams were on the touchlines for girls' Hockey matches and *vice versa*. An ill-judged leading article in *The Times* on girls' education led the Headmaster to write in reply showing that the article was insecurely based. At a time when politicians asserted that there was no such thing as society, the School continued to be a community. Borlase continued to teach that money and the pursuit of money were not the highest good. As the Headmaster put it at Speech Day in 1994: "The prosperity of the nation and the future of our society depend more on the ability to cooperate, to work within a team, to subordinate personal interest to the common good, than to selfishness and self-interest." Service to the community was exemplified by the generosity of teaching both in the classroom and on the sportsfield. Pupils showed it in their response to and support of each other. The Youth Award Scheme gave Sixth Formers the opportunity to work in schools and hospitals, and for younger children to work with Cub Scouts and Brownies. The international perspective was not forgotten either. Sixth Formers had presentations and lectures on South Africa and the Middle East. The Headmaster created links between Borlase and a school in Ramallah and the Prophet Elias Community College in Northern Israel, which caters for children of all faiths.

The year of 1995 was marked by a production of *The Merchant of Venice*. "The audience marvelled that no line, no word was lost or gabbled, but each player acted his or her role with understanding, sensitivity and conviction. Jack Bootle's portrayal of the sad and agonised figure of Shylock was quite memorable, and none of us shrinks from applying the word excellent to this production," opined the Headmaster. (Jack is now the Head of Specialist Factual Commissioning at the BBC, covering Science, Natural History, History, and Religion and Ethics.) The Wind Band similarly excelled.

In his final Speech Day address in the summer of 1996, the Headmaster thanked the Rector of Marlow for allowing the School to use the great Parish Church for assemblies at the beginning and end of each term:

"Listening to the Upper Sixth sing the hymns and join in the prayers of their final assembly reminded me of the immense value of an act done together as a community, which acknowledges that there is something bigger, higher and more demanding than our own individual selfish interests." He was pleased that, at the end of the Spring Term, the assembly in the church had provided the opportunity to celebrate the Passover — the lesson from The Torah was read by a prefect who was a practising Jew — and also the Last Supper. He reported on the sporting successes during the year, citing Rugby, girls' and boys' Hockey, Cricket and Rowing, in which the Senior Quad reached the final of the Public Schools' Cup. He was pleased to report that the campaign to change the age of transfer to secondary schools from 12 years to 11 years, in which Borlase had participated, had been successful. He paid tribute to Dr Peter Phillips, the chairman of Governors, who had supported the innovations of the previous eight years, which had led to an increase in numbers in the School from 450 to 850. He paid an especial tribute to the Deputy Headmistress, Mrs Crittenden, who had worked tirelessly to ensure that the change to co-education had been a success. He said that excellence in every field had always been the aim of the School, not least in academic results. The average Universities and Colleges Admissions Service (UCAS) score per candidate improved by 2.0 points in 1994, by a further 1.8 points in 1995 and was set to improve further in 1996. "I anticipate that within two years, the A level results in this School will place it in the top half dozen of maintained co-educational schools in the country." He announced that there was to be a major building programme in 1997–1998, "to replace the awful temporary accommodation and to provide space for the admission of 11 year olds". He left his final tribute to the pupils themselves. "The members of this School, almost from their first day, catch and contribute to an atmosphere of purposeful learning, liveliness of mind and courtesy of expression, which makes this School outstanding."

In September 1996, Laurence Smy left Borlase to work for UCAS, and Mrs Crittenden took over as the Acting Headmistress until April 1997, when she also left the School.

The Modern Era (1974-2024)

DR PETER A. HOLDING (1997–2018)

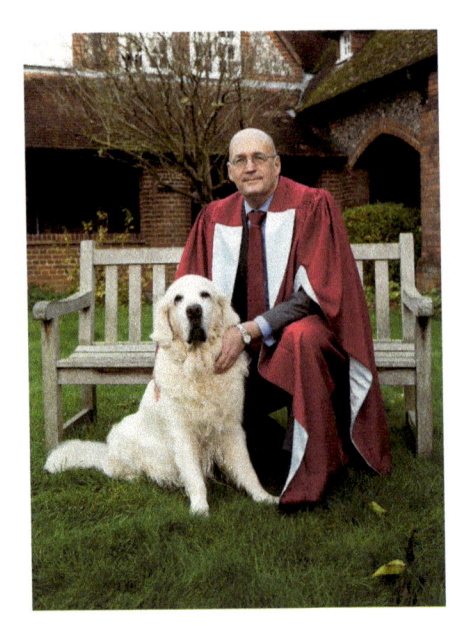

3.3.1. Dr Peter Holding (Headmaster 1997–2018)

Dr Peter Holding became Headmaster in April 1997, having been appointed to the post the previous October. A dual citizen of the USA and the UK, he had been educated both in the USA, gaining a BA and a PhD from the Universities of Pennsylvania and Michigan, and in England, gaining MAs in Shakespeare Studies and Education from Birmingham and the Open University, respectively. Dr Holding had previously worked as Head of Drama at Forest School in London, Head of English at Rugby School, and Deputy Head at Lawrence Sheriff School in Rugby. He had also been involved in running a House at Rugby School. He arrived with the first of several Golden Retrievers — Will, Tom, and Henry — each of which became an ever-present sight around the School during his tenure as Head.

Dr Holding joined the School shortly after the completion of the Modern Languages block, begun by Laurence Smy. The School had also just had its first inspection under the relatively new government-directed inspection scheme, Ofsted. His period as Head was marked by two decades of steady expansion, as well as a number of other important developments. The construction of the Audrey Moore building, named after a long-serving Governor and resident of Shelley Cottage, completed in 1999 on the site of the dilapidated post-World War II canteen, left the School with only one remaining temporary building, where Art was transferred as the School lost the tenancy of the nearby Booth Building, which it had leased from the Holy Trinity Trust. The Audrey Moore building provided a home for the English department and the Sixth Form Common Room, and initiated a process of departmental consolidations as each was given its own base around the School.

The Audrey Moore building's construction ran parallel to the reintroduction of 11 year olds, as Buckinghamshire switched back from a 12+ system to the more traditional 11+ system. This change resulted in an immediate increase in the School size from just over 800 to nearly 950 students. Over the next twenty years, the School size would grow by another 200, largely owing to the rapid expansion of its Sixth Form, from around 200 to in excess of 400. Borlase became a destination of choice for students from a great many other local schools, a mark of the continuing increase in its popularity since it had been threatened with closure in the 1980s.

Other building projects followed, most notably the construction of a new building on the site of the outdoor swimming pool. This loss was greatly regretted, because the pool had been a popular amenity, but the challenges of continuous expansion on a limited site left the School with few alternatives. Funded in part through the generosity of more than 100 private donors, mostly Old Borlasians and parents, as well as a major gift by Old Borlasian Garry Weston (OB 1939–1944), this building provided a new home for the Performing Arts, with a purpose-built Theatre to seat 250, as well as Music rooms, both on the first floor, with a centre for Art and Design on the ground floor. The new building was formally opened on 7 December 2006 by HRH The Duke of Gloucester.

As these buildings came into use, opportunities for further consolidations occurred, and bases for Business & Economics and History were created, along with the transfer of Biology to join the other Science subjects in the North building, adjacent to Home Meadow. However, by the end of the first decade of the new millennium, the continuing expansion of the Sixth Form

3.3.2. The Audrey Moore building, including the School Canteen, completed in 1999

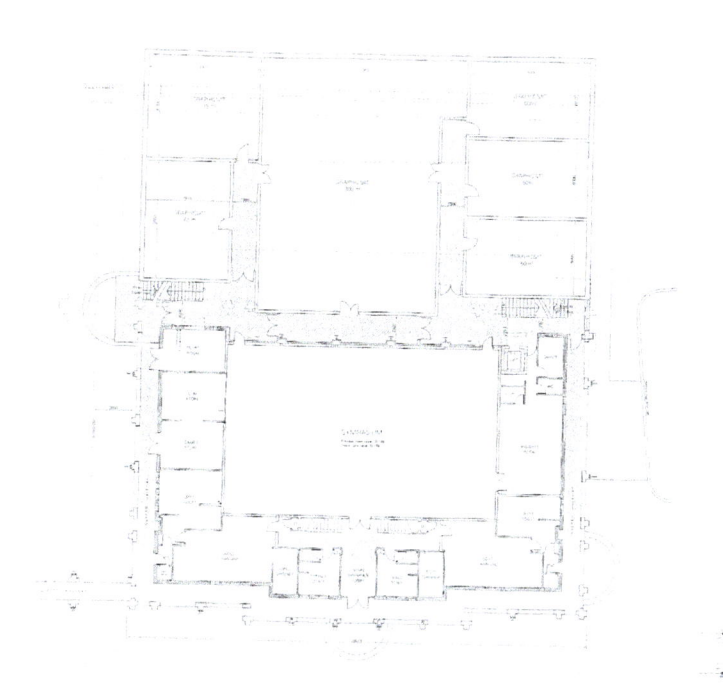

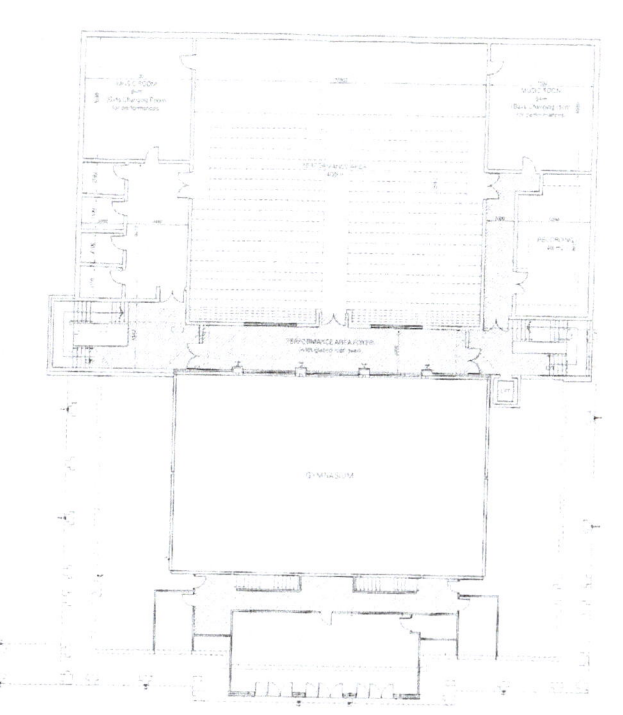

3.3.3. The Weston Building for Technology and the Performing Arts, opened in 2006 by Gary Corcoran (Chairman of Governors), Judge Charles Elly (Chairman of Trustees and President of the Old Borlasian Club), HRH The Duke of Gloucester and Dr Peter Holding (Headteacher)

The Modern Era (1974-2024)

meant that yet more building was needed. Fundraising began again and, after a nearly 10-year campaign, the School was able to commission Borlase parent and architect Tom Russell to design an innovative modern building to house the Sixth Form and provide additional Mathematics teaching space as well as a café for School use. The challenge was to build on the existing crowded site and, as a result, the building was located in between three existing structures: the Hall and the Science and Maths buildings. The white cubed building, officially opened in September 2016, was a substantial departure from the traditional brick and flint architecture of Borlase's original buildings, but provided an elegant solution to the lack of open spaces for building.

Apart from being a period of expansion and related building works, the period from 2000 to 2020 was marked in particular by two other broad trends, both developed in response to central government decisions. Since the 1988 Education Reform Act, schools in England had enjoyed a growth in their autonomy, with a progressive reduction of Local Authority control. This process accelerated in the first decade of the twenty-first century, with progressively less support from the County. These changes resulted in greater freedoms over budgets and curriculum design, and the School began to introduce new subjects as well as a huge expansion in the wider curriculum, including sports, clubs and societies. This expansion was in turn linked to the second major development by the Department for Education: to encourage schools to identify a particular aspect of their curriculum in which to become designated a 'specialist school'. Building on its already rich traditions in Drama and Music in particular, the School opted to become a Specialist School for the Performing Arts in 2005. The School was able to create a second Deputy Headteacher role to lead the development of Performing Arts; in September of that year, Kay Mountfield joined the School, and she would later succeed Dr Holding as Headteacher. Dance was added to the curriculum, with two new Dance Studios located in what had recently been the Biology Department. The sounds of music and footsteps echoed through the windows above the archway and out on to West Street. The decision to develop the Arts was also driven by a desire to have a greater role in the local community, and outreach work into all the local schools to support the Arts became a core part of the School's identity in this decade.

The decision to become co-educational had brought huge benefits to the School, but it also presented challenges. Throughout the 1990s, although the size of the School grew, the actual numbers of boys declined with full co-education. Competing on an even footing with the traditional local sporting rivals, such as John Hampden, the Royal Grammar School and the other Bucks grammar schools, became more challenging and simultaneously there was an inevitable demand for provision for girls as well as for more co-educational activities. For every traditional sporting success from the past, there rapidly became a demand for, and then an expectation of, success for girls. The two traditional core Borlase sports of Rowing and Hockey particularly felt the pressure, and Dr Holding took the innovative decision to introduce specialist professional coaching for each, first with Dave Currie as Director of Rowing in 2007 and then with Mike Irving as Director of Hockey in 2010. The steady stream of individual and team successes was thereby continued, and the names of girls joined the growing list of Hockey and Rowing internationals on the honours boards in the Cloisters.

The search for yet more facilities began. Indeed, the search for a new permanent base for Rowing began as early as 1995, when Borlase parent and volunteer coach, Richard Bedingfield, identified more than 35 potential locations along the river near to Marlow, and quiet investigations began to identify a viable site. This process continued throughout the next 25 years and would eventually result in the creation of a joint venture with Great Marlow School and the identification and purchase of a site near to the A404 bypass and opposite Longridge, where Rowing will be given long-term security of tenure, nearly 150 years after it began at the School. Finding new facilities for Hockey proved slightly less difficult, as the School was able to become a partner with Marlow Sports Club in their development of the facilities on Pound Lane, about half a mile from the School.

3.3.4. The new Sixth Form building, opened in 2016

3.3.5. Dr Peter Holding retired as Headmaster in January 2018

Sports and the Performing Arts thrived throughout Dr Holding's tenure, with a constantly expanding range of Music, with multiple choirs and instrumental ensembles as well as a thriving academic option leading to GCSEs and A levels. The School began to see a steady stream of Borlasians going on to study Music, Drama and Dance at higher education, including elite Academies. The wider curriculum also expanded hugely, linked in part to the growth of the Sixth Form, but also to the growing commitment by the School to education in the widest sense. This ambition had long been part of the School's ethos, growing from its origins and the motto *Te Digna Sequere*, but it now came ever more firmly to the foreground. Societies with foci ranging from Physics to Feminism, from Young Enterprise to World Challenge, and from Debating to Design all flourished. Borlasians became known as incredibly busy people.

Academic success in its more traditional sense also thrived, as the School performed consistently towards the top of national league tables for both GCSEs and A Levels. During this period, it continued to be the norm that Borlase students would progress to university and increasingly to elite institutions, including, of course, Oxford and Cambridge Universities, but also Performing Arts academies, as well as to institutions specializing in everything from Technology to Psychology.

By 2012, when the School was recognized as Outstanding in its next Ofsted report, Borlase was the most oversubscribed school in Buckinghamshire and was asked to shrink its catchment area to alleviate pressure on places. As part of a redrafting of all Bucks school boundaries in 2015, it agreed to this reduction, resulting in fewer children attending from Maidenhead and High Wycombe. The pressures of this growth in popularity had created tensions with local residents, who felt that they were missing out on their local School, forgetting that Borlase had traditionally taken boys from much further afield. These changes eased the pressures slightly, but the School continued to be heavily oversubscribed. The period of threatened closure for the School seemed a distant memory.

In 2015, the Governors agreed to yet another recommendation for change from Dr Holding, and the School became an Academy. The Academy movement, first introduced in the early 2000s, had gained momentum around 2010. Academies had yet greater autonomy from Local Authority control and were funded directly by central government. They also had greater curricular freedoms. In 2016, Borlase converted from being a single Academy to being part of the Marlow Education Trust, a Multi-Academy Trust, yet another central government innovation, and another step towards full autonomy. The School effectively became a government-funded charitable company, in some ways taking it back to its original foundations. This change allowed the School to expand its commitment to working in partnership with local schools and had as its founding aim the furtherance of education for children in the Marlow area, not just at Borlase. It immediately joined with Beechview Primary School in High Wycombe and began discussions with other schools in and around Marlow.

Dr Holding retired as Headmaster in January 2018, to become the CEO of the Marlow Education Trust, but expansion proved a slower process than originally anticipated and, with the advent of the coronavirus disease 2019 (COVID-19) pandemic, further expansion was put on hold for several years.

KAY L. MOUNTFIELD (2018–2023)

Kay Mountfield was appointed as Deputy Head in 2005 to lead the School's new commitment to developing the Performing Arts and making Borlase a centre of excellence for both students and the Marlow community. Kay's passion for music, dance, drama, literature and all things creative had been developed while growing up in Wales; she had studied English with Drama at Royal Holloway College, University of London, and Education at Swansea University. She taught English and Drama at The Windsor Boys' School, was Head of Drama at Edgbarrow School, and moved to Head of Sixth Form, Head of Drama and later a Senior Leader at Windsor Girls' School, before joining Borlase. She had also directed operas for Windsor and Eton Opera and founded the Royal Borough Youth Opera,

The Modern Era (1974-2024) | CHAPTER 3 | 113

3.4.1. Miss Kay Mountfield (Headteacher 2018–2023)

and was producing annual performances at the Farrer Theatre in Eton College. She continued to lead the Youth Opera until 2012, with many Borlasians in the casts.

When Dr Holding retired as Headteacher of the School in January 2018 to lead the new Multi-Academy Trust, Miss Mountfield stepped into the Acting Head role and, in April, was appointed by the Governors as the first female Headteacher at Borlase on a permanent basis (Mrs Crittenden having been the Acting Head in 1996–1997). Mr James Simpson, who was Kay's Acting Deputy, was also appointed into the permanent position and, supported by an excellent and established senior leadership team, the School reviewed its curriculum, with Heads of Department having ownership of the design of its content and sequencing. Teaching and learning pedagogy was developing quickly, and the lexicon around learning strategies reflected this change. Research into metacognition and the role it has in empowering students to learn and remember excited the Staff at Borlase; as a Teaching School, Borlase was training excellent teachers and building the skills of the established team. In 2019, High Performance Learning awarded Borlase with World Class School Status. Dr Ben Parsons led on Teaching and Learning, with Rachael Holmes driving the Values and Character Education. From the Curriculum Review, a new Curriculum Vision and Purpose was established and embraced across the team of specialist teachers at the School: 'Inspire, Empower to Shape the Future'. Borlasians continue to be taught by inspirational teachers who are experts in their disciplines; recruiting and growing these teachers in times of recruitment crisis became a focus of the School. Miss Mountfield believed wholeheartedly in the talent of Borlase students and their ability as independent learners to extend themselves with the right encouragement and empowerment. The academic societies that had started with the Medical Society (MedSoc) and the History Society in 2010 had blossomed over the years into a culture of more than 30 societies.

The Extended Project and The Production Arts BTEC had been introduced by Miss Mountfield when she was Deputy Head to extend more able students; it became clear that all Borlase students benefited from these extension opportunities.

In 2019, Borlase was selected by the Department of Education to be one of only nine Modern Foreign Languages (MFL) Hubs working with the National Centre for Education in Languages. The bid and the work were led by Mrs Jenny Hopper, then Head of MFL, who continued to develop MFL pedagogy. The School played a key role nationally in developing National Centre for Excellence for Language Pedagogy (NCELP) resources for teachers around the country throughout the pandemic and beyond. Mrs Hopper also received a German Teacher Award in 2022 from the Embassy of the Federal Republic of Germany for services to German Language teaching.

In 2018, the Governors, chaired by Charlotte Redcliffe, supported Miss Mountfield's request to change the School's Admissions Policy to try to increase access to a grammar school for children in receipt of Pupil Premium (government funding for disadvantaged pupils to improve educational outcomes). Ten places were ring-fenced for children in the catchment area who could gain a place with a lower score in the 11+ test. The School set up a programme of workshops for children in local primary schools to study Maths, Science, English and Dance in the summer terms.

The Governors also approved Miss Mountfield's request to bid for Expansion Funding for Grammar Schools; this was the first time a government had supported Grammar School expansion since the start of their phasing out in 1965. Borlase was highly oversubscribed, and there was a need to create provision for a small number of children in the villages near Stokenchurch who could not access a grammar school due to the distance rule. The School had been accepting an additional 25 children into Year 9 for many years, and this additional funding would enable the School to bring the extra intake forward into Year 7. With the introduction of the extra form of entry came the opportunity to bid for funding from the Department for Education to accommodate the students. The only new building for which the School would have a chance of receiving planning permission on the site was a Sports Hall, and there had been plans discussed and set out over recent years but the plans required funding. Building a Sports Hall would enable the School to repurpose other buildings that had become unfit and insufficient for the School where there was a need for specialist teaching spaces, and to expand catering and pastoral care resources. The bid was submitted in 2018 and, just in time for Christmas, the School was awarded £1.7 million to develop the Sports Hall.

It became apparent that £1.7 million was not going to cover the costs of the Sports Hall that the School wanted and needed and the further developments to support the School. The School had long been achieving excellence in sport while managing training with limited resources and having to play fixtures off site. Miss Mountfield made a number of determined appeals to Buckinghamshire Council for support. Over the coming months, she secured a further £1.9 million from local government; a bid to The Weston Foundation led to a further £100,000 of support, which was followed by many donations from individual Borlase families, alumni and businesses. At the same time, the Head and the Business Manager were submitting bids to the National Schools Condition Improvement Fund and, in 2019–2020, were successful in bringing in more than £2.5 million to renovate the Cloisters roofs and heating and the Chapel heating. (Most Old Borlasians will remember seeing their breath in front of them when they sang in Chapel during the winter months; the under-pew heating can now be switched on for a much more comfortable experience!)

There followed a season of substantial building and renovation that coincided with one of the School's most unusual and significant challenges in its 400-year history. The COVID-19 pandemic took the lives of hundreds of thousands of people around the world and changed day-to-day experiences for everyone. Another major casualty of COVID-19 was the education and personal development of children. In 2023, the world is still in the recovery period.

COVID-19 Pandemic
2019–2020 was Miss Mountfield's second full year as Headteacher. The academic year had started well, with outstanding achievements in the 2019 exams; Sport was thriving across the School, with a new 'Sport for All' vision, and Borlase was excelling in competitive Sport. A new Director of Rowing had been appointed to lead the School's success as a sculling centre, and the Performing Arts had reached another new high point with the success of the School's Musical, *Sweeney Todd* by Sondheim. On 5 March 2020, the School had a two-day assessment for the Quality of its Teaching and Learning and Leadership by Challenge Partners and was recognized as 'Excelling' at all levels. The calendar was packed with an annual programme of events, and Year 11 and Year 13 students were getting ready for their final exams.

On 19 March 2020, the Prime Minister, Boris Johnson, announced that all schools in the UK were to close the following day and that all GCSE and A Level Examinations would be cancelled. The COVID-19 pandemic had taken its grip worldwide, and all plans and the usual routines of Borlase life were put on hold. The following day, everyone came to School to pack their bags with anything they needed from their lockers and classrooms. The School Captains, Callum Kunchur and Georgia Tuke, put together a Leavers' Tribute overnight, and Year 13 gathered in the Hall for an assembly. They watched their seven years of Borlase celebrated in a showreel and stood up to sing the School Song, led by Miss Mountfield. Each year group came into the Hall with their teachers and were given their final assembly before saying goodbye, uncertain of what lay ahead. It was a very emotional and confusing morning; Year 13 and Year 11 students and teachers in particular had to process a complete change of focus regarding exams.

Miss Mountfield recalls how several students spoke to her in that moment of hurried departure, telling her that they did not want to go home and leave School and their friends. The School immediately leapt into action; Borlase was not going to lose its unique School community. That was a commitment made by the leadership team and all the Staff on Friday, 20 March 2020.

Borlase@home
Over the weekend, Miss Mountfield met with James Simpson and the Senior Leadership Team. Mr Simpson had been a great champion of Google Education and had established a strong culture of using the Google Education platform for learning at School; every child already had a laptop or Chromebook and a School Google account. On Monday morning, the Staff came into School to pack up their belongings and for some emergency training. The IT team stripped computers out of classrooms and offices to enable all Staff to work at home; James distributed visualizers (document cameras) to teachers and ordered more to be issued as soon as possible. Teachers were given a crash course by Mr Simpson and Dr Parsons on live Google Meet lessons; they emptied their rooms of what they needed and left the site.

That Monday evening, Miss Mountfield communicated with all Borlase parents and students that Borlase@home would be open for live teaching the following day — it would start with Tutor Time and Chapel Assembly, and all lessons would be delivered live into children's homes. There was an extraordinary will from everyone to make this work. Teachers met daily online after teaching to keep developing their pedagogy and technical skills. There was a commitment to keep all aspects of School life going — the Sports Staff developed Borlase@home training programmes and extracurricular opportunities; Mr Seth Miall, Director of Music, and Jenny Chislett, the Performing Arts Technician, developed an extraordinary programme of Music created online, and events went ahead — weekly Chapel, Key Stage Assemblies, Arts Dinner, Speech Day, Parents' Evenings, the Borlase Boost (a fundraising campaign to promote physical and mental health during lockdown) and Concerts all continued. VE Day was

3.4.2. Members of Cantorum participating in Borlase@home Music during the COVID-19 pandemic

The Modern Era (1974-2024) | CHAPTER 3 | 115

3.4.3. The new Sports Hall and Hockey pitch on Home Meadow

celebrated, and the School engaged in discussions on Black Lives Matter with subjects relating to their curriculum. For a glimpse of what Borlase@home looked like, visit the School's YouTube Channel, which still has virtual assemblies and celebrations online. It includes some moving choral recordings painstakingly edited into Zoom and, with his characteristic exuberance, Mr Miall engaged the staff in a version of *Hey Jude* sung from their living rooms around the area.

A whole new language for learning developed as Staff and students learned to mute and unmute, and use Pear Deck (an online interactive presentation tool) and other discussion strategies. The Senior Leadership Team were determined to keep the regular rhythm of School going for all children, considering the children we wanted to have return to School — confident, connected and ready to adjust back to normal School life whenever that would be. Tutors met children every morning; the pastoral Staff held safeguarded mentoring and support sessions with individuals, and School counselling continued and developed online. The Head and Deputy Head Boys and Girls had a task like no others previously, and Leon Tasch, Imogen Baguley, Olly Gale and Charlotte Farmer rose to its demands: academic societies and clubs met daily online, and friends presented papers on Politics, Astrophysics and everything in between.

The Borlase parents were incredibly appreciative and supportive. Many were having to support home-learning for younger children and manage their own jobs online; knowing that their child was attending a full day of lessons via Borlase@home was reassuring. In many ways, the months of Borlase@home brought our School community closer together, and parents gained some insight into the world of the classroom as it took place in their kitchens and living rooms. Some even listened in to live-streamed Chapel assemblies!

Another extraordinary and exceptional feature of Borlase@home was the Staff's commitment to teaching Year 11 and Year 13 to prepare them for A Levels and university, even though they had no exams. Teachers completed their courses and, for Year 11 and the 250 external applicants, there was a whole programme of pre-Sixth Form learning delivered to them, each with their individual Borlase Google accounts set up by Mr Simpson.

The School recognized the challenges of students and Staff being online and on-screen for long days so, in May, the School day was shortened to give children and families time in the afternoon to go out and take exercise on those long, hot summer days of 2020.

3.4.4. Completion of the new Sports Hall: Kay Mountfield and James Simpson (Headteacher and Deputy Headteacher, centre), with Chris Duggan (Director of Sport, far left), Catt McLeod (Finance Director, third from left), Tom Russell and his team (architects, right) and members of Glencar Construction

From March to July, the School was eerily empty. Classrooms and Cloisters were silent; Colonel's Meadow was bathed in sunshine but abandoned by human life; there was no singing or music to be heard from the Theatre. The Library area was open for the children of Key Workers, and this provision was extended to students who found learning at home challenging and those whose home Wi-Fi was unreliable. Miss Rhian Williams, the Designated Safeguarding Lead at the time, led Key Worker School, and she, Miss Holmes and Miss Mountfield were in School virtually every day, including holidays, supported by a Senior Leadership Team rota and rotas of Sports and administrative Staff.

While the School was quiet, this was an ideal time to proceed with the building development, if the resources and building contractors could be made available. The architect, Tom Russell, had designed the Sports Hall building, which included a Fitness Suite and Sports Science classroom, and was ready to proceed. To build the Sports Hall, the School needed to replace the playing field footage and could do this by taking up the tennis courts on Quoitings, which were in need of a complete overhaul, and laying a grass football field in their place. This meant laying new tennis/netball courts on the land at the top of the School, above Home Meadow. The Hockey AstroTurf had served the School well but was not big enough to accommodate the School's enormous Hockey programme led by Nathan Monk, Director of Hockey, and Kevin Chappell. With the additional funds raised, the School could have a much larger Hockey AstroTurf laid on Home Meadow next to the new Sports Hall. With the country in complete lockdown, some decisions had to be made around the availability of materials but, importantly, construction workers were allowed to work. The building proceeded, and Tom Russell's stunning Sports Hall rose up while the students studied at home. Via Borlase@home, Miss Mountfield presented the Sports Lottery, which raised a further £50,000 towards kitting out the Hall. For much of the lockdown, the Cloisters were also clad in scaffolding as the roofs started to be replaced. When the students returned to School in September 2020, the work was almost finished.

CAGs and TAGs

With the cancellation of exams, the School was plunged into another challenge. The Secretary of State for Education, Gavin Williamson MP, announced that schools would have to allocate Centre-Assessed Grades (CAGs) to students based on evidence gathered across the academic year. Previous mocks and tests could be used, and greater value was to be given to tests taken nearest to the lockdown and sat under controlled conditions. There was very little information for schools and students, and Staff were in a limbo as Ofqual (the Office of Qualifications and Examinations Regulation) and JCQ (the Joint Council for Qualifications) gradually produced advice and guidance. However, when the guidance came, there were vast tomes to plough through, and schools effectively became examining boards and appeals bodies for their own students. Louise Walder, then Director of Studies, now Deputy Headteacher, pored through pages with the Head and the Examinations Officer, Lesley Haldane. The Government dictated the process, which included teachers blind marking and moderating all work before reaching a final grade that needed to reflect previous grades achieved by schools. The Borlase Staff worked tirelessly at this task; the work was relentless. The classes of 2020 had no opportunity to revise for final examinations; their grades had to be based on the evidence that schools had in March.

Borlase submitted their marks in line with Government guidance, and the results for GCSE and A Level looked to be marginally better than those for 2019, with the usual year-on-year improvement. However, on Results Day, the School and students were presented with a very different picture. Gavin Williamson had instructed Ofqual to apply an algorithm to schools' grades intended to, it was said, ensure fairness. When Borlase received their A Level results, they were lower than any results that the School had ever achieved and considerably lower than the grades submitted. Almost 80% of students had missed their university offer. Miss Mountfield and her team were furious; there was outcry across the country where thousands of state school students had been deprived of the grades honestly awarded to them. Meanwhile, on the websites of several independent schools, there were flagrant celebrations of increases in A* grades by 60%! The only channel of appeal was for schools to put forward a case for any subject in which they felt that the algorithm had unfairly distorted the marks; this was just about every subject at Borlase. Louise Walder and Maths teachers Mark Campbell and Bevan Marchand began the laborious process of analysing subject by subject what had happened to the numbers.

Meanwhile, Kay rallied the press, being interviewed on Radio 4 and being published in *The Daily Telegraph*. Working through the night, Mr Campbell cracked the algorithm and identified how it had been applied to larger set sizes only. Borlase, like many large state school sixth forms and sixth form colleges, had been hit hard, whereas independent schools with small class sizes had been ignored. To make it worse, where schools had submitted inflated grades, they had not been moderated by Exam Boards and were instead left unchallenged. As Mrs Walder presented the findings to Miss Mountfield, she had an opportunity to speak on BBC News 24. Live on air, they exposed the flaws in the algorithm and accused the Government of robbing state school students of their grades, while allowing others to claim higher grades. Mr Campbell's bell curve was shared with the nation. Half an hour later, the BBC called the School to tell them to listen to a Government announcement. CAGs were reinstated, and almost all Borlase students attained their university places. When GCSE grades were awarded, CAGs were immediately accepted. This brought its own complications — Year 12 ended up with almost 240 students — but the School managed to make it work.

The workload of CAGs was surpassed only by the unconscionable system of Teacher-Assessed Grades (TAGs) that followed for the academic year 2020–2021. TAGs were put forward by the Department for Education as the solution to disrupted learning and missed time at school. This time, schools were asked to design assessments, mark assessments and moderate them across the year — while still being told that there may possibly be final examinations. Students experienced the incredibly stressful and protracted process of permanently sitting tests that would count towards their final grades. The government was slow to tell them that they would not sit external exams in addition to the continuous assessment, adding to the uncertainty and anxiety. Borlase students and Staff were remarkable in their stoicism and resilience. Mrs Walder again led the process, and teachers spent what added up to months of time setting, marking, moderating, recording and then filing boxes and boxes of work that filled the Staffroom. Schools were again examiners and managing appeals.

Bubbling and Social Distancing

The 2020 lockdown had been a long stretch. Much as Borlase@home had done its best to keep everyone safe and together online, being able to come back to live School after the summer holiday was everyone's aim. To bring everyone back in September meant another transformation of the School; Borlase would be ready for this new world, and the School resembled a dystopian commune. Before the return, the Senior Leadership Team had rewritten the School systems and risk assessments again, and teachers had to develop another completely new way of teaching.

Without vaccinations, the protection for adults and young people were social distancing, washing of hands (while singing the School Song!), ventilation and wearing of masks. Following Government guidance, students needed to be put into 'bubbles'. In secondary schools, bubbles had to be whole year groups — there was no other way of managing more than one thousand children on a site. This meant separating year groups from one another from the moment they arrived to the moment they left School. To achieve this, the School day was restructured to create six rolling break times across the day. To create the spaces, Miss Mountfield had three 200-square-foot marquees erected on Colonel's Meadow: one would be a very well-ventilated Dance Space; the others would be break spaces to keep year groups apart. Mrs Walder devised a new timetable with three long lessons per day, and the leadership team were effectively on a continuous break-supervision duty that lasted three hours.

In the summer holidays, Ray Kipping and the site-management team had erected Perspex screens around all teachers' desks and had cordoned off a 2-metre area around them. They installed outdoor sinks and put up orange signs everywhere indicating how and where to stand 2 metres apart. The biometric fingerprinting system was replaced by a card reader, and differently coloured lanyards were ordered for each year group so that Staff and students could easily tell to which bubble children belonged. In classrooms and all spaces, there were bottles of sanitizer and COVID-19 cleaner and reams of paper towels. Children would wipe down their desks as they arrived at each class and again as they left. No books or paper were used for work; everyone submitted their work via Google Classrooms. Staff could not stand within 2 metres of any child or each other, and students stuck to seating plans so that the School would always know which child had been within 2 metres of any child who tested positive for COVID-19.

Staff could not meet each other. They operated in individual bubbles to try to avoid passing the virus on to one another. Despite the majority of the working population still 'working from home', teachers and support Staff returned to School. Mr Nicholls made hundreds of clear-plastic face visors in Technology for teachers to wear, so that students could read their lips. He also made hundreds for the local primary schools in the area, and these were distributed to teachers who were also very nervous about the return. Wearing cloth masks or clear Perspex visors and blue rubber gloves, they taught classrooms of students also wearing masks, confined to their individual desks. However, everyone was so glad to be back. After months of speaking to one another via screens, it was joyous to see children running around on the fields again and talking masked face to masked face.

The Borlase Staff again showed incredible resilience and determination to give their students the best educational experience that they could have. Lessons were prepared to make a two-hour stint engaging and, at break times, students could resume extracurricular activities. The hands of the PE Department Staff were raw with wiping down Hockey sticks, oars and balls to enable sport to take place. All fixtures and competitions were cancelled, but all sorts of creative ideas were tried to bring fun and competitiveness into year group sport. Mr Miall was absolutely determined that Music performances would go ahead and would be back live: this was another focus for Borlase. Unable to have students singing or playing next to each other, rehearsing a choir required extraordinary management. Year groups of singers were spread out over the three huge marquees, all open to the elements. Mr Miall set up his electric piano on the field and ran from one marquee to the other to keep people in time. Instrumentalists sat spaced apart, with brass and wind musicians directing their instruments through open windows!

September to December 2020 was a bumpy ride for all schools. As the weather became cooler, the COVID-19 case numbers started to rise again. The daily bulletins from Matt Hancock MP (Secretary of State for Health) and Professor Chris Whitty (Chief Medical Officer) showed the R number increase, and death rates in the UK were in the tens of thousands. There was genuine fear and anxiety. However, having been home for a whole term once, nobody at School wanted to go back to that. The School ran a tight operation. If a Staff member or student experienced any symptoms of COVID-19, they had to stay home and test using a PCR testing centre. Any child or adult who had spent more than 10 minutes within 2 metres of that

3.4.5. Outdoor music concert in December 2020

person, or had been face to face with that person, also had to go home. The isolation period was 10 days. Matron, Nicky Day, and the Head's PA, Claire Woodgate, managed the COVID-19 register on a daily basis, recording the isolation dates and return-to-School dates. If students were at home and well, they could tune in live and be part of their lessons via Google Meet.

As the School moved into December, a new wave of COVID-19 struck the School, and Miss Mountfield and Mr Simpson would go into classrooms on a daily basis to extract students to send them home. Children would be spaced apart in the Cloisters waiting to be collected by parents; some kept smiling, others fought back the tears. In the last week of term, the choirs went to All Saints' Church to rehearse for the Carol Service that they had been working on in those windy marquees all term. Miss Mountfield recalls seeing the despair on the faces of Dr Parsons and Mr Miall as singer after singer was required to quarantine: "Not our best tenors!". The service went ahead together with an outdoor music concert performed to families in cars, supported by Brand Events. Again, Borlase was out on its own, delivering an outstanding programme of Music to be enjoyed in the homes around Marlow and far beyond as grandparents and relatives watched the live-streamed service from around the world. The identification of positive COVID-19 cases continued into the holidays, and it was the responsibility of schools to keep informing parents of any 'close contacts' who had to isolate for 10 days. On Christmas morning, the Senior Leadership Team had to call a number of families to inform them that their child needed to be isolated from the family for Christmas — these were tough times.

In the Christmas holidays, Boris Johnson presented schools with another new challenge. The vaccination was still in development and, in the meantime, testing had become the next-best solution to keep children in schools and get the country back to work. The Department for Education announced that schools would be issued with Lateral Flow Test kits and that all children would need to be tested three times in order to come back to school. They would need to be tested weekly. Another transformation for Borlase! Kay went to see Ray Kipping, who was immediately up for the challenge and sourced plywood to construct a test centre of cubicles. A vast army of volunteer parents and teachers were recruited to come into School and train as testers, processors or guides to be ready for the return. Again, the wider Borlase community pulled together. There was a collective energy to make sure that our young people were able to carry on coming to School, whatever it took.

Lockdown 2: Borlase@home
On 1 January 2021, the Government announced that schools would not be opening for the start of term; it would be 8 March before Borlase could open its gates again. The next term of Borlase@home was a challenge for everyone. The School had done this before, and the novelty of doing everything online had worn off. The enthusiasm for virtual learning had certainly waned, and the Year 11s and Year 13s in particular were anxious about what they would face in terms of exams. The Staff soldiered on with online teaching; this time

3.4.6. COVID-19 testing cubicles

3.4.7. Concert in Higginson's Park at the end of the summer term 2021 more of them came into School and taught from their empty classrooms, because teaching a class from their living rooms while managing family life had added further challenges. The work of the pastoral team was stretched online as students started to struggle. Key Worker School expanded as students just needed to come in occasionally to be with people.

Teachers prepared online assessments for exam groups but these were difficult to manage, and mock exams were delayed to give students the opportunity to have live assessments. There was incredible uncertainty as schools awaited clarity from Gavin Williamson on assessment — schools would be given papers with elements of courses removed, but information was held back, making planning impossible. Borlase students just carried on learning, completing courses via online lessons and working hard independently.

The long, dark days at home and hours of screen time were taking their toll, so Borlase developed the #DoSomethingDifferentDay. All lessons were cancelled on 10 February 2021, and students had online cookery classes from Tom Kerridge's head chef, lessons on cake-making from Burgers of Marlow, a nature trail from wildlife presenter Chris Packham, and opportunities to do all sorts of offline crafts. That helped everyone into half-term.

The Government confirmed that schools could return on 8 March. There was still a lot of fear across the country as the vaccination was just starting to be rolled out. Teachers were not vaccinated, and it would be April before 12–18 year olds would receive the vaccination. Before Borlase could bring students on site, the testing had to be completed; the testing centre had been built for January, and the volunteers just needed to be recalled. Students and Staff were tested twice before 8 March, coming into School three days apart. They lined up — socially distanced — to be tested. Their last tests were done in class on 8 March, and School was able to start on day one. Teaching and learning were back into bubbles and social distancing until the summer term, when positive case numbers began to fall and the School resumed its five-lesson days. Borlase reintroduced outdoor Sports and Dance, and the summer term culminated in a wonderful open-air concert at Higginson's Park supported by Brand Events, who had provided all the Marlow schools with a stage. It poured with rain but spirits were high as everyone sat on deckchairs under umbrellas.

In the 400-year history of Sir William Borlase's Grammar School, never had the physical operations been so changed and never had the emotional lives of young people and the adults who supported them been so tested. The School could be enormously proud of every member of its close community — students, Staff, parents and governors. However, the effects of COVID-19 and the simultaneous exponential growth of dependency on social media that developed in that period presented to young people and adults new challenges and opportunities.

Back on Track

For the years after the pandemic, the School made a commitment to ensure that Borlase students did not miss out on either their academic learning or, to support this, their personal development. Miss Holmes' role as Assistant Head focused on personal development, and she introduced an outdoor education experience for all year groups to support wellbeing and the development of confidence. Sport resumed with a full list of fixtures, and Mr Miall put on two musical shows in a year — one for seniors and one for juniors. Supporting Mental Health became a substantial part of the School's role, and the School's work with young people's Special Educational Needs became, and continues to be, a focus and a strength of the School.

The opening of the Sports Hall, Fitness Suite and wider outdoor Sports Campus allowed for other buildings in the School to be repurposed. The old Gymnasium became a training space for the thriving Rowing programme, with the old training room and adjoining changing rooms being given to Music for teaching, recitals and peripatetic teaching rooms. The infill building was divided into two floors of Maths teaching spaces, and the Sixth Form returned to the bigger study spaces in the C Block Library area for private study. In the Hall Block, a new suite of 30 gender-neutral toilets was installed (better toilets had been top of the students' list of improvements needed for decades!).

The Cloisters rooms were converted into a Pastoral and Learning-support Hub, with counselling rooms and a decompression space. Rooms were created for Language Assistants where there had been a block of toilets, and a new Computer Room was created to accommodate this subject, which was growing in popularity at all levels.

In January 2023, Miss Mountfield announced that she would be stepping down as Headteacher at the end of the academic year. As her successor, the Governors appointed Mr Ed Goodall, previously the Deputy Headteacher of Dr Challoner's Grammar School. The Governors, supported by Dr Holding, the Performing Arts Staff and the new Headteacher, renamed the theatre The Mountfield Theatre in recognition of her work in the Performing Arts over 18 years at the School.

3.4.8. Kay Mountfield with School Captains Helena Kennedy and Sacha Smith outside the renamed Mountfield Theatre

Further building work was undertaken in 2023 to make the buildings fit for purpose going into the School's 400th anniversary year. A mezzanine level was added to the School Canteen to increase capacity, and the 1950s School Hall was converted into a study area for the Sixth Form. The opportunity was taken to remodel the south side of this building to be more in keeping with the Chapel quadrangle. Two stained-glass windows commemorating the 400th anniversary were generously donated, one by Barbara Robson and Rosalind Woollard (daughters of Old Borlasian Stuart Lever) and the other by the School Trustees. The windows were designed and crafted by Petri Anderson, who previously made the south window of the School Chapel.

In addition, after 20 years of research and planning, permission was finally granted for a new boathouse to be built for the combined use of Borlase and Great Marlow Schools. The boathouse was designed and developed by architect Tony Compton (OB 1957–1964) and will be situated near to where the Marlow bypass bridge crosses the Thames.

3.4.9. Designs for the stained-glass windows commemorating the School's 400th anniversary and the new School Boathouse

PERFORMING ARTS AND SPECIALIST SCHOOL STATUS

There are references to choirs and orchestral performances at Borlase in the earliest editions of *The Borlasian* magazines of the 1880s, and the 'Blue Boys' of Borlase walked to All Saints' Church in Marlow, where church singing was no doubt part of their wider education. Over the centuries, Borlase maintained a steady tradition for putting on concerts and staging annual productions in a range of venues; photographs included earlier in this book show performances of Shakespeare's *As You Like It* and *A Midsummer Night's Dream* being performed in 1905 and of Sheridan's *The Rivals* being performed in 1925. By 1928, the tradition of performing an annual School play was established, with plays being performed in the original School Hall in the Cloisters (which became classrooms and is currently the Drama Studio) and then in the School Hall from the 1970s through to the Theatre being opened in 2006. Plays were directed by enthusiastic teachers, Heads of English and even Headteachers, as you will have read in earlier chapters.

When Dr Peter Holding was appointed Headteacher in 1997, he came from a background of teaching Drama and English and was keen to strengthen the position of the Arts on the curriculum and beyond. Drama and Music were taught at GCSE and there were some excellent instrumental ensembles. One of his first appointments was a new Director of Music in 1997.

Patrick Gazard (Director of Music 1997–2009)

With the appointment of Patrick Gazard in 1997, the School saw an explosion of Musical Theatre. Over the space of six years, the tiny stage in the School Hall hosted productions of *Kiss Me, Kate*, *The Pajama Game*, *The Mikado* and *The Mystery of Edwin Drood*. Each production had its own stories associated with it. The on/off relationship in *Kiss Me, Kate* was mirrored in real life ("That slap sounded uncomfortably realistic to me!"). The complex combination of construction and lighting used to create *The Pajama Game*'s knife board was so effective that it led at least one younger member of the audience to question whether or not the actors were throwing real knives at each other. *The Mikado* was modernized and relocated to Waterloo station (though keeping the vast majority of Gilbert and Sullivan's words and music intact) and had a cast that included a future Hamlet for the Royal Shakespeare Company and one of the School's Sports teachers — and all delivered in the same week as an Ofsted inspection. Patrick Gazard also achieved a first at Borlase by writing an original oratorio, *The Fall of Troy*, with Hugh Robson for a cast of soloists, chorus and orchestra and performed for two nights in October 2004.

These were the days of the CD, which recorded the development of Borlase music over those years. Discs included *The Borlase Sound* in 1999; two *April in Venice* CDs chronicling 2002's Jazz and Gospel Choir tour to Italy; and two CDs courtesy of Young Enterprise companies in 1998 and Forte in 2004, the former finishing with *Just Our Bill*, which opened with a new arrangement of *Snakehips Swings Again* (a tribute to famous wartime bandleader and Old Borlasian Ken 'Snakehips' Johnson). Competition success put the School on the local and national map, and the years 1999–2003 proved to be prolific for two of Borlase's senior groups. Firstly the Jazz Orchestra: Music for Youth finalists in 1999, which led to a summer appearance at the Royal Festival Hall, and finalists again in 2003. That was matched by the remarkable rise of the Gospel Choir, formed at the turn of the millennium by student Lauren Keenan, before being named top Senior School Choir at the Sainsbury's Choir of the Year just two years later.

Patrick Gazard initiated the concept of student leadership, which has been developed by the following Directors of Music and has become a feature of Music at Borlase. A few more firsts: 1998 saw the start of the biennial House Music Competition; in 2001, Gazard's original jazz piece *Five Gold Rings*, composed as a tribute to Marlow's Olympian Sir Steve Redgrave, was premiered at the Marlow Town Regatta. In 2002, the School enjoyed a visit from international concert pianist Wayne Marshall to 'christen'

3.5.1. The cast of an early twentieth-century School play in the Cloisters

the new grand piano and, in the spring of that same year, the Upper Sixth 'Bondsongs' routine unwittingly started the tradition of the Leavers' Medley. Alongside all the above, there were the numerous concerts and events, both in and out of School, where our musicians continued to spread the message that, if music was your passion, Borlase was the place to be. In the Music department with Patrick were Jacqui Martinez, Melanie Macfarlane, Robina Redgard-Siler and an outstanding and loyal team of visiting peripatetic music teachers, without whom Borlase would not have had such a wonderful set of young musicians with whom to work. Their legacy lives on, both in terms of the students they inspired — at least four are current Heads of Music and one is a West End Musical Director — and in terms of the musical tradition that followed and continues to this day.

Specialist School Status
In 2003, the Governors supported Dr Holding's decision to apply for Specialist School Status for the Performing Arts. The Specialist Schools and Academy Trust had been launched initially by John Major in 1993 but was developed into a flagship policy of Tony Blair's 1997 Government. Schools could apply for grants, which came with an annual commitment of an extra £129 per pupil for four years to be spent on developing opportunities in the specialist area for the benefit of the school and the wider community. This money paid for resources to be developed but, above all, it paid for time to be given to Staff to run and develop programmes. Dr Holding submitted a successful bid, which was to have a substantial effect on enriching the School's culture and the Arts around Marlow. He planned to submit a further bid for Science when invited.

To support the delivery of his ambitions, he spearheaded the design, fundraising and building of a new centre that would house a Theatre, Music Rooms, Recording Studio, and Design and Technology Suite. The Drama Studio was converted into a Dance Studio ready for the introduction of Dance as a separate subject. In September 2005, he created a second Deputy Headteacher role to lead the specialism and gave Kay Mountfield the freedom and support to drive a creative curriculum, with Dance joining Music, Drama and Art as a weekly lesson for all Key Stage 3 students and available at GCSE and A Level. Music Technology and Production Arts BTEC also became Sixth Form options, making it possible for Borlase students to discover and develop passions and talents that would shape their lives and characters. Borlase is deeply proud of the many students who have progressed to Music and Drama conservatoires, top Dance schools such as London Contemporary, Trinity Laban and Rambert, becoming professional performers, or just continuing their love of the Arts. Claire Hindley was appointed as the first Head of Dance, and she developed an ambitious curriculum for the School, including cross-curricular work with Chemistry, Physics, Geography and Languages and much more! She took contemporary Dance to local primary schools, supported by A Level dancers and started a tradition in which the primary school pupils would perform in the Borlase Theatre.

To address the School's commitment to develop the Arts in the community, Borlase planned to set up a Theatre Company in Residence. Simultaneously, Miss Mountfield was looking for someone who could help her to introduce a qualification to recognize the amazing work being done by enthusiastic Borlasians in sound and lighting. Mark Hartley, Head of Production Arts at Amersham and Wycombe College, came to School for an informal conversation about the BTEC; he left having decided to teach Production Arts to Borlase students and to establish a new Marlow Youth Theatre Company, 'JAM Theatre', based at Borlase. After 17 years, JAM Theatre continues to thrive in Marlow. Michael 'Tocky' Tock was one of the first students to complete the BTEC at Borlase. Highly innovative and passionate about theatre technology, Michael was operating and often making the lighting and special effects for Borlase productions; he left with a Distinction and used this qualification to support his place reading Engineering at York University. Borlase has gone on to produce many students who have gained places at the Guildhall School of Music & Drama, the Royal Central School of Speech and Drama, the Liverpool Institute for Performing Arts and other top conservatoires and who are now running West End shows.

With Performing Arts Status, Borlase was able to employ a full-time technician. Jenny Chislett, who joined in 2007, brought a wealth of talent to the School, leading the Technical Theatre Club for students from Year 7 who would go on to train with Mark Hartley in the Sixth Form. The School installed a computerized sound and lighting system and developed resources alongside the talent and experience of the students; Borlase production values, with bespoke sets and technical support, became widely recognized. Drama, Music and Dance all grew at the School, both on the curriculum and as extracurricular activities.

In 2010, the new coalition government stopped the funding of Specialist Schools after a Comprehensive Spending Review. However, Borlase was committed to continuing its programme of excellence for the Arts and, likewise, to investing in Science. The Borlase School Fund, entitled 'Above and Beyond', was changed to 'Here and Now'. Borlase parents continue to support the funding of wider opportunities via the Here and Now fund. The School is dependent on their generosity and the unstinting enthusiasm and dedication of Staff who deliver the full programmes, volunteering their time.

Dance
The first Head of Department, Claire Hindley, set the standard for Dance at Borlase and continues to teach at the School part time. She was joined by Kirsty Ashby, who became Head of Department when Claire started her family, and Dance has grown and thrived under their years of leadership. The Elite Dance Company EVOLVE was established, with students auditioning to be part of the company and working with different professional choreographers to create highly innovative dance. The School has more than ten Dance Companies, with small ensembles covering a range of Dance styles. Their work, including stunning original choreography, is shared and celebrated in the annual Dance Show. Dancers have performed at festivals and Dance shows alongside professional companies. One of the School's annual highlights is the Year 8 Strictly Come Dancing

3.5.2. A Year 7 Dance project 'The Lost Words' in 2018, and A Level dancers, led by Josh Bojarzin, performing original contemporary dance choreography

3.5.3. The EVOLVE Elite Dance Company and A Level dancer Harry Fayers in 2022

Competition, which began in 2008. The School is transformed into the Blackpool Ballroom, and guest judges are invited to sit alongside School stalwarts who have to prep their knowledge of fleckerls and heel turns. Introducing Dance to boys and girls from Year 7 opened up Dance to young people with no previous experience. A Boys' Dance Company was established by Mrs Ashby, which grew to include more than 60 male dancers. Central to its success is the presence of senior male dancers working alongside beginners, who ensure the chain for having a passion for Dance is not broken. Some of the Boys' Dance Company's most memorable achievements were their pieces in 2014 and 2018 to mark 100 years since the start and end of World War I. In 2022, Savanna Ranmarine was appointed Head of Dance; her department still includes Mrs Hindley, Mrs Ashby and now ex-Borlase Dance student Holly Lidgate.

The Modern Era (1974-2024)   CHAPTER 3 | 125

Music

Performing Arts Status allowed Music to grow on the curriculum and beyond, positioning Borlase as the School to which to apply to study Music. In 2009, Dr Ben Parsons was appointed as Director of Music. Having studied at Cardiff, Oxford and Cambridge Universities, Dr Parsons was not only an excellent academic teacher of Music, he was also a talented orchestral and choral conductor. He developed the Borlase Symphony Orchestra and Strings Orchestra and he set up a Junior Orchestra to grow the musicians who would feed into the senior ensembles. A separate Concert Band was established, and smaller ensembles for Brass, Wind and Strings led by students soon followed. The students quickly rose to the challenge of exciting professional repertoire. Highlights over the years included Mozart and Beethoven overtures, Prokofiev's *Romeo and Juliet Suite*, Elgar's *Cello Concerto* with student cellist Alexander Garrett, and string suites by Elgar, Grieg, Holst and Tchaikovsky.

Dr Parsons introduced the formal Nine Lessons and Carols Service that has become a much-loved tradition at All Saints' Church attended by Borlasians and their families every Christmas. An excellent choral director, he grew Cantorum to a choir of more than 100 voices and introduced a programme of seven choral groups that were designed to be progressive in terms of challenge of repertoire and age group as students grew through the School. The programme included the male broken-voice choir, Madriguys. He also introduced the tradition of inviting an Alumni Choir to form, with one rehearsal in the afternoon, before performing at the Carol Service for families in the evening.

Working with Mark Hartley and Jenny Chislett, Ben also built on the School's enthusiasm for Rock Music, and the School was able to convert the Drama Studio in the Cloisters into a Cavern Club-style venue for the Rocktober concerts. Ben worked with a team of talented Music teachers in his time as Director of Music, including Melanie Macfarlane, Claire Carter and Natalie Long. He also continued to develop the in-house peripatetic Music service. The loyalty, commitment and generosity of instrumental and vocal teachers in sharing their musicianship with students has become a defining feature of the Music Department.

In 2016, Dr Parsons was promoted to Assistant Headteacher. This was a great boon to the Performing Arts as it retained his talent in the Music Department while opening up a vacancy for a new Director of Music. The School was delighted to appoint former Head Boy, Seth Miall, to the role in January 2016. As an alumnus of the School, Seth's career at Durham and Cambridge Universities and in teaching had been followed with interest; he had been Musical Director of Durham University's acclaimed Musical Theatre Company since his first year! Seth brought a further new wave of energy, enthusiasm and talent to grow Music and Performing Arts and lead Borlase through some challenging times.

Mr Miall consolidated on the fantastic work by Dr Parsons, looking to maintain the numbers involved in musical groups and a high quality of performance, while continuing to develop further opportunities. He grew choral music further and particularly invested in junior musicians: his new choir, Youth Voices, was immediately popular, burgeoning into almost 100 girls and boys in Years 7–9. Mr Miall also looked to expand the junior musical production and also revived a large

3.5.4. Dr Ben Parsons with Phoebe and Isabella Mansell

3.5.5. Madriguys performing in 2013

3.5.6. The Senior Strings Orchestra in 2018, directed by Dr Ben Parsons, leader Mary-Anne Grego

School Concert Band, which would meet twice per term and prepare performances for the Autumn and Senior Concerts. Other senior groups such as the Symphony Orchestra, Senior Strings, Gospel Choir, Chapel Choir and Madriguys continued to thrive. The Alumni Choir also grew to the extent that the School now has to hold two evening Carol Services each Christmas.

Building on the introduction of 'Rocktober' a few years earlier, Mr Miall looked to increase the numbers of students involved in contemporary and rock music, introducing a weekly 'Rock Club', to give students the opportunity to form bands and to compose their own songs. A few years later, the Rock Music scene is flourishing, with several bands performing at venues in the local and wider community.

Borlase's rich affinity with Jazz Music — initially developed by Patrick Gazard and further enhanced by Mark Hartley — gained a new dose of energy when Mr Miall appointed Mr Simon Davie as Director of Jazz Bands and a Brass Peripatetic Music Teacher in September 2017. Under Mr Davie's leadership, Jazz Music at Borlase has substantially expanded, with both a large Jazz Orchestra for senior musicians and a Jazz Band for those with less experience, the latter giving students the opportunity to develop initial improvisation skills and an understanding of Blues and Jazz harmonies. The 'Jazz Night' has become a firm favourite with students and parents alike, and the Jazz Orchestra has been in increasing demand for performances at events outside of School. The strength of both Choral and Jazz Music in the School is to be celebrated, with a Cantorum and Jazz Orchestra International Music Tour to Tuscany in July 2023 — the first Borlase Music tour since 2002.

In a time of substantial change in education nationally, Mr Miall oversaw the revision of the School's Music curriculum and the introduction of new specifications for GCSE and A Level in 2018. Contrary to national trends, Borlase has continued to be the place for students to study the subject beyond Key Stage 3, with more than 90 students currently studying Music at GCSE across Years 9–11 and more than 20 studying it at A Level.

As we have heard, the COVID-19 pandemic and associated restrictions provided the Music Department with a range of challenges; however, Mr Miall and the Music Department were adamant that students' musical education needed to continue. In addition to adapting curriculum teaching to enable students to take part in Music lessons in their homes, no matter what resources they may have had, Mr Miall organized a programme of virtual ensemble performances in Spring 2020, edited by Mrs Chislett, which were uploaded to the School's YouTube channel. Peripatetic Music lessons, provided by fourteen teachers, also continued online. As soon as they were allowed, in-person rehearsals started again — albeit at first in marquees and in strict year-group bubbles. Mr Miall was determined that the Borlase Carol Service — such an important part of the Borlase tradition — took place in December 2020. Despite an increasingly bleak national picture, with the support of Miss Mountfield and All Saints' Church, the Music department was thrilled to undertake a socially distanced virtual Carol Service, with the students involved spread around the church. That same Christmas, the Jazz Orchestra and choirs performed in an outdoor concert at Marlow Rugby Club, organized by Brand Events.

These performance opportunities were so important in giving the students a sense of normality and enjoyment in what was a very difficult time. They also meant that musical activities never ceased and made the job of rebuilding Music and the Arts from September 2021 a little easier. Some restrictions were still in place in July 2021, and Mr Miall worked with JAM Theatre and Brand Events in organizing a Summer Concert in Higginson Park, featuring

3.5.7. Mr Seth Miall with Joe Parkinson

The Modern Era (1974-2024)　　　　CHAPTER 3　|　127

3.5.8. The annual Senior Music Medley, satirizing the Performing Arts Staff in 2017

all ensembles. The nature of the concert meant that we were likely to battle the elements — indeed it rained very heavily all evening — but that did not dampen the spirits of the hundreds of students involved, nor the parents watching on deck chairs under umbrellas!

Almost two years later, the Music Department is fully back in action, with no fewer than 20 extracurricular Music clubs taking place on a weekly basis, involving over half of the student body, and more than 250 students taking peripatetic Music lessons. In 2022, Mr Miall was promoted to Associate Assistant Headteacher and Director of Performing Arts and Music, to lead a team that included a new Head of Drama and Dance.

Drama
Drama was already a strength at Borlase, with decades of passionate teachers giving Borlasians opportunities to tread the boards. Performing Arts Status and the new facilities enabled the Head of Drama, Suzanne Davie, to raise production values to a new level. Productions included *The Beggar's Opera*, *Lysistrata* and *Dr Faustus*. Her plays pushed boundaries and challenged actors and audiences. Suzanne also developed opportunities for junior students, running weekly clubs and empowering Sixth Formers to lead them. At the same time, Drama GCSE and A Level grew. Borlase alumni progressed onto Drama Colleges and trained as professional actors, writers, comedians and directors. Borlase had become a training school for teachers, and Lauren Anderson, a former student, trained with Suzanne and later returned to be Head of Department when Suzanne decided to become part-time. More plays followed, including a staging of *Charles III*, a play in iambic pentameter that looked ahead to the tragic reign of the then Prince Charles. In 2022, Mr Berj Tekerian was appointed as Head of Drama and, in his first term, staged an impressive production of Miller's *A View from the Bridge*.

Musical Theatre
Mr Gazard had established a tradition of performing Musical Theatre at Borlase. When Specialist Status arrived, Musical Theatre grew into collaborative extravaganzas, bringing together the outstanding talent of Musical Directors, Heads of Drama and Dance, Mark Hartley, Jenny Chislett and Miss Mountfield. The team was privileged to work with so many wonderfully talented and committed musicians, actors, singers, technical designers and operators, many of whom went on to set up productions in universities and drama colleges and continue in professional careers.

Annie Get Your Gun came first, starring Chris Weeks (currently touring as Buddy in the Musical of that name) and Sophie White. This was followed by *The Pirates of Penzance* set in a school with our current Director of Music, Seth Miall, then Head Boy, playing the lead as the 'Very Model of a Modern College Principal'! *Fiddler on the Roof* was Dr Parsons' first show and was staged on the traverse with a beautiful set influenced by Chagall. Remy Osman was the perfect Tevye in this moving telling of the story; Miss Mountfield's expanded cast gave him six daughters. Lazar Wolf was played by Oliver Taylor who would go on to be President of The Cambridge Footlights and then to write his own sitcom for Channel 4 called *Everyone Else Burns*. The 2013 production of *Les Miserables* set in the round is still spoken about in revered tones — it had an outstandingly talented cast of actors and musicians, many of whom are now performing professionally. Then came *Cabaret* with Chris Murphy, now a successful baritone, who raised eyebrows in his gold lamé hot pants; and *Kiss Me, Kate*, including the amazing 'Too Darn Hot' jazz song and dance sequence choreographed by Kirsty Ashby. Mr Miall's first musical was the sophisticated Cole Porter classic, *Anything Goes*, which had the cast of more than one hundred tap-dancing on board ship, and he followed this with a very ambitious production of Sondheim's *Sweeney Todd*, which Borlase students were ready for and delivered to West End standard. Mr Miall also revived the Junior Musical opportunity on a major scale with *Beauty and the Beast* and *Guys and Dolls*, having directed *Joseph* with juniors when he was a student at the School.

3.5.9. Productions of Annie Get Your Gun, *starring Chris Weeks, in 2006;* Les Miserables *in 2013;* Beauty and the Beast, *starring Charlie Boobyer, Ava Sherwood Rogers and Joe Parkinson, in 2016; and* Oklahoma, *starring Georgie Hill and Tom Hughes, in 2021*

Borlase musicals have enormous casts, are characterized by lots of company work, and whether it was written in or not, there is always room for a ballet to make sure that the dancers have a platform. It would be impossible to name the many great performers, technicians and front-of-house teams who made and make up the Performing Arts families at Borlase. The Borlase YouTube Channel will give you just a flavour of their work.

Chris Weeks (OB 2001–2008)
"Many people think of Borlase as a high-performing academic School, which of course it is, but it was the Performing Arts that brought Borlase to life for me. I got to play Frank Butler in *Annie Get Your Gun* and MacHeath in *The Beggar's Opera*, as well as singing with the Barbershop and my own Jazz group. These roles and experiences gave me confidence in myself and made me feel valued in a way that I had never felt before. Suddenly, I felt like an equal in the room. I am currently playing Buddy Holly in the UK tour of *Buddy: The Buddy Holly Story*, and I can see the threads of all the skills that I use on stage leading straight back to Borlase. The School has led thousands of students to Oxford, Cambridge and other top universities but it has also given me the building blocks that have led me to my acting career. I'll always be grateful for that."

3.5.10. Chris Weeks (left)

The Modern Era (1974-2024)   CHAPTER 3 | 129

Ell Potter (OB 2007–2014)
"The Performing Arts department at Borlase is where it all began for me. Thanks not only to its myriad School productions (which seemed of a higher quality than plays I would later stage at drama school, or even professionally) or the termly concerts (where I would spend most of the night running around backstage trying to remember which ensemble was performing next: did I need my saxophone or my choir folder?), but thanks also to the quiet, protective quality of the place itself. It was a place you could just … be. I am not ashamed to say that when I occasionally (read: often) skipped PE on a Wednesday afternoon, I would head up to the recording studio and practise piano instead. Or exchange YouTube videos of jazz musicians with Dr Parsons and whoever else was there. Or find the resident sleeping bag (every studio needs one) and have a nap under a desk. It was not that I hated PE — it was fine — I just always wanted to be in the Arts department, because I never felt safer, more creatively held, than I did there. It was a haven. These days, I still spend lots of time in recording studios, where I have found a new kind of escape by narrating audiobooks. I am an actor and writer and use the skills that Borlase sowed in me every single day. I feel incredibly lucky that Borlase was where I found my feet."

3.5.11. Ell Potter performing with Sam North

FOREIGN LANGUAGES

After founding the School in 1624, Sir William Borlase left instructions in his will to appoint a schoolmaster to "teach twenty-four poor children to write, read and cast accounts". No mention of languages, either ancient or modern, appears here, but it was commonly accepted in the grammar schools established by wealthy merchants, nobles and guilds that the paid schoolmaster would teach Latin and sometimes Greek.

While Latin remained a staple on the curriculum, there followed a greater demand for skills and education to equip boys for the commercial world. Successive government Education Acts in the second half of the nineteenth century led to a broadening of the curriculum. School records from 1879 show Latin and another European language (French) on the curriculum.

The twentieth century saw a further revision of the languages offered. German was introduced to the School after the arrival of W. O. Robertson (Staff 1931–1951), and Greek was also taught. German and Greek were 'opposing' O Level options from 1957 onwards, but Greek seems to have been phased out in the early 1970s.

It was not until September 2000 that Spanish was introduced at Borlase, whereas Latin was no longer taught from around 2002. Since then, and in line with national trends, Spanish has become the most popular language and is currently followed by German and then French. Mandarin Chinese was introduced in 2011 and continues as an enrichment subject after School, with a handful of candidates completing the GCSE each year.

In December 2018, after a successful bid to the Department for Education, Borlase became one of nine lead schools for the National Centre for Excellence for Language Pedagogy — an exciting, Government-funded project to implement the findings of the Modern Foreign Language (MFL) Pedagogy Review (2016). Borlase MFL Staff led our hub with four contrasting schools in Buckinghamshire and worked alongside teams from 40 other schools nationally to develop, train teachers and teach French, Spanish and German with new resources. We also ran in-person and online training courses regionally and nationally as part of the project, which was completed in March 2023. The project's work has also led to a revised GCSE qualification for French, German and Spanish that will first be taught from 2024.

However, what is currently taught and examined on the curriculum can never fully reflect the diversity of languages and experiences that we share in our Borlase community. In our student body, we now have just under 100 students whose mother tongues represent 38 different languages. We support exam qualification requests for those in which qualifications exist — for example, Polish, Italian, Russian, Japanese and modern Hebrew — but we are enriched immeasurably by our students' knowledge of many heritage languages.

Beyond the Curriculum

Our current MFL curriculum statement states all the skills that we and our predecessors have sought to encourage inside and outside the classroom. We foster an enjoyment in exploiting links, patterns, commonalities and differences in languages to be able to communicate effectively. We show learners how to adapt to real situations; how to plan, communicate, persevere and take risks; and how to become an expert listener and a great observer. Above all, we want our learners to develop a sense of excitement, wonder, empathy and respect towards other cultures. It is thanks to our predecessors, our current MFL colleagues and parental support that Languages at Borlase continue to do this.

The Borlasian magazine records walking holidays in Germany starting in the late 1950s, led by Norman Bateman. The first German exchange visit was in 1967 with the Friedrich-Wilhelm Schule in Eschwege. Several visits were recorded through to the early 1970s.

Meanwhile, several rowing exchanges from the late 1960s and early 1970s between Borlase, Great Marlow and the Marly-le-Roi rowing clubs became the foundation of the official Town Twinning between Marlow and Marly-le-Roi in 1972. We believe that the exchanges have taken place with Collège Louis Lumière in most years since.

German exchanges were relaunched officially between Borlase and Gymnasium Saarburg in 1994. Spanish exchanges were established firstly with Monzon for several years, and subsequently with Colegio Pablo VI in Avila from 2014.

What better way is there to appreciate wonder, empathy and respect towards other cultures than by spending time with families and friends in those cultures? Notwithstanding the hiatus of the COVID-19 pandemic, the pressures of Brexit and the additional challenges with safeguarding regulations, we are proud that we have the support of our parents, pupils and partner schools in maintaining and extending these links — such a precious commodity in a world in which technology extends reach, but personal links are potentially being eroded. And there is more: the Sixth Form study trips, work experience, film trips and so many others. Perhaps top of the list for thanks are the Staff, both past and present, who have made these opportunities happen.

To stimulate the cultural links further, we have enjoyed a series of Languages Showcases, which celebrate the rich heritage of our languages and their pervasive influence in culture, music, dance, humour and our increasing breadth and depth of multinational celebrations. And the whole School enjoys the annual MFL Bake Off in celebration of the European Day of Languages, with students making cakes from every corner of the globe and fundraising in aid of sign language charities.

MFL in the Next 400 Years?

But what of the future of Languages at Borlase? Which languages shall we be teaching in 2124 and beyond? How can we be sure that we shall be equipping our students for their futures, developing them to become global citizens?

The past 10 years alone have sped up the changes and challenges at an unprecedented rate — Brexit, with its initial negative effect on language learning, the COVID-19 pandemic and its extra challenges for teaching a communicative discipline, the war in Ukraine, and global political insecurity and uncertainty. Nevertheless, the resilience, innovation and creativity that language learning brings gives us confidence that languages and linguistic skills will prevail because, in whatever language on offer, Borlase teaches the building blocks on which accurate, effective and successful communication is built, and the aims in our curriculum statement support all the additional life skills that language learning brings.

To illustrate the power and reach of languages, we have alumni with languages and linguistic degrees working in artificial intelligence, national security, international refugee support, government and diplomacy, marketing, consulting, international aid agencies, translation and interpreting, and music and the arts on an international scale. A wall display in our department gives just a flavour of the current potential for linguists — very different from those in 1624, and an opportunity for you to imagine what that list might look like in 100 years' time.

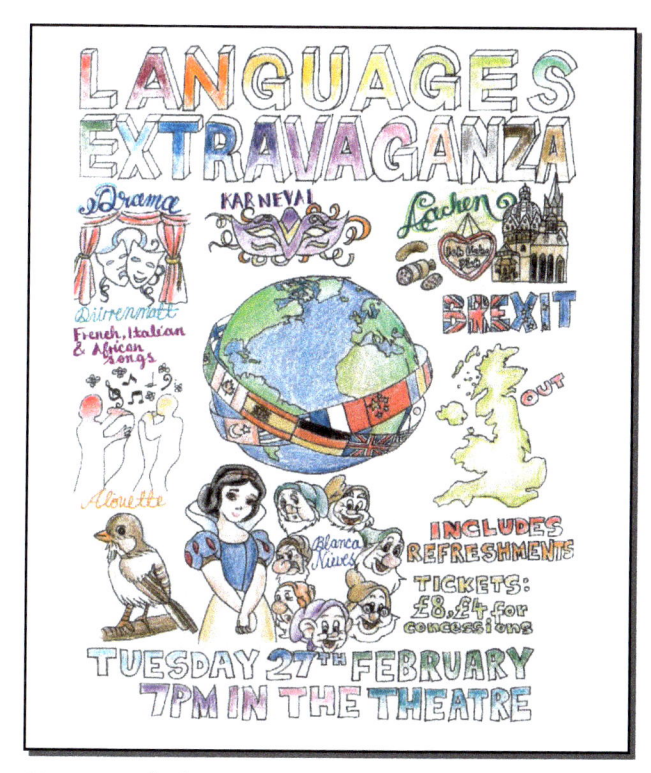

3.6.1. A poster for the Languages Extravaganza in 2016, drawn by Victoria Chong

3.6.2. In 2018, Borlase students took part in an international competition with students from Marlow's twin towns: Marly-le-Roi in France and Leichlingen in Germany. The task was to submit a short story or piece of artwork on the theme of soldiers returning from the front in 1918 and 'their return to peace'. This painting was submitted by Nicola Chmielewska.

3.6.3. Wall display in the Modern Foreign Languages department listing career opportunities

SCHOOL CURRICULUM AND PEDAGOGY

At 400 years old, Borlase is a special place to learn and teach. Looking back at the curriculum followed by those founding students who were introduced to the rudiments of Mathematics, English and Latin, there has been enormous change. However, the principle of providing young people with a stimulating education to empower them to have a better, brighter future and to make a difference and the values of *Te Digna Sequere* have remained constant. Students and teachers share a love of learning and a clear sense of collective purpose as a modern selective School. Visitors and new students and teachers often remark on the openness of current Borlasians to new ideas and skills, their willingness to reflect on how they learn and teach, and on the excitement that they demonstrate about their work. This has always been true of Borlasians at their best, but in recent decades, we have aimed to create a learning environment where *all* students and teachers can be inspired through a varied and challenging curriculum to feel the sense of achievement and empowerment that quality learning brings. In the face of changing Government agendas for education (and ever-tighter budgets), Borlase has held strong in its belief in this great ambition. In 2018, and again in 2022, we explored what this distinctive educational culture meant for young people today. This work resulted in a shared Curriculum Statement 2022 that sets out how we learn and teach at Borlase today:

The Borlase Curriculum provides a breadth and depth of academic learning and cultural experience to excite and extend all our students, including SEND [Special Educational Needs and Disabilities] learners and disadvantaged learners. It is rich in knowledge and in opportunities to develop creativity, instilling a life-long enthusiasm for learning.

This distinctive Key Stage 3 creative curriculum is rich in cultural learning and empowers all our pupils with important, valuable skills that support personal and academic development; these include creative intelligence, independent thinking, collaborative skills, resilience, confidence, leadership, time-management, interpretation and empathy.

In Years 9–11, learners have an enriched Key Stage 4. They study their subjects as disciplines; teachers inspire them with ideas outside and beyond the GCSE specification. There are trips, visits, practical explorations and independent research projects that enrich the learning experience and promote deeper understanding for all learners including SEND and disadvantaged learners — learners are not on a five-term conveyor belt moving towards an examination.

This leads on to an intellectually inspiring and empowering Key Stage 5 where students have a wide choice of academically challenging subjects that lead them on to aspirational destinations to follow their passion. Their studies are extended by independent projects and wider learning, and their journey to being an independent learner is facilitated through academic and organisational skills learned in tutor time. The curriculum includes opportunities to contribute to the community through mentoring and volunteering; to develop leadership through running societies and clubs; and to understand and prepare for the wide range of possible future destinations they might choose.

Our curriculum is delivered by passionate, specialist teachers who encourage aspiration, intellectual curiosity and the exploration of their subject disciplines inside and beyond the classroom. It promotes a love of reading and literacy and develops oracy. It includes a broad range of supercurricular and extracurricular opportunities which ignite and extend students' interests, enthusiasm and skills across a wide range of endeavours, including those linked to academic subjects, to sports, the arts, engineering, artificial intelligence, public speaking, creative writing, entrepreneurialism and so much more.

The Borlase Curriculum develops our students' understanding of how they learn, enabling them to be effective independent thinkers and learners; it empowers them with positive strategies to prepare for examinations that support mental and physical wellbeing.

The Borlase Curriculum supports the Borlase culture and values, developing character based on, and instilling a sense of, moral and social responsibility. It teaches ethical leadership, reinforcing respect and kindness towards oneself, others and the environment.

The Borlase Curriculum inspires and empowers all our students to be happy and successful and to have the skills, knowledge, values and confidence to shape the future.

A World-Class School
In 2019, our learning culture was recognized by a designation as a 'World Class School' by the High Performance Learning organization. We were recognized for a long-standing programme of Staff and student training in the latest thinking from neuroscience and psychology about how we learn, known as metacognition. Borlasians know not only what they are learning, but also how and why they are learning. Teachers and students have been open to exploring what cutting-edge research can tell us about how the brain learns well (and less well). This has played a large part in our development of how students with SEND learn at School: deliberate 'chunking' of knowledge into manageable learning, planning that considers cognitive load, scaffolding and models which enable students with SEND to achieve highly, and the use of technology in creative ways.

A Creative School
Borlase is a creative place to learn in all subjects. Since gaining Specialist Status in the Performing Arts from the Department for Education in 2005, Borlase has developed a curriculum that champions the Arts throughout the School, including weekly separate Key Stage 3 lessons in Music, Dance, Drama, Art and Design, taught by specialists. At a time in School funding when many other schools have made tough decisions to reduce Arts provision, Borlase has retained a fine reputation for valuing the unique contribution of these disciplines to young lives. This happens in the classroom on taught GCSE, A Level and BTEC Theatre Technology courses, with student uptake bucking national trends, and it also happens through our enrichment programme. Our students are consumers and makers of the Arts. The effect of the Arts on students' lives is direct and widely felt. At the time of writing, cuts to the funding of national Arts institutions in this country continue to challenge their influence on future generations.

Lockdown Learning
During the COVID-19 pandemic in 2020–2021, learning and teaching remotely brought new challenges and opportunities for teachers, students and parents. These were unprecedented for all schools, most of which remained open even during the two World Wars. Borlasians showed true grit in adapting to new approaches to technology and pedagogy. With our real classrooms locked down, we found new ways to learn, to present learning, and to assess understanding and give feedback, and support and enrich the curriculum. We were well placed to navigate this new world as a result of the work that we had done for years to foster a sense of resilience, risk taking and independence in our students and our Staff. Our students were able to be flexible in adapting their learning to an online platform, and teachers felt confident to share their pedagogical thinking with classes, exploring new media together, and sometimes co-planning. Their level of metacognitive understanding meant that feedback, delivered in news ways, continued to be relevant and to drive progress. There is little doubt that our students' ability to continue their education with comparatively little disruption is a result of the School's commitment to values and attitudes that have characterized it for a decade or more. Borlasians continued to be excited by learning, to make progress, and be ready for their next steps. When teachers and students returned to their physical classrooms, they took with them the lessons of lockdown, and a more fluent and creative approach to using the tools offered by technology.

Our deeper understanding of how young people learn has meant some exciting changes to how Borlase teachers teach. A whole-school Curriculum Review between 2018 and 2021 challenged us to consider not only what we taught and why, but also the sequence of learning over time. We agreed that Borlasians should be *inspired and empowered to shape the future*; we refined a robust knowledge and skill-based curriculum, within which we develop disciplinary skills of problem solving, thinking critically, being creative, and working in collaboration.

Collaborative Professional Learning
In recent years, teachers have enjoyed working in collaborative groups, known as TLCs (Teacher Learning Communities), where they have explored cutting-edge ideas about teaching and learning in the context of our students. Our teachers have demonstrated genuinely insightful reflective practice, enthusiasm to try new things, and generosity of spirit. These qualities have made Borlase a natural choice for new teachers to train to teach and begin their careers as Newly Qualified Teachers (now known as Early Career Teachers). Our excellent reputation in training and teacher development resulted in successful bids to become a Teaching School Alliance, SCITT (School-

Centred Initial Teacher Training) Lead School, and Modern Foreign Languages Hub. Borlase teachers continue to help to shape the careers of their colleagues and often direct the national agenda in their fields.

Borlase is an exciting and forward-looking place to learn and teach. As we survey our recent and more distant history, we can be certain that learning and teaching will continue to change so that our young people are prepared to shape their futures. In the coming years, teachers and students will undoubtedly see changes to how they work: they will need to understand the effect on learning of artificial intelligence and develop new technological skills; hone the critical thinking skills to engage with cultural–political debates around what constitutes core knowledge in our times; and respond to the opportunities and skills of future labour markets. We hope to have shaped a learning culture in which our teachers and pupils are ready for the challenge.

ASPECTS OF SCHOOL LIFE

House System

The House System at Borlase has long been an established feature of the School's culture. Borlase students have been placed in the Houses of their families one, two, three and even four generations before them, perpetuating that deep sense of pride and identity that Borlasians feel towards their Houses. The first reference in *The Borlasian* to the four original Houses competing in sports was in 1911 — Britons, Danes, Normans and Saxons, with Normans being the House of the Sentry Hill boarders. Vikings and Romans were added as the School expanded at the start of the twenty-first century. The House System at Borlase serves as a mechanism for creating communities within communities; Staff Heads of House and student House Captains lead assemblies and motivate their House community to engage fully in the life of the School. Borlasians enjoy participating in life, and the House system encourages everyone to be a participant whether they excel or whether they are out of their comfort zone. The traditional inter-House competitions have included the key sports of Rugby, Football and Cricket, with Athletics in the summer and the annual Cross Country run. The School House system is now more vibrant than ever — House Music, House Dance and House Drama include every House member; House Public Speaking and House Chess are fiercely contested; and Sports Day has expanded to include all sorts of activities alongside Athletics, including Croquet, Ultimate Frisbee, and House stalls running everything from hook a duck and cake bakes to throw a sponge at a teacher.

In 2022, Julien Bussell, President of the Old Borlasian Club, presented the House Captains with Shields in the House Colours to be displayed in the Stuart Lever Room alongside the silver cups and trophies.

3.8.1. House shields being presented by the Old Borlasian Club to House Prefects in 2022 and displayed in the Stuart Lever Room

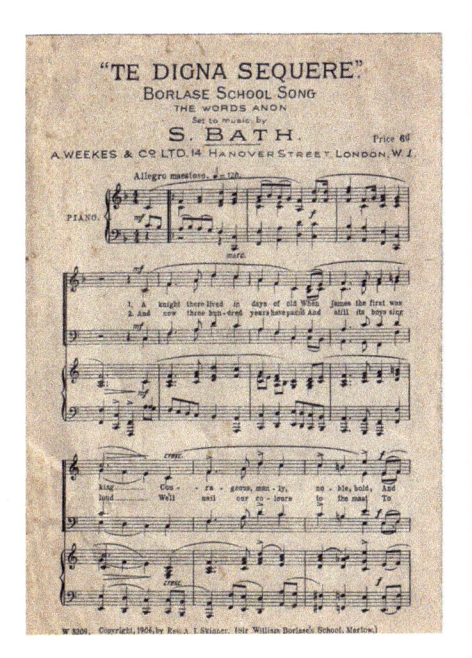

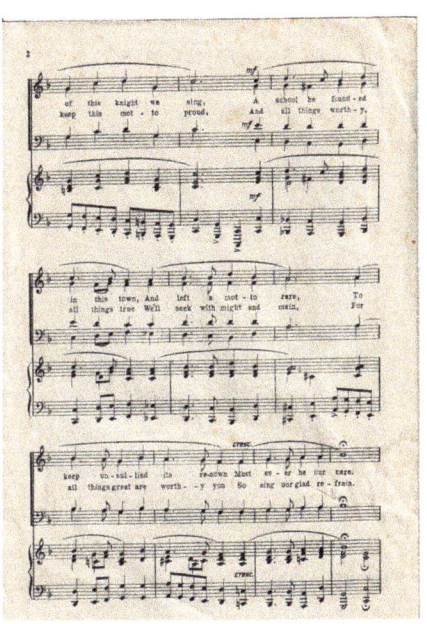

3.8.2. The Borlase School Song, written by the Rev. A. J. Skinner and set to music by Dr S. Bath

School Songs and Founder's Prayer

The School Song, named after the School motto *Te Digna Sequere*, meaning 'Follow things worthy of thyself', was written in the 1920s by the then Headmaster, the Rev. A. J. Skinner, and set to music by Dr S. Bath. The third verse was added by Mr Russell Sage in the 1970s. The Song is still sung at important School occasions, such as the Old Borlasian Club's Annual Dinner.

Te Digna Sequere

A knight there lived in days of old,
When James the First was king;
Courageous, manly, noble, bold,
And of this knight we sing;
A school he founded in this town,
And left a motto rare;
To keep unsullied its renown
Must ever be our care.

*Follow things worthy, follow things true,
Follow all things that are worthy of you;
And let the song
Ring loud and long,
"Te digna sequere"
"Te digna sequere."*

And now three hundred years have passed
And still we all sing loud:
"We'll nail our colours to the mast,
To keep this motto proud,
And all things worthy, all things true
We'll seek with might and main,
For all things great are worthy you,
So sing our glad refrain."

The years roll by and still we sing
The same old stirring song;
With youthful zeal our voices ring
Although the years grow long;
And in our memory those we knew
Their voices raise again,
With them in friendship ever true
We sing our glad refrain.

A hymn was also composed by Skinner and Bath to be sung on the last day of the term, although this practice has died out.

We thank Thee now, O Father,
On this our final day,
And ask Thee for Thy blessing,
To guide us on our way,
That changing school for days of rest,
Thy Spirit still may be our guest.

And may our days of leisure
Be filled with Love divine,
Our works and words bear witness
That we, O Lord, are Thine,
The feeble creatures of Thy hand
Who follow still their Lord's command.

And then for those our comrades
Whose schooldays now are o'er,
As boyhood's haunts are fading
For some far distant shore;
Give them Thy help, O Lord, to-day,
To fight the foe, and work, and pray.

The lives are not forgotten
Of those who once were here,
And left behind examples
And memory ever dear.
Grant us, O Lord, to follow still
The things most worthy of Thy will.

3.8.3. A Hymn for the last day of the term, written by Rev. A. J. Skinner and set to music by Dr S. Bath

The Modern Era (1974-2024)

CHAPTER 3

Finally, *The Borlasian* magazine of 1924 records a Founder's Prayer, which again has fallen into disuse.

Almighty God, always to be praised for the dead as well as for the living, we bless Thy Holy Name for Sir William Borlase, the founder, and for all other benefactors of this school, and pray Thee to continue their work and prosper it exceedingly. Give Thy grace to both masters and scholars, that all who teach may be diligent in their stewardship, and that all who learn may so use these Thy gifts in their youth that they may glorify Thee in their manhood and bring forth fruit abundantly to the benefit of their fellow men. Guide us all, O Lord, with Thy counsel, and afterward receive us with glory for the merits of Thy dear Son, Jesus Christ our Saviour. Amen.

Chapel Organ and Harpsichord

Borlase is fortunate in possessing, uniquely among Buckinghamshire grammar schools, both a fully functioning pipe organ and a two-manual harpsichord. The organ is housed in the School Chapel and the harpsichord in the Wethered Room.

Both of these venerable members of the keyboard family have quietly (and when the occasion demands, noisily) played their part in the Borlase community over the years. It is fair to say that, owing to great social change over the past hundred years or so, understanding of the function of these instruments is perhaps not as widespread as it once was, so it is worth starting with some basic explanations.

An organ is, in essence, a wind instrument; air is blown by mechanical means through pipes which vary in length and thus pitch. Organ music is played on keys identical in appearance to those of a pianoforte; rows of keys are called *manuals* (from the Latin *manus*, the hand). Some organs, including our own, also have pedals, which are played by the feet; the pedals are simply another row of keys. Access of air to pipes is controlled by means of 'stops', which are operated by the organist from the console. The more stops that are pulled out, the louder the sound.

The harpsichord does not have such a long history as the organ, the first instruments appearing only in the later Middle Ages. It is more like a harp than an organ, inasmuch as its sounds are made not by wind but by strings plucked by *plectra* — small pieces of quill, plastic or metal attached to a *jack*. Like the organ, it has manuals (usually one or two, occasionally three) and, very rarely, pedals. Its sound cannot be varied by touch and in this respect is more like the organ than the piano. Owing to the greater suitability of the piano for performing music of the Romantic era, the harpsichord gradually became extinct at the end of the eighteenth century but underwent a revival in the twentieth. Much organ and harpsichord music is interchangeable.

The history of the organ is intimately bound up with religious worship. Its function is primarily devotional, as an accompaniment to hymns, anthems, psalms and carols, as well as for the performance of voluntaries before and after services. The Borlase organ is interwoven with the life of the Chapel, the spiritual heart of the Borlase family. The harpsichord, by contrast, is mainly used for chamber music and has a largely secular function and repertoire.

Although the foundation stone of the Chapel was laid in April 1914, it was not until 1953 that the organ was installed at a cost of £2,153 — a very large sum in those days. It has remained central to the life of the Chapel from that time onwards. The formal ceremony took place on 28 June that year at the Dedication of the War Memorial. The instrument was built by Frederick Rothwell and Sons and has been tuned and maintained for many years by Shepherd and Sons based in Edgware. It has been played in Chapel by a number of organists, including (until 1997) Mr David Colthup, whose extensive knowledge and expertise enabled him to add to the already existing specification (the stops, accessories and compass of the instrument). These additions included a Tuba and two sets of Mixtures, both now fallen into disuse.

For the past twenty years, the organ has been played by Mr Hugh Robson, a former Oxford Organ Scholar and much-loved member of the English Department. Borlasians still sing hymns in assemblies in the morning, and organ music is played before and after the assembly. The organ is also used for the Remembrance Day Service and for Leavers' Chapel in May, as well as for concerts and for other commemorative events and services. Over the years, it has been employed in the teaching and preparation of students for Associated Board examinations.

Like many septuagenarians, the organ is starting to show signs of its age. Recently, the wind pressure dropped to such an

3.8.4. The Chapel Organ and School Harpsichord

extent that its customary throaty roar dwindled to a pathetic bleat. The Shepherd brothers discovered that the fan belt had decayed to such an extent that it was barely functioning; thanks to the resourcefulness of Mr Kipping, who replaced the belt with a pair of elasticated tights, the motor became fully operative once more and the organ recovered its full volume. The general repair of the instrument will inevitably necessitate further attention in the coming years if it is to continue to be played as it has been.

The current School harpsichord was purchased from Morley and Sons in 2007. Previously, the School possessed an instrument built by Mr Colthup and was in full use until 1998. Sadly, it was badly damaged and rendered unplayable and so, thanks to Miss Mountfield's generous contribution from the Performing Arts budget, a new instrument was acquired as a replacement. It was constructed in the early 1960s by the Latvian-born harpsichord maker William de Blaise (1907–1978), according to the musical tastes of his day. In this twentieth century renaissance of harpsichord construction, less attention was given than nowadays to questions of supposed 'authenticity': unusually the de Blaise instrument possesses a so-called 16' 'stop' (by analogy with organ pipe lengths), which gives extra depth and volume. It was at first housed in the Theatre but later moved to the Wethered Room, where it has remained ever since. Like the organ, it is used on an occasional basis. As with the organ, a small number of students have received lessons and taken Associated Board examinations on the harpsichord. Its main function now is in the annual Advent Concert, when it is used for solos and ensembles.

The future of the organ and harpsichord, both at Borlase and beyond, is bound up with the future of European society, from which these instruments emerged, and of whose culture they are an expression. Like the instruments themselves, the music composed for them was the product of a sense of a social and religious identity that is rapidly changing. Whatever the future may bring, the intrinsic beauty of organ and harpsichord music will hopefully ensure that these instruments continue to be played and appreciated by generations of Borlasians in the years to come.

Remembrance Day Services

Recognizing the sacrifice made by the many young alumni of Borlase in the two World Wars and subsequent conflicts has been an important tradition at the School since the memorial to the fallen of World War I was installed in the School Chapel. A service is held annually in the Chapel and is attended by members of the Old Borlasian Club. Until recently, this service included veterans who served in World War II, who would share their stories with the School. The School continues to mark this important occasion with the laying of poppy wreaths during the service by the School Captains, the President of the Old Borlasian Club, and a guest of honour from the armed forces. The whole School gathers to observe the two-minute silence outdoors, with the *Last Post* and the *Reveille* played by a student trumpeter.

In 2014, the School marked the centenary of the start of World War I with an exhibition for the public, inviting the community and alumni back to School to read the stories of the fallen, which had been researched by Ilona Cains (Director of Development) and members of the Marlow History Society. The School also staged an immersive piece of theatre written to mark the occasion. It opened with the audience watching the shooting of Archduke Franz Ferdinand in a 1900s car lent by Old Borlasian Jimmy Platt, from Platt's Motors in Marlow. The audience then walked through the School, watching the recruiting officer call up boys to war in the Cloisters, walking through a hospital scene in the Hall, and past the dramatic and moving shooting of a deserter. The Boys' Dance Company represented battle in their powerful contemporary dance in the Theatre, and the audience moved from there to hear boys singing *Keep the Home Fires Burning* in the semi-darkness, standing among white crosses on the Chapel Lawn. The performance ended in the Chapel, with current Borlasians reading the Roll Call before Cantorum sang *In Paradiso*.

Mr Peter Heywood, Design and Technology teacher for more than 30 years, designed and made a receptacle from English oak that holds six ceramic poppies from the Tower of London exhibition 'Rivers of Blood', one for each Borlase House. The poppies are now placed in position by Year 7 students as part of the Remembrance Day Service each year.

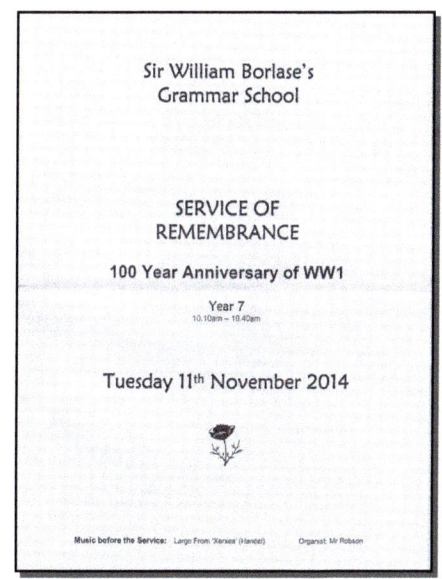

3.8.5. Service of Remembrance in the School Chapel in 2014, marking the 100th anniversary of the start of World War I

3.8.6. The Remembrance Day poppies and oak receptacle crafted by Peter Heywood

The Modern Era (1974-2024)

Orders and Reporting

At the start of the twentieth century, students would be seated in classrooms in order of ability. End-of-term reports, which determined where students sat, consequently became known as 'Orders' — a term that continues to be used today, despite students no longer being ordered by examination results. In the first editions of *The Borlasian* from the 1880s, it was possible to publish class lists of all the boys at the School, together with their marks and attendance record for the year. This practice subsequently ceased, but end-of-year reports continued to be routinely issued to each student.

Here, we reproduce the School reports from three generations of the Compton family: Ron (OB 1925–1932), Tony (OB 1957–1964) and Andre (OB 1985–1989).

Ron went on to study French at Reading University but did not complete the degree course. He took a job in insurance and, after serving in the RAF during World War II, he returned to the insurance business and eventually established the first insurance brokerage business in Marlow in the late 1950s. Ron was a dedicated Old Borlasian and served as President of the Old Borlasian Club.

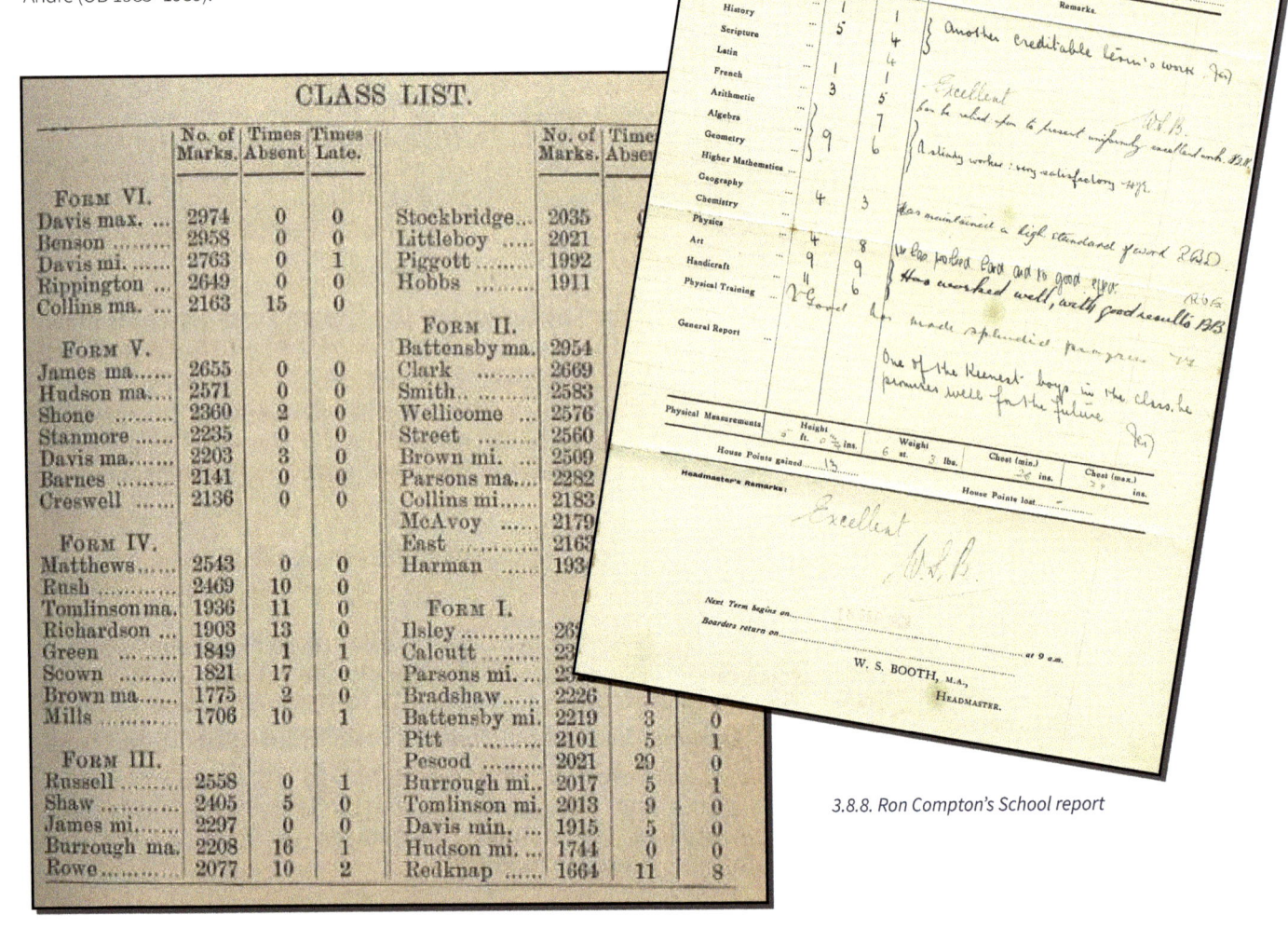

3.8.7. A class list published in **The Borlasian** *of 1885*

3.8.8. Ron Compton's School report

138 | CHAPTER 3 — The Modern Era (1974-2024)

Tony studied Architecture at Thames Polytechnic in London during the Swinging Sixties. He qualified as an architect and eventually set up the practice of Compton Lacey in Maidenhead in the late 1980s, dealing with a wide variety of projects nationwide. Like his father, he is a dedicated Old Borlasian, serving on the committee for more than 30 years and acting as Secretary and twice as President of the Old Borlasian Club. He is also a past Governor and now a Trustee of the School. (He did "do better" in the end!)

3.8.9. Tony Compton's School report and a photo of him with Rowing trophies

The Modern Era (1974-2024)

CHAPTER 3 | 139

After an honours degree in European Studies from Nottingham Trent University (or 'Polytechnic' as it was when he joined), Andre's career has predominantly been in the creative design sector, establishing his own design agency called Handstand in 2008, which is still active and thriving. His love and natural academic ability for writing continues, in both creative and commercial formats. Andre says: "Roy Smith always had faith in me, when many in the Staffroom kept their distance! He does not, however, seem too impressed with this report. Sorry, Roy!"

3.8.10. Pages from Andre Compton's School report

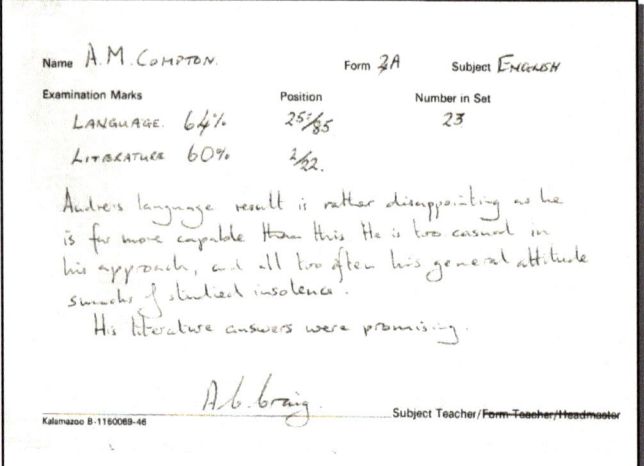

School Uniform

In the eighteenth century, the Borlase School uniform was blue, resulting in the nickname the 'Blue Boys', with red braid hemming and a blue cap with a red tassel. The material was bought from the shop of William Hawes and cut to fit the boy by James Field at the House of Correction.

In *The Borlasian* of 1887, the uniform of 1836 was recalled by Robert H. Smith. "The Blue Boys wore a uniform at Church parade on Sundays. It was formed of a piece of very rough blue cloth, with two holes cut in it for the arms to pass through, and a piece of red tape to fasten it around the neck. We also wore a round shallow cap of the same material, with a narrow red tape band. Thus attired, we were the sport of all the other boys in the parish." By 1904, under the Rev. A. J. Skinner, the boarders went to Church on Sundays in top hats and Eton suits with stiff collars.

Later in the twentieth century, boys wore a blazer with the Borlase coat of arms on the

3.8.11. Borlase boys on Church parade in c.1904, and an advert for School uniform from Morgan's Outfitters of Marlow in the 1940s

3.8.12. Edward John Hawkins in the 1920s; Peter Wiseman (a boarder at Sentry Hill 1966–1968); and a selection of School caps

The Modern Era (1974-2024) CHAPTER 3 | 141

pocket, School cap and a black tie. In the 1980s, the tie was replaced by one that was red with blue stripes. With the introduction of girls to Borlase, an equivalent uniform was introduced for them: a black jacket, black skirt, white shirt and tie. After a time, the girls approached Mrs Crittenden, the Deputy Headmistress, to request the introduction of a bit of colour. The decision was taken to allow girls to wear a red cardigan. However, this caused some controversy among the boys, who approached Mr Banner, the Acting Headmaster, with a petition to be allowed to wear jumpers. Mr Banner was not going to allow that, but he told the boys that he would consider their request. A few days later, he called the boys in and told them, "I have thought of the ideal solution: we have no objection to you wearing red underpants!" In the twenty-first century, six variants of the lower School and Sixth Form ties were introduced, with the stripes indicating the School House to which the student belonged.

3.9.13. In the latter part of the twentieth century, lower School students wore red ties with blue stripes (with the addition of the School coat of arms to indicate the awarding of School Colours). Sixth Formers wore black ties with the School coat of arms (with the addition of gold stripes to indicate the awarding of School colours). In the twenty-first century, the colours of the six School Houses were incorporated into the stripes of the lower School and Sixth Form ties.

3.8.14. Gold Medal winners, many of whom were School Captain

3.8.15. R. H. Webber, School Captain in 1930

142 | CHAPTER 3

The Modern Era (1974-2024)

School Captains

Year	Captain		Year	Captain	Captain
1930	R. H. Webber		1978	Stuart Walker	
1931	S. W. Maskell		1979	Owen Greedy	
1932	H. G. Montey		1980	Chris Britt	
1933	L. G. Hogg		1981	Andrew Boyle	
1934	G. M. McCorquodale		1982	Martin Fewell	
1935	G. M. McCorquodale		1983	Neil Hart	
1936	F. C. Salter		1984	Lance Robinson	
1937	D. G. Tew		1985	Stephen Brown	
1938	E. H. W. Hersee		1986	Andrew Gamble	
1939	B. P. Skinner		1987	Steve Robinson	
1940	R. C. R. Cox		1988	John Adcock	
1941	V. G. Brewer		1989	Phillip Lee	
1942	A. G. Chubb		1990	Philip Dennis	
1943	W. G. Tinker		1991	Charles Richardson	
1944	C. J. Fullbrook		1992	Warren Gibbon	
1945	E. K. J. Darville		1993	Jeremy Tribe	
1946	E. B. Carne		1994	Charles Evans	Katherine Nicholson
1947	W. R. Walker & W. E. Cudd		1995	Alexander Venn	Caroline Lee
1948	A. S. Payne		1996	Jack Bootle	Fiona McFarlane
1949	A. P. Townsend		1997	Daniel Lawes	Tracey Eales
1950	M. E. Davis		1998	Francis Mussai	Andrea Hill
1951	B. J. Platt		1999	Tom Weaver	Saskia Corder
1952	D. Bailey		2000	Peter Latham	Claire Sharpe
1953	B. J. Bond		2001	Max Buckland	Nicole Armitage
1954	D. J. Allaway		2002	James Valentine	Kate Adlington
1955	R. W. West		2003	Gregory Lim	Nicola Bye
1956–1957	D. P. Dandridge		2004	Hugh Miall	Charlotte Longstaff
1957–1958	D. P. Dandridge		2005	Matt Lawrence	Henrietta Oliver
1958–1959	J. P. Meacher		2006	Alex Jamieson	Phillippa Lasocki
1959–1960	C. Smyth		2007	Joshua Cooke	Jenny Jones
1960	M. J. Kemp		2008	Joe Dowling	Hannah Bungey
1961	M. J. Muir-Smith		2009	Seth Miall	Katrina Foster
1961–1962	P. Flowerday		2010	Hugh Stevens	Christina Cameron
1962–1963	J. White		2011	Mitch Byrne	Ellie Field
1963–1964	L. H. R. van Schaik, D. E. Coventry		2012	Remy Osman	Molly Snowe
1964–1965	S. D. Sharp		2013	Josh D'Arcy	Sofia Green
1965–1966	P. S. Belding		2014	Olly Seber	Beth Potter
1966–1967	D. R. Brown, W. G. Plackett		2015	Akil Hashmi	Georgie Whitaker
1967–1968	N. J. Harding, C. H. Sharp		2016	Joel Watson	Frankie Butler
1968–1969	C. H. Sharp		2017	Jed Thorpe	Milly Minter
1969–1970	C. H. Sharp		2018	Jack Broadbent	Mary-Anne Grego
1970–1971	C. B. F. Hall		2019	Alex Lyons	Alexandra Rowlands
1971–1972	C. B. F. Hall		2020	Callum Kunchur	Georgia Tuke
1972–1973	J. P. Crockett, M. J. Richards		2021	Leon Tasch	Imogen Baguley
1973–1974	R. T. C. Austin, C. N. Davey		2022	William Tucker	Shivani Shrestha
1974–1975	C. N. Davey		2023	Joel Taylor	Anne Irving
1976	A. P. Cowling		2024	Sacha Smith	Helena Kennedy
1977	David Harvey				

The Modern Era (1974-2024)

SPORT

400 years of Sport at Borlase has in many ways been reflective of the role of Sport in wider society. Before the nineteenth-century obsession with games in public schools, most sporting pursuits would have been considered unworthy and pervasive. But, as at other schools like Eton, Harrow and Rugby, team games and other athletic pursuits started to grip the attention of the students and Staff at Borlase in the late nineteenth and early twentieth centuries. The rows of Cricket and Football shields down the ceiling of the Cloisters bearing the names of 1st team members are clear evidence of the importance that the School attached to Sport.

In 2021, Borlase saw the opening of a new and exciting Sports Hall, and it is incredible to think that there would have been similar, if not more, excitement in 1912 at the opening of the new Swedish Gymnasium in the Cloisters (now the Stuart Lever Room). This investment, together with facilities such as a rifle range, the Fives court (now a caretaker's tool shed!), an outdoor swimming pool (now covered by the Theatre), and a carefully prepared cricket wicket on Colonel's Meadow, is ample evidence of the importance that was placed on Sport at Borlase during the twentieth century. A plethora of silver inter-House challenge cups (now on display in the Lever Room) for pretty much anything and everything to do with Sports complemented

3.9.1. Association Football on the Colonel's Meadow, c.1900

3.9.2. Sports shields in the Cloisters, recording the names of 1st team players

3.9.3. Anthony 'Tinny' Townsend claiming a new School record in the Shot Put at Sports Day 1948

3.9.4. Sport in the 1950s: Rugby Union in 1959 on a muddy Colonel's Meadow; the 100-yard dash at Sports Day; and a view of the Tennis Courts, with the Home Meadow beyond

the expansion in facilities. Many of these cups are still competed for today.

A notable athlete of the late 1940s was Anthony Patrick Townsend (OB 1944–1950), ironically nicknamed 'Tinny' (Tiny) on account of his great height. He excelled in the sports of Shot Put, Discus and Javelin. In July 1948, Tinny claimed a new School record for the Shot Put (which would remain unbeaten for many years) and came second in the same event at the All England Sports. In the same year, he took 13 wickets in the School's 1st XI and was awarded half-colours for Cricket. The following year, he became School Captain and was awarded the Gold Medal. He captained the 1st XV Rugby team and won both the Shot Put and Discus in the Bucks Athletics Championships. Later in life, Tinny served as Honorary Secretary of the Old Borlasian Club from 1962 to 1985 and became President of the Club in 1973. He also held the position of Grand Master of the Borlase Masonic Lodge.

By the 1950s, Rugby replaced Football as the major winter game — a decision that was deplored at the time by some Old Borlasians! However, it was a necessity as the School was growing in numbers (30 could play Rugby at any one time, instead of only 22 playing Football).

During the 1960s, the School acquired more land (Quoitings) to provide for greater sporting participation. It was during this period too that Hockey was growing from a

The Modern Era (1974-2024)

CHAPTER 3 | 145

3.9.5. A Gymnastics display as part of the annual Speech Day in the 1960s

rather minority pursuit to a highly popular and successful Sport at the School. By 1974, Hockey teams were not only winning most of their matches but individuals were beginning to win national awards. Tennis, Cross Country, Badminton, Sailing, Swimming and Athletics were now also being well represented, providing a sporting opportunity for everyone. Nevertheless, the annual Sports Day firmly remained the major social and sporting fixture of the year, as it does to this day.

In the 1980s, successes in Rugby, Hockey and Rowing continued, with national titles being achieved. Under the leadership of Alan Black (PE master) and his Staff at the time, a wide choice as well as elite success were the order of the day.

With the arrival of girls at Borlase at the end of the 1980s, a growth in the range of Sports on offer was inevitable. By the turn of the millennium, the School saw developments in many aspects of School Sport in terms of both participation and elite success. Opportunities to try different Sports, such as Netball, Horse Riding and Golf, emerged. Cooperation with Marlow Sports Club was an important development in School Sport, as the demand for varied facilities was constantly changing. The Boat Club grew from strength to strength and, in the twenty-first century, the School appointed specialist directors of Rowing and Hockey to help to deliver a top-class programme for boys and girls. The other major games were now Netball and Rugby, and Football had re-emerged as a popular and successful Sport. The annual Sports Day also diversified and embraced many other Sports, such as Ultimate Frisbee and even Croquet, in addition to the traditional track and field events.

3.9.6. The boys' Hockey team were National Champions in 1988

3.9.7. A variety of sporting success at Borlase in the twenty-first century: a girls' double scull winning at Women's Henley in 2008; a boys' Hockey team winning a national title in 2010; the first Borlase boys' Football team to win the Bucks Schools Football Association County Cup in 2015; an award-winning girls' Football team in 2022; a girls' Tennis team in the national finals in 2012; and Danes winning Sports Day in 2014

The Modern Era (1974-2024)

CHAPTER 3 | 147

3.9.8. A diverse range of elite sport at Borlase in the 2020s

As the School moves towards its 400th anniversary, we are seeing continued and sustained successes in so many major and minor Sports. Dedicated and specialist Staff together with a School ethos that continues to engage and connect with the positive values associated with sporting participation at all levels mean that Sport will, no doubt, continue to play a special and vital role in Borlase life and in shaping the future of the School.

Rowing

On a summer's day in 1921, a group of boys asked the Headmaster, the Rev. Skinner, whether they could form a crew to compete in the Public Schools' Fours event at Marlow Regatta. Permission was given, and the crew raced and were beaten finalists — quite an achievement! Thus, Sir William Borlase's School Boat Club was born, having officially competed in an open rowing event. However, boys had been rowing recreationally at Borlase as far back as the late nineteenth century and had in-School races between the Houses and between day-boys and boarders. In 1892, 30 boys were recorded as rowing. The Old Borlasian section of *The Borlasian* from 1913 records that Marlow Rowing Club was well served by Old Borlasians. For many years after 1921, regatta racing was confined to entering only the event at Marlow Regatta and private fixtures against other schools. The boats that the boys used would have been heavy clinker coxed Fours — very robust, but hard work for lightweight, teenage boys. In 1925, the average weight of the 1st Four was nine and a half stone (60 kg).

Until the 1930s, rowing outings were courtesy of Marlow Rowing Club, which provided boats, equipment and some coaching and allowed the boys to use their facilities. Borlase rowers were, in effect, the early junior section of Marlow Rowing Club. As interest in rowing grew, the Boat Club expanded, acquired a few boats of its own, and training became more serious. However, there were no great successes in the 1930s, and Borlase competed only at local regattas. In 1938, the School acquired the lease on

3.9.9. An original Borlase Boat Club badge

3.9.10. A Borlase Four in 1929

148 | CHAPTER 3 | The Modern Era (1974-2024)

3.9.11. The House Challenge Cup for Rowing, presented by A. R. A. Heath in July 1934

3.9.12. Borlase Boat Club in 1952, with Russell Sage at the back right and the Viking Ship trophy (awarded to the winners of the Junior Eights at Reading Regatta) in the centre

a rather rundown, small boathouse on the town side of the river, which gave them the independence that they needed. They boated from there until 1957, when the lease was not renewed and Marlow Rowing Club kindly took Borlase Boat Club back and gave them the use of one of the bays in their boathouse. Coaching had been carried out by willing masters but, in 1934, Mr Russell Sage joined the School and took control of the Boat Club as master-in-charge of rowing, not knowing that he would continue in that role for 40 years, raising the standards of rowing and putting it on a firm footing as an established Sport at Borlase. The first proper inter-House rowing competition was held in 1934, with a trophy awarded to the winners.

In the 1950s, the Boat Club started experiencing some success at regattas and at Head races, mainly rowing in Eights. The first regatta win in 1950 in the Public Schools' Fours event at Reading Regatta, repeated again in 1951, was followed by a few more victories that year. Russell Sage was ably assisted at this time by Francis Smith, an Old Borlasian who in later years introduced Steve Redgrave to rowing at Great Marlow School. The stroke of the 1st Four and Club captain in 1951 and 1952 was Jim Platt (of Marlow garage fame and long-time supporter of rowing in the town). In the late 1950s, the Club was concentrating on rowing in Eights and, in 1959, the elusive win at Marlow Regatta was finally achieved by a promising School 1st Eight, which had more successes that year. Single sculling began to be encouraged in a small way, and two trophies were given to the School for the senior and junior sculling competitions.

Although there were no outstanding results in the early 1960s, the Boat Club did produce an outstanding oarsman in Mike Muir-Smith who, in 1964, became the first of only two Old Borlasians to row in the men's Oxford and Cambridge Boat Race. In 1964, he was in the winning Cambridge crew and he later went on to become a Great Britain international. The introduction of weights training and circuits in the late 1960s led to higher levels of fitness, and standards in competition improved. The Club also acquired two matched single sculls, allowing boys to become more proficient at sculling.

The early 1970s saw inevitable changes in the Boat Club. 1970 was pretty much the last full season of rowing in Eights, and a gradual transition to competing in Fours occurred, although an Eight was still entered for the Princess Elizabeth Cup at Henley Regatta and four Eights rowed in the early-season Schools' Head of the River race in 1971. With a very active Club, there was always a need for more boats and equipment. Sponsored rows became a popular way of raising money and they helped the Club to purchase two Fours and an Eight at this time.

Mr Tony Craig took over the role of master-in-charge of Rowing in 1972, continuing until 1994. Craig further increased the popularity of rowing at the School, and success came with it. Russell Sage stepped back but still continued with some coaching until 1976, when he retired. A newly acquired Eight was rightly named 'Russell Sage'. Like Mike Muir-Smith, several Old Borlasian rowers have gone on to greater success. Chris Langridge became the second Old Borlasian to row for Cambridge in the Boat Race in 1975. Nigel Read achieved enormous success in the 1970s as a lightweight oarsman, rowing in the Great Britain lightweight Eight at several World Championships, winning bronze in 1975, silver in 1976 and gold in 1977 and 1978. He competed in that event again in 1979 and

3.9.13. The J16 'Grand Slam' Crew of 1988: Geoff Roy (bow), Stuart May (2), Chris Bingham (3), Anthony Temple (stroke) and Guy Dinsdale (cox), coached by John Stebbings; and the 1st Eight competing in the Princess Elizabeth Challenge Cup at Henley Royal Regatta in 1990: S. Hillier (bow), N. Corbett (2), P. Gill (3), A. Leslie (4), M. Furlonger (5), S. May (6), G. Roy (7), A. Temple (stroke), G. Dinsdale (cox), coached by J. Stebbings

1980. Nigel became the first Old Borlasian world rowing champion.

Under Tony Craig's leadership, training including gym work was taken more seriously, which led to fitter crews and better results. In the late 1970s, parent support became very important to the Boat Club spirit, and many parents got involved in fundraising. Together with local business support, more and better boats and equipment could be bought, particularly for the younger age groups.

The 1980s were considered a golden period for Borlase rowing, when many crews achieved wins at the National Schools' Regatta and National Championships. Tony Craig's coaching team included David Ravens and, later on, John Stebbings. The emphasis was now on racing in Fours. In 1983, the 1st Four won the Fours Cup at the National Schools' Regatta and, in that year, the Club amassed 23 wins, including 13 wins in Fours. One outstanding achievement in 1984 was Lance Robinson winning the Visitors' Challenge Cup at Henley Royal Regatta as the stroke of a composite Four with Shiplake College. Lance went on to become a Great Britain junior international. The bar had now been raised, and the aim was wins at the National Championships and even representation at the Home Internationals. The 1984–1985 season saw 35 wins, with 22 of them in Fours.

An important acquisition in 1985 was the Club's first coaching launch. Until then, coaching had been done from the bank, either by bike or by running along the towpath for the fitter coaches. Following crews in a launch allowed better monitoring, but also improved the safety of crews. In the late 1980s, increased fitness, the use of small boats and the introduction of sculling led to even higher standards. 1988 was the 'Grand Slam' year, with a Four winning the Schools' Head of the River, the National Schools' Regatta and the National Championships. The same crew went on to represent England in the Anglo-French match. During this period, sculling became as successful as sweep-oar rowing. Individual rowers and scullers from the Club reached a high enough standard to compete for British Junior selection.

The early 1990s saw the new intake of girls to Borlase wanting to experience rowing, and they soon proved to be the equal of the boys' crews. This period also saw the general introduction of crew sculling events and, in 1994, sweep-oar rowing was banned for J14s and J15s in favour of sculling. This opened up more competition opportunities for boys and girls. It was in crew sculling that the girls would prove to be successful. Nevertheless, the senior boys occasionally put an Eight together to have a tilt at the Princess Elizabeth Cup at Henley, but without success. By this time, Borlase had become well established as one of the top rowing schools in the country.

1994 was another landmark year for the Boat Club, with the retirement of Tony Craig after 22 years as master-in-charge of Rowing. John Stebbings wrote of him: "Tony's role as master-in-charge of Rowing during this time … cannot be underestimated. His personal dedication to School rowing has been remarkable." Tony's departure eventually brought about a change over the next few years in the ways in which the Boat Club was

3.9.14. *The girls' J15 Coxed Quad that won the Schools' Head of the River Race in 2002: Nicola Spencer (bow), SJ Howard (2), Angharad Rego (3), Amy Tinley (stroke), Carolyn Johnson (cox), Charlotte Cox & Richard Bedingfield (coaches); Lizzie Tinley, Borlase's first girl to win a world rowing medal, with Rowing master Tony Craig*

run and crews were coached. In the following few years, several teachers managed and coached the Boat Club, but the days of Russell Sage and Tony Craig were long gone, and volunteer non-teacher coaches became necessary to cope with the large number of pupils wanting to row.

In 1997–1998, a promising boys' crew with no coach was taken under the wing of Russ Thatcher, a coach at Leander Club. This was the beginning of a change for the Club and the start of employing professional coaches. That boys' Quad became very successful and attracted more boys into the Borlase–Leander squad, producing several Great Britain trialists and eventually seven who represented the country. At this time, Dr Peter Holding (the new Headteacher) and Richard Bedingfield (a parent coach) were looking at the future development of the Boat Club and the need to have its own base.

The end of the twentieth century saw the beginning of the professional coaching era and the start of a search for an independent home for the Boat Club. This quest was to take more than 20 years before planning permission for a new boathouse was finally achieved. The introduction of rowing for Year 8 required more coaches and more boats. Russ Thatcher became the first professional coach for a short time, and then the position of Director of Rowing was created, with Charlotte Cox (ex-captain of Marlow Rowing Club) taking on the role. On the water, the girls' squads were holding their own against the boys and had a first-ever regatta win in Eights and started to win at the National Championships level. In 2001, Lizzie Tinley was the outstanding girl sculler who competed for Great Britain in a Quad in the World Junior Championships, thus becoming Borlase Boat Club's first female international rower.

2005 was a milestone year for the Club. Borlase had to leave Marlow Rowing Club after almost 50 years due the increase in numbers using the Club and the busyness of the Marlow stretch of the Thames at the weekends. The Boat Club was now committed to finding a new permanent home, and the search for a suitable site continued in earnest. The lower Cookham reach below the lock was favoured because it would provide a less busy and longer reach for training. Upper Thames Sailing Club at Bourne End came to the rescue and hosted the Boat Club for most of 2006 but then another move became necessary, this time to Longridge. Ali Brown, an ex-international lightweight, had taken over from Charlotte as the Director of Rowing and had the difficult task of keeping the Club going during all the upheaval of moving. It was hoped that the stay at Longridge would be a temporary arrangement; however, Borlase was joined by Great Marlow School and RGS High Wycombe, and Longridge became the home for schools' rowing for many years.

In 2007, Dave Currie, another successful ex-international lightweight oarsman, took over as Director of Rowing but, like Ali Brown, after building his experience as a coach he moved on to Abingdon School. During this period, an Easter training camp became popular and was sometimes held abroad. The boys would still aim for the Fawley Cup at Henley Regatta, but any great success would elude them. However, Dave's success as an international was a new influence for the youngsters, and membership of the Boat Club rose to 100.

One young, aspiring coach replaced another in 2010 when Robin Dowell took over as Director of Rowing. He proved to be a highly inspirational coach and brought great success for the Boat Club's senior crews in the following years. During his term between 2010 and 2015, the boys' Quad achieved an exceptional run of results in the Fawley Cup at Henley Regatta. After being the losing semi-finalists in 2011, they won the event in 2012, were losing finalists in 2013, and then won the

The Modern Era (1974-2024)   CHAPTER 3

3.9.15. Borlase winners of the Fawley Cup at Henley Royal Regatta in 2014 and 2015

event in 2014 and 2015. These results placed Borlase sculling right at the top of junior rowing in the country, and several Borlase scullers were being selected to compete for Great Britain at the junior level. Having grown his reputation for success, Robin inevitably moved on to coaching Great Britain juniors and then coaching the national squad in Switzerland, where he tragically died in late 2022 during a coaching session.

On a happier note, at the end of 2022, planning permission was finally achieved for a new boathouse in a field next to the Marlow bypass bridge. This joint project with Great Marlow School had taken more than 20 years to find the right site for the schools. The Boat Clubs will at last be able to move from their temporary home at Longridge into their own permanent base just across the river as soon as the boathouse is built. In 2023, Sara Helin became the first female rower from Borlase to participate in the Oxford and Cambridge Boat Race (sadly losing to Cambridge) and was also the President of the Oxford University Women's Boat Club.

The Director of Rowing is currently Phil Gray, an experienced coach who took over the Boat Club during the period of the COVID-19 pandemic, when there was relatively little rowing activity. Post-pandemic, interest in rowing at Borlase is stronger than ever, with around 200 pupils rowing (having grown from 140 in 2020). Phil is supported by four salaried coaches, and the Parent Support Group is as important as ever in providing valuable help, ranging from fundraising to organizing events.

Borlase rowing continues to go from strength to strength. Having celebrated the centenary of the Boat Club in 2021, it confidently looks forward to another 100 years of enjoying being on the water and success in racing.

Hockey

Hockey was first played at Borlase in the 1890s. Only a few fixtures were completed, and a plea was made in *The Borlasian* for more matches because players were keen and "a good oak stick" could be bought for a shilling. However, the request does not seem to have been heeded and the Sport died out, although apparently a few Staff and pupils played for Marlow in the early 1900s. The game restarted at Borlase in the late 1960s, but the 'modern era'

3.9.16. The 1972 Borlase Hockey team

dates from 1972, with the founding of a Hockey Club at the School and the development of a proper fixtures list. Even then, Hockey was a rather clandestine affair: Rugby was the only 'official' winter Sport, so matches had to be arranged out of School — until the selection of the then-Headmaster's son (chosen on merit!) caused Hockey to be viewed more favourably.

The 1970s: the beginning

Progress was swift right from the start. In September 1972, David Wedd was asked whether he would 'look after' the Hockey team. He agreed, and Rob Atkinson told Wedd that he should be the captain. As Wedd was new to the School and had not even learned the names of all the would-be players, he went along with the decision, which proved to be an excellent one: Atkinson was a natural leader. That first season, the XI won 13 matches. The only defeat was by the Royal Grammar School, a top Hockey school already, and their kindness in giving a first-team game to a School side with no known record was remarkable, and paved the way for an important rivalry later on, which proved beneficial to Hockey in both schools.

It was not really surprising that the 1972 Borlase team did so well, for there was plenty of ability, which only needed channelling properly. Team selection was easy, as Wedd had just 12 players from whom to choose (!), but of those 12, Chris Davey was later to gain his 'blue' at Cambridge, while Pat Land was to become the School's first international and later a formidably successful coach.

The following year, Borlase took part in the recently instigated Green Shield Rose Award scheme, a series of skills tests against the clock. As a 'new' Hockey School, without a huge commitment of fixtures, the players had plenty of time to practise skills and, rather to their surprise, found that they had achieved one of the highest scores in the country. As a result, Borlase began to be noticed. The success of the 1st XI also meant that a lot of younger boys were keen to start Hockey and, as a result, the newly constituted U14 XI had a very encouraging year, followed by an even better 1974, in which they were unbeaten in 14 matches.

Ken Pappin had by now joined the Staff. He had a good Hockey background and a flair for coaching. For more than a decade, until his other duties as housemaster and head of department prevented him from giving due time to Hockey, he and Wedd were able to run five teams (although not all at once). In the spring of 1975, Wedd and Pappin crossed to Holland with that year's fine U14 side, for the School's first overseas Hockey tour. The hosts were the Evergreen Club of Maassluis, near Rotterdam, and the visit was a great success, although the omens had not been good when the authorities at the Hook of Holland at first refused to accept Ken Pappin's green Irish passport! The U14s played eleven matches during the tour and won the Maassluis tournament. More importantly, they stayed with Dutch families and made many friends, so the hosts were invited back to England for the following Easter — a fixture that was to continue non-stop for more than twenty years, alternating between Maassluis and Marlow.

Other 'milestones' came and went quickly. Bisham Abbey gained a fantastic new Sports building and two artificial pitches, which in those early days Borlase was able to use a great deal. Even more important was the starting of a 3AS team at Marlow Hockey Club, in which promising young players from the School and the district were able to play together, against adult opponents, in a side reinforced by four 'veterans', all of whom still possessed reasonable skills and had considerable experience, if no longer the speed and fitness of youth! David Wiltshire was the tireless organizer and manager, while Brian Wadley, Wally Locke and David Wedd also played. It was a remarkably successful team, which at one stage won ten successive matches against adult sides from other clubs. It was also most enjoyable to play in, and Wedd believes it proved of equal benefit to the School and to Marlow Hockey Club. The development of the club's Colts sides prospered in parallel with the 3AS and things happened speedily. In 1977–1978, the School had three international players; the following year, Borlase became U18 Bucks champions while Marlow Colts won the Mercian League, both for the first time; and a year later, the U14s became Borlase's first-ever South of England winners.

The 1980s and 1990s

Borlase was becoming an 'important' Hockey School, and one of the first to play regularly on artificial grass, as Bisham Abbey's red grass miraculously transformed into two wonderful Astro pitches. The 1983–1984 season brought Borlase's first national title, when the U16s beat City of Portsmouth in the final at Coventry. Two years later, the School had one of its best-ever seasons: Borlase won the Weybridge Sixes for the first time, and Marlow Colts won the Mercian League again; no fewer than ten boys from the School were selected for the South East of England U14 team and it was hardly a surprise that Borlase's U14s, captained by Paul

3.9.17. The first Borlase U14s Hockey team to visit Maassluis

The Modern Era (1974-2024)

3.9.18. The Borlase boys' Hockey team became European Champions in 1991

Way, became National Champions. Neil Brown, Owain McGuire and his younger brother Phil all played against Wales at Willesden as a prelude to the Hockey World Cup, which was being held in England. It was also the year of *I Ran The World* for Famine Relief, so, on the day, Borlase and Royal Grammar School Hockey teams ran together from Handy Cross to Bisham Abbey, where the sides split half-and-half and played a two-hour match for charity. In the summer holidays, two Colts teams went to Ghent, Belgium, for the first of many visits to the La Gantoise Club.

The Borlase team that had become U14 National Champions in 1985–1986 followed that up by winning the U16 title for the next two years, and the U18 championship for the two years after that. This was not the end of their success, for in 1990–1991, they won the National Indoor U18 title and at Easter 1991 went to The Hague to represent England in the European U19 championship. They won (of course!), and are still the only British school to do so — but it was the way that success was achieved that stays in the mind. It is very seldom that tournament winners also win the Fair Play trophy. Their supreme achievement was the defeat of the Russian national side, by 4–1, with some astonishing Hockey. The 'European' Tournament was the last time that remarkable squad played together — with a few (but very few) changes each year, they had won six National and one International Championships in six seasons and finished, as a School side, with an overall record of Played 110, Won 100, Drew 10, Lost 0. Paul Way was captain of five of these championship-winning teams; eight of the boys played for England at schools level, and one for Wales, while Simon Nicklin and Howard Hoskin not only played throughout the six years, but also both went on to be picked for Great Britain.

In 1990, Jonnie Robinson joined the Staff. He was a League player and Cambridge 'blue', who brought many new ideas to coaching in the School, especially with regard to indoor Hockey, and his rapport with the players was brilliant. Borlase was now co-educational, and in the 1990–1991 season, Jonnie was a key figure when the first girls' U16 XI represented the School. Their enthusiasm brought them an unbeaten first season; in their second, they produced four County players; and in only their third year of School Hockey, they reached the U18 National Indoor Finals at the Crystal Palace. Some start! Anna Bennett became Borlase's first female international — and, indeed, before leaving School, she had been picked for the full England side, at that time the first schoolgirl ever to be so honoured.

3.9.19. The first Borlase girls' Hockey team were unbeaten in their first season

Soon, Jonnie Robinson had a young family of his own, so could not give as much time to Hockey as he would have wished, but the remarkable momentum kept going, for Welsh internationals Rob Stevens and Chris Davies now joined the Staff. Rob's sociable attitude and playing experience proved useful to the boys' teams, whereas Chris, helped by Claire Lewis, took over the girls' coaching with such flair, allied to good organization, that in 1993–1994, the U18s reached the Indoor Finals again, and in the following year, the U16s went a stage further, outdoors, by winning the National title. In the same season, that team's exuberant captain, Naimh Staunton, became the School's first Irish international.

Throughout the rest of the 1990s, both boys' and girls' teams regularly won County and South of England titles, without adding to their tally of nine National Championships. The girls' teams, in particular, seemed almost permanent participants in the Indoor Finals, and on one occasion both U16 and U18 teams reached that stage together, an astonishing achievement for a School with so few players — and no indoor hockey resources! Chris Davies had now been joined as coach by Allison Fountain (soon to become Ellis), but despite their skills and enthusiasm they could never quite wrest the title from the very experienced *club* sides that had begun to dominate the 'nationals'.

On 12 May 1992, to celebrate the School's 20th year of Hockey, a Borlase Past and Present side played a match at Bisham Abbey, against a team drawn from the Great Britain players who were training for the Olympics in Barcelona. The Borlase side was captained by Chris Maskery, the School's first full international, and the result was a startling 7–7, with Phil McGuire scoring five. For the first and only time, the entire School trekked over to Bisham Abbey during lesson time, to watch the match. On 22 January 1996, *The Times* carried a lengthy article on Borlase's Hockey successes as its 'Sport in Schools' feature.

During the 1990s, Phil McGuire, Simon Nicklin, Howard Hoskin and Anna Bennett all played many times for the full Great Britain side, and Phil, Simon and Anna represented Great Britain in the Olympic Games.

Some thoughts in 2002
It is harder now to equal the results of previous decades, and many things have contributed to this. The School is much bigger, but although many people play Hockey occasionally, as part of a widened National Curriculum, the academic requirements are so demanding (for pupils and Staff) that out-of-School coaching is much reduced and fewer play 'seriously'. Bisham Abbey now has only one Astroturf pitch, which is seldom available, and in any case the cost of hiring it is exorbitant. Borlase is lucky to have the small 'tennis-courts' Astro area — but without floodlights, winter training after School is very difficult! And the lunch break has become steadily shorter (35 minutes shorter than it was in 1972). No longer are there regular exchange visits with Dutch or Belgian teams, for a variety of reasons, and although there have been three tours to Barcelona, each very worthwhile, that venue is too far and too expensive for an annual visit. It is hard to overstate the value of overseas competition, for experience and motivation! Between 1976 and 2000, the School was host to more than thirty teams from eleven countries, and made nineteen overseas tours. Perhaps even more worrying, however, has been the trend (necessity?) for pupils to get weekend jobs, so that many very able players no longer turn out for County matches or inter-school competitions — and these games are where the experience, and rewards, come from. They are also where the role models develop.

Something from the early days that would be hard to equal now was a sense of 'involvement'. To begin with, the only way the Borlase teams and Marlow Colts could pay for their kit, training, fixtures, travel, etc. was by taking part in sponsored events. There were sponsored games, sponsored dribbles, sponsored runs — and indeed there was even a sponsored 24-hour game at Marlow Hockey Club (which in pouring rain ruined one pitch so completely that not a single game had to be cancelled during that season because 'it couldn't get any worse'!). Ken Drucquer at the sports shop reduced the cost of all kit for young Hockey players. Enterprising parents ran jumble and car boot sales. The School's minibuses were used for free transport for School, Club and County matches and when these were not available a gang of parents' cars came to our aid. The players were tough, too! So that they did not have to waste practice time at Bisham Abbey after School, they ran the 1.5 miles there and back as part of their fitness regime, and three times per week lunch breaks were sacrificed to competitive circuit training.

Also, in the past, excellent coaching and umpiring was done by senior boys and girls, with 'poachers-turned-gamekeepers' very prominent! The most argumentative of junior internationals often seemed to have a sympathetic attitude to, and understanding of, would-be players, and Howard Hoskin, Simon Archer and James Davies, in particular, had they been less effective players, could easily have become top-level umpires. And over the years, one of the reasons for Borlase's success as a Hockey School was the number of really good coaches who emerged *from the players*. Ian McIntosh, Danny Poulsen, Paul Way, Jon Owen, Nick and Peter Latham, Niamh and Cormac Staunton, Catherine Howard, Andy Watts, and Chris and Ben Land — the list is a long one: these and many more spent countless hours coaching, to a very high standard indeed. It meant that on weekday evenings, under the Bisham Abbey floodlights, two adults (sometimes only one) could supervise the busy and energetic coaching of 60 budding Hockey players. It is indeed much harder to organize this kind of thing on a regular basis today, but it would be sad if such an important tradition were to disappear. Perhaps if the planned floodlit Astro pitch is indeed built nearer to Borlase, this will allow these practices to be restored.

On 22 June 2002, a 'festival'; was held to celebrate 30 years of Borlase hockey. It was a pleasant and successful day, with some excellent games and an enjoyable get-together afterwards. It was good to see so many players who had contributed so much to the history of Borlase Hockey over thirty years, obviously relishing the occasion.

The twenty-first century
Kevin Chappell arrived at Borlase in September of 2002 to take over boys' Hockey from a PE teacher called Ollie Jones, who had been at the School for only one year, having taken over from David Wedd. Jones certainly left an impression on the boys at the time; Ollie Pruden would often talk of Jones' 'Zen Hockey' philosophy.

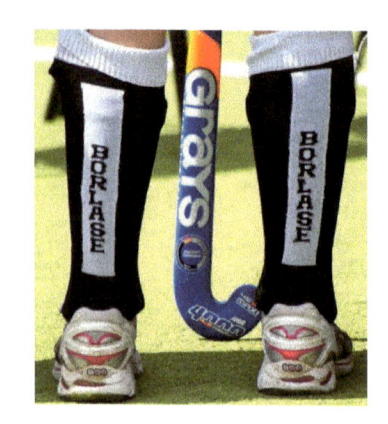

3.9.20. Borlase Hockey kit

Other Hockey staff at the School were extremely supportive and full of advice. Karen Brown (who later coached the Great Britain women's Hockey team to gold at the Rio Olympics) ran the girls' teams (when she was not locked in her office, doing her other role as examinations officer). She produced some fantastic teams. Karen coached at Borlase from 1999 and 2005 and was good friends with Assistant Head, Sophie Cheston, who helped to coach the teams and run tours in her time at the School between 1998 and 2006. They both made sure that Kevin Chappell understood the tradition and heritage involved in Borlase Hockey. Together, they took a great team up to the National Indoor finals that contained all three Philp sisters (Sophie, Abi and Lulu — in Years 7 and 8 at the time!), Roisin Orchard, Ella Bunt and Jenny Hopkins (captain).

The School also had a fantastic boys' 1st XI in 2002, thanks to David Wedd's legacy, although as alluded to previously, it was tough to get them to give up their Sunday jobs to come and play in the County Tournaments. However, they had no problem committing to the King Edward's School Bath Tour. Andy Watts was England U18 captain at the time and, between Chris Land, Steve Harding and him, they certainly kept Zen Hockey alive. Bertie Buxton and Nick Worthington would sit on either side of the goal waiting, while those three worked their magic to put it on a plate for them.

Karen Brown left Borlase in 2005, and Rachel Tabone took over the girls' coaching. Tabone and Chappell were both full of gratitude to the Hockey Support Group, a select crew of parents who helped to raise funds and guide Hockey in the right direction. The most common debate at the meetings was whether we should push a level of Hockey that was achievable for all or a production line of international players; somehow we managed to keep doing both simultaneously. A huge thank you must go to Alan Harding, Nigel and Sally Woolven, Julian Stanford and Julie Swales who chaired this group.

The Woolven family turned out to be a decent set of athletes, with Tom representing England U18 Hockey, Becky representing Great Britain Equestrian teams, Jenna going all the way through to Great Britain U23 Hockey, and Pippa representing England Athletics in the steeplechase. They were all great Hockey players of their time.

Tours were in high demand, and the boys' and girls' 1st XIs went to Valkenburgh, Holland, in 2003 and again in 2010. There was also an U14 tour to Amsterdam in 2008 — a trip that has now become commonplace for that age group. The tour paid off as the boys' U14s came back and went on to win National Bronze, led by their captain, Sam Burroughs.

3.9.21. Sam Burroughs in the National semi-final against Kingston Grammar School at Bisham in 2008

3.9.22. The three musketeers: Marriot, Tricker and Whitaker

Tabone was blessed with the three musketeers, as she called them: Beth Marriot, Zoe Tricker and Georgie Whitaker, who were the core of a very good girls' group who went all the way through the School together, ably assisted by Abby Griffiths and Immy Brown from the year below.

One of the best initiatives that the Hockey Support Group came up with was to put in place a new role of 'Hockey Community Coach'. Great Britain player John Peckett was the first to be appointed to this role in 2006 and was tasked with not only coaching at Borlase but also running an initiative for primary schools designed to improve the quantity and quality of Hockey that our feeder schools were getting. Simon Bond took over this role in 2007 and had an immediate effect, as our girls' U16s (containing the three musketeers) won a National Bronze Outdoor Medal and then our boys' U14s were crowned National Outdoor Champions in 2010. Some stand-out names from that squad include Jack Clee, goalkeeper Callum Haismann, Josh Rollett, Jack Turner (U16 Hockey Writers' Player of the Year and now a Great Britain player and coach at the School) and captain James Veitch.

In September 2010, the Community Coach role was upgraded to Director of Hockey, a combined venture for Marlow Hockey Club and Borlase. Mike Irving took on the role, and it felt like a genuine step up for Hockey in the local area. Mike certainly knew his indoor Hockey and, in 2013, the boys' U18s won the National Schools' Championship. The team contained many of the boys' U14 gold medallists from 2010, combined with the likes of Noah Sharples from the year above; they were a force to be reckoned with. Two years later, they got Bronze with Sam North at the helm and Jack Turner again pulling the strings.

It turned out that the combined role was an unachievable task for one person, so in September 2015, the full-time Director of Hockey role was made exclusive to Borlase, and Nathan Monk took on the position. In the summer term before the commencement of his role, Monk worked with a number of Borlase students at the Junior Regional Performance Centre in Oxford. The likes of Toby Bruce, Elliot Killington, Murray Whitaker and the Tylers were all part of the Oxford squad, and Monk was excited to know that he would be working with them, and many other fantastic Hockey players, during the next academic year at Borlase. Bruce, Killington and Whitaker would all go on to represent England U16s that season.

Monk enjoyed working with the girls' U18 group in his first year at Borlase, which was a fantastic combination of talent and hard work, including England players Frankie Butler and Freya Bull as well as some who had only just picked up a Hockey stick! The squad epitomized Borlase Hockey and the characters that the School develops.

Soon after Monk started, the Hockey Support Group disbanded, with the aim of getting a fundraising group off the ground. The Friends of Borlase Hockey group was formed in 2016, and thanks must go to Gill Towell and her trusted army of parent supporters, who set about raising money for equipment, kit, video analysis software and subscription grants. The fundraising efforts of this group continue to this day, and more than 160 tickets were sold to parents and Staff members for a quiz night in the School Hall in February 2023. Many parents have supported the Friends of Borlase Hockey group over the years, especially Gill Towell, Lisa Arnold, Jo Gurney and Ness Hill.

Jo and Ness were instrumental in the success of Borlase Hockey's 50th anniversary celebration in September 2022, recognizing 50 years of Hockey at the School since 1972. We welcomed more than 220 guests, including alumni, parents and Staff, to the fantastic event in the new Sports Hall. Welcome drinks accompanied by a Borlase Jazz band took place on the Cloisters lawn, before a three-course meal served by current students in the Sports Hall. It was great to

3.9.23. The girls' U18 Hockey squad from 2015–2016

3.9.24. The Friends of Borlase Hockey Group

The Modern Era (1974-2024)   CHAPTER 3 | 157

hear from Old Borlasians Pat Land, Keith Packer, Jack Turner and Jenna Woolven, while Frankie Butler stole the show with her incredible speech about her life so far. Thank you to everyone who attended that momentous occasion.

Borlase Hockey continues to compete at a national level. The girls' U16 indoor team reached the National Finals in 2016, and the boys' U18 indoor team finished third a couple of years later. In 2023, the boys' U16 and girls' U18 indoor teams both reached the National Finals in January and finished fifth and third respectively. Both U16 teams had runs to the National Cup quarter-finals, and the boys' U13s have just qualified for the National Finals in May, after being crowned regional champions in March.

The boys' U18s have set the tone with their commitment, focus and energy. Despite missing out on a National Final to an overtime corner during the indoor season, they are training up to three times per week as the National Plate semi-final awaits. Freddie Pollard has done a fantastic job of galvanizing his troops, a real throwback to the days of Burroughs and North.

Equally as pleasing is the continued growth of the Club. Borlase now has approximately 320 Hockey players and is regularly fielding A–D teams in the U12 and U13 age groups. More than 220 Hockey fixtures were played in the 2022–2023 season, and the School entered teams in county, regional and national tournaments at all levels. The second intercontinental Hockey tour to South Africa is planned for summer 2023, following the resounding success of the first tour in 2018.

Borlase also continues to work in primary schools with Marlow Hockey Club, a link that is as strong as ever. The primary school programme has gone from strength to strength thanks to the hard work of Kate Porter, Lee Morton and Luke Stone over the years. From four schools in 2015, there are now nine schools involved in the programme.

The fantastic new facilities onsite — a half-pitch AstroTurf on Home Meadow, which sits beside the new Sports Hall — have added another dimension to what we can offer.

3.9.25. Boys' U18 Indoor Hockey National Finalists in 2018

3.9.26. Members of the Hockey Tour to South Africa in 2018

Thank you to everyone who contributed to the Pitch Lottery, an excellent initiative that helped to pay for the majority of the equipment now used in the Sports Hall and on the AstroTurf.

Borlase Olympians

Mark Buckingham	1988 Seoul	Rowing (Men's Coxless Four)	4th
Simon Nicklin	1992 Barcelona	Field Hockey (Men's)	6th
Phil McGuire	1996 Atlanta	Field Hockey (Men's)	7th
Anna Bennett	1996 Atlanta	Field Hockey (Ladies')	4th
Rob Williams	2012 London	Rowing (Men's Lightweight Coxless Four)	2nd
Jonathan 'Jono' Clegg	2016 Rio de Janeiro	Rowing (Men's Lightweight Coxless Four)	7th
Jack Beaumont	2016 Rio de Janeiro	Rowing (Men's Quadruple Sculls)	5th
	2020 Tokyo	Rowing (Men's Quadruple Sculls)	2nd
Tom Dean MBE	2020 Tokyo	Swimming (Men's 200 m Freestyle)	1st
		Swimming (Men's 4 x 200 m Freestyle Relay)	1st

3.9.27. Recent Borlase Olympians: Anna Bennett, Rob Williams, Jono Clegg, Jack Beaumont and Tom Dean; Tom and Jack pictured at the 2020 Tokyo Olympics (delayed to 2021 because of the COVID-19 pandemic) with their three medals

The Modern Era (1974-2024)

CHAPTER 3 — The Modern Era (1974–2024)

CHAPTER 4
THE OLD BORLASIAN CLUB AND ALUMNI

A BRIEF HISTORY OF THE CLUB

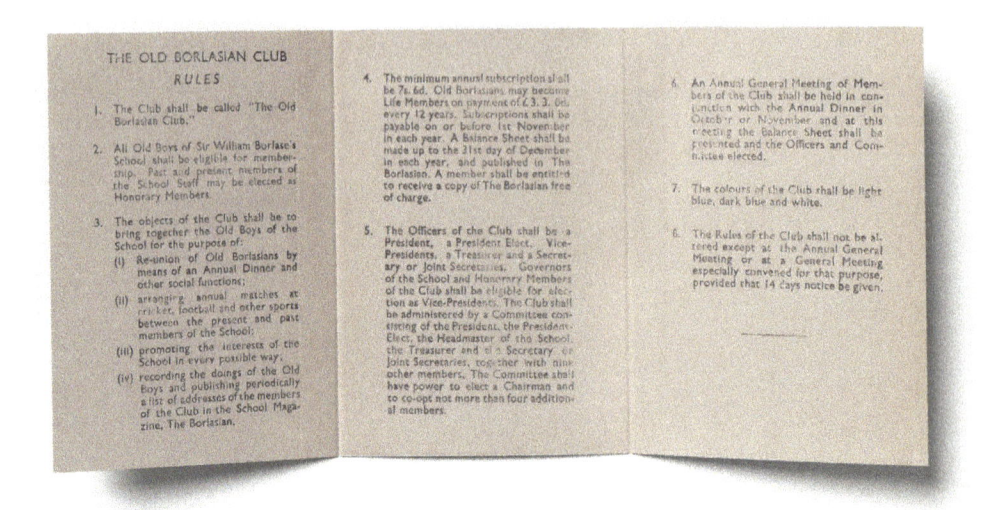

4.1.1. A booklet containing the Rules of the Old Borlasian Club

The Old Borlasian Club was founded on 21 March 1907 by the Headmaster of the School at that time, the Rev. A. J. Skinner. Within the rules of the Club, drawn up on 9 April in that year, four objectives were defined.

Primarily, the Club would exist to promote and facilitate the friendship of Borlasian schoolmates after they had left the School, especially by means of an Annual Dinner. Then follows the arranging of sports fixtures between present and past members of the School. The promotion of the interests of the School in every way possible by its past pupils was the next intention and, finally, it was deemed important to record the activities of Old Borlasians and periodically to publish a list of the addresses of members.

The first officers of the Club were elected: the Rev. Michael Graves (the former Headmaster) as President, Alfred Davis as Treasurer, and Frank Harman as Secretary. Membership cost 2/6 per annum (including a copy of *The Borlasian* magazine), which was no small sum in Edwardian Britain and suggests, quite accurately, an air of affluence and privilege.

So, in those serene and peaceful few years after its foundation, the Old Borlasian Club firmly established its roots. It fulfilled its objectives, and Annual Dinners were held in London that were well attended by Club members. These dinners developed a ritual of their own. During the meal, the President 'takes wine' with pupils of the successive Headmasters. This ceremony enables Old Borlasians to identify their contemporaries for (as R. H. Sage put it) "baldness, beards or even avoirdupois can often render men unrecognisable after the lapse of years". When eating is finished, there are the Loyal and Silent Toasts. Then follows the Toast to the School, proposed by a distinguished Old Borlasian, which is answered by the Headteacher, who reviews the progress of the School over the past year. The School Song is sung. A Toast to the Old Borlasian Club is proposed, to which the President responds. Meanwhile, the Toovey Loving Cup (see below) circulates around the tables. Finally, the President introduces the President-elect and invests him with the Presidential medallion, a legacy from the Rev. A. J. Skinner.

4.1.2. The third Annual Dinner of the Old Borlasian Club, held on 1 June 1910 at the Holborn Restaurant; the Rev. Michael Graves presided

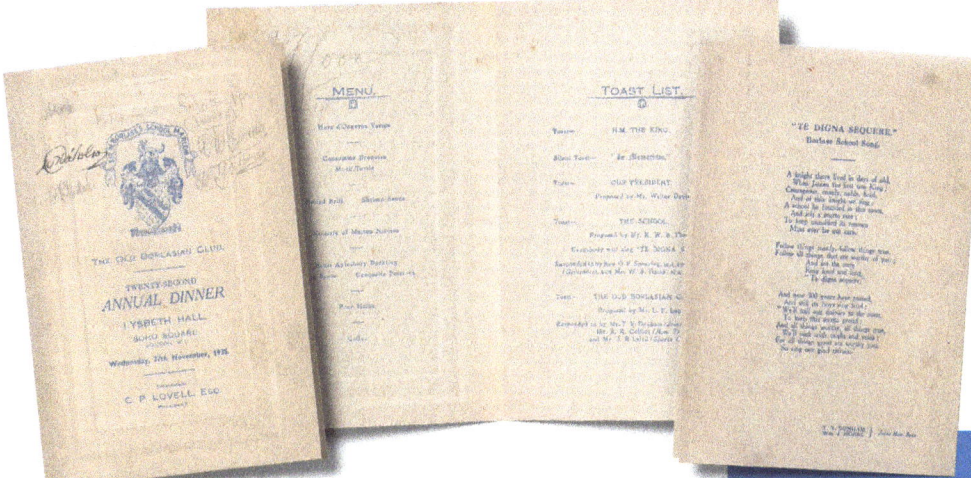

4.1.3. A menu card for the twenty-second Annual Dinner of the Old Borlasian Club, held on 27 November 1935 at Lysbeth Hall, signed by some attendees

Inevitably, the School moved on to new phases in its life and, after 1947, the privilege of attending Borlase was thrown open to a wider population of boys and eventually, in 1987, also to girls. The well-being of the School is always present in the Club's deliberations and, over the past 115 years, many opportunities have been taken by Old Borlasians to fill a gap in the needs of the School, with a variety of gifts of equipment or cash. In the twenty-first century, the Club contributed to School fundraising campaigns to repair and re-tile the Chapel spire and to build the new Sports Hall.

4.1.4. Plaque marking the centenary of the Chapel in 2014 and the contribution of the Old Borlasian Club to refurbishment of the spire

The Old Borlasian Club and Alumni

CHAPTER 4

4.1.5. Stained glass in the south window of the Chapel, donated by Stuart Lever

This spirit of giving is epitomized by the gift in 1998 from one prominent Old Borlasian, Stuart Lever (OB 1939–1944), of a stained-glass window above the main entrance to the School Chapel, with the theme 'The Pursuit of Excellence and the Helping Hand' — most appropriate for a Chapel that had been built as a War Memorial. Lever also initiated the School Development Fund. As he put it, "The Development Fund is the outstretched hand. The Helping Hand puts something into it."

In 2007, The Old Borlasian Club celebrated its centenary, and Stuart Lever presented the School with a stained-glass roundel, designed by Alfred Fisher and crafted by Petri Anderson. The roundel was unveiled at the Annual Reunion on 12 July 2007 and it hangs on the staircase to the Theatre.

4.1.6. The Old Borlasian Club centenary roundel, donated by Stuart Lever; photographed are Bill Bates, Dennis Paton, Ron Compton, Mrs Nora Compton, Monty Seymour, Andy Howland (President) and Tony Chubb

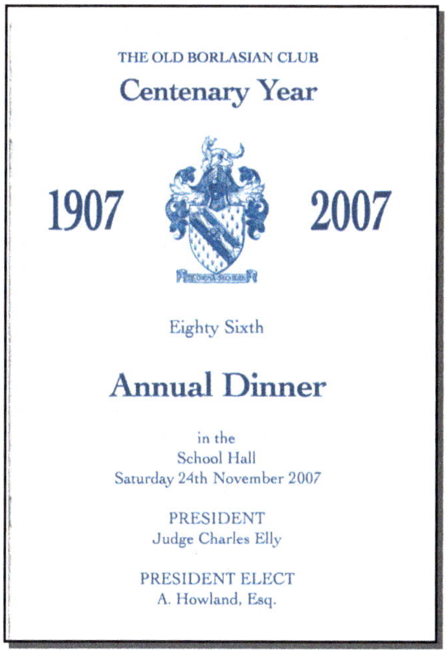

4.1.7. Menu card for the Centenary Dinner of the Old Borlasian Club, held on 24 November 2007 in the School Hall

Old Borlasian sides have played the School at various sports over the years. Football and Cricket matches in the early twentieth century were later joined by Hockey, Rugby and a Rowing regatta. There has even been an Old Borlasian Croquet competition! Gradually, the combination of health and safety concerns and logistical problems has resulted in these annual fixtures being abandoned. However, an Old Borlasian XI played the School 1st XI at Cricket in June 2022 (the Old Borlasian team won!), and it is hoped that this fixture will be restored as an annual event.

The Old Borlasian Club is pleased to support the School in many ways. For some years now, the Club has paid for the prizes that are awarded at the annual Sport Dinner, Performing Arts Dinner and STEM Fayre, in addition to the annual Old Borlasian Club prize, which is presented at Speech Day to "the pupil who, irrespective of success in school, shall have proved himself by his general conduct and bearing during the past year to be a credit to the school" (nowadays, of course, girls are also eligible!). The Club continues in its mission to nurture what W. S. Booth called 'The Borlase Spirit'.

4.1.8. Old Borlasian versus the School sports fixtures: an Old Borlasian Cricket team in the 1930s (note Ken 'Snakehips' Johnson in the centre of the back row); an Old Borlasian Football match on Colonel's Meadow in 2009; an Old Borlasian Cricket match in 2022

The Old Borlasian Club and Alumni — CHAPTER 4 | 165

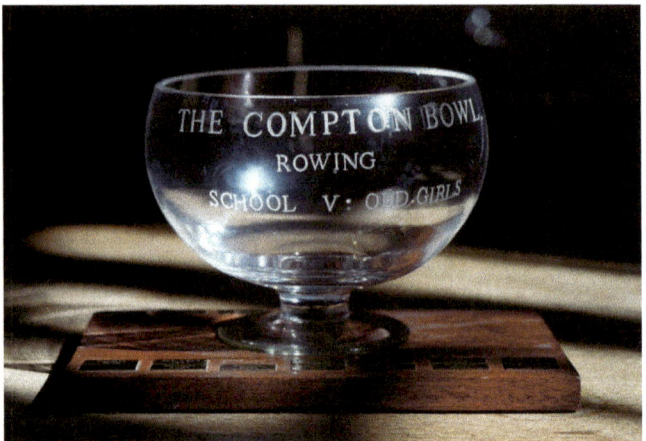

4.1.9. The Turk Plate and Compton Bowl, presented at the Old Borlasian Regatta

4.1.10. Examples of prizes funded by the Old Borlasian Club: the Ronald Bates Cup for the Old Borlasian Prize awarded at Speech Day, a Sports Cap awarded to 1st Team Captains at the annual Sports Dinner and a 'Boscar' (Borlase Oscar) awarded to winners at the annual Performing Arts Dinner

OFFICERS OF THE CLUB

The Presidents of the Old Borlasian Club are listed below. Their names are inscribed on the Toovey Loving Cup and on an honours board in the Cloisters.

Presidents

1907–1933	Rev. Canon M. Graves	1987	B. A. C. Keal
1934–1935	C. P. Lovell	1988	L. S. Dandridge
1936	F. W. Rowe	1989	T. Kelly
1937	T. R. Toovey	1990	S. M. Lever
1938–1945	B. T. Dickson	1991	A. J. Dean
1946–1947	F. B. Harman	1992	R. C. Child
1948	P. J. Rowe	1993	B. C. Wilson
1949	T. V. Dunham	1994	G. R. Fuller
1950	A. H. Harman	1995	A. Compton
1951	A. G. Taylor	1996	C. M. Winter-Taylor
1952	L. F. Lunnon	1997	D. J. Jameson
1953	J. W. Shaw	1998	W. H. Findlay
1954	E. A. Milner	1999	F. L. Thomas
1955	J. C. Davies	2000	R. R. Smith
1956	H. D. Cronyn	2001	D. C. W. Banner
1957	A. L. Wood	2002	D. M. Stainton-Ellis
1958	C. W. W. Jefkins	2003	P. J. Allen
1959	F. H. N. Layton	2004	E. J. Brown
1960	F. B. Cleare	2005	A. Howland
1961	W. W. Macdonald	2006	R. C. Elly
1962	H. P. Day	2007	A. Howland
1963	E. A. G. Moores	2008	A. H. Stafford
1964	A. C. G. Smith	2009	S. K. Funnell
1965	A. G. Laws	2010	P. Hogg
1966	W. R. Compton	2011	D. P. Dandridge
1967	F. G. Wigmore	2012	G. B. S. Lim
1968	R. G. Bates	2013	J. G. Cooke
1969	A. G. Chubb	2014–2015	A. Compton
1970	J. C. Gardner	2016–2017	C. L. Funnell
1971	F. J. Turk	2018–2019	C. A. Wells (née Nixon)
1972	J. E. Hinton	2020–2021	J. J. Bussell
1973	A. P. Townsend	2022–2023	G. B. S. Lim
1974	E. J. Lampard		
1975	D. Wight		
1976	R. H. Sage		
1977	K. J. Lawton		
1978	V. G. Brewer		
1979	R. H. Hobden		
1980	Rev. A. J. M. Saint		
1981	P. F. Todd		
1982	G. J. White		
1983	E. V. Sturt		
1984	J. W. Barry		
1985	M. E. Seymour		
1986	J. D. S. Hester		

Honorary Secretaries

1907–1911	F. B. Harman
1911–1913	F. A. Sloan
1913–1922	T. V. Dunham
1922–1946	T. V. Dunham & W. J. Hobbs
1946–1962	E. A. G. Moores & A. L. Wood
1962–1964	A. P. Townsend & A. L. Wood
1964–1985	A. P. Townsend
1985–2016	J. W. Barry
2016–2022	A. Compton
2022–	C. A. Wells (née Nixon)

4.2.1. The Old Borlasian Club President's medallion; on the reverse is inscribed: "Remember the Rev. A. J. Skinner BA. One of the Founders of the Club and Headmaster 1904–1927"

Current Committee

Dr Gregory Lim (OB 1997–2003) (President)
Dr Cathie Wells (OB 1990–1992; Staff 2000–2004, 2008–2010) (Honorary Secretary)
Grant Taylor (OB 1978–1982) (Honorary Treasurer)
Andy Barron (OB 1998–2000)
John Barry (OB 1948–1956)
Julien Bussell (OB 1978–1984)
Ilona Cains (Director of Development) (co-opted)
Tony Compton (OB 1957–1964)
George Cook (OB 1995–2002)
Chris Funnell (OB 1975–1978)
Simon Funnell (OB 1972–1979)
Ed Goodall (Headteacher) (*ex officio*)

The Old Borlasian Club and Alumni

STUART LEVER ROOM

4.3.1. Stuart Lever, whose bequest to the School enabled the creation of an archive and memorabilia room; he played for the Rugby 1st XI in 1943–1944 (front row, second from left)

Stuart Mordecai Lever was born in 1927 and attended Borlase between 1939 and 1944. He was an enthusiastic member of the Athletics, Rowing and Rugby teams. He recalled his pride at scoring the School's first-ever try in a match against a team from Bomber Command. After School came National Service in the Army Intelligence Corps, mostly spent in post-war Vienna, Austria. He then went up to Magdalen College, Oxford, to read Economics and Philosophy, before qualifying as a Chartered Accountant. He was Master of the Worshipful Company of Glaziers from 1992–1993 and, as we have already heard, he presented the School with a stained-glass window for the Chapel and a roundel to commemorate the centenary of the Old Borlasian Club, of which he was President in 1990–1991. Lever died on 4 February 2018, aged 90 years, and left a substantial legacy to the School in his will. The Old Borlasian Club decided to use the bequest to create a history and memorabilia room in the Cloisters (originally the Swedish Gymnasium), which now bears Lever's name. Many of the School's treasures are displayed in this room, including the Toovey Loving Cup, belonging to the Old Borlasian Club.

Toovey Loving Cup

Thomas Reginald Toovey was born in 1883. Believed to be a local boy from Wycombe, he

4.3.2. The Stuart Lever Room in 2023 and a collection of the silver trophies on display in the room

4.3.3. Thomas R. Toovey MBE, who donated the Loving Cup

joined Sir William Borlase's School in about 1894 and gained employment with Thames Conservancy in 1897. When it was established in 1909, the Port of London Authority took over management of the tidal Thames. Toovey transferred to this new body and was promoted to Assistant to the General Manager by 1924.

During the Great War, Toovey had been appointed secretary of a government committee organizing employment of labour battalions at the docks when civilian labour became short. His services in this position and his services in connection with the Special Constabulary earned him the MBE.

With his extensive knowledge of London's docks, which were an easy target for Gotha bombers and Zeppelins during the war, Toovey was commissioned by the government of the day to organize and further improve the defences of the port against air raids and enemy action. Such were his plans that they were adopted for the rest of the ports in Britain and elsewhere, notably Australia. He was no stranger to those parts as he had visited New Zealand and Australia in 1924 in an official capacity. Toovey retired from the Port of London Authority in 1937, at which time he received his decoration — but his retirement was short-lived, as we read below.

To accompany all his influential attachments to many of the oldest guilds of London, Toovey, a Freeman of the City of London, was soon to add the prestigious honour of being elected President of the Old Borlasian Club. He served as President-elect in 1936 and duly acceded to the Presidency in 1937. However, duty called and, by 6 November, Toovey was on board S.S. Orford on his way to Australia and New Zealand as a representative of the Port of London Authority. Toovey retained this post until June 1948.

The Old Borlasian Club Annual Dinner in 1937 was held on Wednesday 24 November at Lysbeth Hall, Soho Square, London. As Toovey wished, Mr C. P. Lovell was his representative at the evening's proceedings. A radio telegram of greeting was despatched to the new, but now absent, President on board S.S. Orford, and a menu card was signed by all the members and sent later by airmail.

At the following year's Annual Dinner, after the Silent Toast had been drunk, Lovell announced that Toovey, whose Presidency ended at this dinner, had presented the Club with a large silver loving cup to commemorate his year in office. The Toovey Cup has the School's Coat of Arms inscribed on it and is on permanent display among the treasures and various artefacts held in the Stuart Lever Room. It was traditionally used by all who attended the Annual Dinner "to drink to the health and success of Old Borlasians overseas". Around the base are engraved the names of all former Presidents of the Club.

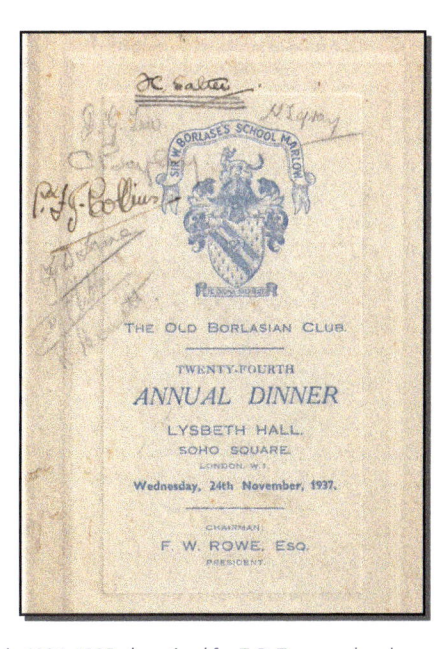

4.3.4. C. P. Lovell, President of the Old Borlasian Club in 1934–1935, deputized for T. R. Toovey when he became President in absentia at the Annual Dinner held on 24 November 1937

The Old Borlasian Club and Alumni | CHAPTER 4 | 169

BORLASE MASONIC LODGE

Freemasonry, like Borlase, started in a major way in England when James I was King. King James became a Freemason at the Lodge of Scone in 1601, two years before he took the English crown and, throughout his reign, Freemasonry started to become very fashionable.

side of the Cloisters and at the founding and consecration of the School Chapel.

Booth had fought in World War I and found the Lodge in Salford, Manchester, that he joined in 1921 to be a great comfort to himself and other ex-servicemen in terms of comradeship and support after the horror of the trenches.

Therefore, he resolved to form a Borlase Lodge for "his boys", as he called them, returning from World War II.

There were 16 founders, including Booth, and he was the first Master. The other founders were: Rev. D. J. Amies, R. E. Batting, J. E. L. Griffith, L. C. Haddon, A. H. Harman, J. Howland, L. R. W. Long, W. W. Macdonald, E. A. Milner, H. F. Nottage, P. J. Rowe, J. W. Shaw, G. C. Smith, W. D. Taylor and A. Wellicome. All the founders were Old Borlasians who mostly had fought in World War I or World War II and were members of Marlow Lodge, Wycombe Lodge or other Masonic Lodges in the district. Each founder contributed 10 guineas as a founder's fee, approximately a month's salary at the time.

It is thought that the Old Library (now the Staffroom) was designed so that it could be used as a Masonic Lodge, with stairs going up by three, five and seven and an alcove at the top outside the door in which the Tyler (or door keeper) could sit. In the 1940s and 1950s, that alcove was home to a half suit of armour (now in the Wethered Room). The Library was where Borlase Lodge was consecrated and where it met for the first few years after its founding on 2 March 1946.

Borlase Lodge still operates from the Masonic Centre in Marlow, but has now amalgamated with Norman Arches Lodge, another Old School Lodge founded by alumni of the old High Wycombe Technical Institute. The combined Lodge is now called Thames Schools Lodge, but still bears the Borlase number, 6216, in the Register of the Grand Lodge of England and is keen to maintain its relationship with the School. Over the years, most of the membership has been alumni, parents, teachers and others with School connections and still accepts people connected with the School if they are interested in Freemasonry.

4.4.1. Ceremonial Masonic laying of the foundation stone of the Assembly Hall on 13 October 1909

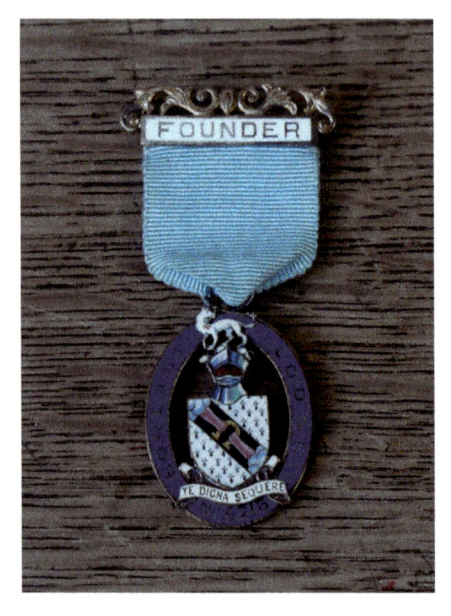

4.4.2. A Masonic Jewel presented to each of the Founders of the Borlase Lodge, No. 6216

The book cannot possibly reference all of them, but below are the stories of just a few Old Borlasians whose achievements represent the spirit of *Te Digna Sequere*.

4.4.3. The staircase to the Old Library (note the progression of steps) and the half suits of armour (now in the Wethered Room)

2nd Lt Basil Arthur Horsfall VC

Basil Arthur Horsfall (1887–1918; OB 1903–1906) was born on 4 October 1887 and grew up with his three older brothers in Chapman House, Darley Road, Colombo, in what was British Ceylon, now Sri Lanka. His father was a wealthy tea merchant and, like most of the British families based in Ceylon, sent their four sons back to Britain for their secondary education in England.

Edward Francis was at Borlase between 1897 and 1901; Cuthbert William was at the School from 1897 to 1902. Godfrey Lock was the third brother who was closest in age to Basil — he arrived in 1902, and Basil joined him in 1903 at the age of 15 years. They therefore enjoyed two years at Borlase together. At that time, there was a boarding house at Borlase that was home to about 30 boys. However, it is not clear whether all four Horsfall boys were boarders.

From references in *The Borlasian*, we know that Basil and his brothers were keen sportsmen. Cuthbert was in the Cricket 1st XI in 1902, and he also won the long jump on

4.5.1. Second Lieutenant Basil Arthur Horsfall VC

4.5.2. Horsfall (front row, second from the right) in 1906

The Old Borlasian Club and Alumni · CHAPTER 4 · 171

Sports Day in 1902. Basil played Football and Cricket. Indeed, he was captain of the Cricket 1st XI in his final year. The Headmaster, the Rev. A. J. Skinner, described Basil's cricket performance in *The Borlasian* of 1905: "Very useful bat, powerful hitter, good field. Fine, medium right hand bowler. Too impatient to make runs. Lately has developed a habit of playing over balls on leg stumps with disastrous results at nets, at least."

After leaving Borlase in 1906, Basil returned to Ceylon, working firstly in rubber but then began work in the Civil Service. He also joined the Ceylon Engineer Volunteers and qualified in signalling. When war was declared in August 1914, he at once applied for permission to go to England and enlist to fight. He was rejected at first because his role in the volunteers was considered to be of national importance. In July 1916, he finally received permission and joined the 1st Battalion of the East Lancashire Regiment, where his eldest brother, Edward, was already serving.

Basil reached France in February 1917, and he was immediately made the Commander of a Platoon within C Company, led by his brother Edward. On 11 May 1917, the Company were called to take part in an attack on the Chemical Works at Roeux, near Arras, a heavily fortified German strongpoint where several British attacks had already been repulsed. Both brothers were wounded early in the action, Edward more seriously. Basil, finding himself the senior officer in the Company, took command and held it together for five hours until relieved by a senior officer of another Company. Fainting from loss of blood, Basil consented to go to the dressing station. At the age of 30 years, this was his first experience of the front line. Basil was evacuated to hospital in England.

On 24 October, Basil discharged himself from hospital and returned to fight in France, despite General Haig himself recommending that he stay in England to recover. He transferred to the 11th (Service) Battalion of the East Lancashire Regiment, which famously became known as the 'Accrington Pals'.

A period of relative calm preceded the early months of 1918, arousing suspicion and expectation that the Germans had something up their sleeve. Sure enough, with 22 divisions frontline (385,000 men) and 22 more divisions in reserve, Operation Michael was launched on 21 March 1918 under a cloak of fog, with a massive bombardment of high explosive and gas shells. A huge front from Arras southward to Saint-Quentin (50–60 miles) was blown open, sending the Allies reeling.

Basil's company (part of the 31st Division) was rushed forward on 22 March in a fleet of buses to help to close the rift in the front line and were dropped near Boisleux-Saint-Marc, a village already under threat. In the next 4 days, the Battalion was ordered to fall back to new positions, such was the German pressure. At dawn on 26 March, they took up a position in hastily-prepared trenches at a crossroads between the villages of Ablainzevelle and Moyenneville and were now in the foremost line of the British defences.

Artillery fire (including some 'friendly fire') began the day on 27 March. With rapid changes in tactics and the speed of advance of the enemy, the direction of battle occasionally changed. With the fall of Ablainzevelle now on his right flank, Basil's company rebuffed an enemy attack but he himself received a serious head wound. With two other company officers killed and one seriously wounded, he led his platoon to a second counterattack and recovered his position. When the order to withdraw was given, he was the last to leave, exhausted but insisting he could have held on longer, had it been necessary. Basil fell on the way to the safety of the bank of the Cojeul River. His body was never recovered. His Victoria Cross citation in the London Gazette of 23 May 1918 concluded: "This very gallant officer was killed when retiring to the positions in rear." He is commemorated together with 35,927 other men who died in the Battles of Arras and who have no known grave.

Casualties in this 16-day struggle totalled 163,000 British, 77,000 French and at least 240,000 Germans. By 5 April, after terrible carnage, the Kaiserschlacht (Kaiser's Battle) lost its impetus and Allied victory was assured. The Battle of Amiens from 8 to 11 August saw the final turn of the tide, and the Allied offensive would continue, more or less steadily, despite many more vicious battles elsewhere, for the next 100 days until the Armistice on 11 November 1918.

On 12 February 2004, a service was held in the Chapel and a plaque was unveiled on the front of the School to commemorate Basil A.

Extract from a letter to Mr Charles Horsfall from Colonel Arthur Rickman

Dear Mr Horsfall,

I am so sorry that my letter of April 4th has not reached you telling you of the magnificent manner in which your son died … Hearing that the other two platoon commanders on the ridge were both killed and the other platoon commander wounded he refused to leave his men. Throughout the day, a very heavy fight continued. Twice your son lost his position but each time he counterattacked, driving back the enemy. He held his ground though his company had lost 135 out of the 180 engaged. I sent instructions for your son to retire. He received the instructions and carried them out, himself remaining behind to supervise the retirement. During the retirement he was unfortunately killed close to the ridge he had held so gallantly for days. His body was placed in a trench just beside where he fell, and we were driven back 1,000 yards and until yesterday the trench has been in German hands ever since. I am afraid his personal belongings which he carried on his person were left with him. The action was intense and it would have been impossible to have searched the dead under such withering fire of both artillery and machine gun fire.

Alas your son has gone in earning for his battalion the undying fame of a Victoria Cross. Beloved by all. Respected by all. Splendid endurance and a record of the greatest gallantry under the most adverse conditions. His name will be forever remembered by his regiment and by all who had the honour to know him.

Extract from a letter to Horsfall's parents from King George V

It is a matter of sincere regret to me that the death of 2nd Lieutenant Basil Arthur Horsfall, late 3rd attached 11th Battalion East Lancashire Regiment, deprived me of the pride of personally conferring upon him the Victoria Cross, the greatest of all rewards for valour and devotion to duty.

George R.I.

Horsfall VC, a century after he had attended the School as a pupil. On 27 March 2018, exactly 100 years after Horsfall's death, another service was held in the Chapel, and a framed tribute to him, containing a replica VC medal, was presented to the School by the Mayor of Marlow on behalf of the Marlow Remembers WW1 Association.

Major Jack William Shaw MBE

Jack William Shaw (1891–1968; OB 1904–1908) was born in 1891 and was educated at Sir William Borlase's between 1904 and 1908 and then at London University. During his time at School, Shaw won various trophies for Athletics and Swimming, some of which are displayed in the Lever Room. He was also an accomplished oarsman and rowed at Henley in 1913, 1914, 1919, 1920, 1921 and 1923, becoming a member of Leander Club. He stroked the Marlow Rowing Club Service Crew, which beat the Australian crew in 1919. He also played Football for

4.5.3. Basil A. Horsfall's Victoria Cross and the memorial plaque to him in the Chapel

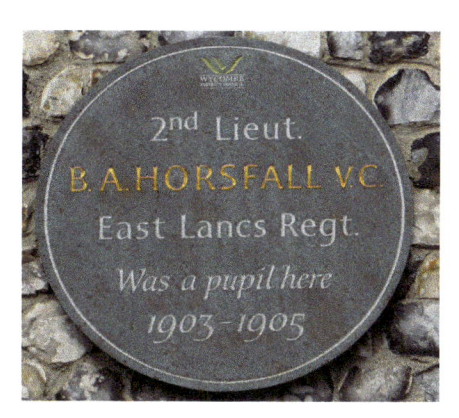

4.5.4. In 2004, a plaque was unveiled on the front of the School to commemorate Basil A. Horsfall VC and, in 2018, a replica VC medal was presented to the School (from left to right: James Simpson, Deputy Headteacher; Chris Funnell, President of the Old Borlasian Club; Jack Broadbent, Head Boy; Mary-Anne Grego, Head Girl; Kay Mountfield, Headteacher)

The Old Borlasian Club and Alumni | CHAPTER 4 | 173

Marlow, Maidenhead United and Slough Town,

4.5.5. Major Jack William Shaw

4.5.6. A Marlow Eight from 1912, with J. W. Shaw in the 2 seat

and was 'capped' on several occasions for Berks and Bucks. Shaw was also a middleweight boxer for the 43rd Light Infantry in Ireland.

Shaw joined the Army in 1910 and served with various regiments (2nd King Edward's Horse; the 1st, 2nd and 4th Buckinghamshire Battalion and the 6th, 7th and 9th Battalions of the Oxfordshire and Buckinghamshire Light Infantry). On 14 August 1916 while serving in France, Shaw was selected for the Royal Flying Corps and he returned to England to train as a pilot. He was back in France by 25 October 1916 as a qualified pilot, with just 11 hours of solo flying experience. Nevertheless, he served with distinction with the 22nd and 40th Squadrons, bringing down five German aircraft on the Western Front. The French awarded him the Croix de Guerre.

On 7 June 1917, his plane was shot down during the Battle of Messines in Belgium. Lieutenant Shaw was photographed with members of the German naval squadron at Torhout, including the pilot, Kunstler, who had shot him down earlier that day. Shaw's boots and flying kit had been confiscated as a precaution against his escaping.

Shaw was detained in a prisoner-of-war camp at Freiberg, Germany. By September 1917, he had established a code in his correspondence back to England (prisoners were allowed to write two letters and four postcards per month). One of the earliest messages contained the intelligence that the Zeebrugge Mole 'sheds' were not, as had been thought, bombproof — information obtained from a senior naval officer who had come through that place. Shaw's mother took the message straight to the Admiralty and, from that time until the end of the war, that code remained in operation between Shaw and the authorities.

Shaw attempted to escape from the camp in Freiberg but was recaptured and sent to Holzminden Punishment Camp, near Hanover in Saxony, which was the worst prisoner-of-war camp in Germany and, rather like Colditz Castle in World War II, had a reputation for being inescapable. The commandant of Holzminden, Hauptmann Karl Niemeyer, was reported to be capricious, unfairly punitive and particularly brutal.

The camp held 550 officers and 100 orderlies and, after it opened in September 1917, there were 17 escape attempts in the first month alone. All were unsuccessful. In November that year, the prisoners began digging a tunnel that would run under the camp's perimeter wall. The barracks consisted of two *Kasernen* (buildings) 'A' and 'B', and the tunnel started from under Kaserne B, beneath the British orderlies' quarters, in a spot that the Germans never visited and which was partitioned off. Officers

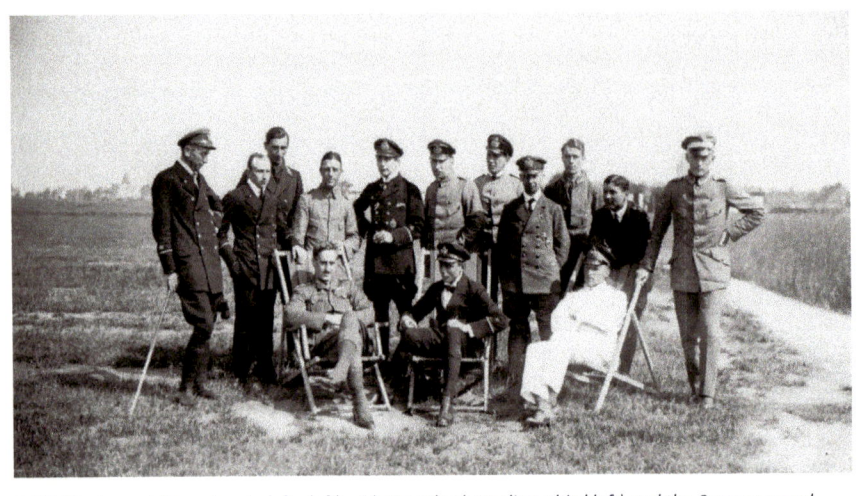

4.5.7. Lieutenant Shaw (seated, far left) with Kunstler (standing, third left) and the German naval squadron that had shot down his plane over Belgium

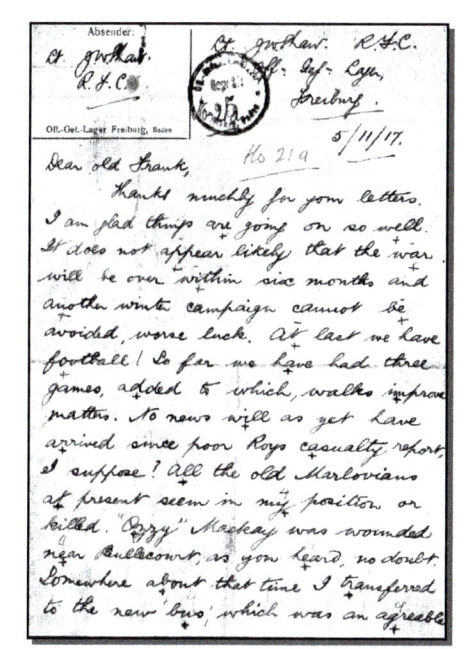

4.5.8. One of Shaw's coded letters home from the prisoner-of-war camp in Frieberg; decoded, the message reads "Paine to Admiralty. Zeebrugge Mole sheds not bombproof"

4.5.9. Holzminden prisoner-of-war camp, with British prisoners and German guards

changed clothes with the orderlies during the day, went to their quarters, and excavated with shovels or pieces of hard tin, but were in their own rooms by nightfall, where frequent counts of the prisoners were made at any hour of the night. The tunnellers worked in three-hour shifts, in teams of three, using trowels, chisels and a 'mumptee', an instrument with a spike on one end and an excavating blade on the other. The loosened earth was moved in basins by a pulley system, then placed in bags made from old shirts and hidden. A crude ventilating shaft was made from biscuit tins, and electric torches supplied the light.

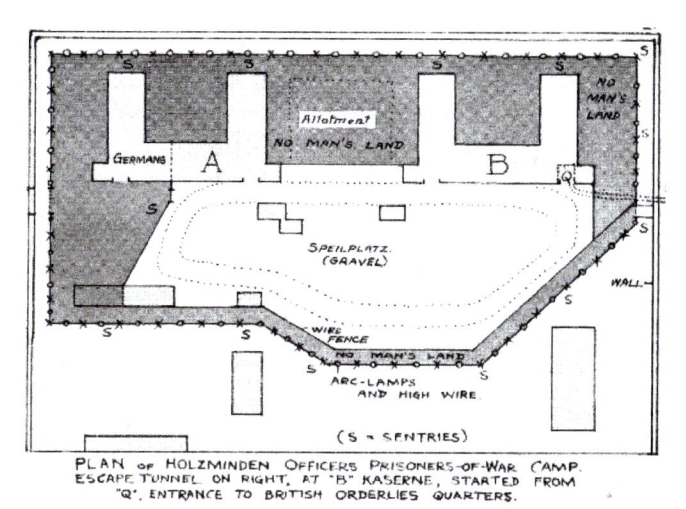

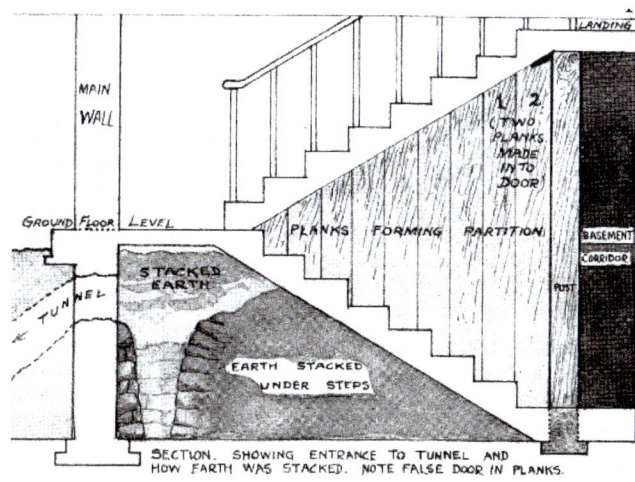

4.5.10. Sketches drawn by Shaw depicting the layout of the camp and the excavation of a tunnel

4.5.11. The opened tunnel at Holzminden Camp, Germany

4.5.12. Jack Shaw as a member of the Old Borlasian Club committee in 1948

The prisoners were assisted by three German administrators at the camp: a mailman who became known to the soldiers as 'the letter boy', a man who supplied torches and was dubbed 'the electric light boy', and a female typist who passed on information because she was infatuated with an airman. The captives had a room at the barracks in which they made imitation German army uniforms and used a basic camera to forge identity documents.

The would-be escapees were careful not to talk about the tunnel with fellow detainees, meaning that fewer than half of the prisoners at Holzminden knew of the existence of the tunnel, which was 60 yards long and 6 feet deep, before it was opened on 23 July 1918. That night, 60 officers began the escape attempt, with 29 getting away through a nearby field of rye, but the tunnel collapsed on the 30th man, blocking the escape route. Shaw was the next man in the queue and had to turn back.

Of the 29 escapees, 19 were rounded up and taken back to the camp, partly because the alarm had been raised by the farmer whose rye field had been trampled. The remaining 10 made a successful run to neutral territory, led by Wing Commander Charles Rathborne, who hid on board a train and reached the Dutch frontier after 3 days. The 10 successful escapees were awarded medals at Buckingham Palace by George V. It was the biggest escape from Germany in the whole war. At the end of the war, Shaw and his fellow remaining prisoners were released from Holzminden and returned by train and boat to England, eventually docking at Hull.

After the war, Shaw served in Cork, Ireland. In 1924, he married Phyllis Muriel Townsend, and they had a daughter, Rosemary Frances, in 1926. Shaw retired from the Army in 1930 but served in military liaison during World War II, which earned him the MBE. Later in life, Major Shaw served as President of Marlow Football Club, was a Commandant of the Bucks Special Constabulary, had a long-standing association with the British Legion, and was a founder-member of the Borlase Masonic Lodge. He was a Governor of the School and a member of the Old Borlasian Club committee, serving as President in 1953–1954. He died at his home in Marlow in February 1968, aged 76 years.

John Arbuthnott, 14th Viscount of Arbuthnott

4.5.13. The 14th Viscount of Arbuthnott

John "Jack" Ogilvy Arbuthnott (1882–1960, OB 1895–1900) was born in Montrose on 15 September 1882. He attended Borlase between 1895 and 1900. Before the outbreak of World War I, he spent several years in Canada, where he owned a ranch. He enlisted in the Calgary Light Horse, a unit of the Canadian Army, in February 1917, and later served as a lieutenant in the Welsh Guards. He succeeded to the title Viscount of Arbuthnott on the death of his father, the 13th Viscount, in 1920. Lord Arbuthnott represented viscounts at the Coronation of Elizabeth II in 1953, having also attended the Coronation of George VI in 1936. He served as Lord Lieutenant of Kincardineshire from 1926 until his death and sat in the House of Lords between 1945 and 1955 as a representative peer for Scotland. He was one of the earliest members of the Old Borlasian Club. Lord Arbuthnott died on 17 October 1960.

Sir Arthur Frank Kirby KBE, CMG

Arthur Frank Kirby (1899–1983; OB 1910–1915) was born in Slough on 13 July 1899. His father had been a lamplighter and porter on the Great Western Railway (GWR) at Reading, and his grandfather had also worked for the company. At Borlase, his nickname was 'dynamite', not because of his abundant energy, but owing to his 'Slough-cockney' accent! He was still at School when World War I broke out in 1914. Kirby served with the London Rifle Brigade in 1917 and was wounded at the Battle of Flanders. On demobilization, he was one of the first special trainees of the GWR, continuing in the family tradition.

In 1928, he entered the Colonial Service as assistant secretary to the Gold Coast Railways in Australia, where he worked for 10 years. In 1938, he became assistant superintendent of the line with the Kenya and Uganda Railways. In 1942, he moved to Mandatory Palestine and was appointed general manager of the Palestine Railways. In 1945, the Jewish Resistance Movement launched a war against British administration and sabotaged the Palestine Railways network at 153 locations. Trains, bridges and stations were bombed, and even Kirby's car was stolen at gunpoint. Nevertheless, Kirby rescued the railway from the verge of collapse, first to function as an efficient wartime service and then to reorganize it to meet the anticipated peacetime needs and to ensure a smooth transition to the new administration when the British withdrew from the Mandate in May 1948. Whereas some British political figures adopted a 'scorched earth' policy when handing over to the new State of Israel, Kirby was meticulous in his efforts to maintain a fully functioning railway system. He then returned to East Africa as superintendent of the line. He was later the Assistant Commissioner for Transport and then the general manager of the East African Railways & Harbours Corporation, before being appointed the East African High Commissioner.

In 1957, Sir Arthur spoke at the Jubilee Dinner held to mark the 50th anniversary of the Old Borlasian Club, and he was the Guest of Honour at Speech Day in 1961. He died in Hove on 13 January 1983.

Ken 'Snakehips' Johnson

4.5.14. Sir Arthur Frank Kirby

4.5.15. Ken 'Snakehips' Johnson

Kenrick Reginald Hymans Johnson (1914–1941; OB 1929–1931) was born in Georgetown in what was then British Guiana (now Guyana) on 10 September 1914 and was sent by his father, a doctor and the country's Medical Officer of Health, to be educated in England. He arrived at the age of 15 years to be a boarder at Sir William Borlase's School. He excelled in his studies and distinguished himself in the School Cricket team and in the Football team as a goalkeeper, standing at a height of six feet four inches. He later studied Law at London University but his interest developed into dance and he took tap dancing lessons from Buddy Bradley, an American choreographer who had worked with stars such as Lucille Ball, Eleanor Powell and Fred Astaire. Johnson's fluid and flexible style earned him the nickname of 'Snakehips' and

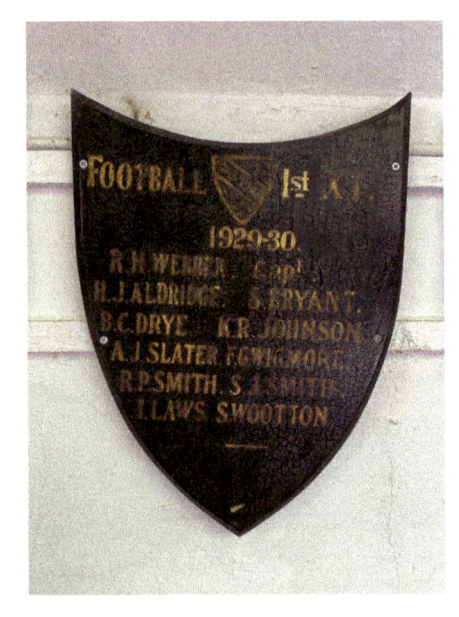

4.5.16. Ken Johnson (back row, centre) in the 1st XI Football team and the shield from 1929–1930 in the Cloisters that bears his name

he would dress in a white suit with a flower in the lapel.

Contrary to the British music scene at the time, Johnson was largely interested in jazz, particularly the swing movement in America. He eventually made a trip to the USA in 1934 and acquired some film work in New York as well as cabaret in Hollywood. It was during a trip to Harlem that Johnson was exposed to the orchestras of Cab Calloway and Fletcher Henderson, which inspired him to organize one of his own. Hence, Johnson's journey from dancer to bandleader began in 1936.

The first incarnation of Johnson's orchestra was known as 'Ken Johnson and his Rhythm Swingers' and consisted of Joey Deniz (guitar), Abe Clare (bass), Freddie Greenslade (trombonist) and Tom Wilson (drums). Four new players from Johnson's native West Indies arrived in 1937, including saxophonist and clarinettist Carl Barriteau. The group then became 'The West Indian Orchestra', and the group embodied Johnson's desire to recreate the American swing sound. The West Indian Orchestra were well received throughout England; they were regarded as one of the top swing bands in the country by 1940, having received exposure through radio broadcasts on the BBC and a television appearance.

Johnson attended the Old Borlasian Club Annual Dinner in 1938 and was mentioned in *The Borlasian* later that year: "Ken Johnson, whom we were pleased to see at the Dinner, has frequently broadcast with his Orchestra, and often 'tops the bill' at leading Music Halls".

Johnson was an inspirational dancer with an extraordinary sense of rhythm. He injected a strong rhythmic element to the music, similar to Duke Ellington's jungle style, and the performances featured his dancing as well as the music. The rhythmic element was taken up by the musician. In traditional big bands, star players would play musical duets with each other, but in Johnson's band, the musicians would duet with the dancer. He would leap up and down staircases and play head-to-head dance/sax duets with individual players. The dance performance was enhanced by creating intricate sets of steps, ladders and obstacles to be danced on, over and under. There are many recordings and some films that show him dancing at the front of the band. The other big bands caught on, and adopted his style of local and Latin influences.

By 1941, the West Indian Orchestra became the house band at the Café de Paris in London's West End and it was here, in the midst of the Blitz, that Londoners came to experience the swing music of The West Indian Orchestra.

Although the Café de Paris was a tiny venue, it was accessed via a long and steep staircase that went underground and provided a feeling of sanctuary for the wartime residents of the West

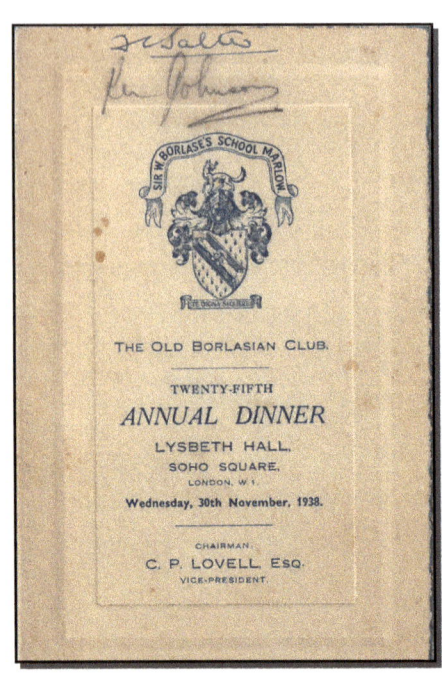

4.5.17. Menu card for the Old Borlasian Club Annual Dinner in 1938, signed by Ken Johnson

178 | CHAPTER 4

The Old Borlasian Club and Alumni

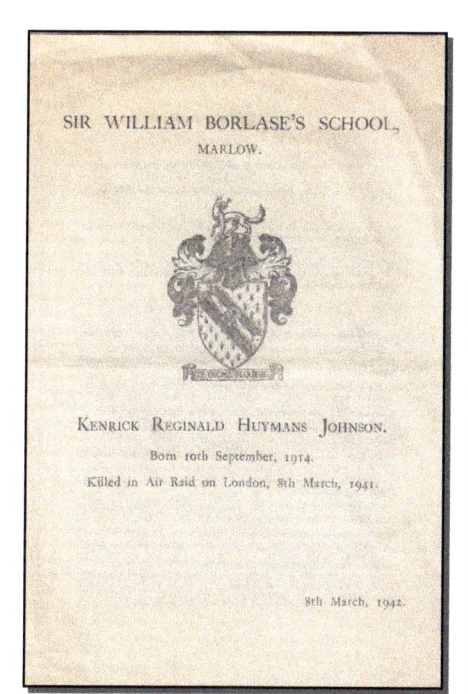

4.5.18. Pew sheet for a Memorial Service for Ken 'Snakehips' Johnson held in the School Chapel on 8 March 1942 (one year after his death), and plaques to commemorate him in the Chapel and on the front of the School

End seeking respite from the darkened streets of the black-out.

On 8 March 1941, during a usual Saturday night performance by Ken Johnson and his orchestra at the Café de Paris, the area between Piccadilly Circus and Leicester Square was strafed with bombs. One of the bombs fell through an air shaft into the club before exploding, shattering the glass ceiling and killing over 30 people as well as injuring a further 80. Buckingham Palace was also hit in the same raid. Survivors were taken to the Charing Cross hospital, but Johnson was not among them. One eyewitness recalled how he found Johnson, unmarked by any outward signs of injury, with a flower still in his lapel. He was 26 years old.

'Snakehips' was cremated at Golders Green in a service attended, despite the war, by more than 300 musicians and other mourners. Without any publicity, his ashes were returned to Borlase at the request of his family and are immured in the School Chapel. Johnson is commemorated in the Civilian War Dead Roll of Honour at St George's Chapel in Westminster Abbey, on a memorial at Golders Green Crematorium, and on a plaque on the front of the School. One of the Borlase music prizes awarded annually at Speech Day is named in his honour.

By the time of Johnson's death, jazz had developed from its roots in New Orleans and Chicago. It is now recognized that the exotic and exciting style of Snakehips and his bands greatly influenced the big band scene in England well into the 1950s, through the skill and dedication of those players who had managed to survive the war. The extraordinary paradox is that much of this was due to the influence of a man who never played the music, but who danced it with great brilliance and communicated his love for it to musicians and audiences.

Jazz at Borlase: the Snakehips legacy

Martin Joseph Kemp (1942–2022; OB 1953–1961) recalls being exposed to jazz at Borlase in the 1950s.

In 1919, the Original Dixieland Jazz Band, led by trumpeter Nick LaRocca, then probably the most famous jazz band in the USA, and possibly the first to establish jazz as a distinct musical genre, arrived by boat at Liverpool to start a summer tour. This visit was a sensation, introducing Dixieland jazz to the British public and ending with a private concert for the Royal Family.

The band and its players became famous in both the UK and the USA, but one little-known fact is the identity of the young British musician

4.5.19. Martin J. Kemp

who took over the piano for the first part of the tour, after the band's American pianist fell ill in Liverpool. At short notice, his place was taken by Harry Shalson, a pianist and singer who integrated successfully with the band, and played until the American player recovered. I got to know about this only because, in the early 1950s, Harry and his family, including his son, Vaughan Shalson, moved into a house next to us in Bath Road, Taplow, and Vaughan, who became a friend of mine, told me all about it between games of billiards.

After the tour, Harry went on to achieve fame as a popular singer with a typical 1920s 'whispering' style, making many records, and eventually changing to a career in business in the late 1930s. Curiously, therefore, his career overlapped with that of Ken 'Snakehips' Johnson, but as far as I know, their paths never crossed.

I started at Borlase in 1953, coming from Winbury Prep School, where my love of music had formed. In my second year I was shown a School clarinet and was told I could borrow it. I was thrilled, but then found I could not have it, because my parents could not afford lessons at three guineas for ten. It was then that I made friends with Richard Booth, a very genuine person and a great pianist, whose father played the clarinet, and who offered me free lessons. By this time, the clarinet had been given to someone else, but my family agreed to save so that I would be able to have a clarinet to learn on. For two years my family saved and, in the meantime, I played excruciating violin. Eventually, I got my clarinet.

There was a Jazz Club at the School in the years after I arrived that played records. One of those involved was David Dandridge, who was Head Boy in my early years at the School. They mostly played New Orleans tracks, full of blues banjos and gravelly voices. My own love of jazz also developed from listening to my father's extensive record collection. My brother, Steve, and later my younger brother, Jerry, also attended Borlase. Steve was a very good singer and could pick up and play any instrument straightaway, but never pursued it, and Jerry joined in our musical activities on drums.

Mr Peirce, the Music teacher, was an interesting character because, although enthusiastic, he seemed to me to be tone deaf. He also taught Scripture and failed to convince me that everything in the Old Testament should be taken literally.

Richard Booth accompanied me on my first School concert and tried unsuccessfully to interest me in jazz and a particular blues singer called Little Richard. We lost touch and, years later, I found out what I had been missing as I joined the Borlase 1953 group just after he died. Borlase had many musical students while I was there.

Borlase acquired a further connection with jazz when young Vaughan Shalson became a pupil at the School. Vaughan, a few years younger than I, followed me first to Borlase, and then to Cambridge where he studied Engineering. He eventually squared another circle by settling in the USA.

In 1957, almost simultaneously with Vaughan's arrival at School, Humphrey Bryson, a mathematical genius in my year, and I, together with the Haynes brothers and others, formed a Jazz Band at Borlase whose initial style took us back full circle to the original Dixieland Band's jazz of the 1920s. In this, we were spurred on by the success of the Traditional Jazz ('trad') revival. The jazz at which we threw ourselves, with rather more enthusiasm than skill, was the exciting, noisy hubbub of the 'trad' boom, a rather inaccurate attempt to revive 1920s jazz. 'Trad' took over from rock'n'roll, and had everybody dancing. We played New Orleans jazz on Thames river boats, at dance halls and at local regattas.

We were an odd mixture, mostly from Borlase, including the Haynes brothers, both trumpet, and Ed Sloan, a very skilful trumpet player. They tended to get in each other's way. Humphrey Bryson played piano/banjo and knew far more jazz than I did, but let me run the band, and Chris Robinson, a skilled jazz guitarist inspired by modern jazz giants such as Miles Davis and Charlie Parker in the USA, played beautiful modern jazz guitar. The rest of us scratched around.

After one concert, when we asked the caretaker to play drums (he refused to play a second time), we enlisted my overexcited brother Jerry, who used to thrash the drumsticks three or four times high in the air, sometimes catching them but often failing, so that they were smartly confiscated by members of the audience. We had two bass players: non-Borlasian eccentric Rupert Allan, who had a home-built bass, and Alec Harrison, whose family had forbidden bass guitar playing on religious grounds. To avoid detection, he used to lower himself out of his window with his electric bass attached in order to escape to gigs.

We played for anyone who would have us. We were fairly chaotic, and our audiences often got something they were not expecting. I remember escaping from a dance hall where the rather rough audience had been expecting Elvis Presley covers and were throwing things at us, and on another occasion trying to play unexpected strict tempo quicksteps at the Odney Club to a disappointed audience in dinner jackets. Also, in total darkness, unsuccessfully trying to pick out my band members from the huddle of supine bodies, male and female, on the deck of a riverboat that had run aground, so that we could play a second set (I never did find them).

After Borlase, I went on to St John's College, Cambridge, where despite an admissions tutor warning me that the College disapproved of jazz because of the debilitating effect it had on the mind, I formed the Windy City Seven band with friends, including Humphrey Bryson. After leaving Cambridge, I pursued a career as a lawyer in Westminster and Cambridge, but was accompanied at every step by an inescapable passion for playing jazz in almost every possible style. This also led me, 25 years after leaving Borlase, to teaching jazz improvisation as a volunteer in schools and at residential courses.

Martin was a member of the Old Borlasian Club committee and died in October 2022, aged 80 years.

Monty E. Seymour

Monty E. Seymour (1914–2017; OB 1926–1930) was born on 11 May 1914 in the farmhouse of Monkton Farm in Little Marlow. He attended Borlase between 1926 and 1930, before becoming a successful pharmacist in High Wycombe. Having served in India and Burma during World War II, he played an important role in setting up the Wycombe branch of the Royal British Legion and served as its President for more than 50 years. He became President of Wycombe Wanderers Football Club in 1966 and, again, served in the role for more than 50 years. He was made an Honorary Burgess of the town in 2002.

4.5.20. Monty Seymour, with Celia Blakeway-Phillips (Director of Development), celebrating his 100th birthday at Borlase in 2014, and on his pony Tommy, with dog Jack, just before he attended Borlase

He was President of the Old Borlasian Club in 1985 and, for many years, he was the longest-lived Old Borlasian. In 2014, a party was held at the School to celebrate his 100th birthday. Monty recalled how he used to travel to School on his pony. Seymour died on 12 January 2017, aged 102 years, and many Borlasians attended his funeral in All Saints' Church, High Wycombe.

Dr Henry Charles King

Henry Charles King (1915–2005; OB 1928–1930) was born in London on 9 March 1915. School records show that King was admitted to Borlase as pupil number 1208 on 23 May 1928, his father Edward King was a master baker and that the King family lived at 21 West Street. For his thirteenth birthday, his father presented Henry with a copy of Robert S. Ball's *The Story of the Heavens*, beginning Henry's life-long interest in astronomy. After soliciting assistance from an optician and his Science teacher, he built the first of many telescopes and proceeded to carry out surveys of the night sky. He used his home-made telescopes from the roof of his West Street home and soon filled his bedroom with drawings of the Universe.

The Borlasian from King's time at School shows that he won the Geography prize in 1929 for his essay *English Life in the Middle Ages*. He also took part in the School play *Le Jeune Traitre* as a soldier, performing the play in French. King (or 'Kingy' to his School friends) was also an accomplished athlete, winning the 1929 Junior Sports Competition. Perhaps more surprisingly, King went on to win the special prize for Divinity in 1930, with an essay entitled *New Commentary on Holy Scripture*. All this paints a picture of a very serious-minded young man. King left Borlase in December 1930 after gaining School Certificates in English, History and Physics and, appropriately enough, started work at Bateman Opticians in Maidenhead.

In 1932, he moved to Sutton Avenue in Slough, near to Observatory House, former home of the great astronomer Sir William Herschel, who discovered Uranus in 1781. Henry contacted Lady Constance Lubbock, Herschel's granddaughter, and was granted

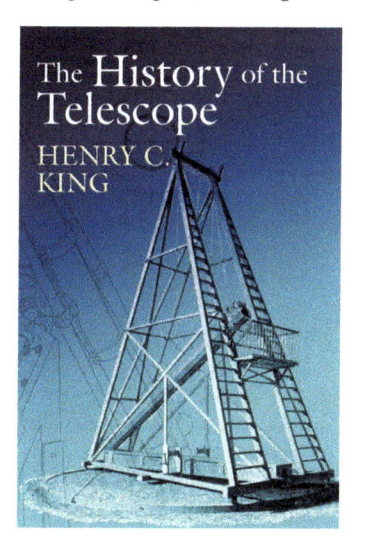

4.5.21. Henry C. King, astronomer and author of *The History of the Telescope*

permission to use the historic books, letters and papers in the Herschel library. He also built an observatory and proceeded to build telescopes and observe variable stars. During World War II, he was Inspector of Aeronautical Instruments for the Ministry of Aircraft Production at Ruislip.

At London University, King received a degree in Astronomy and Mathematics, then his MSc and PhD degrees in the History and Philosophy of Science. King's major published work, *The History of the Telescope*, was written mostly during World War II, using resources limited to those in London and Oxford, making his achievement all the more remarkable. In 1951, the manuscript was the thesis for his PhD at the University of London and was subsequently published as a book in 1955. It remains one of the definitive works on the subject and is still in print. Indeed, King's output of astronomy books and journal articles was prodigious, many of them focusing on telescopes, optics and planetariums.

Henry then began his career in ophthalmic optics, in both industry and education. King became Senior Lecturer in Ophthalmic Optics at Northampton College of Advanced Technology (now City, University of London) for seven years in the early 1950s. He was also President of the British Astronomical Association from 1958 to 1960 and a Fellow of both the Royal Astronomical Society and the British Optical Association. King was also a member of the British Society for the Philosophy of Science and the British Society for the History of Science.

In 1956, King became the first Scientific Director of the London Planetarium, itself the first public planetarium in the UK. Standing on the site of a former cinema that was bombed during World War II, the copper-roofed building was opened by the Duke of Edinburgh in 1958 as a part of Madame Tussaud's. King would often present lectures, taking his audience on magical trips to the stars, inspiring many children who heard these talks to pursue their interest in astronomy.

In 1968, King moved to become the first Director of the new McLaughlin Planetarium in Toronto, Canada. King remained in this post until 1976. Henry's other major book, *Geared to the Stars*, written with John R. Millburn and published in 1978, was an exhaustive history of orreries (clockwork models of our solar system), astronomical clocks and planetariums. Again, it is regarded as the definitive work on the subject.

Henry and his wife Mary, whom he had married in 1939, retired back to England in 1980. Sadly, the McLaughlin Planetarium was closed on 5 November 1995, and the London Planetarium closed in 2006, despite much protest. King died on 30 July 2005.

Garry Weston CBE

Garfield Howard 'Garry' Weston (1927–2002; OB 1939–1944) was born on 28 April 1927 in Toronto, Canada. His father, W. Garfield Weston OC (1898–1978), was the owner of George Weston Limited food conglomerate, which included Associated British Foods and Fortnum & Mason. Garfield Weston served as MP for Macclesfield during World War II and, in the summer of 1941, gave the School a beautiful oil painting by Montague Dawson (1890–1973) of a clipper ship under full sail, with the caption "It isn't the gale, but the set of the sails, that determines the way you go", which is from a poem by Ella Wheeler Wilcox (1850–1919).

Garry Weston moved to England at the age of 4 years, and both he and his older brother, Granger, attended Borlase. The Westons were a large family of nine children who lived in a fine house at Hambledon, but in no way were they waited on. They were brought up in the tradition of working hard.

Stuart Lever was stroke of the School 1st Four in 1944, and Garry was at bow, and Lever recalled that they learned teamwork together and, in particular, that good timing made for efficiency (and avoided a jab in the back from the oar behind).

Weston and Lever both went up to Oxford to read Philosophy, Politics and Economics, and Lever remembers his first time as Weston's guest at New College in Hall for dinner. When they had finished slurping their soup, there was a motto at the bottom of the bowl, "Manners maketh man".

At the age of 22 years, working in his father's business, Weston invented the Wagon Wheels biscuit. He became managing director of Ryvita in 1951, but left in 1954 to co-found the Weston Biscuit Company in Australia. He returned to the UK to manage Associated British Foods, serving on its Board of Directors from 1949 and taking over as company chairman in 1967. He remained on the Board until 2000.

He served as head of the Garfield Weston Foundation, which has given generous aid to a multitude of good causes, including the School, and assisted many initiatives to get off the ground. The Foundation's best known and probably most generous donation was £20 million to the British Museum in 1999.

Outside of business, Garry was a very retiring person and lived in simple style. He kept in contact with the School and was a trustee of the Borlase Trust. He died on 15 February 2002.

4.5.22. W. Garfield Weston and his Old Borlasian son, Garry Weston

Judge R. Charles Elly DL

Richard Charles Elly (1942–2021; OB 1952–1960) was born on 20 March 1942. After attending Borlase, Charles trained as a lawyer, graduating from Hertford College, Oxford, and the College of Law in London. On qualification, he became a partner at a law firm in High Wycombe. Initially specializing in criminal law, he then broadened into different areas of the law.

Having served the Berks, Bucks & Oxon Local Law Society as Secretary, Treasurer and then President, Charles was appointed as the President of the Law Society of England and Wales for 1994–1995. Subsequently, he became a member of the Lord Chancellor's Advisory Committee on Legal Education and Conduct. He was a Governor of the College of Law for 16 years from 1984 to 2000.

In 1998, he was appointed a Circuit Judge, first at Kingston, and then at Reading, being Designated Family Judge for Berkshire, retiring in 2012. He was awarded an Honorary Doctorate of Law from Kingston University. Having practised at his law firm for 35 years and serving as a full-time Circuit Judge for 15 years, Charles was honoured by his appointment as a Deputy Lieutenant of the Royal County of Berkshire in 2011.

He was dedicated in his service to his church community, undertaking almost every role in his local parish of St John the Baptist, Cookham Dean, serving as a churchwarden on three separate occasions and taking up the role of vice-chair of the Parochial Church Council. He was Lay Chairman of the Maidenhead Deanery Synod, a member of the Oxford Diocesan Synod and Bishop's Council, and Chair of the Diocesan Trustees (Oxford) Ltd.

Charles was President of the Cookham Society for 10 years from 1987 to 1997, served as Chair of the Berkshire Gardens Trust, and chaired the local village club and horticultural society. He had a keen interest in the arts, particularly opera and ballet, and was heavily

4.5.24. Charles Elly (second from right), with the Head Boy Alex Venn, the Headmaster Laurence Smy, and the Head Girl Caroline Lee, in 1995, and the plaque in Chapel commemorating him

The Old Borlasian Club and Alumni

CHAPTER 4 | 183

involved with the National Association of Decorative and Fine Arts Societies.

Despite his many and varied professional and community commitments, Charles remained a loyal Old Borlasian. He served for many years as a Governor of the School and was Chairman of Governors from 1996 to 2001. He stepped down to become the first Chairman of the Borlase Trustees and subsequently Chairman of the Marlow Education Trust. He was the President of the Old Borlasian Club from 2006 to 2007, the year in which the Club celebrated its centenary.

Charles, who had been receiving treatment for advanced systemic mastocytosis, died on 27 March 2021, aged 79 years.

Prof. Richard Hugh Britnell FRHistS, FBA

Richard Hugh Britnell (1944–2013; OB 1953–1957) was born on 21 April 1944 in Wrexham and attended Borlase until 1957, when his father was appointed Headmaster of a primary school in Lavendon and Richard moved to Bedford Modern School. He went on to become a professor in the History Department at the University of Durham and an important figure in the study of the economic and social history of the Middle Ages. The following text is adapted from an obituary in *The Guardian*.

As we struggle with current financial crises, we might be tempted to look fondly back to times when Economics were plain and simple. The Middle Ages are sometimes imagined as a time of self-sufficiency, when we grew our own crops and made our own bread. Richard Britnell, who has died at the age of 69 years after a long illness, made his name as an historian by showing that trade and money played a central part in mediaeval life.

His book, *The Commercialisation of English Society, 1000–1500*, set out clearly and comprehensively the view that change, most rapid in the thirteenth century, was driven by markets, urban growth and expanding trade. The inhabitants of even the remotest village and the most traditional feudal lord sold their surpluses of grain, wool and animals, and as money flowed, better methods of keeping accounts were introduced, farmers specialized in the most profitable crops, and industries multiplied in both country and town. Those reading Richard had to banish from their minds a picture of slow-witted peasants concerned solely with routines of ploughing and planting. They were, for example, often making decisions about the sale and purchase of parcels of land.

Richard's student days at Clare College, Cambridge, from 1961 to 1966, had coincided with a period when the ups and downs of the mediaeval economy were thought to depend on the expansion and decline of population. The idea had a strong logic, but did not explain the dynamics behind, for instance, the rise of towns. As a research student, he analysed landed estates in Essex, explored their sales of grain, and then moved on to look at weekly markets, which operated not only in towns but also in villages in growing numbers in the thirteenth century.

He immersed himself in the records of the important provincial town and port of Colchester — *Growth and Decline in Colchester, 1300–1525* was published in 1986 — while at the same time keeping track of the farming and rural society of eastern England, both during the period when Colchester was booming, and when its prosperity diminished. All of this culminated in the book on commercialization, which surveyed five centuries of history, and used general economic ideas applied to evidence relating to the whole country.

There had been a general trend among economic historians in the 1970s and 1980s to give mediaeval trade and towns more prominence, but Richard summed up the whole process, gave it a sharper focus, and developed it into a new explanation of change. The concept of commercialization received the stamp of his authority, and the book is still much quoted. He went on to further high-quality work on markets and society, but also ventured into political history, especially in the years around 1500.

After Cambridge, at the age of 22 years, he was appointed a lecturer at Durham University and there he stayed, initially in the Economic History department, in which he taught mainly the modern period, and then in History. He became a Professor in 1997, but six years later ill-health forced him to take early retirement, and for 10 years as Emeritus Professor he continued to publish and to be involved in the University and the city. He was elected a Fellow of the British Academy in 2005.

Not many academics can be said to have moved the boundaries of their subject, yet no-one meeting Richard encountered any pretension or flamboyance. He was restrained and modest in manner, but you were soon aware of an acute mind and great reserves of wisdom. He was careful in his writing and presentations and criticized (usually gently) those who ventured into rash or unjustified generalizations. He was a skilled organizer of conferences, in which he quietly established a friendly atmosphere. He nurtured some talented postgraduate students, helped research assistants to find jobs, and edited or co-edited books of essays (nine in all) to which scholars at the beginning of their careers contributed.

Richard found time to co-operate with other disciplines. For example, he became interested in literacy and language, on which he collaborated with his wife, Jenny, herself a lecturer in French at Durham, whom he married in 1973. Unknown to most of his academic friends, he enjoyed acting, played the piano and organ (serving as organist in his local church), and helped to run Durham's Rotary Club. He died on 17 December 2013.

4.5.25. Richard Hugh Britnell

Borlasian Parliamentarians and Diplomats

Authority and politics ran strongly in the Borlase family since the time of the Norman Conquest. Sir William Borlase was MP for Aylesbury, and many of his descendants were also MPs, including his second son, Henry, in memory of whom the School was founded. However, it is not until 321 years later that we trace a pupil of the School being elected to Westminster. A total of three Old Borlasians served as MPs in the modern era.

Lt Col. George Burnaby Drayson (MP for Skipton 1945–1979)

4.5.26. George Burnaby Drayson

George Burnaby Drayson (1913–1983; OB c.1924–1930) was born on 9 March 1913 and attended Borlase in the second half of the 1920s. Drayson served with the Royal Artillery in World War II in the Western Desert. He was captured in 1943 and taken into captivity. Despite the tide turning in the Allies' favour, Drayson was held as a prisoner of war in Northern Italy. However, in the company of a fellow escapee, he tramped 500 miles down the length of the peninsula until he reached the Allied lines, now advanced from North Africa to Italy.

Drayson held the rank of Lieutenant Colonel when he left the Army. In July 1945, very soon after the war in Europe ended, a General Election was held. In a shock result, Winston Churchill and his Conservative-led coalition were cleared from office in favour of Clement Atlee's Labour Party.

Drayson won the Skipton seat for the Conservatives from Hugh McDowell Lawson, of the short-lived Commonwealth Party. During his career as an MP, Drayson was also a member of the London Stock Exchange from 1935 to 1954, the Royal Agricultural Society and the Livestock Export Council of Great Britain. He was also invited to attend the Moscow Economic Conference in 1952.

Drayson was the Guest of Honour at Speech Day in July 1948 at the invitation of Mr Booth, then Headmaster. Stories of his military career captured the imagination of the audience, who were reminded of the ration cards and famous red petrol, which Drayson likened to the 'Tizer' bought by the pupils at Mrs Tidy's Tuck Shop.

Drayson remained an MP until 1979 and died on 16 September 1983.

Timothy Simon Janman (MP for Thurrock 1987–1992)

Timothy Simon Janman (OB 1969–1975) was born on 9 September 1956 and was a Marlow boy whose mother and stepfather, Irene and Jack, lived first in Station Road, Marlow, and then Oak Tree Close. Tim's proximity to the railway station later engendered, not unnaturally, a young boy's interest in trains, which he developed while at Borlase.

Janman attended St Peter's Church of England Primary School in St Peter's Street and Holy Trinity Junior School in Wethered Road. In 1967, when his stepfather was posted to Singapore with the RAF, Janman ended his primary school days in RAF Changi Junior School, where he successfully took his '11 plus', which earned him a place at the only existing RAF Grammar School. Changi is close to the infamous prison used by the Japanese in World War II.

He returned to Marlow in 1969 in time to join the Second Form. Ernest Hazelton was Headmaster, Janman's form master was M. Mercer (English), and Janman was placed in Normans. In the Autumn of 1972, when his stepfather was posted to RAF Brize Norton, Janman became a boarder at Sentry Hill.

Of the teachers whom Janman met, several remain firmly in mind for particular reasons. Tony Craig afforded Janman the proud moment of coxing the Borlase 1st Eight in 1975 at Henley. Other sports were not quite Tim's cup of tea and he particularly disliked Rugby, as he was a very keen Footballer but Football was not yet officially played at Borlase. However, he did take a leading role in the Debating Society and got his colours for Debating and Rowing as well as half-colours for Chess.

The teacher who made a deep impression on him and whom he remembers most fondly was Rod Hamer (Art). Janman was already a strong Conservative, but Hamer steered Janman to a strong belief in small government, free markets and disciplined monetary policy supported by an independent Bank of England. Luckily, Janman's ability at Art was sub-zero and most of his Art lessons were spent discussing Politics and Economics with Hamer and having to endure interruptions from the rest of the class who actually wanted to talk about their work! Hamer also quite unexpectedly lent his support to Tim in forming the School Railway Society. The Headmaster deemed that an adult was necessary to take parties of boys to various stations for trainspotting, a popular hobby of the time. Another member of the teaching Staff who influenced Tim was Bob Ogden (Chemistry), known as 'Stan'. He played a big part in Janman enjoying Chemistry and following it through to degree level.

Janman obtained A Levels in Biology, Chemistry and Physics, which took him to Nottingham University to study for a Chemistry

4.5.27. Timothy Simon Janman

The Old Borlasian Club and Alumni

degree. He graduated in 1978. During his final year, he was elected General Secretary and Deputy President of the Nottingham University Student Union for 1978–1979. He was instrumental in the Union boycotting the annual National Union of Students (NUS) Grants demonstration in 1979.

After university, Janman spent nearly 4 years with Ford Motor Company in training and industrial relations roles. Initially based at the Thames Foundry in Dagenham, he also worked in Woolwich and finally at the Ford Transit Van Plant just outside Southampton. None of these plants remains open.

In 1983, wanting a complete change, he successfully applied to join IBM in sales and remained with them, based in Basingstoke, until his election to Parliament. In May 1987, he doubled the Tory majority over Labour in the Shirley Ward to sit on Southampton City Council, but chose to resign after 3 months owing to his success in the June 1987 General Election. He felt that he could not do the residents of Shirley Ward justice while also serving as an MP representing a constituency 100 miles east of Southampton.

Labour's renewed attempts in the late 1970s to abolish Grammar schools, putting Borlase under threat, was one of the main reasons why Tim, still only aged 16 years, decided he wanted to become an MP. He always retained an interest in education and led a campaign in the House of Commons to abolish the NUS closed shop. This resulted in the Government in the subsequent Parliament (1992–1997) legislating to create a Student Union Code of Practice, giving students the right to opt out of NUS membership.

Janman was one of the cheerleaders on the Conservative backbenches that kept up pressure on the Government to abolish the Dock Labour System, which they duly did. He was in the top 30 MPs in the 1987–1992 Parliament for voting attendance, but did not always toe the Government line. He was one of Norman Tebbit's lieutenants in organizing Tory opposition to the 1990 Hong Kong Bill (which saw the biggest Tory rebellion against Mrs Thatcher's Government), and he was one of only 11 Conservative MPs to defy a three-line whip and vote against joining the Exchange Rate Mechanism in 1990.

Overall though, Janman was very much a committed Thatcher loyalist and supported her in the 1990 leadership contest. After losing his seat in 1992, Janman undertook lobbying work for the Shopping Hours Reform Council (SHRC), seeking to neutralize the opposition to liberalizing Sunday Trading law among some Tory MPs. His efforts were highly successful, and the SHRC model is the basis of the law as it stands today. In 1993, he returned to business sales, with Manpower plc. After four very successful years, he left them to go into Executive Search, working for Boyden and then moving to Hoggett Bowers in 2003. He retired in 2016.

Dr Phillip James Lee (MP for Bracknell 2010–2019)

Phillip James Lee (OB 1983–1989) was born in the Canadian Red Cross Hospital on 28 September 1970 to Marilyn and Tony Lee and has an older brother, Jonathon. He attended Clayton Primary School, close to home in Bourne End, where he lived throughout his School years. After junior education, he went on to attend Borlase in 1983 and joined the Britons House. He was keen on his sport and played Rugby, Cricket and (recently re-introduced) Football. Outside School, he played Rugby for Marlow RFC and Oxford University RFC and Cricket with a touring side of School-day contemporaries, the Old Grumblers. He is a keen Queens Park Rangers supporter.

Lee was appointed Head Boy in his last year at School under Roy R. Smith, but finished his time with Laurence Smy after Mr Smith retired due to ill health. For Lee, the age of 14 years seems to have been doubly decisive. He decided that Medicine was to be his career and also felt the urge to achieve some worthwhile service in the public domain. Despite winning a scholarship to St Mary's Medical Hospital in Paddington, his A Level results (Chemistry and Biology) fell short of the level required. Undeterred, Lee pursued degrees at London University and Keble College, Oxford, and deservedly secured his place at St Mary's in 1994.

As the course progressed, Lee spent 12 weeks undertaking an elective (experience abroad) in the hospital of the University of Otago, Dunedin, New Zealand, where he spent time in its well-equipped Intensive Care Unit. This facility contrasted vividly with his next posting, the poorly funded rural hospital of Aitutaki in the Cook Islands. It was stoically run by two dedicated doctors, Dr Aung and Dr May — a husband-and-wife team from Myanmar. Medicines were in scarce supply, and they were often making do with surpluses

4.5.28. Phillip James Lee

from pharmacies and doctors' bags, dutifully collected and despatched from Germany by a friend of Dr Aung, rather than what various medical conditions required. Lee gained valuable experience in the antenatal department and proudly delivered one baby. On his return to the UK, he graduated from St Mary's and then gained much experience in various medical departments of a number of hospitals, including Wexham Park Hospital. In 2004, he qualified as a General Practitioner.

Even before then, Lee's political ambitions took a step forward. Although his father and grandfather had both been Labour stalwarts, he knew that there was little chance of becoming a Labour MP in this area and looked elsewhere for a foothold. He got on a selection list for the Conservatives in Windsor in 2002 for the 2005 election but was not chosen. In 2009, with a record of service on Beaconsfield and Maidenhead Councils up to 2008, Lee stood for selection in the Bracknell constituency and was successful, although the local party was not financially supportive. Lee was selected again for the 2015 General Election and won the seat again. During this Parliament, the Brexit vote threw the Conservative leadership into chaos and, in 2016, David Cameron resigned as Prime Minister and was eventually replaced by Theresa May. Although strongly opposed to Brexit himself, Lee continued to serve and was appointed a junior minister in the Department of Justice.

At this time, Lee had been very vocal in the House and on frequent television appearances and, in the bitterest moments of Mrs May's struggle, he defended her character and reputation despite his being a 'Remainer'. After another Conservative Party leadership election in 2019, Boris Johnson was elected. Lee, who had already resigned from the Department of Justice in 2018, decided he could no longer stay with Boris Johnson and, on 3 September 2019, Lee crossed the floor of the House of Commons and joined other Tory Remainers under the banner of the Liberal Democrats. With Johnson's majority of one suddenly changed to a minority of one and desperate to get Article 50 through the House before the end of the year, he called a General Election, in which Lee lost his seat. Disappointed but not shocked, Lee returned to full-time practice as a GP.

Sir Graham Stuart Burton KCMG

Graham Stuart Burton (1941–2021; OB 1951–1959) was born in Marlow, Buckinghamshire, on 8 April 1941, the son of Cyril Stanley Richard Burton, a civil servant and veteran of World War I, and Jessie Blythe Burton. He was educated at Borlase between 1951 and 1959 and spent a year at Bristol University studying Law. But Law was not for him, and he briefly worked in a pub and later a sawmill, playing Cricket and Hockey whenever he could. In 1961, parental pressure induced him to join the Foreign Office as an executive officer. Burton had a remarkable ability to get alongside people and gain their trust.

In 1964, Burton was posted to Abu Dhabi. At that time, the Gulf states were under British protection, with the 'political agent' an eccentric former army officer, Sir Hugh Boustead. Burton enjoyed recounting his first meeting with Boustead who had never heard of his School and was dismayed to learn that he had attended neither Oxford nor Cambridge, could not ski and had never been to India. However, the two got on and Burton became effectively the agent's *aide-de-camp*. In the absence of telephones, Boustead would summon his staff with a whistle. Three blasts were for Burton, who would leave his prefabricated cabin and trudge across the sand to the residence.

During the genteel coup in 1966, when Sheikh Zayed bin Sultan al-Nahyan displaced his less progressive brother Sheikh Shakhbut, Burton was despatched to block the airfield runway and prevent outside interference. The economic development that followed Zayed's accession brought a flow of oil income and the arrival of movers and shakers from Britain and elsewhere. Serious companies were interested, serious politicians were involved, and serious countries were concerned to oust the UK from its privileged position in Abu Dhabi. One of Burton's tasks, helping to organize the political agent's dinner parties, required some sensitivity. A slip-up with a dinner invitation could produce shock waves that hit capitals when companies complained. Burton had an innate political compass, which was honed in Abu Dhabi. In time, he became commercial officer, with a key part of his work advising on suitable agents for British companies. He was able to see the fruits of this work much later when he returned to Abu Dhabi as British ambassador to the United Arab Emirates.

In 1965, he married Julia Margaret Lappin and, in 1967, they went to Lebanon where he learned Arabic at the Middle East Centre for Arabic Studies in a village above Beirut. He enjoyed the immersion in Lebanese life. The endless Arabic word lists and flash cards were carried everywhere, and he practised the language constantly, often during games of tric-trac (backgammon) beside the petrol pumps with the owner of the nearby garage.

In 1969, he was posted to Kuwait as commercial officer. There was a lot of serious business as well as socializing with the young Kuwaiti set who would one day run the country and captaining the 'Kuwait Casuals' at Cricket. In 1972, Burton returned to London to the Middle East Department and during that posting he 'bridged', passing the Foreign Office fast stream interview.

In 1975, he was sent out to Idi Amin's Uganda for three months to cover the leave of the deputy head of mission. The President spent a lot of time crisscrossing the country to open shops or schools and wherever he went the diplomatic corps went too, which involved driving for hours on dusty and pitted tracks. Anyone even vaguely disparaging the

4.5.29. Sir Graham Stuart Burton

4.5.30. Sir Graham Burton with Sheikh Zayed bin Sultan al-Nahyan in 1990

regime was expelled. During Burton's time there, a British lecturer wrote a somewhat uncomplimentary book but instead of being expelled was imprisoned and sentenced to death. Amin offered to release him if the Prime Minister, Harold Wilson, came to Uganda. After much work behind the scenes by the High Commission, James Callaghan, the Foreign Secretary, went to Uganda to see Amin and escort the lecturer home.

Burton was then posted to Tunis as deputy head of mission. From Tunisia it was something of a culture shock to move in 1978 to New York to take on the Middle East portfolio in the UK mission to the United Nations. Burton excelled in this new role, bringing into play his political skills, knowledge of the Middle East and remarkable ability to get alongside people and gain their trust.

In 1981, he was posted to Libya as counsellor in the embassy in Tripoli, with a mission to restore morale where the rigours of Colonel Gaddafi's rule were not eased by insensitive management. Burton diagnosed a shortage of essential, particularly liquid, supplies, which was remedied by a foreign merchant with a creative approach to invoicing. Burton and his family were under constant scrutiny from the authorities, but he made many Libyan friends and enjoyed his posting. Then, in 1984, shots fired from the Libyan embassy in London killed the policewoman Yvonne Fletcher, relations were broken, and British diplomats left Libya. Burton was on leave in London at the time and helped to handle the crisis from within the Foreign and Commonwealth Office (FCO).

He was then assigned to head the Security Co-ordination Department, a new FCO department to bring all relevant ministries, agencies and police together. It was thought, rightly, that his buoyant personality, so different from the aloof stereotypical diplomat, would inspire confidence among the various bodies with which he was to work. This was important and sensitive work for which he was awarded a CMG in 1987.

In 1987, Sir Antony Acland, then British ambassador in Washington, secured Burton's appointment as consul general in San Francisco because he was "so good with people". There was much there to keep him busy, from an earthquake to Irish matters to Silicon Valley. His love of sport, including an encyclopaedic knowledge of baseball, which he had begun to develop in his New York days, created an instant bond and was key to many enduring friendships with senior businessmen and politicians. The ambassador in Washington approved his visit to London with the San Francisco 49ers on their first appearance at Wembley stadium.

In 1990, Burton returned to Abu Dhabi as ambassador. These were difficult times — the Bank of Credit and Commerce International (BCCI) scandal, the Gulf War — but the friendships made and the trust established during his first posting there endured. "The boy has come back," the merchants said. "The boy is clean." A characteristic of his approach was the attention he paid to the British community. He always said that members of the community would know someone local better than he did and were a valuable source of advice. He had a special knack for putting people at their ease, and for "reading the room" when making speeches.

In 1994, he became ambassador to Indonesia. During his time there, the Free Papua Movement kidnapped a group of Cambridge science students working in the jungles of Irian Jaya (now Papua), the easternmost province of Indonesia, and held them for 128 days together with their Indonesian colleagues. Burton was involved in the negotiations. Eventually, the go-ahead had to be given to Indonesian special forces to attack and the British students were freed. Sadly, two of the Indonesian students were killed, as were eight of the rebels.

In 1997 came Burton's final posting, to Nigeria as high commissioner in Lagos and Abuja. Though far from easy — not least because he insisted on a fortnightly move between the two centres — this posting saw Burton in his element. He had always kept his team close, getting around the offices, offering encouragement and dealing promptly with problems. In Nigeria, he successfully managed a large and complex diplomatic mission as well as befriending people everywhere and making his mark across a fascinating country. He was advanced to KCMG in 1999.

After retiring from the diplomatic service in 2001, he worked for Control Risks and other commercial interests. His charity work was important to him. He was a trustee of Sightsavers for many years and travelled a lot on their behalf. He was also a member of the international board of the Chalker Foundation for Africa. In his final years, although unwell himself, he was a volunteer porter at the Chelsea and Westminster Hospital, enjoying his conversations with patients as he ferried them around the hospital. He died on 15 July 2021, aged 80 years.

4.5.31. Fleur Thomas with two members of the Irish Guards, attending HM The Queen's Birthday Party in Luxembourg, 2022, and with His Royal Highness Grand Duke Henri on the occasion of HM The Queen's Platinum Jubilee

Fleur Thomas

Fleur Thomas (OB 1989–1991) was in the second cohort of girls in the Sixth Form at Borlase. Below, she recalls her time at School and subsequent career.

I never really felt that I fitted in well with my peer group; I wasn't sporty, I didn't live in Marlow, and I wasn't particularly popular. I had 'defected' from Wycombe High School — in those days the High School was concerned about losing their girls to the new mixed Sixth Form at the boys' School. As a 15-year-old contrarian, I was therefore even more determined to leave. Despite not being able to study my chosen subjects (!), I always felt that Borlase was a caring School and a safe environment, and my years there were happy ones. In those days, skill at Sport (especially Hockey and Rowing) was valued above all, whereas for Music, there was only one small poky Music room in the Cloisters. There were three of us in that year at Borlase who were the 'musical' ones, and we put up a strong argument for the award of School Colours for those of us who represented the County in Music (until then Colours were awarded only for Sports). We won that right.

Performing Arts were focused on in the annual School play (*Twelfth Night*, and one of the best times of my life when I played a musician in Mr Stafford's production). I was proud to be a prefect, and enjoyed the hours of study, chat and silliness in the tiny study above the Cloisters — we even repainted it ourselves during the holidays.

My time at Borlase was sadly also marked by the accidental death of two students, Tim Magee and Ben Rimmer. I had been in the School play with Tim, and I took the School bus with Ben. These sad events really affected me and, to this day, I often find myself thinking of them both. Lives not lived.

My career did not go to plan as I sought happiness over the concept of progression in a single route. Nonetheless, I remained close to Borlase for several years after I graduated: it felt like a safety net. In 2000, I became the first female President of the Old Borlasian Club and remained a trustee of various School trusts until taking up my current post.

I learned that it is most important to do what you are passionate about, rather than what you feel you should do, because you are simply most likely to have greater success when you have real passion for what you do. I would never have made the world's greatest surveyor, so it is fortunate that I chose to leave six months in. I would never have had the social skills that I have now, had I not worked as cabin crew for British Airways in the mid-1990s. If I hadn't replied to an advert for a job working with the Reserve Forces in Aldershot in 2002, I would never have ended up in Whitehall. My life path has been winding, exciting and diverse, and I do not regret it.

Through hard work and determination, I have found and created opportunities that I never dared dream about. I was lucky that the right people recognized my hard work and potential, but for people with diverse life experiences like mine, it shouldn't come down to luck. I am now using my privileged position to mentor young people in the Government social mobility and gender networks.

I am currently His Majesty's Ambassador to the Grand Duchy of Luxembourg. Before this post, I worked in the Ministry of Defence and in the Department for International Trade, as it was known then. As a single mother with a non-traditional path, I never could have imagined myself in this role.

I was appointed to my current role by Her Late Majesty Queen Elizabeth II, and currently live in one of the most spectacular homes one can imagine, in one of the most beautiful countries in Europe. I have the privilege of representing His Majesty The King and his Government until April 2025. After that, who knows? I am due to return to the Ministry of Defence, but I'm in my late 40s; there is still plenty of time for a few more challenges and changes.

The Old Borlasian Club and Alumni

Borlasians in Literature and Linguistics

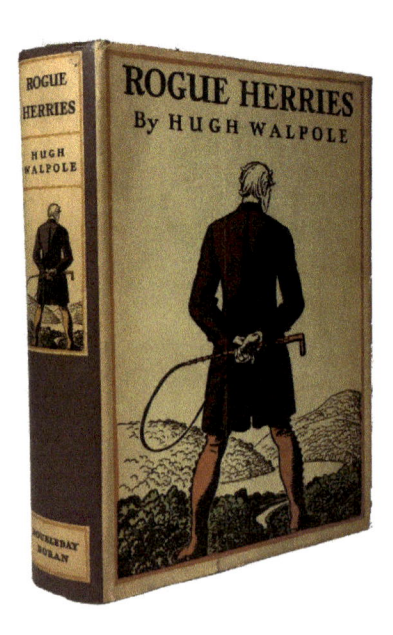

4.5.32. Sir Hugh Walpole, author of The Herries Chronicles

Sir Hugh Seymour Walpole CBE

Hugh Seymour Walpole (1884–1941; OB 1894–1896) was born in Auckland, New Zealand, on 13 March 1884. In 1889, his parents moved to New York and he was initially taught by a governess. In 1893, his parents decided that Hugh needed an English education, and he was sent to a preparatory school in Truro and then moved to Borlase in 1894. His time at the School was not a happy one, and he later recalled being bullied, frightened and miserable. Learning of Hugh's unhappiness, his father moved him to the King's School, Canterbury, and then Durham School. Between 1903 and 1906, Walpole studied History at Emmanuel College, Cambridge.

Walpole published his first novel, *The Wooden Horse*, in 1909. His first commercial success was *Mr Perrin and Mr Traill*, published in 1911. Walpole's poor eyesight disqualified him from serving in the armed forces in World War I, so he accepted a journalistic appointment based in Moscow and became reasonably fluent in Russian. During an engagement in June 1915, Walpole single-handedly rescued a wounded soldier; his Russian comrades refused to help, and Walpole carried one end of a stretcher and dragged the man to safety. For this action, he was awarded the Cross of Saint George. Walpole's novels *The Dark Forest* and *The Secret City*, published in 1916 and 1917, drew on his experiences in Russia. He also published the first of his popular 'Jeremy' novels. Walpole left Russia on 7 November 1917, the day that the Bolshevik Revolution began. For the rest of the war, he worked in British propaganda and was awarded the CBE for his wartime work in 1918.

Walpole remained prolific in the post-war years: between 1918 and his death in 1941, he published 30 novels, 6 short stories, 2 plays and 13 other assorted works. In addition, he began a parallel career as a lecturer in literature. In 1930, Walpole published possibly his best-known work, *Rogue Herries*, a historical novel set in the Lake District, where he now lived. He followed it with three sequels; the four books together were known as *The Herries Chronicles*. In 1934, Walpole accepted an invitation to go to Hollywood to write the scenario for a film adaptation of *David Copperfield*. The success of this film led to an invitation to return in 1936 to write the scenario for *Little Lord Fauntleroy*.

In 1937, Walpole received a knighthood in the Coronation Honours for services to literature. In 1939, he was commissioned to report on the funeral in Rome of Pope Pius XI, the conclave to elect his successor and the subsequent coronation. After the outbreak of World War II, Walpole remained in England, continuing to write. He completed a fifth novel in the Herries series and began work on a sixth. He was diabetic and died from a heart attack at Brackenburn, his home near Keswick, on 1 June 1941, aged 57 years.

As a gay man at a time when homosexual practices were illegal for men in Britain, Walpole had conducted a succession of intense but discreet relationships with other men. He eventually settled in the Lake District with Harold Cheevers, a married policeman, who became his chauffeur and whom Walpole described as "his perfect friend". Walpole was a keen and discerning collector of art. After his death, he left fourteen works to the Tate Gallery and Fitzwilliam Museum, including paintings by Cézanne, Manet, Augustus John, Tissot and Renoir. Sir Kenneth Clark called Walpole "one of the three or four real patrons of art in this country, and of that small body he was perhaps the most generous and the most discriminating". A biography of Walpole was published by Sir Rupert Hart-Davis in 1952.

Chris Bradford

Chris Bradford (OB 1986–1992) is a successful author, best known for children's fiction books. Below, he recalls how his time at Borlase led to this career.

I wore the School motto, *Te Digna Sequere* (Follow things worthy of thyself), on my uniform for seven years. I saw it every day above the gate and in the stained-glass windows. I even studied Latin, so I knew what it meant. Yet little did I know how great an influence this powerful saying would have on my life and career.

My time at Borlase was filled with studying, Drama, Hockey and Rowing. The impact of my teachers would turn out to be crucial in preparing me for my future creative career. Mr Stafford's English lessons laid the groundwork and my passion for literature and writing. His Drama classes also helped to instil confidence and a love of performance that would serve me well for my music career and my uniquely

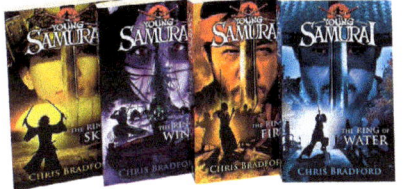

4.5.33. Chris Bradford starting at Borlase in September 1986, receiving a prize for English at Speech Day, and today, as the best-selling author of the Young Samurai *series of books*

interactive author visits. Mr Shannon's History lessons were in a class of their own — bringing to life the past in a way that would enable me to write with true authenticity for my award-winning *Young Samurai* series. My Latin master Mr Thompson not only taught me the foundation of the English language, but also provided lessons for life, such as how to play Golf, network and solve *The Times* crossword! Meanwhile, my biology teacher Mr Stebbings' commitment to Rowing helped to build up my muscles, resilience and determination to overcome the odds. Due to my teachers' and Borlase's ethos, I had the confidence and ability to pursue my dreams — to follow things worthy of myself.

After acquiring an English Literature degree at Exeter University, I travelled the world, volunteering for the charity Raleigh International in Zimbabwe and Nicaragua. Then I embarked on a decade-long music career. With my band, I toured the UK, appeared at the Notting Hill Carnival, released an album and even had the honour of performing for Queen Elizabeth II. These were marvellous times, and I dreamed of becoming a rock star…

But the wheel of fame turned in a different direction. My music career led me to writing a critically-acclaimed book on songwriting: *Heart and Soul*. This opened the door to more music books and then an idea for a story about a young boy who became the first foreign samurai. Thanks in part to Mr Stafford's English lessons, I possessed the necessary skills to write a fiction book. *Young Samurai: The Way of the Warrior* was published to huge success and launched me as a best-selling children's author.

I have since written some forty books, including the award-winning *Bodyguard* series and the *Jake & Jen* phonic books, which are read in a quarter of UK primary schools. My books are published in twenty-five languages, have received thirty-five children's book awards and sold over 3 million copies. My life goal is getting kids reading. This, I believe, fulfils the worthy Borlasian motto of *Te Digna Sequere*.

Max Porter

Max Porter (OB 1993–1999) was born in High Wycombe in 1981. He received a degree in the History of Art from the Courtauld Institute and an MA in radical performance art, psychoanalysis and feminism. His first success in the literary world came when he won the Bookseller of the Year Award while managing the Chelsea branch of Daunt Books. Porter's first book, *Grief is the Thing with Feathers*, was published in 2015 and won various prizes, including the International Dylan Thomas Prize in 2016. It was adapted into a stage play that premiered in Dublin in 2019 starring Cillian Murphy and has been performed in London and New York. Porter has subsequently published three more books: *Lanny* in 2019, *The Death of Francis Bacon* in 2021, and *Shy* in 2023.

4.5.34. Max Porter

Jonnie Robinson

Jonnie Robinson (Staff 1990–2001) taught German at Borlase for eleven years. He recalls his time at the School and his subsequent exploration of the English language, working at the British Library.

In 2023, I was contacted on social media by a former student just wanting to tell me that he still occasionally sings the German definite article declension table to the theme tune of *Byker Grove* (try it – "*der die das die … den die das die … dem der dem den*"). The recollection instantly put a smile on my face, followed almost immediately by a slight sense of regret that, since leaving teaching, I now only occasionally experience such moments of shared enthusiasm for learning. Clearly I may be deluding myself here about the subtext of a light-hearted tweet, but one of the many things that I cherish about my eleven years at Borlase was the refreshingly cheerful and good-natured relationship between colleagues, between Staff and parents and, perhaps most importantly, between teachers and students in the classroom and beyond.

I arrived at Borlase in September 1990 and spent the first few years teaching German in the far terrapin, which in winter resembled an igloo at morning registration and a sauna by afternoon registration, and coaching Hockey at Bisham Abbey. As a lifelong language(s) and sports obsessive, it was a privilege to teach successive cohorts of students, most of whom shared an interest in one or the other (or at least tolerated them with good humour!). It was a genuine pleasure to experience most students responding positively to learning German and encouraging to see a steady rise in student numbers at GCSE and A Level, culminating in a cohort of 32 students studying German at A Level. Yes, 32 A Level German students! I often wonder whether that might represent some kind of record — certainly at Borlase, but maybe even nationally — and I hope one day to see a reversal of the recent decline in students studying Modern Foreign Languages.

On the Hockey pitch, it was fascinating to observe Weddy's Wunderkinder at first hand and an honour to coach the 1991 U18 Boys' Indoor National Champions. It was equally inspiring to witness David's determination to ensure that girls' Hockey had every opportunity to reach similar standards, and I umpired what I think was the first official girls' Hockey match against Amersham College. I also coached the girls at their first major competition — the 1993 U18 Indoor Nationals at Crystal Palace — and was thrilled to see Chris Davies take them to even greater heights when they won the U16 National Title in 1995. Above all, I was always incredibly impressed by, and grateful for, the number of students who took the time to thank me at the end of a lesson, practice, match or tournament — a simple thing, but very much appreciated.

Towards the end of the 1990s, I became increasingly frustrated by decisions made both locally and nationally about the status of German in the school curriculum, so reluctantly began to consider a switch to Higher Education teaching and research. Having completed an MA in Linguistics, I worked as Research Assistant

4.5.35. Jonnie Robinson

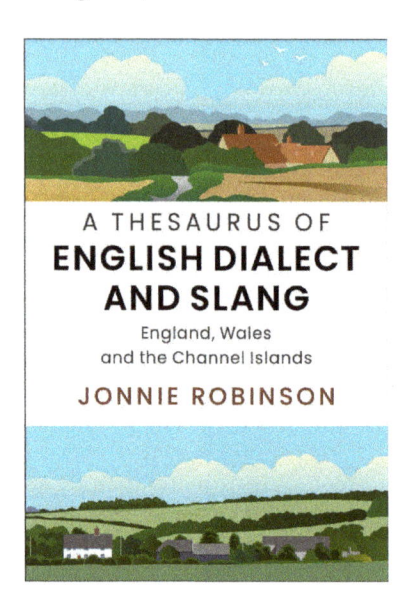

on the archive of the 1950s *Survey of English Dialects* at the University of Leeds, before joining the British Library Sound Archive in 2003. I am currently Lead Curator of Spoken English and responsible for the Library's extensive archive of sound recordings of British accents and dialects. In 2010, I co-curated the world's first major exhibition on the English Language, *Evolving English: One Language, Many Voices*, and have published widely on vernacular English, most recently *East Midlands English* (2018), *A Thesaurus of English Dialect and Slang* (2021) and the *British Accents and Dialects* website. I still enjoy close links with schools and students by running regular workshops at the Library, presenting at conferences and seminars, and organizing an annual English Grammar Day.

I look back on my time at Borlase with great fondness and am proud to have played a very small part in the 400-year history of such a wonderful School. I still occasionally bump into Old Borlasians — most recently at a literary festival in Gateshead — and it is always a pleasure to reminisce. Teaching at Borlase enabled me to pursue my two passions equally and to meet countless engaging people, including many far more talented linguists and sportsmen and sportswomen than I (*sportsthem*, as I suspect Sam Smith might say). My subsequent career inevitably saw a gradual shift in focus towards linguistic research and language documentation, although I coached and umpired junior Hockey at Southgate for many years and our three children regularly play with, and against, Borlasians and Old Borlasians. My interest in sport now manifests itself in the inventory of dialect, slang and jargon that I compile from mainstream press and media sporting discourse and present in an occasional #WordOfTheDay tweet and annual *Sports Word of the Year* blog.

One final linguistic thought as we mark 400 years of Borlase. While I cannot vouch for the first 350 years, I am reasonably sure that when I was teaching, we invariably called the school BORlase (with emphasis on the first syllable); intriguingly, I increasingly hear younger speakers call it borLASE (with emphasis on the second syllable). Funny old game, innit, language? I look forward to future Borlasians contributing to, and witnessing, the continued evolution of the School (and of English and German) in equally exciting and unpredictable ways for another 400 years.

Mark Gloyens and Tim Coombes

Mark Gloyens (OB 1975–1981) and Tim Coombes (OB 1975–1981) are the founders and joint Managing Directors of The Marlow Brewery and Rebellion Beer Company. Mark and Tim met in September 1975 on their first day of School at Borlase. They recollect having an argument over who got a particular locker, which resulted in a brief scuffle, the outcome of which is still hotly disputed. They spent the first two years in the same class with Mrs Cooper for Maths, Mr Welch for History and Mr Banner for Latin, among others. In the third year, the class was split and, although they did not have many lessons together anymore, they remained in contact as they both played Fives during breaktime and Hockey for the School with Mr Wedd as coach. After O Levels, they ended up back in class together as they both chose Maths, Physics and Chemistry for A Level, and in particular they remember sitting at the back of the class in Physics with Mr Bodey and a course book called *Physics is Fun*.

They kept in touch after leaving Borlase in 1981, with Mark going straight on to university to study Chemical Engineering at UCL and Tim taking a year out to travel to Australia, which included working in a winery in the Barossa Valley. Returning home, Tim then started a Civil Engineering course and, during the summer holidays, they got together while playing Cricket for Penn Street Cricket Club and, in 1984, spending a month travelling around Europe by train. It was during this trip, while they were talking about their long-term ambitions, that

4.5.36. Borlase U16 Cricket team in c.1978 (Tim Coombes front row far left and Mark Gloyens front row third from right); Mark and Tim at the Rebellion Brewery 30th Anniversary Brew in April 2023

they first mooted the idea of maybe eventually setting up and running a business together. Tim and his brother Andy (John Andrew Coombes; OB 1967–1973), who is now the Finance Director at the brewery, had set up and run a business buying fish from Billingsgate Market and selling it to local pubs and at a market stall in Wycombe and Amersham. After graduating in 1984, Mark went off to Australia and worked in the same winery as Tim had back in 1982.

The latter years in the 1980s saw Tim and Mark working for large companies. Mark had moved from winemaking to brewing, and Tim pursued a career in sales and marketing. In 1988, the Wethered Brewery in Marlow was closed, which brought to a temporary end over 200 years of brewing in the town. The old brewery really towered over Marlow and was easily the largest employer at the time and a major part of the commercial and social life of the town. One of Mark's earliest vivid memories is of the smell of the old brewery from Higginson's Park, where he spent break times as a 5-year-old pupil at the now closed Dial Close School located next to the George & Dragon pub on the Causeway.

In 1990, Tim and Mark were both beginning to feel it was time to work for themselves, and with the debate over how to redevelop the old brewery site still ongoing, the spark of their idea to restart brewing in Marlow was ignited. Over a couple of pints and a whole crispy duck and pancakes, they thrashed out the idea, wrote a business plan and drew up a partnership agreement. Their attempts to locate the new brewery in part of the old Wethered site in the centre of town were frustrated, so in April 1993, the Rebellion Brewery started brewing on the Rose Business Estate in Marlow Bottom.

After 30 years and now located on Bencombe Farm, the brewery produces approximately 300 barrels per week and employs more than 70 staff, getting close to the scale of the Wethered Brewery when it closed in 1988. Mark's brother Paul Gloyens (OB 1972–1979) is the Engineering Director at Rebellion and has been instrumental in building the state-of-the-art brewery on Bencombe Farm. Tim and Mark have returned to Borlase over the years to take part in industry days and careers talks and are pleased to take on Borlase students for summer and Christmas holiday work.

4.5.37. Nina Hartstone won an Academy Award with John Warhurst in 2019

Nina Hartstone

Nina Harstone (OB 1987–1989) was among the first intake of girls to Borlase in the Lower Sixth and studied History, German and Art. She recalls her time at School and describes her career in sound editing.

I remember my mind being opened by lively political debates in History with Mr Shannon, which gave me a lifelong interest in politics and activism. Jazz musician and Art teacher Mr Hamer set me on my creative path, instilling a love for Renaissance art and developing my appreciation for all forms of music. My time at Borlase filled my head with possibilities!

After completing an Arts degree at Kent University, I grasped every opportunity to work in film, hungry to get my foot in the door. My first job in sound was at Pinewood Studios, making tea and learning about post-production. Over the years, I worked my way up through the ranks of sound editorial, reaching the pinnacle of my career in 2019 when I was awarded both an Academy Award (Oscar) and a BAFTA for my work on the film *Bohemian Rhapsody*. Back in the Sixth Form at Borlase, I could never have imagined that my career would reach such heights, and it is a testament to the power of sparking imagination at a young age. Thank you, Borlase — here's to the next 400 years!

Michael Acton Smith OBE

Michael Acton Smith (OB 1986–1993) was born in Marlow in 1974 and is now a highly successful technology entrepreneur. After attending Borlase, he went on to co-found with Tom Boardman the online gadget and gift retailer Firebox.com, which in 2004 was one of the fastest-growing, privately owned businesses in the UK. In 2004, he launched Mind Candy, which produced the alternate reality game Perplex City. The game was nominated for a BAFTA award in 2006. The following year, Mind Candy launched the online world Moshi Monsters, a multiplayer, role-playing game aimed at children aged 6–12 years. By 2013, Moshi Monsters had more than 90 million users worldwide, and has gone on to produce a range of merchandise and an associated video game, music album and feature film. Moshi Monsters won a British Academy Children's Award in 2013 for best Original Interactive. In 2012, Michael Acton Smith and Alex Tew co-founded Calm, the leading mental wellness brand with the #1 app for sleep, meditation and relaxation. Calm has grown to more than 100 million downloads, was the Apple 2017 app of the year, and is the world's first mental health 'unicorn' (a private start-up company valued at more than $1 billion). Acton Smith received an OBE in 2014

4.5.38. Michael Acton Smith, creator of Moshi Monsters and co-founder of Calm

for services to the creative industries. Below, he recalls his time at Borlase.

36 years ago, I nervously stepped through that impressive arch on West Street for my first day of 'big school' at Borlase. An early highlight that settled the nerves was discovering 'Ye Olde Tuck Shoppe', just outside the School gates. It was rumoured to be centuries old and sharp elbows were needed to fight to the front for a bag of sherbet lemons or cola cubes. It reminded me of the chaotic sweet shop from the original *Charlie and the Chocolate Factory* movie. Roald Dahl featured in my early lessons with Mr Sayer, the high-energy English teacher who helped to spark my imagination and introduced us to the dark and surreal *Tales of the Unexpected*. Dahl's writing and creativity had a big influence and sowed the early seeds for what became the weird and wonderful world of Moshi Monsters.

Another teacher who had a big impact on me was the ebullient Mr Howland. His colourful Maths lessons would mix quadratic equations with in-depth updates on his beloved Oxford FC. Howland's other great contribution was running the Borlase Chess Club and driving us all around Bucks and Berks for after-School matches in a battered minibus. My lifelong love of chess began at Borlase. It is a great game that teaches patience, planning, competitiveness and strategic thinking — all valuable skills that have greatly helped my business adventures, from Firebox in the late 1990s through to the mental health app, Calm.

Sir William Borlase's is a wonderful School, and I am thrilled that my niece is starting there this year. I cannot wait to see how the School inspires the next generation of students over the coming decades.

Dr Paul Hawkins OBE

Paul Hawkins (OB 1986–1993) was born in 1974 and is the founder and Chief Innovation Officer of Hawk-Eye Innovations. Paul took the business from a start-up in 2001 to a business that now employs more than 550 people and is valued in excess of £250 million. Andre Agassi described Hawk-Eye as "the biggest thing that's happened to tennis in the last 20 years". The technology is best known for its use in Tennis, Cricket and Football but it is also used in 24 other sports around the globe.

After leaving Borlase in 1993, Hawkins went on to study Mathematics and Computer Studies at Durham University, followed by a PhD in Artificial Intelligence. He then worked for Roke Manor Research, where the idea of Hawk-Eye was initially pitched and developed. Paul's work has been recognized through his being awarded the "young entrepreneur of the year" and an OBE in 2014 for his services to sport and technology. Hawk-Eye has also received two BAFTAs, one Emmy, one Logie, and three Royal Television Society Awards.

4.5.39. Dr Paul Hawkins, founder of Hawk-Eye Innovations and stroke of an Old Borlasian Four (with David Haldane, Steve Dance and Paul Thomas) rowing in 1992 against the 1st Four from 1952

The Old Borlasian Club and Alumni

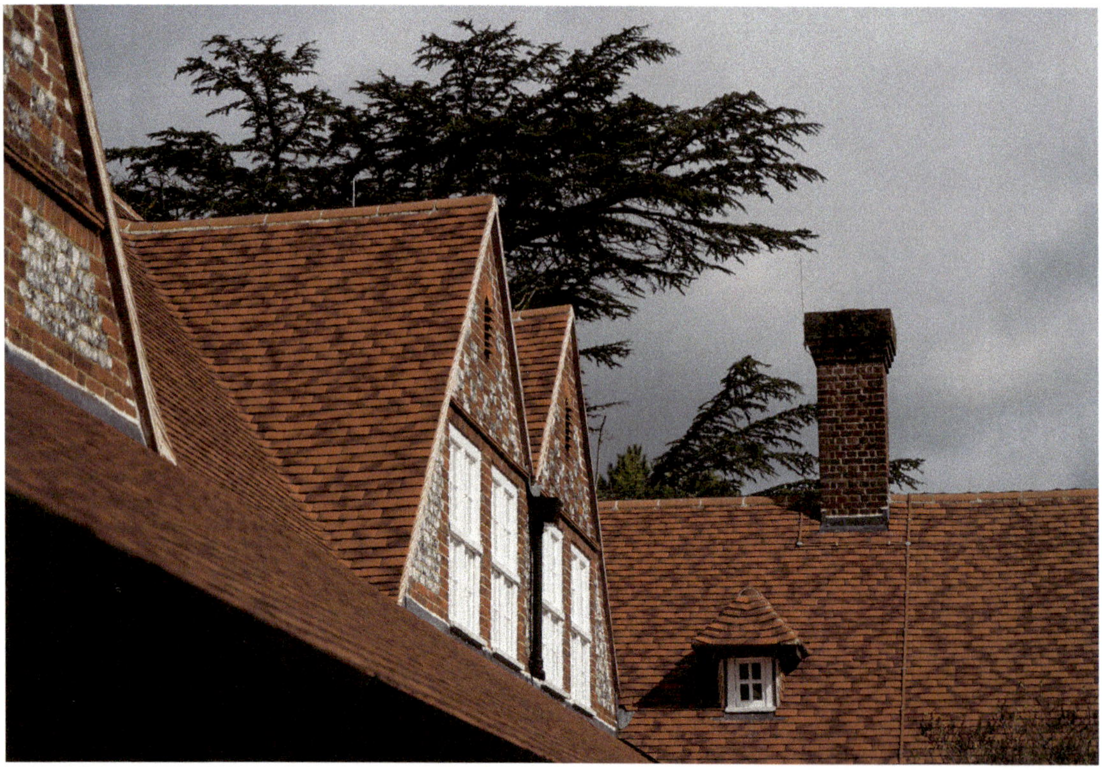

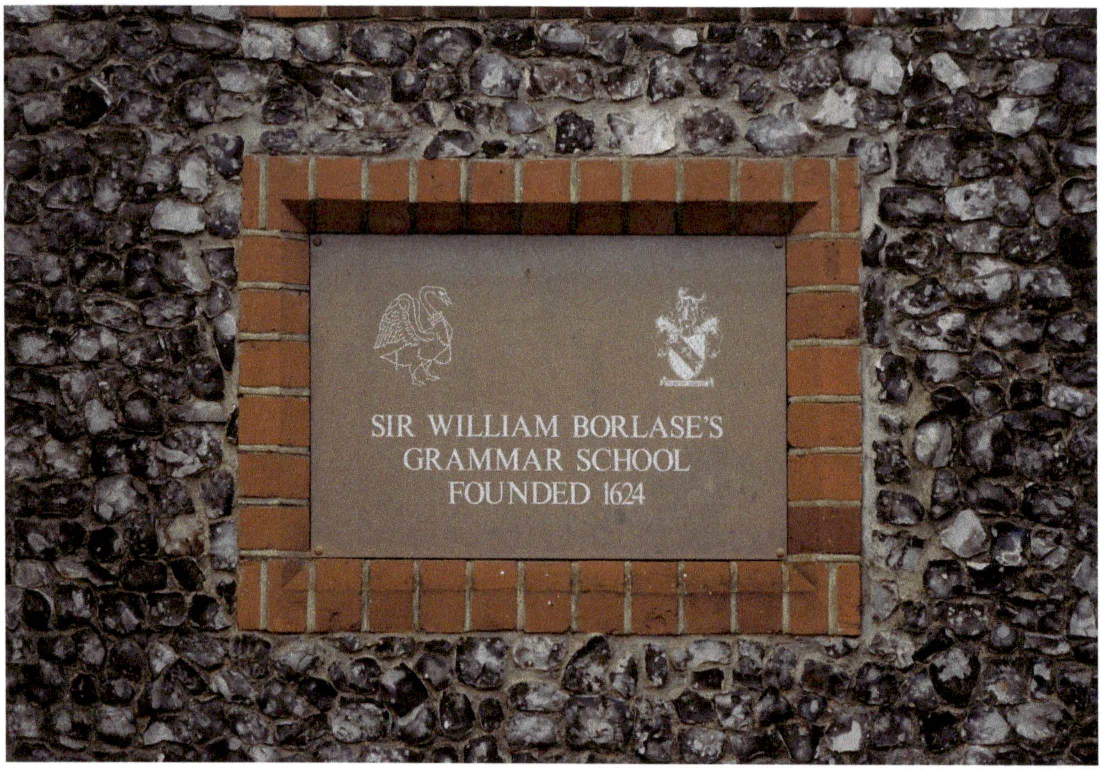
SIR WILLIAM BORLASE'S
GRAMMAR SCHOOL
FOUNDED 1624

CHAPTER 5
STAFF

LONG-SERVING TEACHING STAFF

Below is a list of individuals who joined the teaching Staff of Sir William Borlase's since *The Borlasian* magazine was first published and who served for at least 10 years (up to the end of the academic year 2022–2023). Several members of non-teaching Staff have also given long and dedicated service to the School, which is gratefully acknowledged; however, they are not listed here because members of non-teaching Staff were not historically listed routinely in *The Borlasian* and so their dates of service are difficult to ascertain with accuracy.

Teacher	Length of service	Year appointed
Russell Sage	42 years[a]	1934–1935
John C. Davies	39 years & 4 months	1916–1917
Cynthia Ayres	39 years[b]	1971–1972
Don Banner	38 years	1951–1952
Charles Davenport	38 years[a]	1935–1936
Fred Peirce	38 years	1940–1941
George Dewhurst	37 years[a]	1938–1939
Dennis Paton	36 years	1953–1954
Peter Heywood	35 years	1984–1985
Tony Shannon	35 years	1974–1975
Paul King	34 years +[c]	1989–1990
William Robertson	33 years & 2 terms	1931–1932
Walter Jones	33 years	1929–1930
Bryan Welch	32 years	1953–1954
Brian Teasdill	31 years	1959–1960
Mike Adamson	29 years	1993–1994
William Booth	29 years	1927–1928
David Wedd	29 years	1972–1973
Mary Brooke	28 years & 2 terms	1989–1990
David Colthup	28 years	1967–1968
Fred Davies	28 years	1940–1941
Hugh Robson	27 years +[c]	1996–1997
Norman Bateman	26 years	1957–1958
Tony Craig	26 years	1969–1970
John Stebbings	24 years & 2.5 terms	1983–1984
Karen Rooke	24 years +[c]	1999–2000
Dave Thompson	23 years & 2 terms[b]	1964–1965
Robin Pitman	23 years & 1 term	1942–1943
Jane Blane	23 years +[c]	2000–2001
Mike Jones	23 years	1983–1984
Arlette Kendall	23 years	1973–1974
Rev. Albert Skinner	23 years	1904–1905
Andrew Atkinson	22 years	1979–1980

Teacher	Length of service	Year appointed
B. Birkett	22 years	1919–1920
Dr Peter Holding	22 years	1996–1997
Dr Martin Isles	22 years	1989–1990
Kevin Chappell	21 years +[c]	2002–2003
Wendy Farmer	21 years[b]	1990–1991
Bob Ogden	21 years	1970–1971
Andrew Stafford	21 years	1980–1981
Elena Watson	21 years +[c]	2002–2003
Jane Bungey	20 years & 2 terms	2001–2002
Ralph Stedman	20 years & 2 terms	1921–1922
Suzanne Birkett	20 years	2002–2003
Clare Cooper	20 years	1976–1977
Rev. Sam Day	20 years	1966–1967
Joy Halton	20 years	1969–1970
Barbara Howland	20 years	1990–1991
Dave Tester	20 years	1989–1990
Christine Carter	19 years	1996–1997
Andy Howland	19 years	1989–1990
Craig Robertson	19 years +[c]	2004–2005
Rod Hamer	18 years	1973–1974
Earnest Hazelton	18 years	1956–1957
Kay Mountfield	18 years	2005–2006
Jenny Hopper	17 years	2005–2006
Joe McNally	17 years +[c]	2006–2007
Helen Milne	17 years +[c]	2006–2007
Fiona Pryor	17 years +[c]	2005–2006
Paul Beniston	16 years & 2 terms	1990–1991
Martin Brown	16 years	1988–1989
Rita Bond	16 years	2000–2001
Rhian Williams	15 years & 1 term	2006–2007
Harold Bayley	15 years	1958–1959
Jenny Chislett	15 years +[c]	2008–2009
Sgt Tommy Foreman	15 years	1919–1920

Teacher	Length of service	Year appointed
Malcolm Galloway	15 years	1979–1980
Rev. Michael Graves	15 years	1880–1881
Marshall Hall	15 years +[c]	2008–2009
David McLean	15 years	1960–1961
Rosemary Stops	15 years	1997–1998
Carolyn Williams	15 years	1999–2000
Alison Barraclough	14 years	2000–2001
Alan Black	14 years	1971–1972
David Ravens	14 years	1973–1974
Ken Pappin	14 years	1975–1976
Dr Ben Parsons	14 years +[c]	2009–2010
Roy Smith	14 years	1974–1975
Chris Wright	14 years	1976–1977
Edward Benson	13 years	1888–1889
Edwin Clarke	13 years	1888–1889
Dr Kay Clymo	13 years	1975–1976
Suzanne Davie	13 years[b]	2003–2004
Louise Forrest	13 years	2004–2005
David Hodgson	13 years	1963–1964

Teacher	Length of service	Year appointed
Liz Holmes	13 years	1988–1989
James Simpson	13 years	2010–2011
Suzannah Freer (née Shaw)	12 years & 2 terms	2000–2001
Jill Barnett	12 years	1991–1992
Patrick Gazard	12 years	1997–1998
Hayley Higham (née Yelling)	12 years	1998–1999
Liz Singh	12 years	2005–2006
Malcolm Brownsell	11 years & 2 terms[d]	2002–2003
Fred Handsombody	11 years & 1 term	1885–1886
Ron Boardman	11 years	1977–1978
Stuart Hill	11 years	2009–2010
Jonnie Robinson	11 years	1990–1991
Major Alex Wylde	11 years	1995–1996
Adrienne Crittenden	10 years	1987–1988
Allison Ellis (née Fountain)	10 years	1995–1996
Tony Malim	10 years	1955–1956
Melanie Macfarlane	10 years	2000–2001
Lucy Smith	10 years	1989–1990
Toby Weeden	10 years	2004–2005

[a]Including war service. [b]Over two periods. [c]Still on the Staff. [d]Over three periods.

By tradition, many of the longest-serving members, or those who died while on the Staff, are commemorated with plaques in the Chapel after their death. Those honoured and remembered in this way are shown below.

C. Ayres (Staff 1974–2013)
D. C. W. Banner (Staff 1951–1989)
W. S. Booth (Headmaster 1927–1956)
C. B. Davenport (Staff 1935–1973)
J. C. Davies (Staff 1917–1956)
N. Day (Matron 2007–2021), died while a member of Staff
G. A. Dewhurst (Staff 1938–1975)
C. Elly (OB 1952–1960; Chair of Governors & Trustees 1996–2021)
E. M. Hazelton (Headmaster 1956–1974)
W. F. Jones (Staff 1930–1963)
D. Paton (Staff 1953–1989)
F. W. M. Peirce (Staff 1940–1977)
W. O. Robertson (Staff 1931–1964)
R. H. Sage (Staff 1934–1976)
J. Schofield (Staff 2005–2007), died while a member of Staff
Rev. A. J. Skinner (Headmaster 1904–1927)
R. R. Smith (Headmaster 1974–1988)
B. H. Teasdill (Staff 1959–1990)
B. Welch (Staff 1953–1985)

In addition to the War memorials, several Old Borlasians who died at a young age are commemorated in the Chapel:

E. W. Hester (OB 1913–1915)
David Angus Dickson KM (OB 1906–1911), killed in action 15 October 1914
Basil Arthur Horsfall VC (OB 1903–1905), killed in action 27 March 1918
William Lawrence Tadgell (OB 1932–1935), killed in action 25 November 1939 aged 19 years
Kenrick Reginald Huymans Johnson (OB 1929–1931), died 8 March 1941 aged 26 years
Rupert Archer Jim Keene MC (OB 1934–1937), died 4 July 1950 aged 29 years
R. K. Read, died 5 April 1961 aged 14 years
L. W. Highley, died 26 March 1965 aged 18 years
Tim Magee, died 12 February 1990 aged 16 years
Ben Rimmer, born 1972, died 1990
Robin Graham, born 1988, died 2007
Robert Coates, born 2001, died 8 March 2019 aged 17 years

TRUSTEES, GOVERNORS AND STAFF

These lists are as of August 2023.

Marlow Education Trust

Ian Duguid
Alistair Handford
Dr Peter Holding (CEO)

Rick Krajewski
Fulden Thomas
Gill Towell

School Trustees

Edward Brown (OB 1953–1959) (Chair)
Tony Compton (OB 1957–1964)
Ed Goodall (Headteacher)
The Countess Howe (Lord-Lieutenant of Buckinghamshire)

Dr Gregory Lim (OB 1997–2003)
Joy Morrissey MP (Member of Parliament for Beaconsfield)
Gill Towell (Chair of Governors)

School Governors

Kate Burt
Phil Gray (Staff Governor)
Alex Hodgson (Associate Governor)
Alex Jamieson
Kally Kang-Kersey
Hugh Miall

Charlotte Redcliffe
Tom Russell (Associate Governor)
Phil Sharp
Charlotte Thatcher (Parent Governor)
Gill Towell (Chair)

School Staff

Goodall, E.	Headteacher
Walder, K. L.	Deputy Headteacher, Director of Studies, Maths
Holmes, R.	Assistant Headteacher, Culture & Character, English
Hussain, S. N.	Assistant Headteacher, Director of Sixth Form
Parsons, B. P.	Assistant Headteacher, Teaching & Learning, Music
Hartley, N.	Associate Assistant Head, Head of Sport and PE
Miall, S. W.	Associate Assistant Head, Director of Music and Performing Arts
Parsons, G. C.	Associate Assistant Head, Head of Science and Biology
Addison, J.	Geography
Al-Mashehadani, A.	Computing
Albarracin Seiquer, M. P.	Dance
Alexander, V. L.	Modern Foreign Languages
Archer, S.	Business Studies
Ashby, K.	SENDCo, Head of Key Stage 5, Dance, Music
Barrett-Klikis, S.	Modern Foreign Languages
Black, C.	Psychology
Blackwell, H.	Biology
Blane, J.	Geography
Bodinetz, T.	History, Politics
Bonwick, H.	Head of Key Stage 3 English
Buchanan, R. L.	Biology, Head of Key Stage 3 Science
Campbell, M. C.	Maths
Challis, F.	Art
Chappell, K.	PE
Colville, F.	Head of Modern Foreign Languages
Cork, R.	Modern Foreign Languages
Couch, N.	Head of Physics
Cross, O.	Head of English
Freeman, R.	English
Hall, M.	Head of Art and Design & Technology
Hartley, M.	Technical Theatre
Harker, R.	Music
Hindley, C.	Dance
Hocking, K.	History
Hepner-Logan, C.	PE, Head of Year 9
Holloran, J.	History, Head of Year 10
Hopper, J.	Modern Foreign Languages
King, P.	Head of Geography
Leibowitz, A.	Maths
Manthorpe, H. N.	Physics
Marchand, B.	Head of Maths
McNally, J.	Head of Business Studies and Economics
Mead, P.	Head of History
Milne, H.	Biology
Nicholas, K. E.	Head of Religious Studies, Psychology
Nicholls, G. J.	Design & Technology
Nunan, H.	Biology (part time)
O'Riordan, R. G.	Modern Foreign Languages
Pike, J.	Physics
Privey, L.	English
Pryor, F. W.	Head of Government and Politics
Ramnarine, S.	Head of Dance
Rayner, S. R. C.	Drama and English
Robertson, C.	Head of Key Stage 3, PE
Robson, H.	English
Roman Rojas, B.	Head of Spanish

Rooke, K.	Biology	Groeneweg, P.	School Support Assistant
Sanghera, H.	Maths	Haldane, L.	Exams Officer
Sankara Raman, G.	Chemistry	Hampton, C.	Member Marlow Education Trust
Serrinha, A.	PE	Han, Y.	After-School Club Teacher of Mandarin
Shah, D.	Head of Chemistry	Harper, H.	Foreign Languages Assistant
Shurrock, C.	Maths	Harper, K.	Designated Safeguarding Lead
Stafford, P.	Chemistry	Hazell, J.	School Support Assistant
Tekerian, B.	Head of Drama	Holmes, E.	SIMS Administrator
Topley, A. E.	Maths	Hutchinson, A.	Science Technician
Vijayan, N.	Maths	Joel, A.	Assistant Director of Rowing
Wadsworth, S.	Maths	Kendall, L.	Key Stage 4 Learning Mentor / Teacher
Watson, E.	Maths	Kipping, R.	Site Manager
Win, K.	Head of Computing	Koteles, R.	Cover
		Lewington-Chislett, J.	Performing Arts Technician
Attia, K.	Foreign Languages Assistant	Lidgate, H.	Key Stage 3 Learning Mentor
Bagley, B.	Site Assistant	Lofthouse, J.	Literacy Coordinator
Barkel, D. J. D.	Physics Technician	Longley, C.	Key Stage 3 Learning Mentor
Barrett, A.	Cover Supervisor / Reprographics	Lyons, J.	Receptionist
Bigsby, A. K.	Technician	Macgillivray, L.	Biology Technician
Bownass, K.	School Counsellor	Manthorpe, W.	Cover
Bourton, M.	Director of Operations	Mills, C. M.	Finance Assistant
Brokenbrow Morton, E.	Modern Foreign Languages Administrator	Monk, N.	Director of Hockey
Budge, L. F.	Development Assistant	Moorley, F.	Finance Assistant
Bull, H.	Student Support Officer	Morris, C.	School Administrator
Cains, I. S.	Director of Development	Murgatroyd, K.	Sixth Form Administrator
Cartwright, N.	Senior IT Technician	Neill, R.	Site Assistant
Chaplin, S.	School Administrator	Palombaro, F.	IT Technician
Chawla, A.	Director of IT	Pettigrew, A. U.	Foreign Languages Assistant
Clayton, R.	Sixth Form Administrator	Paton, J.	Exams & Data Administrator
Coates, C.	School Administrator	Reid, T.	Key Stage 4 Learning Mentor
Conan, C. E.	School Administrator	Rigg, S. J.	Key Stage 3 Learning Mentor / EHCP support
Cupitt-Jones, L.	School Administrator	Robinson, S.	Chemistry Technician
Das, J.	Finance Assistant	Rogers, I.	Key Stage 3 Learning Mentor
Davie, S.	LAMDA	Sewell, C.	Hockey Coach
De Matos Sharps, F. R. J.	Sports Games Organiser	Stevens, D.	Attendance Officer / Duke of Edinburgh Lead
Dharwar, R.	School Support Assistant	Summerfield, A.	HR Manager
Dickinson, K.	Data Manager	Thomas, F.	Chief Finance Officer
Donnelly, A.	Key Stage 4 Learning Mentor	Vedadipour, L.	Design Communications
Fortnam, L.	Student Support Officer	Wilds, B.	Site Assistant
Furley, E.	Student Support Officer	Wilson, J.	Netball Coach
Garrow, C.	Receptionist	Wingrove, C.	Careers Officer
Godfrey G.	Art Technician	Woodgate, C.	Head's PA
Goodman, J.	Healthcare and Wellbeing Lead		
Gray, P.	Director of Rowing		

4.5.40. Plaques in the Chapel to long-serving teachers

ACKNOWLEDGEMENTS

CONTRIBUTORS

The first two chapters of this book are based largely on a previous *History of Borlase*, written by J. C. Davies covering the period 1624–1957 and then updated by Russel H. Sage to include the period 1957–1984. I am very grateful to them both for their scholarly research and writing. The remainder of this book is a compilation of contributions from Old Borlasians and others, whom I shall attempt to acknowledge here. I apologize to anyone whom I might inadvertently neglect to mention. Moreover, I accept responsibility for any inaccuracies in the book and all omissions from it.

William Copeland Borlase MP wrote a detailed history of the Borlase family in *The Descent, Name and Arms of Borlase of Borlase in the County of Cornwall*. The Reverend David Miller (former Rector), Anthea Hearn (churchwarden) and Michael Thorn kindly provided information on and photographs of the Borlase memorials in Helston Church. Jane Bungey provided additional photographs from the Cornwall area. Peter Rodger (churchwarden) kindly provided access to Little Marlow Church. Sue Cheetham provided a copy of her article entitled 'William Francis and the Parliamentary Borough of Great Marlow', subsequently published in the *Records of Buckinghamshire*.

Many others contributed to sections of the text: Michael Symons (Boarders at Borlase), Laurence Smy (his tenure as Headteacher), Dr Peter Holding (his tenure as Headteacher), Kay Mountfield (her tenure as Headteacher; Performing Arts; House System), Dr Ben Parsons (Music; School Curriculum and Pedagogy), Seth Miall (Music), Jenny Hopper (Foreign Languages), Hugh Robson (School Organ and Harpsichord), Craig Robertson (Sport), Tony Compton (Orders and Reporting; Rowing), David Wedd (Hockey 1972–2002, reproduced from a chapter in *One Hundred Years of Marlow Hockey Club*), Kevin Chappell and Nathan Monk (Hockey 2002–2022), John Barry (Toovey Loving Cup; profiles of Borlasian MPs), Bryan Wilson (Borlase Masonic Lodge), Martin and Hartley Kemp (Jazz at Borlase), and Andy Howland (Long-serving Teaching Staff). Thanks also to the Old Borlasians who provided profiles of themselves: Fleur Thomas, Chris Bradford, Jonnie Robinson, Mark Gloyens & Tim Coombes, Nina Hartstone and Michael Acton Smith. The profile of Dr Henry Charles King is adapted from an article in *The Borlasian* written by Scott Elcock, that of Prof. Richard Hugh Britnell is adapted from an obituary published in *The Guardian*, and that of Sir Graham Burton is adapted from an obituary published in *The Times*.

I gratefully acknowledge the assistance of Ilona Cains (Director of Development) as well as Harry Elliott, who, among other contributions, digitized the entire catalogue of Borlasian magazines, which provided an invaluable resource. I am grateful to all the editors of this esteemed publication over the more than 130 years that it has been printed. I pay tribute to Stuart Lever, who was a great supporter of the School during his life and, as a result of his legacy bequest after his death, has enabled the creation of the School history and memorabilia room named in his honour. William Edwards took many photographs around the School site, as credited below. I thank Ed Adams and Nick Oulton from Gresham Books for their support during the publication of this book. Finally, I am enormously indebted to members of the Old Borlasian Club committee, including Julien Bussell, who digitized many of the archive photographs, and especially John Barry and Tony Compton, for their unfailing support and advice during the writing of this book and their enduring dedication to the School.

Gregory Lim
September 2023

PICTURE CREDITS

1.1.1. From *Historia Anglorum* by Matthew Paris (c.1253)
1.1.2. Jane Bungey; Jane Bungey
1.1.3. Jane Bungey; Wikimedia; Wikimedia
1.1.4. Jane Bungey [Borlase window]; Michael Thorn, with thanks to the Rector and Churchwardens of St Michael's Church, Helston [Borlase memorials]
1.1.5. Bill Harrison; From *The Descent, Name and Arms of Borlase of Borlase in the County of Cornwall* (hereafter *History of the Family of Borlase*) by William Copeland Borlase MP
1.2.1. Attributed to John de Critz (c.1605), Museo del Prado, Madrid
1.2.2. Abraham Blyenberch (c.1617), National Portrait Gallery, London
1.2.3. Gregory Lim, with thanks to the Rector and Churchwardens of St John the Baptist Church, Little Marlow
1.3.1. *History of the Family of Borlase*
1.3.2. Ibid.
1.3.3. Gregory Lim, with thanks to the Rector and Churchwardens of St John the Baptist Church, Little Marlow
1.3.4. Sir Anthony van Dyck (1637/1638), National Trust Collections
1.3.5. Attributed to Angelica Vanessa Garnett, Sir William Borlase's Grammar School (hereafter SWBGS)
1.3.6. Michiel Jansz. van Miereveldt (1625), National Portrait Gallery, London
1.3.7. Gregory Lim, with thanks to the Rector and Churchwardens of St Mary & St Edburga's Church, Stratton Audley
1.3.8. Follower of John Michael Wright (17th century), Wikimedia
1.3.9. Vicky Summersby
1.4.1. SWBGS
1.4.2. *History of the Family of Borlase*
1.4.3. Ibid.
1.4.4. Ibid.
1.4.5. Ibid.
1.4.6. William Edwards; SWBGS
1.5.1. Buckinghamshire County Archives
1.5.2. B. Birkett, from a painting lent by the Misses Segrave
1.6.1. SWBGS; William Edwards
1.6.2. SWBGS; William Edwards; SWBGS
1.7.1. William Edwards
1.8.1. Copy of an original by John Opie, National Trust Collections; (1800), in the possession of Gregory Lim; (1799), British Museum
1.8.2. Gregory Lim, with thanks to the Rector and Churchwardens of St Mary & St Edburga's Church, Stratton Audley
1.10.1. Joseph Constantine Stadler and Joseph Farington, published in *An History of the River Thames* by John & Josiah Boydell (1793)
1.10.2. Buckinghamshire County Archives
1.10.3. MyMarlow.co.uk
1.10.4. From *The Book of Marlow* by A. J. Cairns (1994), originally published by permission of Cdr O. F. M. Wethered
1.10.5. William Edwards
1.11.1. In the collection of the Dukes of Buckingham & Chandos
1.12.1. Buckinghamshire County Archives
1.12.2. Richard Rothwell (exhibited in 1840), National Portrait Gallery, London; Alfred Clint, after an original by Amelia Curran, National Portrait Gallery, London
1.12.3. In the possession of Gregory Lim; William Edwards
1.12.4. *The Revolt of Islam* by Percy Bysshe Shelley (1818)
1.12.5. The Marlow Society, published in *Marlow A Pictorial History* by Rachel Brown and Julian Hunt (1994)
1.12.6. From *Marlow A Pictorial History* by Rachel Brown and Julian Hunt (1994)
1.12.7. WikiMedia
1.12.8. Savills
1.13.1. Lucy Walters, Barr Build
1.14.1. SWBGS
1.14.2. John Kay (1798), Welsh Portrait Collection at the National Library of Wales; Gregory Lim, with thanks to the Rector and Churchwardens of St John the Baptist Church, Little Marlow
1.15.1. SWBGS
2.1.1. Ibid.
2.1.2. The Marlow Society; SWBGS
2.2.1. SWBGS
2.2.2. Wikimedia (c.1880)
2.2.3. From *Marlow A Pictorial History* by Rachel Brown and Julian Hunt (1994)
2.2.4. SWBGS; SWBGS
2.2.5. William Edwards
2.2.6. Ibid.
2.2.7. Ibid.
2.2.8. SWBGS; SWBGS
2.2.9. SWBGS
2.2.10. Ibid
2.3.1. Ibid.
2.3.2. In the possession of Gregory Lim
2.3.3. SWBGS
2.3.4. King's-Edgehill School/Wikimedia
2.4.1. SWBGS
2.4.2. William Edwards
2.4.3. SWBGS
2.4.4. Ibid.
2.5.1. Ibid.
2.5.2. Ibid.
2.5.3. Ibid.
2.5.4. William Edwards
2.5.5. SWBGS
2.5.6. Ibid.
2.5.7. SWBGS; SWBGS; William Edwards
2.5.8. SWBGS
2.5.9. Ibid.
2.5.10. William Edwards
2.5.11. SWBGS
2.5.12. Ibid.
2.5.13. SWBGS; SWBGS; SWBGS; William Edwards
2.5.14. SWBGS
2.5.15. SWBGS
2.5.16. William Edwards
2.5.17. Ibid.
2.5.18. William Edwards; William Edwards; William Edwards; SWBGS
2.5.19. William Edwards
2.5.20. Ibid.
2.5.21. Ibid.
2.5.22. SWBGS
2.5.23. Ibid.
2.5.24. Wikimedia
2.5.25. SWBGS
2.5.26. Ibid.
2.5.27. *Vanity Fair* (1884); Michael Eagleton; MyMarlow; SWBGS
2.5.28. SWBGS
2.5.29. Ibid.
2.5.30. Ibid.
2.5.31. Ibid.
2.5.32. Ibid.
2.5.33. Ibid.
2.6.1. Ibid.
2.6.2. Ibid.
2.6.3. SWBGS; William Edwards; William Edwards
2.6.4. William Edwards
2.6.5. Ibid.

2.6.6. SWBGS; SWBGS
2.6.7. SWBGS
2.6.8. Ibid.
2.6.9. Ibid.
2.6.10. Ibid.
2.6.11. Ibid.
2.6.12. Ibid.
2.6.13. Ibid.
2.6.14. SWBGS; Michael Eagleton
2.6.15. Michael Eagleton
2.6.16. William Edwards; William Edwards
2.6.17. SWBGS
2.6.18. William Edwards; William Edwards
2.6.19. Michael Eagleton; William Edwards
2.6.20. SWBGS
2.6.21. Ibid.
2.6.22. Ibid.
2.7.1. Ibid.
2.7.2. Ibid.
2.7.3. SWBGS; SWBGS
2.7.4. SWBGS
2.7.5. SWBGS; SWBGS; SWBGS; William Edwards
2.7.6. SWBGS
2.7.7. Ibid.
2.7.8. William Thomas Stothard, British Museum; Gregory Lim, with thanks to Mrs Green
2.7.9. SWBGS
2.7.10. Ibid.
2.7.11. Ibid.
2.7.12. Ibid.
2.7.13. Ibid.
2.7.14. Ibid.
2.7.15. From *Sentry Hill The Boarding House Years 1961–1985* by Michael Symons
2.7.16. Ibid.
2.7.17. Ibid.
2.7.18. Ibid.
2.7.19. Ibid.
2.7.20. Ibid.
2.7.21. Ibid.
2.7.22. Ibid.
2.7.23. Ibid.
2.7.24. Ibid.
2.7.25. Ibid.
2.7.26. Courtesy of Michael Symons
3.1.1. SWBGS
3.1.2. SWBGS; SWBGS
3.1.3. William Edwards
3.1.4. Courtesy of Andrew Stafford
3.1.5. SWBGS
3.1.6. Ibid.
3.1.7. Ibid.
3.1.8. Ibid.
3.1.9. Ibid.
3.1.10. SWBGS; SWBGS
3.1.11. SWBGS
3.1.12. SWBGS; William Edwards; SWBGS
3.1.13. SWBGS
3.1.14. Ibid.
3.2.1. Ibid.
3.2.2. Ibid.
3.2.3. SWBGS; William Edwards; SWBGS
3.2.4. SWBGS
3.2.5. Ibid.
3.2.6. SWBGS; SWBGS; William Edwards; William Edwards
3.2.7. SWBGS
3.3.1. Ibid.
3.3.2. William Edwards; William Edwards
3.3.3. SWBGS; SWBGS; William Edwards; SWBGS; SWBGS; William Edwards
3.3.4. William Edwards
3.3.5. SWBGS
3.4.1. Ibid.
3.4.2. SWBGS/YouTube
3.4.3. Glencar Construction
3.4.4. SWBGS
3.4.5. MyMarlow.com
3.4.6. SWBGS
3.4.7. Ibid.
3.4.8. Ibid.
3.4.9. Petri Anderson; Tony Compton/TP Architects
3.5.1. SWBGS
3.5.2. Ibid.
3.5.3. Ibid.
3.5.4. Ibid.
3.5.5. Ibid.
3.5.6. Ibid.
3.5.7. Ibid.
3.5.8. Ibid.
3.5.9. Ibid.
3.5.10. Ibid.
3.5.11. Ibid.
3.6.1. Courtesy of Victoria Chong
3.6.2. Courtesy of Nicola Chmielewska
3.6.3. William Edwards
3.8.1. SWBGS; William Edwards; William Edwards
3.8.2. SWBGS
3.8.3. Ibid.
3.8.4. William Edwards; William Edwards
3.8.5. SWBGS
3.8.6. Gregory Lim
3.8.7. SWBGS
3.8.8. Courtesy of Ron Compton
3.8.9. Courtesy of Tony Compton
3.8.10. Courtesy of Andre Compton
3.8.11. SWBGS; SWBGS
3.8.12. Courtesy of Edward John Hawkins; courtesy of Peter Wiseman; William Edwards
3.8.13. William Edwards; Hawkinsport; Hawkinsport
3.8.14. William Edwards
3.8.15. SWBGS
3.9.1. Ibid.
3.9.2. Harry Elliott
3.9.3. SWBGS
3.9.4. Ibid.
3.9.5. Ibid.
3.9.6. Ibid.
3.9.7. Ibid.
3.9.8. Ibid.
3.9.9. Ibid.
3.9.10. Ibid.
3.9.11. William Edwards
3.9.12. SWBGS
3.9.13. Ibid.
3.9.14. Ibid.
3.9.15. Courtesy of Rufus Biggs
3.9.16. From *One Hundred Years of Marlow Hockey Club* edited by Graham Sweet (2009)
3.9.17. Ibid.
3.9.18. Ibid.
3.9.19. Ibid.
3.9.20. SWBGS
3.9.21. Ibid.
3.9.22. Ibid.
3.9.23. Ibid.
3.9.24. Ibid.
3.9.25. Ibid.
3.9.26. Ibid.
3.9.27. Olympedia; TeamBG.com; BritishRowing.com; PA Images/Alamy Stock Photo; Alamy; Courtesy of Tom Dean and Jack Beaumont
4.1.1. SWBGS
4.1.2. Ibid.
4.1.3. Ibid.
4.1.4. Gregory Lim; William Edwards
4.1.5. William Edwards
4.1.6. William Edwards; SWBGS
4.1.7. SWBGS
4.1.8. Ibid.
4.1.9. William Edwards; William Edwards

4.1.10. Ibid.
4.2.1. William Edwards
4.3.1. SWBGS; SWBGS
4.3.2. William Edwards; Gregory Lim
4.3.3. *Star (Christchurch)* (24 May 1929); William Edwards
4.3.4. SWBGS; SWBGS
4.4.1. SWBGS
4.4.2. William Edwards; Borlase Lodge
4.4.3. William Edwards
4.5.1. SWBGS
4.5.2. SWBGS
4.5.3. Lancashire Infantry Museum, Fulwood Barracks, Preston; William Edwards
4.5.4. SWBGS; William Edwards; *Bucks Free Press*
4.5.5. Imperial War Museum
4.5.6. SWBGS
4.5.7. *My Attempts to Break Prison* by Captain J. Shaw, originally published in three parts in the *Oxfordshire and Buckinghamshire Light Infantry's Regimental Journal* between 1931 and 1939
4.5.8. Ibid.
4.5.9. Ibid.
4.5.10. Ibid.
4.5.11. Ibid.
4.5.12. SWBGS
4.5.13. Walter Stoneman (1937), National Portrait Gallery, London; Wikimedia Commons
4.5.14. Walter Bird (1960), National Portrait Gallery, London
4.5.15. *Illustrated Sporting and Dramatic News* (6 September 1940)
4.5.16. SWBGS; Gregory Lim
4.5.17. SWBGS
4.5.18. SWBGS; William Edwards; William Edwards
4.5.19. Courtesy of Martin and Hartley Kemp
4.5.20. SWBGS; courtesy of Monty Seymour
4.5.21. Published in King, D. A. Henry C. King (1915–2005). *Journal for the History of Astronomy* **38**, 526–527 (2007); Dover Publications
4.5.22. Garfield Weston Foundation
4.5.23. William Edwards
4.5.24. SWBGS; Gregory Lim
4.5.25. The British Academy
4.5.26. Courtesy of George Burnaby Drayson
4.5.27. Courtesy of Timothy Simon Janman
4.5.28. Courtesy of Phillip James Lee
4.5.29. *The Times* (15 December 2021)
4.5.20. Ibid.
4.5.31. Courtesy of Fleur Thomas
4.5.32. Bain News Service (1900); Doubleday, Doran & Co.
4.5.33. Courtesy of Chris Bradford; Puffin
4.5.34. Lucy Dickens/British Council; Faber & Faber
4.5.35. Courtesy of Jonnie Robinson; Cambridge University Press
4.5.36. Courtesy of Mark Gloyens & Tim Coombes
4.5.37. Courtesy of Nina Hartstone
4.5.38. Courtesy of Michael Acton Smith
4.5.39. Paul Hawkins/Chartwell Speakers; SWBGS
4.5.40 William Edwards

SUBSCRIBERS

Chloë, Dominic & Damien Adams	OB 2017–, OB 2019–, OB 2022–
Mike Adamson	Staff 1993–2023
John Adcock	OB 1982–1988
Jonny, Tom & Lizzy Ainscough	OB 2012–2020, OB 2016–2023, OB 2019–
Charles Allen	OB 1970–1975
David J. Allen	OB 1985–1990
John C. Allen	OB 1956–1963
Johan Andrea	OB 2018–2023
The Arnold Family	OB 2021–
Anna Ayling	OB 2022–
The Barford Family (Ella & Abigail)	OB 2020–, OB 2022–
Jennifer Baron	OB 2016–2023
Andrew Barron	OB 2018–2020
John William Barry	OB 1948–1954
Willem Bateson	OB 2016–2023
Aniela Batterberry	OB 2021–
Zac Bayliss	OB 2016–2023
Alexis Besnard	
Lara Blatt	OB 2016–2023
Annabelle Bilson	OB 2021–
Chris Bingham	OB 1984–1990
Tristan Bishop	OB 1982–1988
Tomasz & Agnieszka Bizior	
Duncan Black	OB 1987–1993
Matthew Blaikie	OB 2003–2010
Michael Blaikie	OB 2000–2007
Adam, Claudine, Raffy, Leo & Elodie Bone	OB 2021–
Connor Botha	OB 2019–2024
Michael Boxall	OB 1954–1961
Andrew Boyle	OB 1975–1981
Chris Bradford	OB 1986–1992
Alexander Britton	OB 2016–2023
Thomas Buick	OB 2016–2023
Jane, Hannah & George Bungey	Staff 2002–2023, OB 2001–2008, OB 2003–2010
Samuel Caldwell	OB 2019–
Rebecca & Sebastian Canton	OB 2017–2022, OB 2019–
David Carvey	OB 1974–1980
Jonathan Cary	OB 1976–1982
Andrew Casey	OB 1995–2001
The Chambers Family	OB 2022–
Kevin Chappell	Staff 2002–
Kush Chavda	OB 2015–2020
Krishni Chavda	OB 2016–2023
Sue Cheetham	
Joanna & Victoria Chong	OB 2017–, OB 2019–
John Clark	OB 1958–1965
Max, Ellie & Sophia Clark	OB 2013–2020, OB 2017–, OB 2021–
Amy Clarke	OB 2019–
George Clarke	OB 2021–
Sebastian Clarke	OB 2022–
Sienna Clarke	
Fiona Colville	
Alexander Coe	OB 2016–2023
Andre Compton	OB 1985–1989
Tony Compton	OB 1957–1964
John Conry	OB 1962–1969
Nicholas Constandinos	OB 2020–
Rafael & Noa Conway	OB 2017–2024, OB 2021–
Tom & Rosa Cook	OB 2020–
Henry & Joseph Coombs	OB 2019–, OB 2021–
Freya Cornish	OB 2021–
Charlotte Coster	OB 1997–2003
Karen S. Courtney	OB 2002–2009
Karl Craig	OB 1994–2000
Tony Craig	Staff 1969–1995
Oliver Crofts	OB 2021–2023
Elsie Crossman	
Steve Dance	OB 1974–1980
Priyanka Das	OB 2020–
Benjamin Davenport	OB 1987–1993
Piers de Jode	OB 2022–2024
David James "Diz" Desborough	OB 1948–1955
Max Dexter	OB 2016–2023
Harrison & Elizabeth Dowley	
Carrie Dru	OB 1997–2003
Dick "Dann" Dunn	OB 1963–1969
Vivek & Vikramaditya Edulakanti	OB 2017–2024, OB 2021–
Gareth Edwards	OB 1996–2002
Craig Elliott & Sinead Lynch	
Donna Elliott	OB 1990–1996
Charles Elly	OB 1952–1960
Fin & Riley Engelberts	OB 2018–2023
Anthony John Evans	OB 1958–1963
Paul Everard	OB 1953–1959
Kristian James Farr	OB 1994–2000
Oliver Charles Farr	OB 1992–1998
Georgina Fernandez Leonard	OB 2016–2023
Philip Ferris	OB 1961–1966
Simon Ferriter	OB 1994–2000
Duncan Fisher	OB 1998–2004
David Flower	OB 1974–1980
Daisy Foley	OB 2016–2023
Monty & Seb Fordham	OB 2020–, OB 2023–
Anthony George Foulds	OB 1973–1974
Theo & Barnaby Froome	OB 2022–
Simon Funnell	OB 1972–1979
Amelie & Kenji Furphy-Yamazaki	OB 2019–, OB 2022–
Paul Edward Garner-Richards	OB 1988–1994
Mike Gellatley	OB 1953–1961
Peter S. J. Gellatley	OB 1956–1963
Ellie Gill	OB 2022–
John Gill	OB 1987–1990
Paul Ginman	OB 1968–1974
Rich Glover	OB 1980–1984
Mark Gloyens	OB 1975–1981
Ed Goodall	Staff 2023–
Ines Graham Usabiaga	OB 2018–2023
Vicky Gray (née Rose)	OB 1991–1997
Lucie Greaves	OB 2020–
Justin Griffith	OB 1960–1966
Joaquin Grundy-Llorenty	OB 2020–
Can Gücümengil	OB 2022–
Piraye Gücümengil	OB 2023–
Laura Gwilliam	OB 1993–1999
Christopher Hackett	OB 2020–
Clara & Ellen Hagstroem	
Lesley & Dan Haldane	
Arabella Hallawell	OB 1988–1990
Sasha Halliwell	OB 2018–2023
India Harris	OB 2023–
Finley Harvey	OB 2022–
Neil Harvey	OB 1989–1996
Addyson-Tyler Hawtree	OB 2022–
Dexter Heap	OB 2022–
Nathan Hendry	OB 2021–
Ellis Henningsen	OB 2021–
Claire Mitchell & David Hermelin	OB 1987–1989
Alexander Hill	OB 2017–2024
David Hill	OB 1981–1987
Georgie Hill	OB 2016–2023
David Hillier	OB 2005–2012
Daniel Hillier	OB 2016–2023
Emily Hillier	OB 2018–
Harley Hillier	OB 2019–
JJ Hillier	OB 2022–
Oliver Hire	OB 1994–2000
Jenny Hopper	Staff 2005–2022
Harriet Howard	OB 2023–
The Howland Family	Staff & OBs 1989–2010
Eden Hunt	OB 2016–2023
Anne Irving	OB 2018–2023
Ron Ives	OB 1944–1949
Alex Jamieson	OB 1999–2006
Holly Elizabeth Jardine	OB 2022–
Emily & Phoebe Jennion Wood	OB 2021–, OB 2023–
Dhilan Johal	OB 2023–

Navraj Johal	OB 2019–	Richard Nelson	OB 1963–1970	Matthew Searle	OB 1972–1977
Jack Johnson	OB 2018–	Sam Newcombe-Malins	OB 1993–1999	Philip Sequeira	OB 1995–2001
Robin S. Johnson	OB 1955–1962	Daniel Nixon	OB 2005–2012	Akmal & Ayaan Shaik	OB 2017–2024, OB 2022–
Stan Johnson		Margaret Nixon	Staff 2000–2023	Daniel Shave	OB 2023–
Silvia Kearey	OB 2021–	John Lloyd Nutt	OB 1962–1968	David Shipp	OB 1951–1958
Sophia Anne Kelleher-Monsen	OB 2020–	Thomas & William O'Connell	OB 2013–2020, OB 2013–2020	William Shipton Jones	OB 2016–2023
Hamish Jack Kennedy	OB 2020–			Ben Skelton	OB 2016–2023
Helena & John Kennedy	OB 2017–2024, OB 2015–2022	David Orchard	Staff 1971–1980	Paul H. Smith	OB 1962–1969
		Richard Osborn	OB 1955–1962	Christopher Smyth	OB 1952–1960
Jamie King	OB 2016–2023	Remy Charles Osman	OB 2005–2012	Emily & Daniella Southgate	OB 2020–, OB 2022–
Jagat Singh Klair	OB 2022–	K. J. Overshott	OB 1951–1959		
Pamela Knight		Mike Oxlade	OB 1968–1974	Reina Kawashima Speirs	OB 2023–
Hudson Knott	OB 2020–	Sarp Ozturk	OB 2023–	Ellie Spicer	OB 2023–
Lisa Kroeff Dixon	OB 2017–2024	Colin Packer	OB 1968–1976	Michael C. R. Stamford	OB 1967–1974
Anna Kroeff Dixon	OB 2019–	Keith Packer	OB 1974–1981	Jemima & Barney Stern	OB 2022–
Maya Kuncher	OB 2016–2023	Alexia Palet-Candelario	Staff 2011–2012 & 2014–2017	Daisy Stevens	OB 2016–2023
Chris Lane	OB 1979–1985			Will & Emily Stubbings	OB 2016–2023, OB 2019–
Christopher Lawton	OB 1985–1991	Phoebe, John, Charlie & Laurie Palmer	OB 2018–		
Sophie Lazenby	OB 2021–2023	Graham Parkins	OB 1989–1997	Dylan Sylvester	OB 2017–2024
Susanne Lewis	Staff 2013–2021	Sumat & Arjun Parmar	OB 2023–	Michael "Stodge" Symons	OB 1961–1965
James Ley	OB 2016–2023	Maya & Gia Patel	OB 2019–	Aurora Taylor	OB 2023–
Gregory Lim	OB 1997–2003	Dennis Paton & Family	Staff 1953–1989	Joel Taylor	OB 2016–2023
Kim A. Lim		Liberty Payne	OB 2022–	Anthony Temple	OB 1984–1990
Lily Lithgow Smith	OB 2023–	Ruby Peacey	OB 2017–2024	Freddie Terrell	OB 2022–2024
Nicky Lloyd (née Pratt)	OB 1987–1989	The Pedder Family		The Thatcher Family	
Georgina Lonergan	OB 2018–	Ruben Picard	OB 2020–	Edward Thomson	OB 2017–2024
Robert Y. Lyn	OB 1961–1968	Michael Pidoux	OB 1958–1965	Polly Thomson	OB 2019–
Dennis Lyne	OB 1954–1961	Jim Platt	OB 1945–1952	Michael & Christine Tock	OB 1999–2007
Alasdair Maclachlan	OB 1990–1995	Frederik Pollard	OB 2016–2023	Michael True	OB 1992–1998
Christopher Howard Marlow	OB 1966–1968	Dom Porter	OB 2017–2024	Sasha Tuke	OB 2021–2023
Elliot Marston	OB 2016–2023	Matthew Porter	OB 2018–	Joe Turner	OB 2020–
Brian Martin	OB 1969–1971	Alan Poskitt	OB 1977–1983	Ana & Ines Graham Usabiaga	OB 2015–2023
C. McClure	OB 2018–	Iain Pressling	OB 1982–1988	Jerry & David Vaughan	OB 1967–1973
Helen McCorry	OB 1989–1992	Ryo & Kai Punwani	OB 2016–, OB 2019–	Mike Waddington	OB 1972–1980
Olivia McDonald	OB 2012–2019	David Ralph	OB 1973–1977	Richard Walton	OB 1981–1986
Gareth Menezes	OB 2019–	Jude Rawlings-Dean	OB 2020–	Justin S. Wark	OB 1972–1978
Paul Merchant	OB 1982–1988	Callum & Anabelle Rayner	OB 2018–, OB 2020–	Victoria Warnes	OB 1994–2000
Colin B. Miles	OB 2022–	Paul Richardson	OB 1954–1961	Thomas Warrington	OB 2019–
Barnaby Mills	OB 2021–	Edward Ridley	OB 2016–2023	Izzy Watson Legtmann	OB 2021–2023
A.B., D.J., S.A.A., I.J. & J.P. Milne	OBs 1942–1982	Jemima Ridley	OB 2016–2023	Andrew P. J. Webb	OB 1977–1983
Andrew Milsom	OB 1964–1971	Trevor Roberts	OB 1959–1966	Christopher Weeks	OB 2001–2008
Isaac Mohammed-Akram	OB 2018–	Freya Rogers	OB 2016–2023	Emily Wells	OB 2016–2023
Eilah Morgan	OB 2021–	Michael Rogers	OB 1978–1985	Oliver & William Whall	OB 2016–2023, OB 2019–
Adrian Morris	OB 1958–1965	Ollie & Tilly Royden	OB 2021–		
Hannah Moxon (née Ferriter)	OB 1998–2004	The Rubim-McKeating Family	OB 2021–	Darren Whatman	OB 1984–1990
Annie Munro	OB 2020–	Michelle Ruddenklau (née Pratt)	OB 1988–1990	Georgia & Will White	OB 2022–, OB 2023–
Rory Munro	OB 2022–	Andrew Rymer	OB 1996–2002	Alfie Wiggs-Steele	OB 2020–
Justin Murphy	OB 1986–1992	Emma Sage	OB 2016–2023	David Willey	OB 1943–1950
Josh Mustard	OB 2019–	Russell Saunders	OB 1985–1989	Felix Wilson	OB 2021–2023
Steve Nattress	OB 1989–1995	Ethan, Guy & Alison Schrecker	OB 2020–	Geoff Wood	OB 1953
Richard Neathey	OB 1972–1979	Edward Scottow	OB 2022	Phil "Woody" Woodward	OB 1962–1967

Join us in congratulating Sir William Borlase's on the celebration of their 400th anniversary!

'Meritas augentur honores Et noblesse oblige'

On behalf of my family and me, as well as I'm sure many governors, teachers, parents, pupils, alumni, faculty and Marlovians and all others who have engaged over what now begins Sir William Borlase's incredible 5th century, we want to congratulate and celebrate Mr Ed Goodall, and all the team and students on their unprecedented 400th anniversary.

The Lacy Family Foundation is honoured to be invited to support the 400th anniversary of Sir William Borlase Grammar School. 400 years is no mean feat. A true testament to the school's dedication to education, excellence and impact in society across many generations, backed by clear and enduring values.

It is incredible to think that Borlase was founded under the reign of King James I, the first monarch of the Stuart dynasty, and predates the precursor to Sandhurst situated just across the road (1802), a true upstart and newcomer! But incredibly likely to have provided the officers for the Duke of Wellington's defeat of Napoleon.

Not to mention bomber command at Danesfield House or photographic intelligence at Watlington House during WW2, nearly 350 years on, or the role in establishing the Paralympics and record of Gold medals in Rowing of Borlase's alumni.

It's hard to imagine a more important time for Borlase to lead from the front as a school itself, partnering within the local educational system, working with the community and preparing the leaders of the future for the local and global challenges of our time. The Lacy Family Foundation is proud to be able to support this anniversary - even in a small way - as part of its focus on sport, education, health, well-being and neurodiversity as vehicles for positive change for current and future generations - a vision Mr Goodall and his team clearly embrace.

Whilst we normally do not publicise our giving or the foundation, we felt it worth showcasing some of the incredible organisations we support in a similar vein; we'd encourage you to visit.

T4 Education

The World's Greatest Teaching Prize was founded by Vikas Pota of T4 & Peter Lacy of Accenture in 2022 to celebrate the pioneering schools and those case studies from which others would learn about: innovation, overcoming adversity, supporting healthy lives, environmental action, community collaboration. It has already proved an enormous success with the end goal environment prize winner in the Philippines alone being rolled out to nearly 1.2 million pupils the day after the award by the Education Minister.

The Tap

Founded by currently serving **Brigadier** Nick Cowley, OBE has a focus on securing work experience internships and placements at some of the world's top companies for those from underprivileged **backgrounds** across London and the Southeast to give them unique experiences and boost their prospects.

Project Everyone

Project Everyone, founded by Richard Curtis of Mr Bean and Love Actually fame, as well as Kate Garvey, the Chief Marketing Officer of the London Olympics and Freud, focuses on communicating the Sustainable Development Goals in a way that is powerful, simple and compelling for 'everyone' including publications and films from Ricky Gervais to Ted Lasso to Jane Goodall.

BecomingX

Founded by former SAS **soldier** and famed global explorer Bear Grylls and fellow extreme explorer Paul Gurney, aims to support educators, students and youth 8-18 with inspiring short videos and stories from Kate Winslet to Wladimir Klitschko to Roger Federer, to Channing Tatum on the science of success and what it really takes to achieve impact.

ELEVATE

Founded by Lorna Solis, an inspiring and award-winning refugee and journalist herself, provides predominantly young girls - mostly from conflict zones and refugee camps - with education opportunities at top institutions such as Harvard, Princeton, UCL etc. with fully paid scholarships to complete their studies as well as highlighting female heroes through short films of pockets of true hope and inspiration in tackling social and environmental challenges.

In addition to the above, we would encourage you to visit the following pages that we have also supported over the last three years:

- Hay Festival Schools Programme
- World Economic Forum (Young Global Leaders)
- Danesfield School
- National Geographic - Pristine Seas Project - Enric Sala
- Marlow United Youth Football Club
- Thirst - Mina Guli
- Ocean Advocate, Patron of the Oceans - Lewis Pugh

Whilst wishing it another 400 successful years seems a little much (!), we are excited about what the future brings for this incredible institution and look forward to getting behind campaigns such as 'Here and Now Fund' along with others who are in a position to do so, to enable greater impact in the future.

Yours sincerely,

Lord Lacy, Baron de Lassy, on behalf of the Lacy Family Foundation.

The Lacy Family Foundation combines the charitable, philanthropic and community-oriented donations across the centuries of the families of both the United Kingdom and France. Tracing its history to Ilbert, Roger and Hugh de Lacy in 1070 currently chaired by Lord Peter Lacy and aligned to the founding principles that honour and merit come from the pursuit of benefit to others and that with privilege and power come responsibility for the many not the few.